SUGAR, CIGARS, AND REVOLUTION

Sugar, Cigars, and Revolution

The Making of Cuban New York

Lisandro Pérez

NEW YORK UNIVERSITY PRESS

New York

NEW YORK UNIVERSITY PRESS
New York
www.nyupress.org
© 2018 by New York University

References to Internet websites (URLs) were accurate at the time of writing. Neither the author nor New York University Press is responsible for URLs that may have expired or changed since the manuscript was prepared.

Library of Congress Cataloging-in-Publication Data
Names: Pérez, Lisandro, author.
Title: Sugar, cigars, and revolution : the making of Cuban New York / Lisandro Pérez.
Description: New York : New York University Press books, 2018. | Includes bibliographical references and index.
Identifiers: LCCN 2017038239 | ISBN 9780814767276 (cl : alk. paper)
Subjects: LCSH: Cuban Americans—New York (State)—New York—History—19th century. | Cubans—New York (State)—New York—History—19th century. | Immigrants—New York (State)—New York—History—19th century. | New York (N.Y.)—Ethnic relations—History—19th century. | New York (N.Y.)—History—19th century.
Classification: LCC F128.9.C97 P47 2018 | DDC 974.7/004687291—dc23
LC record available at https://lccn.loc.gov/2017038239

New York University Press books are printed on acid-free paper, and their binding materials are chosen for strength and durability. We strive to use environmentally responsible suppliers and materials to the greatest extent possible in publishing our books.

Manufactured in the United States of America
10 9 8 7 6 5 4 3 2 1
Also available as an ebook

To Liza

CONTENTS

Introduction

New York Stories

I grew up hearing New York stories. In my Cuban childhood, New York became a city of myths and legends, the setting for all interesting things that ever happened to my family. Back then, I did not appreciate that I was living in a remarkable place and time, the heady Havana of the 1950s. But that was my humdrum everyday childhood world, the one I had always known. By all accounts, New York, which I never visited as a child—now *that* had to be a truly extraordinary place.

My favorite New York family story is the one my father would tell about his first outing in the city. He was thirteen years old and had arrived from Havana on July 1, 1933, on the ship *Morro Castle* with his father, older sister, and one of his younger brothers.[1] The following day, a Sunday, they all found themselves in great seats at the Polo Grounds to watch a doubleheader between the Giants and the St. Louis Cardinals. The scene made quite an impression on my father: it was the Fourth of July weekend and the stadium was festooned with red, white, and blue banners, with a capacity crowd of some fifty thousand cheering on the Giants. It was exactly what he expected the United States to look like. The first game lasted eighteen innings, with Carl Hubbell accomplishing the incredible feat of pitching the entire game, allowing the Cardinals only six hits, no walks, and pitching twelve of the innings perfectly. The Giants won, 1–0. They also won the second game by the same score, but my father did not get to see it.[2] My grandfather stood up at the end of the marathon first game and announced that he had seen enough baseball for one day. They all left for their hotel, the MacAlpin, near Herald Square.

The larger story is how my father happened to be at the Polo Grounds, and in the United States, on that summer day in 1933. He and his brother went to New York to enroll in a private prep school in Long

Island. My grandfather, after whom both my father and I were named, was an orphan from central Cuba who had done very well financially by building a successful leaf tobacco exporting business. By 1933 he was already sixty-two years old and at the height of his business career as the exclusive Cuban exporter for the General Cigar Company in New York. He had just built a spacious home in Havana's most fashionable neighborhood for his wife and ten children, of which my father was the oldest son.

My grandfather's financial connection with New York would have lasting implications for my family, implications that went far beyond economic prosperity. Although one of his daughters was a nun, my grandfather rejected the idea of educating his sons in a traditional Catholic school for boys in Havana. Perhaps because he knew absolutely no English, he was determined to have his children learn the language and the ways of the people in New York with whom he had done business for decades. The location of the school could not have been other than New York, since my grandfather relied on the connections of the president of General Cigar, Bernhard Meyer, the same one who offered the corporate box at the Polo Grounds for the doubleheader. One of Meyer's children, Max, attended Woodmere Academy in Long Island, and so Meyer arranged for my father and uncle to not only enroll there, but also to be boarded at the home of the school's director, Mitchell Perry.

And so it was that my father (and eventually three of his brothers) spent five years studying at a predominantly Jewish prep school, living in a Protestant household, learning flawless English, and accumulating a trove of experiences and anecdotes centered on that other place that shaped his life. That's how I grew up hearing about Sundays in the Polo Grounds or in Yankee Stadium, of the beauty of Penn Station and the majesty of the Empire State Building, of weekend rides on the Long Island Railroad, and about the misery of having to eat beets, cauliflower, and rhubarb pie, but also of the charms of a coed school and especially of one Peggy Cohen.

Years later, when it came time to plan his honeymoon, where else would my father go except New York, to show off the city he knew so well to his bride, who was not Peggy Cohen, but a Havana girl who had never been to New York but had also grown up, as we shall see, with her own set of Manhattan stories. And when it came time to decide on a school for me, it was not going to be a Catholic boys' school, but one of the many American coed schools that by the 1950s had mushroomed in Havana to serve the huge American community as well as the many Cuban parents such as mine who wanted their children to learn English. It is therefore not difficult for me to see how a New York-Havana business partnership, forged early in the twentieth century, would have a determining effect on my life, embedding in my consciousness a clear personal connection with New York.

On my mother's side of the family my ancestral links to New York preceded the twentieth century by quite a bit. My maternal great-grandfather, Ernesto Fonts y Sterling, arrived in New York in 1879 to attend a school in New York's Hudson Valley. He had come under the guardianship of his aunt Hilaria and her husband, the prominent and wealthy Miguel Aldama, who went to New York in 1869 as an exile from the war for independence that had broken out in Cuba.

In the United States, my great-grandfather learned two things that served him well later in life: bookkeeping and, most importantly, English. In 1895 he joined the armed rebellion that started that year against the Spanish, eventually rising to the rank of colonel and serving as the treasury secretary of the government-in-arms. After the war he formed part, as deputy auditor, of the Cuban "sub-cabinet" of Leonard Wood, the U.S. military governor of Cuba, and later as chief auditor of the new Cuban Republic. His English was especially useful when in 1912 he accepted a position as administrator of two U.S.-owned sugar mills, among the largest of the colossal mills that sprung up in eastern Cuba through the investment of New York-based financial concerns.

After a long illness, Colonel Ernesto Fonts died in 1918 at the age of forty-eight, but not before advising his widow, María Luisa, that upon his death she should take their two rambunctious teenage sons (my maternal grandfather, Oscar, was the youngest) to New York and enroll them in New York Military Academy so they would acquire English and discipline. Almost immediately after he died, María Luisa did exactly that. With her pension as a veteran's widow and despite not knowing a word of English, she installed herself in a Manhattan residential hotel and sent my grandfather and his brother up the Hudson River to the military school. She did not return to Havana until the boys had finished high school, some five years later.

During those years my grandfather would spend as many weekends as he could with his mother in Manhattan, where they would take full advantage of the cultural life of the city. Whereas my father's stories were laden with baseball snippets, my grandfather Oscar's tales favored opera and the theater. He would tell me, for example, about going to the Metropolitan Opera House to hear Enrico Caruso sing the role of Radamès in *Aida*. His favorite stage act, however, was one his mother did not care for: the feats of Harry Houdini. My grandfather would also tell the story of how he met my grandmother at a party in Manhattan just before his return to Cuba. She lived in Havana, but was visiting cousins who were longtime residents of New York.

All of those stories of my childhood formed part of an oral family tradition that I can only describe as New York lore and that served to establish my personal connection with the city. It is a connection I have always felt. Several years after my family left Cuba in 1960 and settled in Miami, I took a full-time summer job at a burger place just so I could earn enough extra money to, at last, take my first trip to New York. It was 1968, a tumultuous year, I was nineteen and in college, and I will never forget the mixture of wonder and familiarity I felt during the two weeks I spent exploring Manhattan on my own.

I once regarded my New York connection as unique, perhaps a combination of fortuitousness and my family's socioeconomic status in Cuba. But after some forty years of studying and writing about Cuba, and especially about the Cuban presence in the United States, I have become convinced that my family's experience, far from being isolated or idiosyncratic, was a microcosm of the evolving links between New York and Havana, links that arose early in the nineteenth century and shaped what the Cuban nation had become by the time of the Cuban Revolution of 1959.

When he felt compelled to leave Cuba in 1869, Miguel Aldama, my great-grandfather's guardian, went to New York, a city he had visited many times before and where he sold his sugar and kept sizable financial accounts. The city was already the most important center of the émigré separatist movement and the principal market for Cuban products, especially sugar. With the start of a new century and the Cuban Republic, those well-established nineteenth-century links multiplied as the relationship between Cuba and the United States grew increasingly intimate in all areas of life: political, economic, social, and cultural. While the political strings that connected both countries were pulled from Washington, the far deeper economic ties, with all their social and cultural consequences, were centered in New York. Manhattan banks, financial firms, and corporations were largely responsible for the vertiginous levels of investment that flowed into Cuba, especially in the decades before the Depression. From the devastation of the conflict against Spain that ended in 1898 arose a new Havana elite buoyed by the capital that U.S. firms started funneling into the island through investment opportunities opened up by geographic proximity and, especially, a political climate whose stability was effectively guaranteed by the U.S. government.

That massive infusion of capital, engineered in New York, had a multiplier effect in all areas of Cuban life, from the development of Havana's extraordinary architecture and infrastructure, to the arts, music, and sports, political culture and social stratification, and even to the core of Cuban national identity.[3]

My family's experience was part of that broader process. My great-grandfather's education in New York prepared him to serve in that new Cuban world of the twentieth century. Ernesto's English and understanding of U.S. culture and business enabled him to form part of the U.S. administration of the island and later work as a manager for U.S.-owned sugar properties in eastern Cuba, working jointly with a friend from his war days, Mario García Menocal, a Cornell engineering graduate who would become Cuba's third president. Little wonder that Ernesto's dying wish was to have his sons attend school in New York, perpetuating further the family's cultural connection with the city. When his widow made the bold move of taking her sons to New York, she had many Cuban neighbors to keep her company. The residential hotel where she lived, the Walton, on the southwest corner of Columbus Avenue and 70th Street, was owned and operated by the Quevedo family of Havana, who lived in the hotel, along with nine other Cuban families, most of them with last names that were common among the island's elite.[4]

My father's education in New York was also a product of that reality of twentieth-century Cuba. His father's business acumen in the tobacco industry would never have paid off so handsomely without the capital U.S. buyers took to the island, allowing him to greatly expand his market. Eventually, General Cigar would enter into a corporate partnership with him, investing in upgrading and expanding his processing and storage facilities and increasing his payroll. That permitted him to build that spacious home in the Vedado district of Havana, a home designed and constructed by a prominent New York engineering firm. In sending his sons to study in New York, he was following a well-established pattern among Havana families of the time. And it was not at all unusual to take one's bride to a honeymoon in Manhattan, as did my father, and also Fidel Castro.

This book originated in the realization that my family's experience formed part of a much larger and intricate web of New York-Havana connections. By the beginning of the nineteenth century, New York started replacing Spain as that "other place" in the Cuban consciousness, that place beyond an island's constraining boundaries that sparks the imagination and becomes the primary destination, real or imagined, for those who seek, for whatever reason, to escape or assuage their insularity. It became the place of reference for style, ideas, progress, culture, and economic advancement—in short, the place where horizons could be expanded beyond the possibilities available in a tropical island.

The process of Cuban nation building, which started fairly early in the nineteenth century, was characterized by a distinctly modernist, progressive, and secular orientation. Spain, the colonial oppressor, could not be the model for that process. One revealing symbol of that fact was the triumph in the late nineteenth century of baseball over bullfighting in the scheduling competition for Havana's public arenas. Baseball was embraced by Cubans because it symbolized American modernity.[5]

New York's role in that process was of critical importance to understanding the creation and development of the Cuban nation during the second half of the nineteenth and the early part of the twentieth century. Establishing the role of New York in the development of Cuban culture and society requires detailing the links by which New York exercised that influence. The Cuban community in New York was not only a result of, but also a critical contributor to, the weaving of a dense and complex web of political, economic, and cultural networks that made New York the critical place of reference for the Cubans' sense of modernity and nationhood. "Emigration," as Louis A. Pérez Jr. wrote, "served as the crucible of nation, for many vital elements of Cuban nationality were forged and acquired definitive form in North America."[6] New York, I argue, was the most important "crucible" of Cuban emigration and nationhood in the nineteenth and early twentieth centuries.

Starting fairly early in the nineteenth century and for more than a century thereafter, virtually all significant intellectual, artistic, business, and political figures associated with the construction of the island nation went to New York, some for a lifetime, others for defining sojourns. And it was not just any city, it was New York. From democratic culture, corruption, stark social contrasts and social justice, to jazz and baseball, Cuban New Yorkers were exposed to what New York had to offer: a look at the new patterns of modernity. As Thomas Bender has argued,

> It was in New York . . . that advanced culture and learning first confronted modern urban conditions. Before their counterparts in any of the great European capitals, men and women of learning in New York had to confront the ideology and practice of democracy and unprecedented social heterogeneity.[7]

The Cuban community of New York arose within a broader context of economic and political connections between New York and Havana in the nineteenth century. The volume of ship traffic between the two cities increased tremendously. Cubans went to New York not only to plot revolution against Spain, but also to make a living, importing sugar and tobacco from Cuba, manufacturing or selling cigars, refining sugar or a myriad of other activities, including real estate investment. The separatist war that started in 1868 led to the massive exodus of elites, especially the landed aristocracy, whose lives and properties were threatened by Spanish repression. Their political and economic pursuits maintained them in contact with the homeland at the same time that they became fixtures on the New York social and economic scene. Their weddings and baptisms were lavish events, even by New York standards. Passengers arrived daily from the island to visit their New York relatives and to shop for the latest in manufactured goods and fashions in Manhattan's unparalleled retail emporia. Insurrectionist leaders raised money to outfit expeditions to the island to fight the Spanish. Havana lottery tickets were sold freely on the streets of Manhattan and Brooklyn. Those who in Cuba ran afoul of the law or of creditors were likely to turn up in New York. Decades before Cuban cigar workers rolled cigars in Tampa, they were laboring at their craft in lower Manhattan using imported Cuban leaves.

Near the close of the nineteenth century, New York's Cuban community became the political and intellectual center of the definitive independence movement organized by José Martí. It was a time and a place that defined the future course of the nascent nation. While the community overwhelmingly supported the Cuban struggle for independence, it endured beyond that struggle, into the twentieth century and into another phase of Cuba's—and New York's—history.

The twentieth century brought inextricably close commercial, political, and cultural ties between the United States and Cuba, and New York remained, until 1960, the most important U.S. city for Cubans, drawing to it those who helped shaped the cultural, economic, and intellectual institutions of the young Republic. These included writers, academics, intellectuals, businessmen, artists, sports figures, and, perhaps most importantly, musicians. Cuba's foremost contribution to universal culture was indelibly affected by performance venues and record companies in Manhattan. The busy ship traffic between New York and Havana was soon complemented by air service, one of the busiest of all air routes in North America.[8]

New York's Cuban community had many features of what we now call a "transnational community." The term came into vogue as a major conceptual tool in the study of contemporary U.S. immigration to describe the networks of social, political, and economic relations that immigrants construct that link their societies of origin and destination. "Through these networks," wrote Alejandro Portes, "people are able to lead dual lives. . . . [They] are often bilingual, move easily between different cultures, frequently maintain homes in two countries, and pursue economic and cultural interests that require their presence in both."[9] Challenging the notion that immigrants become "uprooted" when they migrate, the concept of transnationalism recognizes the many ways migrant communities remain connected, on an ongoing and evolving basis, with their locales of origin.[10]

Although this conceptual framework has been applied almost exclusively to contemporary immigrants, some attention has also been paid to the existence of transnational ties between earlier immigrants and their homelands. Nancy Foner looked at how Russian Jews and Italians in New

York at the end of the nineteenth century sustained a myriad of ties with their societies of origin.[11] Nina Glick Schiller recognized the importance of U.S. immigrant communities in shaping and consolidating nineteenth-century nation-states in Europe and Asia.[12] In an edited book entitled *Chinese American Transnationalism*, a group of scholars of the Chinese presence in the United States examine the many ties between Chinese Americans and their homeland during the Exclusion Era.[13]

* * *

In this book, I seek to correct some of the imbalances in what we know about the history of Cubans in the United States before the 1959 Revolution. Essentially, I seek to give New York its due, and place the better-known history of political activism within its broader and lesser-known social, cultural, and economic context. There is an impressive bibliography on the Florida cigar making communities, especially Tampa, and there is an even larger bibliography on the political activities of Cuban émigrés, especially the life and work of José Martí, who lived in New York during the last fifteen years of his life.[14]

But aside from the political activism of Martí and his followers late in the century, the history of Cuban New York is far less known, despite its importance. New York's Cuban community is one case in which a transnational community played a determining role in the very creation, and subsequent evolution, of a nation-state. While that role was most evident in the political arena, both its antecedents and consequences were much broader, extending to the cultural, social, and economic. To study Cuban New York as a transnational community, we must therefore go beyond its often-studied political activities and examine the broader community, something that has not been done in a systematic manner in the case of New York.[15]

There is relatively little in the existing literature that tells us about the Cuban merchants, manufacturers, seamstresses, cigar workers, crafts-men, shopkeepers, laborers, artists, writers, and musicians, white Cubans, Afro-Cubans, stalwart women, Catholics, Freemasons, and even Chinese Cubans who inhabited the city even before the arrival of Martí in 1880. We also know relatively little about how Cuban New York originated and how the city served as the stage for the earliest efforts to extricate Cuba from Spanish control. The transnational social, economic, cultural, and, yes, political connections between Cuba and New York were forged decades before Martí became a New Yorker.

The focus of this book is therefore on what we know least about Cuban New York: its rise and development before it became the stage in the 1890s for the development of the definitive independence movement. I also seek to intertwine the political history with the social and economic forces that continuously shaped the community.

This book represents another of the many studies of how New York developed as an international migration destination and as a global center for commerce, communications, and the spread of modern urban-based values. The story of Cuban New York is therefore not just a Cuban story. It is also a New York story. The importance of New York's trade with the island, the city's cigar and tobacco industry, and the political lobbying and activism on behalf of the Cuban cause gave Cubans a level of visibility within the busy New York landscape, yet their presence in the city has received scant attention in general historical works on New York.[16] In part, this is a function of the absence, as has already been noted, of comprehensive studies of the community. Those writing histories of the city have not had secondary sources on the history of Cuban New Yorkers to draw upon. There is also the perception that during the nineteenth century the story of immigrant and ethnic New York is a European one. Latin Americans only figure into that story toward the middle of the twentieth century.[17] From a demographic perspective, that is fair and accurate, but it shortchanges the full scope of New York's history as a global metropolis.

If the story of Cuban New York is an important New York story, then it is of even greater importance to the history of the Latino presence in the city. The population that has its origins in Latin America will soon account for nearly one-third of New York City's inhabitants, an unprecedented proportion for any ethnic group, even for a city built on ethnic diversity. Cubans, however, now make up less than 2 percent of New York's present-day Latinos. Eight other Latino nationality groups in the city have higher numbers. But, as we shall see, from the time Latin American nation-states were in their infancy, in the early nineteenth century, to the beginning of the twentieth century, Cubans were by far the largest group of Latin Americans in New York. To trace the origins of Cuban New York, therefore, is to uncover the origins of Latino New York.

* * *

The book is divided into two parts, corresponding to the two motors that successively in time were the driving forces in the rise and development of Cuban New York: sugar and war. The first one is sugar, or more precisely, the Cuba Trade, as it was known in New York. I open this first part with my arbitrary starting point for the story of Cuban New York: December 15, 1823, the day Father Félix Varela y Morales arrived at a South Street pier aboard a cargo ship from Gibraltar. During this first period a Cuban community emerged from the flourishing commerce between New York and Cuban ports, trade fueled primarily by Cuban sugar. New York's Cuba Trade preceded U.S. independence, and by the first half of the nineteenth century it was a consequential part of the overall U.S. trade picture. It was this commerce that led to the creation in New York of not only a community of Cuban elites with commercial and mercantile interests, but also a community of craftsmen whose livelihood was connected to the port. This first period also saw the debut of New York as a premier setting for the activities of Cuban separatists, especially those who favored annexing the island to the United States. Some, especially the intellectuals, were exiles, unable to return to the island, but most Cubans, especially the traders in sugar, continually moved back and forth, early examples of true transnational migrants. I close that first part of the book on the day that Carlos Manuel de Céspedes, on his plantation in eastern Cuba, declared the start of a war for independence that was to last ten years.

Just when the Cuba Trade was waning, the war that started in 1868 powered the continued development of Cuban New York. That is the subject of the second half of the book. Many of the former transnational elites became exiles, forming part of an exodus that brought some of Cuba's most prominent *criollo* families to New York escaping the repression and uncertainties that characterized the conflict between Cubans and Spaniards. That exodus exploded the city's Cuban population, making it far more numerous than any of the other Latin American nationalities. The decade of the 1870s represents the demographic high-water mark for the presence of Cubans in New York in the nineteenth century. The efforts of the elite émigrés to help the fighters in Cuba became highly contentious, with the exiles bitterly divided over strategies and personalities as the military situation on the island turned desperate.

Eventually, the deterioration of the island's economy because of the war pushed many Cubans from humbler social origins, especially cigar workers, to migrate to New York. The war lasted a long ten years, and although many Cuban New Yorkers returned to the island after the end of the conflict in 1878, most had already sunk roots into the Manhattan bedrock and stayed. The second part of the book includes a look at Cuban New York in the 1880s, a heterogeneous and seasoned community of cigar workers, craftsmen, and laborers, but also of elites, many of whom had invested their wealth in New York real estate. It was also a community scarred by war, with a notable presence of veterans and widows.

The second part ends with the story of the man who, from New York, organized the next, and definitive, war for Cuba's independence: José Martí. In chapter 8 I insert Martí into the story of Cuban New York with his arrival in the city in 1880 and his subsequent activities during that decade. But I stop short of delving into the well-known story of his activism after 1891 when, through the founding of *Patria* and the Partido Revolucionario Cubano, he intensively dedicated himself to organizing the independence movement that immortalized him in Cuban history. That story has already been extensively documented and I could not possibly do it justice here within the scope of this book. I am more concerned with placing Martí in his New York milieu and, especially, viewing what he did in the city as the final chapter in the long history of Cuban New York in the nineteenth century. That perspective yielded what, to me, turned out to be one of the most revealing results of my research: the exceptional role José Martí played within the entire history of Cuban émigré activism in New York. I personally rediscovered Martí through my work for this book. Let me explain.

In many ways, this book was going to be the not-Martí book. The history of Cubans in New York has been so dominated by the story of Martí, the Partido Revolucionario Cubano, *Patria*, and all the well-known activities surrounding the final independence movement that I felt strongly that the story of the earlier development of Cuban New York needed to be told. This was reinforced when I replied to questions about what I was working on: "I am looking into the history of Cuban New York." The usual response was "Oh, Martí, right." Actually, no, I would counter: Martí was certainly not the first Cuban to live in New York;

he was in fact preceded by a larger and very interesting community of Cubans whose origins say a lot about early Cuba-U.S. ties and about the beginnings of Latino New York. That's the untold story I wanted to tell.

But my intent on leaving Martí out of this story was also rooted in a reaction to what I had been taught as a Cuban schoolboy, that is, that the man was a demigod. I was in kindergarten when Cuba celebrated the centennial of his birth in 1953. In my class in *artes manuales*, we had to cut out a picture of Martí, place it in a frame, and decorate the frame. When I got home, I held the picture behind my back and approached my mother: "I have a picture here of someone; guess who it is." "Is it a picture of a woman or a picture of a man?" my mother asked. I thought for a moment. "No," I replied, "it is not the picture of a woman or of a man . . . it is a picture of José Martí." From what I had been taught, this Martí could not have been a mortal; such was the magnitude of his myth among Cubans. I do not remember a time in my life when I did not know how to recite from memory his poem "La rosa blanca" as well as many of his *Versos sencillos*, yet I do not recall ever having consciously memorized them. It's as if I had been born knowing every word of those poems.

During my undergraduate college years I became interested in the study of Cuba, which led me to reexamine and question all preconceptions of Cuban history that I had acquired in my childhood in Cuba and especially during my teenage years in Miami, where I lived after leaving Cuba with my parents. Miami is an émigré community that has idealized the lost homeland. With the intellectual hubris typical of many college students, I was intent on casting aside what seemed like myths about the island's exceptionalism and the prowess of its revered historical figures, Martí foremost among them. I saw the existing biographies of Martí as outright hagiographies and I tried to take a more critical, or at least more realistic, view of his life and work. When I started the Cuban New York project years ago I therefore had no predisposition to center it on Martí. I perceived there was a much larger and older story besides his, and that was the story I wanted to tell. Besides, as I mentioned previously, enough has already been written about his revolutionary activities in the city, leaving little possibility of adding any new scholarship.

I am glad I made that choice and that the book centers on that earlier, largely untold, story. But I discovered that in the story of Cuban New

York there is no ignoring Martí, despite my efforts to do so. My research on the decades prior to Martí's arrival led me to appreciate the political and social tradition in which Martí labored and just how much he creatively and drastically departed from it when he crafted his historical movement for Cuban independence. As I traced the patterns of émigré activism that preceded and followed him, I realized that Martí's political work and thought were truly extraordinary and stand out as unique exceptions to those patterns. To be sure, the man was no demigod, but he combined an unwavering commitment to a cause, one for which he was willing to sacrifice literally everything, with an exceptional talent for communicating and organizing, and one additional and critical element: a gift for political analysis and foresight. He was unlike any Cuban exile who preceded him and who followed him in the quest for a better Cuba. I fully admit that as a result I have now come full circle on Martí, somewhere close to the sense of awe I felt about him when I was in kindergarten.

I am telling a story, so I decided that an epilogue was more appropriate than a conclusion. Rather than attempting all-encompassing generalizations or observations, I opted for an epilogue to tie up the loose ends of the nineteenth-century story of Cuban New York. As the century was coming to a close, Spanish colonialism ended and Martí's worst nightmare was under way. I have entitled the denouement of the story "Martí Should Not Have Died," after the popular song of the same title, because that is the theme that best ties the loose ends together as events clearly demonstrated Martí's exceptional foresight.

* * *

As with any book with a broad scope, this book will no doubt disappoint readers who may have wished to see this or that aspect of the story of Cuban New York receive more extensive treatment in the book. I am cognizant that in telling this story I have had to be selective and limit the coverage of some historical figures and events that were part of this period of Cuban and New York history and that admittedly deserve more attention. For example, I researched the stories of more Cuban New York families than those I finally included in the book. To include them all would have taken the narrative into too many byways, disrupting its flow.

That the book cannot possibly capture the full richness of the story of Cuban New York in the nineteenth century may be one of its greatest contributions. My hope is that this sweeping account of the development of this important yet neglected community will provide a strong foundation upon which further research and writing can be based. There are indeed many more stories to be told of Cuban New York, many more investigative avenues that flow from this book that need to be pursued. There are some gaps that can be filled with research into collections I have not tapped, especially those in Cuba. This book will have served an important purpose if it stimulates more research on Cuban New York and the origins of the Latino presence in the city.

One of the reasons I was attracted to this topic was precisely its freshness. There is a huge scholarly bibliography on Cuba in almost every humanities and social science discipline. As someone who has been studying the island and its diaspora for more than forty years, I found it invigorating to enter an area of research in which I learned new things every day, things that I never knew and that apparently no one else knows either, or, at least, no one has written about them. As if clamoring to have their story told once I started looking for them, Cuban New Yorkers have started popping up everywhere: musty books, microfilms, brittle newspapers, historical markers, digitized collections, archives and manuscripts, legal proceedings, cemetery records, real estate transactions, passenger lists, census questionnaires, baseball box scores, advertisements, directories. I found evidence everywhere that more than a few Cubans walked the streets of the city in which I now live and did things that ranged from extraordinary to banal, from comic to tragic, and from noble to criminal. And their presence in the city needs to be told, for it is part of the history of Cuba and the history of New York.

PART I

Sugar: 1823–1868

1

The Port

Cuba, while still belonging to Spain, became more and more
an economic dependency of the United States in general and
of New York in particular.
—Robert Greenhalgh Albion, *The Rise of New York Port*[1]

The winter of 1823–1824 was relentless, keeping New York's streets iced
and slippery for most of the season. No one walking along South Street
those cold days was likely to have noticed the frail priest with the tenta-
tive gait of an old man, supporting himself tenaciously on the arm of his
younger companion. Nor would anyone have turned their heads toward
the two men as they chatted in the unmistakable inflection of the Spanish spoken in Havana. It was a familiar sound on the city's waterfront.

Father Félix Varela, however, was not an old man. He had just turned
thirty-five. But walking on icy streets was not something he had done
before, and until he became accustomed to it he relied on the steady arm
of his teenaged former student, Cristóbal Madan.[2] Learning to walk on
the frozen and snowy streets of a cold city was probably not a skill Varela felt he would need for very long. After all, he found himself in New
York almost by accident. He was one of a handful of passengers who
on December 15, 1823, disembarked at the South Street piers from the
Draper, a cargo ship that had set sail from Gibraltar.[3] Varela had sought
refuge in the small Mediterranean English colony to escape the wrath of
a vengeful Spanish king. Reinstated on the throne by French troops, Ferdinand VII immediately rolled back the progressive measures the Spanish parliament had forced him to adopt, measures that had given hope
to Cuban liberals that Spain would grant the island greater autonomy
and abolish the slave trade. Defying the Cuban slave owners, Varela was
in Madrid as one of three elected deputies from the island arguing for
those reforms before the parliament.[4] Once King Ferdinand regained
power, however, the Cuban priest became a special target of the mon-

arch's reprisals. The *Draper* happened to be one of the first ships Varela was able to catch out of Gibraltar. He probably regarded New York as a temporary place of refuge until he could return to Havana and resume his teaching duties in philosophy and constitutional law at the San Carlos Seminary.

But the Spanish Crown had a long memory for enemies. In the end, learning to walk on icy streets proved useful: Varela spent the next twenty-seven winters in Manhattan. He never returned to Cuba.

The arrival of Félix Varela in New York on that cold December day in 1823 can be regarded as the beginning of the Cuban presence in New York, or for that matter, in the United States. The founder of two downtown churches and an eloquent defender of the rights of Catholics and the Irish at a time when they faced serious challenges from "nativists" and "anti-Papists," the Cuban priest played a critical role in the development of the New York archdiocese.

But to understand the origins of the city's Cuban community, one must go further back in time than the arrival of Varela, all the way back to the eighteenth century. As with most Cuban stories, it begins with sugar. As with most New York stories, it begins with the port.

* * *

Father Varela arrived at a thriving harbor, and New York's trade with his native island contributed in no small measure to the bustle on the waterfront of lower Manhattan. The same year the priest arrived, 1823, ninety-seven passenger ships had arrived directly from seven different Cuban ports, more than half of them from Havana.[5] Several ships were engaged regularly in transporting passengers to and from the island. The brigantines *Packet* and *Abeona*, for example, made five and four round trips, respectively, from Havana to New York that year, while the schooner *Blue Eyed Mary* made several trips to and from Matanzas.[6] In that decade, from 1821 to 1830, there were more passengers arriving in New York from Cuban ports than the number of passengers arriving from all the other ports of Latin America and Spain combined.[7]

Underlying that passenger traffic were the extensive and long-standing trade relations between New York and Spain's island colony, commercial ties older than the United States itself, dating back to a British military victory in 1762. On January 4 of that year, during a long and costly conflict with France, the English declared war on Spain because Madrid had sided with the French.[8] King George's forces set out to deal a fatal blow to the Spanish by capturing the city that for nearly two centuries had served as the axis of Spanish shipping in the New World.

Havana at the time was the third-largest city in the Western Hemisphere, behind only Lima and Mexico City, and much larger than New York, despite having no precious mineral resources in its hinterland.[9] It had acquired its size and importance because of its strategic location in the Caribbean. It was Spain's premier port and shipyard in the Americas, the place where Spanish royal ships from Veracruz and Cartagena, laden with the treasures of the Spanish colonies on the mainland, were gathered and outfitted for the convoyed transatlantic voyage to Spain. It was also the first stop for the ships carrying goods, passengers, and news from the mother country. Lima and Mexico City were relatively isolated; in contrast, Havana's position at the crossroads of the Spanish empire gave it very early a reputation as the center for all kinds of business and commerce, legitimate and not-so-legitimate. As with all major port cities, it had acquired a character that was both cosmopolitan and tawdry.[10] The city was the center of Spanish power in the Caribbean, and the English knew that capturing it would be a serious setback to the Spanish and the French, not to mention the possible economic benefits of controlling a busy trade center. Havana, as one historian put it, "was reputedly rich in booty."[11]

Because of its importance, Havana was a walled and heavily fortified city. Yet, on August 13, 1762, the Spanish captain-general of Cuba, Juan de Prado, surrendered the city to the English after troops commanded by Lord Albemarle from the naval expedition led by Admiral George Pocock laid siege to Havana in a bold military maneuver that caught the Spanish unprepared.[12] Albemarle assumed control of the city as if he planned to stay forever. But after only eleven months, the English departed in accordance with the peace treaty signed with France and Spain.

Those eleven months, however, marked the beginning of a transformation in Cuban history. While the English occupation was detested by the residents of Havana loyal to Spain, the *criollos*, the Cuban-born descendants of the Spanish, were discreetly delighted to see the English arrive. Eager to expand their economic horizons beyond the constraints imposed by the Spanish Crown, the *criollo* oligarchy welcomed the English merchants who, as Hugh Thomas observed, made an "immediate descent" upon the island.[13] The consequences were also immediate. Under Spain, the traffic into Havana had been dominated by the royal ships carrying the treasure and goods from the mainland, with only about fifteen commercial vessels entering the harbor each year. During the eleven months of the occupation, however, more than seven hundred merchant ships entered Havana, many of them from the English North American colonies.[14]

The floodgates of commerce between Havana and the rest of the world had been flung open, and the Spanish Crown found it difficult to close them after resuming control of the city. It was not for lack of trying. Laws and royal decrees during the 1780s sought to retain Madrid's economic control over the colonies, especially in the face of mounting trade with North America. One such measure limited the number of days foreign vessels could remain in Spanish American ports.[15] But the restrictions proved futile. Cuba was far from Spain, and the nearby North American colonies were able to provide much-needed supplies. The economic interests of the colony prevailed over allegiance to Spain, even among the Crown's officials on the island. Foreign-owned ships carrying slaves, for example, were allowed to dock in Cuban ports.[16]

Two events that occurred in the remaining years of the eighteenth century helped to intensify Cuban-North American trade relations: the independence of the thirteen English colonies and the Cuban sugar boom.

Even in the throes of the American Revolution, the importance of trade with Cuba was recognized by the Congress of the Confederation when in 1781 it appointed an agent "to reside at Havana, to manage the occasional concerns of Congress, to assist American traders with his advice and to solicit their affairs with the Spanish government."[17] When independence from Britain was achieved, trade with Cuba could develop unfettered by European interests and conflicts.[18] The Napoleonic wars, blockades and closures of continental ports, occupations of colonies, and other actions disruptive of commerce left the United States as a neutral trading partner for Cuban merchants and producers.[19] Leaving the British empire also meant that the Americans had to aggressively expand their markets as they lost the protectionism that the English exercised over the products of their colonies.[20]

Increasingly isolated by the European wars, unable to supply its Caribbean colonies with all their needs, and incapable of absorbing all of Cuba's productive capacity, Spain relented in its efforts to curb U.S.-Cuba trade. In 1797 the Spanish Crown formalized what had thus far been a tacit approval of U.S.-Cuba trade through a royal decree that authorized commerce with "neutral" ships.[21] During 1798, the year after the royal decree, 431 American ships anchored in Havana, compared to only 97 Spanish ships, and even some of those Spanish vessels were cleared for the United States.[22] In 1801, 824 U.S. ships entered Cuban ports.[23] "Cuban-American trade," observed Bernstein, "exceeded the island's commerce with Spain."[24] Cuba was a Spanish colony, but by the start of the nineteenth century, its ports, especially Havana, were in the service of the trade with the young American nation.

As the eighteenth century closed, another development served to multiply the volume of trade between Cuba and the United States: the start of the boom in the island's sugar production. What became known as Cuba's sugar revolution transformed the island's economy and society and tied Spain's colony closer to the United States, particularly New York.

Beyond the walls of Havana lay a vast countryside whose full agricultural potential remained largely unrealized for centuries as the Spanish focused on the precious mineral resources of the mainland and assigned Cuba the role of transportation hub. When the British invaded Havana, nearly three hundred years after Columbus set foot on Cuba, one-fourth of the population of the entire island was still clustered around Havana's piers, facing the harbor, and walled off from the hinterland.[25]

The nascent Havana *criollo* oligarchy had largely been responsible for the piecemeal development of the sugar industry in the region outside the city. At the time of the British occupation there were fewer than a hundred sugar mills in the area.[26] Cuba was nowhere close to having a true plantation economy on the scale that had been developed in the neighboring British and French island colonies. In terms of both land and number of slaves, the Cuban mills were relatively small, with modest production and rudimentary technology.[27] The cane grinder itself, or *trapiche*, was a primitive apparatus with three triangulated vertical rollers powered by an animal.[28]

Sugar lagged behind many of Cuba's other agricultural products.[29] Large cattle estates in the east central region of the island had long been producing cured beef that the English and the French bought to feed the large slave populations of their colonies in the Caribbean. Tobacco farmers were already engaged in producing the quality leaves that were among Cuba's earliest and most coveted exports. Scattered throughout the island were the *estancieros*, largely subsistence farmers who made a negligible contribution to Cuba's exports.[30] Cuba's fertile lands were therefore not intensively cultivated and agricultural production was insufficient to make the island a true exporting colony. It carried a heavy trade deficit, especially in its commerce with the United States, importing manufactured goods, textiles, and foodstuffs, especially flour. The explosion in sugar production toward the close of the eighteenth century changed all that. Cuba now had something to sell, and the United States, especially New York, was buying.

Manuel Moreno Fraginals, in his seminal work *The Sugarmill*, first published in 1964, traces the origins of the sugar revolution to the sudden and direct access by the Cuban planters to the British slave trade.[31] It was the sinister underside of the commercial opening caused by the occupation of Havana:

> With the English occupation, the plantation concept of the British Antillean colonies took root in our island. . . . For the first time the Creole oligarchy negotiated directly with the English slaver. In former days, slaves were sold through Spanish merchants or usurious and rapacious middlemen. . . . Under English domination the Liverpool merchant brought his Negroes from his Jamaica depots for direct sale in Havana.[32]

The cheap and massive importation of slaves was the trigger for the sugar boom. The biggest constraint on the growth of the small mills had been the lack of labor.[33] "Sugar development," Moreno Fraginals argued, "depended on the slave trade."[34] From 1764 until 1790, some 33,500 slaves were introduced into Cuba, and that was only the beginning of a massive importation of Africans.[35] In 1789 the Spanish Crown, recognizing the importance of slavery for the development of its colony and bowing to pressure from the *criollo* oligarchy, removed all existing barriers to the free commerce in slaves.[36]

As the availability and supply of slaves increased, so did the need for more acreage on which to grow the cane stalks. The *criollo* planters acquired large amounts of land south and east of Havana, into the Matanzas region. They pushed out small farmers and tobacco growers as they developed sugar estates that eclipsed the small mills based on the *trapiche*.[37]

Growing more cane in turn meant expanding the productivity of the grinding process. In the mills' sugar houses, where the cane was ground and its juice processed, the planters prided themselves on using the latest chemical and mechanical innovations. Two developments in the closing years of the eighteenth century greatly enhanced the technology of sugar production. One was the discovery, in Louisiana in 1795, of the process for granulating sugar. The other was the application of steam power to drive larger and more efficient cane grinders. The expansion in productive capacity created an even greater demand for slaves. It was a vicious cycle that fed on itself. What had once been a small sugar production system with a paternalistic slave regime now became a system of large plantations and factories in which the slave was reduced to a mere factor of production to be exploited to the fullest. Cuba's new sugar regime not only ground cane, it also ground slaves.[38]

At the very end of the eighteenth century another event gave the sugar revolution a further push: the slave rebellion in the neighboring French colony of Saint-Domingue. The rebellion led to the creation of the first independent nation in Latin America and the Caribbean, Haiti, but it devastated its sugar industry. Saint-Domingue had been the world's leading sugar producer, and the sudden and total loss of its production capacity created a huge void in the world sugar market and a sharp increase in prices.[39] The rush to get in on the profitable sugar market fueled even further the self-feeding cycle of slaves-land-technology. "Avarice and boundless ambition to become wealthy," as Moreno Fraginals wrote, characterized the "explosive awakening" of what he called the "sugarocracy," the *criollo* oligarchy that would become Cuba's newest elite.[40]

As the nineteenth century opened, all the factors were in place for the explosion in Cuban sugar production. In 1761, the year before the

British occupation, the 98 small mills in the Havana region combined to produce only slightly more than 4,300 tons of sugar, with an average production capacity of 49 tons per mill. In 1792, at the cusp of the sugar transformation, total production had already multiplied to 13,800 tons. But even that increase was insignificant compared to what would happen during the first half of the nineteenth century. By 1860 total production reached 515,741 tons. Nearly three-fourths of the 1,318 mills in the country were either mechanized or semi-mechanized, with an average production of 432 tons per mill. The 64 fully mechanized mills were responsible for about 15 percent of the total production, with an average production per mill of 1,176 tons. "The nation," wrote Moreno Fraginals, "became a burnt offering to the god sugar."[41]

It is impossible to overstate the impact of the sugar juggernaut on Cuba. The sugarocrats multiplied their wealth, spending conspicuously, purchasing titles of nobility, and building fabulous homes in Havana. The old Spanish port city, which for more than two hundred years had stayed within the confines of its protective walls, broke through those walls as it transformed itself from a shipping hub to a true trade center, exporting the products of a large cash crop grown in its hinterland.

The most evident impact of the sugar revolution on Cuban society was demographic. The census of 1774 showed that nearly three centuries after the Spanish set foot on Cuba, the island's population amounted to only 171,620. Slightly over 20 percent were slaves. But by 1827, only fifty-three years later, the total population more than tripled, to 704,487, with slaves now representing in excess of 40 percent of the population. Just fourteen years later, in 1841, the population passed the million mark and the proportion of slaves continued to rise.[42]

The explosion in population, wealth, sugar production, and exports occurred at a time, as we have already seen, when the United States was already Cuba's major trading partner. The Americans were therefore on the ground floor of the new expanding Cuban sugar economy. U.S. merchants immediately opened offices in Havana and Matanzas, the two northern Cuban ports serving the sugar-producing region. They extended credit to the planters and became their agents, shipping sugar products to the United States and importing U.S. goods.[43] Industrial machinery was in special demand in Cuba as the planters continually upgraded and expanded the productive capacity of the mills.

As its population boomed and the Cuban economy moved closer to a monoculture, the need to import foodstuffs increased dramatically. Also in demand were luxury items that helped the sugarocracy exhibit its new wealth: the latest fashions, carriages, furnishings, and so forth. The United States was the nearest and preferred provider of all those goods, as well as the largest market for Cuba's sugar.

Throughout the first half of the nineteenth century, trade between the United States and Cuba boomed. In 1830 alone, 936 U.S. ships entered Cuban ports.[44] By 1835 commerce with Cuba reached such proportions that it became an important factor in the total U.S. trade picture. Roland T. Ely, using the annual reports of the U.S. Treasury Department, came to the following conclusion:

> The combined value of exports and imports for the Cuba trade consistently ranked third or fourth place relative to the total commerce of the United States between 1835 and 1865.[45]

At first, New Orleans, Boston, Philadelphia, and Baltimore vied with New York for the flourishing Cuba trade. But in the end New York ended up with the lion's share of the commerce with the island, especially in sugar. By 1860 the port of New York was handling almost two-thirds of all sugar entering the United States.[46] The key to New York's dominance was its capacity to turn a hefty profit through the further industrial processing of the raw sugar.

Cuba exported raw brown sugar, the product of a process by which cane syrup was partially crystalized and then poured into containers with holes in the bottom to allow molasses, a by-product, to slowly drain off. The residue in the container was raw brown sugar. According to Robert Greenhalgh Albion, the sugar arriving in New York from Havana was in its "clayed" form, that is, it had been formed in conical pots that after draining were sealed with moist clay and crated in large wooden boxes. The sugar from Matanzas, on the other hand, was referred to as "muscovado," shipped as half-ton units, the residue of crystalized syrup poured through large hogsheads or casks.[47] No matter what its packaging, however, it was all raw brown sugar that was marketable only to the poorest consumers. The real profit was made by selling it as refined white sugar and packaged in a large cone or loaf.[48] The profitable refining process was done in New York, which even before the Cuba Trade had established itself as the nation's refining center.

In 1689 New York had the first sugar refinery of the North American colonies, and by 1855 there were fourteen plants operating in the city.[49] From 1845 to 1860 the port of New York exported an average of 1.8 million pounds of refined sugar annually. In 1860 alone it exported 4.7 million pounds.[50] Other U.S. port cities did not have New York's capacity to refine Cuba's sugar. Spain had no refineries at all, which explains its lack of interest in cornering its colony's production of raw sugar.[51]

New York's advantage extended to another sugar product, molasses. Most of the imported molasses came from Cuba, and New York brought in more of it than any other U.S. port.[52] While some of the molasses was sold directly to consumers in the Northeast, a good portion of it was distilled into rum. New York was second only to Medford, Massachusetts, in the United States in its rum production, providing yet another opportunity to profitably increase the value of imports.[53]

Besides raw sugar, New York was also interested in Cuban cigars, which became fashionable among the men in the city. In 1860, 243 million cigars came in through New York harbor, more than half of all U.S. cigar imports, and most of them from Havana.[54] Albion states that as many as a million cigars would arrive in a single ship from Cuba's capital.[55] New York would also import Cuban tobacco leaves as the number of cigar factories multiplied in lower Manhattan and New Yorkers, especially German immigrants, turned Cuba's unprocessed imports into a manufactured product.

New York's exports to Cuba were, of course, much more diverse than the products arriving from Cuban ports. As noted earlier, the island's increased population and wealth and its dramatic shift to a single crop economy meant that the demand for a wide range of products that New York could provide increased sharply. Cuba had to import practically everything. The sugarocrats bought machinery for their mills, fine linen and clothing for themselves, furnishings for their new mansions, carriages in which to be seen around Havana, and large amounts of foodstuffs, especially flour, to feed their slaves.

The key players in New York's trade with Cuba were the counting houses that lined Manhattan's waterfront. A combination of trading office, warehouse, accounting firm, credit agency, bank, and investment

Figure 1.1 South Street from Maiden Lane, showing the piers and the location of the counting houses. Source: Miriam and Ira D. Wallach Division of Art, Prints and Photographs, New York Public Library Digital Collections, digitalcollections.nypl.org.

manager, these mercantile establishments typically had employees or representatives operating out of offices in Havana and Matanzas. The counting houses cultivated relations with the Cuban planters, extending them credit, acting as their shipping and commission agents, selling their sugar, and purchasing goods in New York on their behalf.

The Cuban sugarocrats came to depend on the New York merchants. The sugar boom was predicated on the expansion and increased complexity of the productive capacity of the mill. This swelled the costs of production without a financial infrastructure on the island to provide the necessary mercantile support. Credit was therefore a particular problem for the planters as they continually invested in land, slaves, and technology. Moreno Fraginals estimated that the amount of investment it took to launch the sugar boom exceeded 15 million pesos, "the highest figure for any business of the period anywhere in the Americas."[56] The New York merchant became both agent and banker for the planter.

Albion argues that the merchants of South and Wall Streets applied to the Cuban sugar planter the same formula they used to deal with cotton producers in Georgia and Alabama. The merchants would advance credit against the next crop, enabling the planters to invest in slaves and New York-made machinery, but usually keeping them in a state of permanent indebtedness to the merchants.[57]

Regardless of whether or not the relationship between merchant and planter was exploitative, one thing is certain: the counting houses and their agents forged links between Cuba and New York that went beyond the commercial sphere, establishing the basis for a profound and extensive exchange of not only goods and money, but also of people and culture.

Louis A. Pérez Jr. has demonstrated how the commercial ties had an impact on creating a considerable American presence in Cuba early in the nineteenth century.[58] The introduction of U.S. technology into the island, especially in the transportation, communication, and production sectors, was accompanied by large numbers of American engineers and technicians. Cárdenas, a port in the Matanzas region, became known as the "American city."[59] By 1826 Havana already had an English-language commercial weekly, the *Mercantile Weekly Report*.[60]

The flow of people and culture, however, also occurred in the other direction, and Cubans started coming in greater numbers to the United States, especially to New York, where the commercial connection with Cuba was strongest. Spearheading that flow were boys and young men from wealthy families seeking an education and work experience, and the counting houses had a direct role in bringing them from Cuba. In many cases, the merchants, at the request of their Cuban clients, would make the arrangements for the sons of merchants and planters to be enrolled in boarding schools in the New York area. The counting house would also temporarily employ young Cuban men in their own operations in New York, a sort of internship that would enable them to learn English and become familiar with modern business operations.[61]

Of all the New York counting houses, the one that had the most profound and sustained influence on the Cuba Trade was Moses Taylor and Company. Established in 1832 and located at 44 South Street, Taylor's counting house conducted business with Cuba for more than fifty years. Many of the company's records have survived and form a massive collection housed at the New York Public Library's Rare Book and Manuscript Division. They provide a fascinating glimpse into how commerce forged the social, cultural, economic, and political links that kept New York and Cuba bound together throughout the nineteenth century.

* * *

Moses Taylor was a fourth-generation New Yorker, born in Manhattan in 1806 to a family of English descent. His father, Jacob, was a cabinetmaker prior to becoming one of John Jacob Astor's most trusted associates in the real estate business. Later in life Jacob served as city alderman and state prison inspector. Although the family was comfortable, the young Moses was not born into wealth and started making his way in life as an apprentice clerk in the mercantile business.[62] By the time he died in 1882, his estate was conservatively estimated at $35 million. Moses Taylor's business career was emblematic of the transition from capitalist mercantilism to industrial and financial capitalism.[63] Although in his later years he concentrated more on banking, rising to the presidency of City Bank, his firm never totally abandoned what had been responsible for his initial financial success: the Cuba Trade.

Taylor's first break as a clerk came when he was hired by the mercantile house of G. G. and S. S. Howland, at the time the most important New York house specializing in the Latin American trade. By the time he was twenty-six, Taylor had a thorough familiarity with the burgeoning commerce with Cuba and, with the aid of Astor, he established his own counting house.[64]

Taylor specialized in importing Cuban sugar, serving as consignor for shipments made to his counting house on South Street. For several years he even owned some of the ships that made regular runs to and from Cuban ports. Roland Ely estimated that by 1865 Moses Taylor and Company "had captured something like one-fifth of the entire sugar trade between Cuba and the United States."[65]

But despite Taylor's best efforts to stay focused on sugar imports, the Cuba Trade made specialization very difficult. It was a business that rested upon the cultivation of relations with merchants and planters in Cuba. In the absence of mercantile institutions on the island (the first commercial banks did not appear until the 1850s), the key to successfully sustaining those relations was to provide the merchant and planter in Cuba with a broad range of business and personal services. The House of Taylor found itself acting as representatives of its Cuban clients for everything from selling sugar consignments to procurement and shipment of U.S. goods to the island, banking and investment services, and even the handling of personal matters of little economic utility for the firm, such as facilitating the education of children in New York and arranging for vacations in the United States. No other New York counting house was as successful as Taylor's in developing such a broad set of contacts with Cuba.

Part of that success was due to Taylor's insistence that the firm not invest in Cuba. Unlike other New York counting houses, Taylor and Company did not purchase any land or mills in Cuba or invest in any commercial venture there. Furthermore, the one service he refused to provide planters was to advance them credit on future crops.[66] Consequently, Taylor was never in competition with any of the Cuban merchants who did extend such credit, nor did he place himself in a potentially competitive or exploitative relationship with the planters. That is probably one reason his Cuban clients had an unwavering faith in the integrity of the operations of Moses Taylor and Company, something that is palpable in the correspondence found in the firm's archives. The Cuban planters and merchants entrusted the South Street firm with their sugar, cigars, money, investments, purchases, and even their wives' New York shopping trips and the education of their children in the United States. A great deal of the trust in the firm was earned not just by Taylor, but also by two associates whose personal qualities and contacts made possible the penetration of the Cuban market: Henry Augustus Coit and Percy R. Pyne.

Taylor knew Coit from the days when they both worked at the Howland firm. Coit was a nephew of the Howland brothers and was their representative in Havana, dealing primarily with that city's most important mercantile and credit house, the Drake Brothers. When the Howland firm reorganized and Coit was excluded as a partner, Taylor gave him an office and clerical assistance at 44 South Street. It was a great move: Coit started steering business in the direction of the Taylor firm.[67] Whereas Taylor had a gruff and businesslike demeanor, Coit was a gregarious and sociable man who had built a strong network of contacts during the years he lived in Cuba. He spoke Spanish and was sensitive to the importance of personal relations in doing business there. Taylor never learned Spanish, nor cared to, and, amazingly for someone who depended so much on the Cuba Trade, did not once visit the island. Coit enjoyed going to Havana and would travel there frequently on Taylor's behalf, sending back to New York letters detailing new trade possibilities. He would also suggest to Taylor certain goodwill gestures toward his Cuban contacts, such as sending a client a barrel of apples as a gift, something Taylor probably would have never thought of doing.[68] Coit would also recruit buyers for Taylor's consigned sugar shipments during his working summer vacations in Saratoga Springs, New York's fashionable playground of the time.

Coit left the firm, and the business world, when he was ruined in the Panic of 1857. Taylor was forever grateful to him. Coit and his socialite Boston wife never had children, so Taylor named one of his own Henry Augustus Coit Taylor.

Replacing Coit as the principal point man in the Cuba Trade was a young man Taylor had hired as an apprentice clerk and promoted over the years to the administrative levels of the counting house, Percy R. Pyne. An enterprising man and excellent manager with great social skills, Pyne learned Spanish and took over the day-to-day operations of the firm's business with Cuba. He eventually became Taylor's son-in-law, succeeding him at the head of the firm when Taylor died in 1882.

Moses Taylor and Company did business for many years with the biggest names among Cuba's merchants and planters. These included the Drake Brothers, regarded as Havana's foremost merchants and bankers and owners of two sugar mills in Matanzas.[69] Other prominent last names among Cuba's sugarocrats who were Taylor's clients include Iznaga, Baró, Moré, and Ajuria.[70]

Taylor's biggest client, however, was Tomás Terry, who maintained a close business and personal relationship with Taylor that started in 1838 and lasted the rest of Taylor's lifetime.[71] Terry built his fabulous fortune on a variety of sugar-related financial operations, including the commerce in slaves. He focused his efforts on the rapidly developing southern region, around Cienfuegos, where he owned several mills. He made most of his money, however, not by producing sugar, but by extending credit to other planters in the region (usually at exorbitant rates), and exporting sugar products and importing machinery for mills.[72] Moses

Taylor and Company was his agent in New York for all exports and imports. Ely estimated that by 1865 Terry was invoicing Taylor for about $1 million a year in sugar and molasses.[73] Toward the end of his career Terry learned from Taylor that there was even greater money to be made, with less risk, by investing in Pennsylvania coal and in U.S. securities.[74] Taylor would handle all those investments from a massive account that Terry kept with him at 44 South Street. Terry is an example of a Cuban client who made the jump with Taylor from trade to industrial and financial capitalism. For Terry, as with other Cuban clients of Taylor, New York started replacing the sugarcane fields of Cuba as their primary focus of investment, and a progressively greater amount of Cuban venture capital was finding its way to Manhattan.

The most fascinating items in the Moses Taylor archives are not the ledger books that detail large financial transactions, but rather the innocuous documents and letters that illustrate how the social and cultural ties between New York and Cuba emerged in the wake of this bustling commercial activity. Taylor, Coit, Pyne, and their associates functioned as more than just merchants of goods and investors of capital. They were agents in a much broader transnational exchange. Part of doing business with Cuba was to effectively act as cultural brokers.

There are the letters, for example, from Don Sebastián Peñalver y Sánchez, third Marquis of Casa Peñalver, the owner of El Narciso, one of the largest sugar estates on the island.[75] The marquis was emblematic of what Moreno Fraginals called "the sugar mill as intellectual adventure."[76] Despite depending on agriculture and slave labor, the sugarocrats saw themselves not as a feudal class, but as an enlightened bourgeoisie with a worldly orientation, attuned to the latest intellectual trends and especially the latest scientific and technological innovations that could be applied to their mills.

In the first of two letters, written from Havana in English and dated February 10, 1849, the marquis thanks Taylor for the recent sales of his sugar in New York under terms Peñalver found very favorable. He asks Taylor to buy for him a sugar grinder and a couple of agricultural implements ("Gidder harrows"), which, he specifies, are to be purchased at A. B. Allen, 191 Water Street.[77] In another letter a few days later, Peñalver adds to his order some "trifles" that Taylor is to also procure for him and ship to Havana as soon as possible, charging all costs to his account:

1 map of the world
1 Lévy, *Histoire Général* (bound in leather)
2 *Études de Géographie* de Lévy
2 *Atlas* de Lévy, partie moderne et partie ancienne
1 *Encyclopédie universelle*, 22 volumes, last edition
1 *Encyclopedia Britannica* 21 volumes quoted $160
1 ditto *Americana*, 14 volumes
The last two English encyclopedias must be of the last edition, and have a print very legible so they don't fatigue the eyes. Begging to excuse the trouble, I remain respectfully,
your most obedient,
Sebn. de Peñalver[78]

Cuba's sugar aristocracy may have had a worldly orientation, but by the nineteenth century that world did not come to them through Madrid aboard a royal ship, but through a New York counting house and aboard a U.S. merchant vessel.

In 1863 Tomás Terry had one of his employees ask Percy Pyne to spend from four to five thousand dollars from Terry's account for the purchase of a set of earrings, brooch, and necklace that Terry wished to give to his daughter for her wedding. The selection of the pieces was left entirely to Pyne's judgment.[79]

Another client, José Alcázar, exchanged several letters with Moses Taylor and Company in 1868 requesting that the firm fill an order for various items to be used in the Tacón Theater, at the time Havana's largest and most elegant venue for the staging of plays and concerts.[80] The order included wall-mounted candelabra, books of blank tickets and a stamping press for printing tickets, fifty wardrobe locks, and matting for the theater's passageways.[81]

Trolling Manhattan for candelabra, wardrobe locks, jewelry, and French encyclopedias was not, however, among the most bothersome tasks that the staff at 44 South Street had to perform for Cuban clients. Far more challenging had to be attending to the constant stream of boys and young men who were sent by clients to study and work in the United States in the care of the counting house. They were usually placed in schools in New Jersey or the Hudson Valley, away from the corrupting influences of the city and where they could learn English rapidly.

Taylor's charges had to be received at the dock, enrolled in a boarding school and transported to it, and outfitted with winter clothing and other necessities; and provisions had to be made for periodic disbursements of tuition, board, and allowances. The Taylor firm was in effect *in loco parentis* of the children sent by their clients, and had to deal with any problems that might arise. Tomás Terry's sons, for example, were even placed under the legal guardianship of Taylor during the years they were studying in the United States.[82]

As one might expect from privileged children suddenly thrust into the austerity of a boarding school, away from family and friends and in an unfamiliar culture, problems arose constantly. Master Enrique Céspedes was enrolled in Nitchy's Institute in West Bloomfield, New Jersey, for only four months when in October 1858 he had to be withdrawn from the school for his behavior. The frustrated school director wrote to the Taylor office,

> I fear it will be attended with some difficulty to find a school for him, where he will be happy and improve at the same time. He is very passionate and has no friends among all my pupils, and is irritable at the slightest and gentlest hints, not even reproaches.[83]

Enrique was the son of a friend of one of the partners in the Manzanillo firm of Torres, Reigadas, and Company, whose sugar was each year consigned to Taylor. In the letter that Enrique carried with him aboard the *California* to New York, Taylor is asked to place him in a school where he can learn English, French, bookkeeping, and "whatever other branches of instruction he is inclined to learn," stressing that he should be in a place where he has no possibility of conversing in Spanish with anyone so that he may quickly learn English. All expenses, including an allowance of four dollars a month, were to be charged to the Manzanillo company's account with the Taylor firm.[84]

After Enrique's problems at the New Jersey school, Taylor's staff enrolled him in a school in the Hudson Valley. He was constantly sending them letters demanding more money for expenses. Dealing with Master Céspedes must have been exasperating for the personnel at 44 South Street, who undoubtedly had more profitable activities that required their attention. When his father requested that they buy him a gold watch as a present, Enrique insisted that he be sent the fare to go to the city so that he could pick out the watch himself. When the office refused, he wrote letters to Taylor insinuating that the venerable multimillionaire counting house owner was pocketing part of his allowance. After about sixteen months in this second school he was also asked to leave by the director in a letter to Taylor and Company:

> I find myself obliged to call your attention to our somewhat eccentric young friend Enrique Céspedes. . . . I can not . . . retain him another quarter. . . . He is becoming daily less and less amenable to either kindness or rule, and his particularly treacherous character and readiness at all kinds of subterfuge renders him a dangerous inmate.[85]

Upon receiving a copy of the letter, and without even waiting for a decision from Enrique's father, Torres and Reigadas wrote to Taylor asking that the youngster be placed on the first ship to Havana so as to "liberate you as soon as possible from the impertinences that, much to our sorrow, this young man has caused you."[86]

Master Céspedes was probably not the most troublesome of Taylor's Cuban charges. That distinction may have belonged to Baltasar Velázquez, who was enrolled by Henry Coit in 1845 at the Poughkeepsie Collegiate School. The school was a favorite of Coit for boarding Cuban students. José Aróstegui, José de Lavalette, and the brothers Francisco and J. Loynaz, among others, preceded Velázquez at Poughkeepsie and apparently were good students, since their files have few complaints against them. Velázquez apparently also did well during the four years he attended Poughkeepsie, but after he graduated and left Poughkeepsie for Manhattan for the return trip to Cuba, he dropped out of sight. School director Charles Bartlett, alarmed, wrote a letter to Coit:

> I learned this morning . . . that Mr. Velázquez has not sailed yet for Cuba. I greatly fear his attachment to a young lady, who left this place for the city two days after he left, is the occasion for his remaining in the city. . . . The girl is old enough to be his mother. She is rather pretty in full dress, and is very fascinating in her manners. . . . I think you had better send him home by the first vessel which sails.[87]

Older students were frequently enrolled in St. John's College, as Fordham was then called. Jesuit discipline apparently dealt effectively with many of the behavior problems. Martín Ruiz de Palacios, who was entrusted to Percy Pyne by a client in Sagua la Grande, was enrolled at St. John's in 1858. In his attempt to spend some vacation time in Manhattan, Ruiz apparently convinced Pyne to send him eight dollars, ostensibly so he could visit a friend in the city. The money arrived in a letter sent by the Taylor firm to the school's chief disciplinarian, a Jesuit who replied the following:

> We should not have the least objection to grant Master Ruiz the desired permission; yet as he does not intend to visit any friend but wishes rather to have a *frolic* with a few other Spanish boys of his own age either at the Metropolitan or at the St. Nicholas Hotel, we think it better not to grant his request. We withheld both the letter and the money, which he does not need for College expenses. It has been credited. Master Ruiz has occasionally spent a day in the city with some other students, but always accompanied by one of our gentlemen; he therefore cannot complain that we have not afforded him any means for his amusement.[88]

Ruiz's file also contains a report on his academic progress, signed by R. J. Tellier, S.J., president, with the following annotations (in Spanish): "he does not regularly conform to the smoking prohibition," and "from time to time he uses indecorous expressions."[89]

Taylor's staff would also place young Cuban men in unpaid internships with firms that had some connection with the Cuba Trade. Ramón de Céspedes (no apparent connection to the infamous Enrique) was placed at the West Point Foundry in Cold Spring, New York, in April 1855 after studying engineering for a few months at a school in New Canaan, Connecticut.[90] Located on the Hudson about forty miles from Manhattan, the West Point Foundry was one of the country's largest ironworks, producing military ordnance, steam engines, pipes for water systems, and the cast-iron used in the facades of many Manhattan buildings.[91] It was the most important manufacturer of the sugar grinders the Taylor firm would buy for clients in Cuba. The steam-powered grinder at Tomás Terry's Esperanza sugar mill, for example, was purchased by

Taylor in 1858 from West Point.[92] Working at the foundry afforded a young Cuban such as Ramón the opportunity to learn not only about business operations but also about the design and construction of the machinery so critical to Cuba's sugar industry.

De Céspedes reported to Pyne that he had found room and board with a family in Cold Spring for $4.50 a week.[93] Despite a monthly allowance of thirty dollars, De Céspedes would pepper Pyne with letters asking for additional money for expenses such as boots and winter clothing, alleging that he was "peniless" [sic].[94] He returned to Cuba in March 1856.[95]

Assuming the demanding role of caretaker in the United States for these and many other Cuban youngsters was obviously a necessary and worthwhile burden for Moses Taylor and his associates. The file that the firm kept on boarding schools in the New York region, with brochures and letters from headmasters, was almost as large as the file it had on sugar refiners and sugar equipment manufacturers. It was quite simply an important part of the firm's operations and one that reflected its Cuban clients' interest in educating their children in the lives and ways of the country with which they conducted the bulk of their business. It was a phenomenon not limited to Moses Taylor and Company. In 1850, one New Yorker estimated that nearly two thousand young Cubans had already been educated in U.S. schools, adding that "their ideas and customs upon returning to the island are more North American than Spanish."[96]

* * *

The business of the South Street counting houses had created a bridge between lower Manhattan and Cuba. On the back of New York's Cuba Trade rode an extensive network of social contacts that would cement the New York-Cuba connection and begin the process by which New York—and by extension the United States—replaced Spain as the "other" place in the Cuban consciousness. That substitution, which had already occurred in the commercial arena before the end of the eighteenth century, would rapidly expand to the social, cultural, and political spheres. It was the basis for the rise on the island of Manhattan of a community that for most of the nineteenth century remained the largest concentration of Latin Americans east of the Mississippi.

2

Exiles, Sojourners, and Annexationists

> I am here, my dear Marquis, in this metropolis of social
> equality and commercial arrogance they call New York.
> —María de las Mercedes Santa Cruz y Montalvo in a letter
> to the Marquis de Pastoret, 1844[1]

Cristóbal Madan y Madan was a teenager when he arrived in New York aboard the brigantine *Emma* from Matanzas on June 24, 1822.[2] His family's origins were in Waterford, Ireland, where the name was probably spelled Madden. Cristóbal's grandfather migrated to Havana by way of the Canary Islands around the time of the British occupation of the city, the right moment to get in on the ground floor of the sugar boom. The family lived in Havana, but its mills were in the Matanzas region. Cristóbal was named after his maternal grandfather, who was also his father's uncle. Cristóbal's father, Joaquín, had married a first cousin, Josefa Nicasia Madan. Joaquín and Josefa had six children, of which Cristóbal was the youngest and the only male. After his wife died, Joaquín married yet another first cousin, Josefa's sister. They had no children.[3]

As with many other young men from Cuba's sugarocracy, the young Cristóbal went to New York to learn English, study, and gain experience in the city's mercantile world. Arrangements were made for him to intern as a clerk in the counting house of Jonathan Goodhue, a New Englander who had moved to South Street from Salem and was engaged, years before Moses Taylor, in importing sugar from the mills of the Madans and other Cuban producers.[4] Goodhue and Company was located at 44 South Street, the same address where Moses Taylor would later establish his counting house.[5]

On a cold day in December 1823, the sixteen-year-old Madan heard Goodhue, in an excited voice, summon him to the front of the office. There, in a meager coat peppered with snow, stood Father Félix Varela, an acquaintance of Goodhue and Madan's former philosophy teacher in

Havana. The Cuban priest and intellectual had gone directly from the dock of the *Draper* to the one place in the city where he knew people from his days in Havana: a South Street counting house.[6] Madan arranged lodging for Varela at a boardinghouse on Broadway. For days thereafter he took his former teacher on walks near the piers, steadying him as Varela became accustomed to walking on the icy streets.

Only two months before Varela arrived in New York, a handful of Cubans living in the city decided to meet with Simón Bolívar, the man who had just ended Spanish colonialism in much of South America, to persuade him to send part of his army to Cuba and liberate the island. They were led by one of the first exiles in the city, José Aniceto Iznaga, a young man from a wealthy landowning family of Basque origins that had established itself in Trinidad, in southern Cuba, in the early part of the eighteenth century.[7] Known for his impetuousness, the young Iznaga had run afoul of the authorities on the island for his many challenges to colonial rule, and was forced to move to New York in 1819.[8] Together with his brother Antonio and other members of an embryonic New York Cuban community, they would periodically meet at the Manhattan home of Bernardo Sánchez to hatch plans for wresting Cuba from Spain.[9] On October 23, 1823, six of them, including Iznaga and a young Cuban who was studying in New York, Gaspar Betancourt Cisneros, left the city aboard the *Midas* for La Guayra, on the northwest coast of South America, for their meeting with the famed liberator. Iznaga paid for the group's travel expenses.[10]

Needless to say, nothing came of the scheme, but it marked the debut of New York as the prime staging area for the plots and campaigns of Cuban émigrés in their struggle against Spanish colonialism. It was a struggle that would last the rest of the century.

* * *

By the time he arrived in New York, Father Félix Varela had an established reputation as an educator, philosopher, and advocate of Cuban separatism.[11] During the first two years he lived in the United States, he wrote extensively about Cuba, arguing for a change in the political status of the island and the need to abolish slavery.

Varela's early writings in the United States circulated in a serial he founded entitled *El Habanero*. It was described on the cover as a "politi-

Figure 2.1 Félix Varela. Source: "Félix Varela," *Juventud Rebelde*, June 5, 2017, www.juventudrebelde.cu.

cal, scientific, and literary paper written by F. Varela." Seven issues of *El Habanero* were published between 1824 and 1826. The first three were printed in Philadelphia, where Varela lived for a few months in 1824, and the last four in various printing houses in Manhattan. Each issue had twenty-five to thirty pages on sheets that were folded into a size that could fit into envelopes.[12] The idea was to send as many copies as possible of *El Habanero* to Havana.

Varela's bold essays calling for a new social and political order for Cuba did reach the island and had a notable impact. But with the reinstatement of King Ferdinand to the throne and the loss of much of Spain's empire to independence movements, the Crown did not want Cubans thinking about change. The island's colonial governor, Francisco Vives, was given extraordinary emergency powers to deal with any manifestations of disloyalty to His Majesty.

Governor Vives did more than just ban *El Habanero*. Varela had already been sentenced to death *in absentia* for his part in the ill-fated and progressive Spanish legislature of 1822–1823.[13] With the publication of *El Habanero*, Vives decided to apply the sentence. An assassin was dispatched to New York in the spring of 1825. One of Varela's biographers identified him as "One-Eyed Morejón" of the Havana police and one of Vives's "thugs."[14] Varela's sympathizers in Havana alerted their friends in New York, and the plot was foiled by the vigilance of Varela's Irish parishioners, who had befriended the priest and had no sympathy for colonialists. The one-eyed Spanish-speaking stranger no doubt had difficulty passing unnoticed in the Irish neighborhood and returned to Havana, presumably without earning the 30,000 pesos Vives promised him for the job.[15] Although the attempt on Varela's life did not materialize, it was clear that he could not return to Havana.

That same year, the president of Mexico, Guadalupe Victoria, invited Varela to sail to Veracruz aboard a Mexican warship that was due to arrive in New York. The president offered the protection of his government for as long as Varela wished to live in Mexico. The priest declined the generous invitation, preferring to stay in New York. It was a decision that spoke volumes about the place that New York had come to occupy in the Cuban economic, political, and cultural landscapes. No doubt Varela would have felt more comfortable leaving New York. During those first years in the city he did not adjust well to the cold weather or to the language, which he found difficult to learn. "The whistling sound of English," he wrote at the time, "rings in my ears like impertinent flies, making it hard to write comfortably in Spanish."[16] And yet, when offered a privileged opportunity to move to a Spanish-speaking warmer country, he chose to face New York's climate and language. That choice was to be repeated in subsequent decades by exiles who wished to stay close to their native island and remain active in its affairs. In terms of economic, political, and socio-psychological distance, the closest place to Cuba was New York. Varela would remain there for almost thirty years, eventually conquering English to the point of speaking it almost without an accent.[17]

As soon as Varela returned to New York from Philadelphia, in 1824, he accepted an offer from New York's first resident bishop, the Irish-born John Connolly, to do pastoral work in the diocese. He was assigned to St. Peter's Church on the corner of Barclay and Church Streets and moved into a nearby house at 140 Fulton Street.[18]

At the time there were only two Catholic churches in Manhattan besides St. Peter's: the old St. Patrick's Cathedral, at Mott and Prince Streets, and St. Mary's, a small church near Grand Street. Only six priests

manned those churches, serving some thirty-five thousand parishioners.[19] During subsequent decades, the New York diocese experienced
tremendous growth, fueled primarily by Irish immigration. The talented
and dedicated Cuban priest quickly emerged as a key player in shaping
that growth.

Varela's contributions to the New York diocese were critical at a time
when the Catholic Church faced extraordinary challenges. In the 1830s
there was a vicious revival of anti-Catholicism among Protestant funda-
mentalists. The sermons and writings of some of the "anti-Papists" even
fueled acts of vandalism and arson against Catholic churches in New
York and New England. Varela recalled one incident in Boston when his
dinner with that city's bishop was interrupted by shouts and gunfire in
the street. Bostonians were celebrating the acquittal of virtually all of the
defendants accused of burning down an Ursuline convent in Charles-
town, just outside the city. The celebration turned ugly when shouts
went up asking for "the heads of the Catholic priests."[20]

Varela witnessed another incident in which some five hundred parishioners of the old St. Patrick's Cathedral surrounded the church
in anticipation of an attack by a mob intent on burning the building.
Bloodshed was narrowly averted when the municipal authorities intervened.[21] Varela wrote that religious tolerance exists only legally in the
United States, otherwise "it is an abominable hypocrisy to pretend to
have tolerance."[22]

But the Cuban priest was not intimidated by the climate of religious
intolerance and violence. Whatever New York's anti-Catholics could mus-
ter against him paled in comparison to what he had already experienced.
Varela had narrowly escaped the grasp of Ferdinand's troops in Spain, the
executioner waited for him Havana, and he was targeted by an assassin.
"I am perfectly cured of the malady of fright," he once wrote.[23] He summoned his training as a theologian and philosopher and his skills in ex-
pository writing and took up the role of defending the Church in the area's
Catholic publications, especially the *Truth Teller*. In 1830 he founded the
Protestant Abridger and Annotator, primarily to respond to attacks made
in *The Protestant*, a newspaper of the Presbyterian Church in New York.
He also founded the *Catholic Observer* and the *New York Weekly Register
and Catholic Diary*.[24] He battled with the Public School Society, which
funneled public education funds exclusively to Protestant schools.

Varela's courageous defense of the Church rapidly made him the intellectual leader in the small but growing New York diocese and he became a favorite of the new bishop, the French-born Jean DuBois. But Varela's most lasting contribution to the New York diocese was the founding of two downtown parishes, greatly expanding the number of parishes to accommodate the growing influx of Irish immigrants. It all started when he learned that an Episcopalian church at 33 Ann Street was for sale. There was a generous offer on the property from a group of horse riders looking to establish a clubhouse. The Episcopal elders, however, were willing to sell Christ Church for less if it remained a house of worship. Varela raised funds from prominent Catholics in the city, among them several wealthy Spaniards and Cubans, and bought Christ Church for $19,000.[25]

Christ Church was dedicated on July 15, 1827, by Bishop DuBois, and became Manhattan's fourth Catholic parish, with Varela as its pastor.[26] Eventually he acquired the adjacent building, 45 Ann Street, and opened there a day school for boys and girls that offered not only religious instruction, but also classes in grammar, crafts, music, French, and Spanish.[27] In that adjacent building he also established modest living quarters for himself and the assistant pastor, Joseph Schneller, an Austrian ex-Jesuit described by one source as "irascible," and who eagerly joined Varela in his intellectual polemics with the city's anti-Catholics, serving as editor of the *Weekly Register and Catholic Diary*.[28] Varela lived at 45 Ann Street from 1829 to 1834.[29]

A noteworthy aspect of the establishment of Christ Church was the manner in which Varela legally structured the ownership and administration of the parish. An issue that at the time divided lay Catholics and the Church hierarchy was control of the parishes. Unlike the situation in most of the world, U.S. Catholic congregations exerted control over their parishes through boards of trustees in a manner similar to Protestant churches. Bishops were always battling the lay trustees for control.[30] Although rooted in American ideals of democracy and independence, the "trustee problem" also had economic origins. Catholic congregations usually raised the money to establish parishes and then sought to maintain financial control through a corporation run by a lay board. The only prerogative bishops had was the appointment of priests, and even that was frequently questioned.[31]

Varela witnessed at St. Peter's the conflict between the bishop and the parish's trustees. Accustomed to the strong hierarchical structure of Spanish Catholicism, the Cuban priest found the American model bizarre, akin to the flock giving orders to the shepherd. He was evidently not ready to apply to the religious area the spirit of independence so evident in his writings on the political destiny of Cuba. Since Varela raised the money for Christ Church and executed the purchase, he placed the property in the name of the bishop and created a parish board that elected the Cuban priest as chairman. The arrangements Varela made for diocesan control of Christ Church became the norm for parishes established in Manhattan in subsequent years, giving the bishops greater authority over congregations.[32]

Christ Church had a short history. On Sunday, October 27, 1833, while Father Schneller was administering communion, there was a loud rumble as a large fissure spread across the interior wall of the church.[33] Excavations for a construction project near the church had undermined its foundations. Makeshift services were held at 45 Ann Street and at a location rented by Varela at 208 William Street. But it was clear immediately that the old Episcopalian house of worship had to be abandoned. Two fires, one in 1834 and another, probably part of the Great Fire of December 16, 1835, finally destroyed the building.

Two parishes emerged from the destruction of Christ Church. To replace it, the diocese bought land on St. James Street, between Madison and Chatham Streets, in the vicinity of the Five Points area, and constructed an imposing Romanesque church on the site, a structure that stands to this day. It was officially named Christ Church, but became known as St. James. Part of the funds for the new church came from the sale of the property on Ann Street. The new church was to serve the parishioners of the old Christ Church, but many of them considered the new location of their parish to be too far north and east. Although he was to be transferred to St. James once it was built, Varela wanted to remain with his congregation.

One of Varela's staunchest supporters, the Swiss restaurateur Giovanni Delmonico, came to the rescue. Only a few years before, in 1827, he and his brother Pietro had opened a restaurant at 21–25 William Street. With the help of their nephew Lorenzo, they would turn Delmonico's into a New York culinary landmark that survived well into the twentieth century.[34]

The story goes that one day as Delmonico was walking along Chambers Street, just east of Broadway, he noticed an auction under way for the sale of a church building, the Dutch Reformed Presbyterian Church. Knowing the predicament of Varela and his flock, he placed the winning bid, $56,000, leaving a cash deposit. Delmonico's impulsive action was both good news and bad news for Varela. It was a fine building and its location was perfect for keeping together his Ann Street congregation. But the price tag gave Varela pause. Eventually, however, Delmonico and the other generous benefactors who formed the new parish's board came up with the down payment, a mortgage was secured, and the purchase of the building went ahead.[35] Because of the size of the mortgage, Varela apparently chose not to turn the property over to the bishop, placing it instead under his own name, thereby taking personal financial responsibility for it.[36] Apparently enough funds were secured for Varela to purchase a modest house just around the corner, at 23 Reade Street, to serve as rectory and residence. He would live in that house for the rest of his years in New York.[37]

A cry of protest went up in the city's anti-Catholic circles when it was learned that the old Dutch Reformed church had fallen into the hands of the "Papists."[38] Ignoring the outcry, Varela renamed it the Church of the Transfiguration of Our Lord. On March 31, 1836, months before St. James was completed, Transfiguration Church was inaugurated with Varela as pastor.

Varela was rising to prominence within the leadership of the Catholic Church in the United States. By 1829 he was already serving as vicar general of the New York diocese. During the two years that Bishop DuBois was in Europe, Varela and the other vicar general, John Power, his former colleague at St. Peter's, had responsibility for the administration of all diocesan matters.[39]

When DuBois prolonged his stay in Europe, it was rumored in New York that he did not intend to return and that he was quietly lobbying the Vatican to have Varela replace him.[40] The rumors were totally unfounded, but they alarmed Spain's representatives in the United States, who had been keeping a close watch on Varela's growing influence within the New York diocese. Francisco Tacón, the Spanish minister in the United States, sent a letter on March 14, 1830, to his superiors in Madrid charging that Varela, a known enemy of Spain, was conspiring with DuBois to assume the New York bishopric.[41] Spain's minister of state immediately instructed his Vatican ambassador to communicate to the Holy See the concern that "this bad Spaniard and worse priest," who has maintained "intimate and criminal relations with . . . agitators," not be allowed to "realize his ambitious designs."[42] The response from Cardinal Albani, the Vatican's secretary of state, was that the New York bishopric was not vacant and therefore no consideration was being given to Varela, but should he be proposed in the future for an appointment, the concerns of His Majesty's government "will not be forgotten."[43] The Spanish recognized Varela as a pioneer voice for Cuban independence and they were relentless in their persecution of him.

One reason the Spanish were always vigilant of him is that despite the growing burden of his pastoral and administrative duties, Varela continued to write, thereby maintaining a presence among Cuba's leading thinkers. In addition to his numerous intellectual skirmishes with the detractors of Catholicism, written in English and published in religious publications, he wrote in Spanish primarily for his compatriots on the island. An essay or review by Varela would occasionally appear in one of Cuba's journals. In New York he updated and printed several editions of his most important philosophical work, *Lecciones de filosofía*, first published in Havana in 1819. He also found time to translate into Spanish Thomas Jefferson's *Manual of Parliamentary Procedure* and *Elements of Chemistry Applied to Agriculture* by Humphrey Davy, books that Varela considered important for the political and economic future of Cuba. Both translations were printed in New York in 1826.[44]

In 1835 the printing house of William Newell, at 162 Nassau Street, produced the first volume of a planned three-volume work by Varela, *Cartas a Elpidio*, written in the form of letters to a fictitious friend. Varela's intention was to call his countrymen's attention to what he considered the most important problems plaguing society. The first volume dealt with the causes and negative effects of impiety. The second volume, on the distinction between religion and superstition, and the damage done by the latter, was printed in 1838 by G. P. Scott and Company, located at the corner of John and Gold Streets. The planned third volume, on fanaticism and its contribution to despotism, was never written, apparently because Varela perceived that the first two were not well received in Cuba. The two published volumes, however, were eventually recognized as important contributions to Cuban philosophical and theological thought.

By the 1840s Varela had settled into the demanding routine of a parish priest in a diocese with a booming population of needy immigrants. He became involved in many charitable projects, among them the Half-Orphan Asylum, incorporated as the Asylum for the Relief of the Children of Poor Widows, located in Greenwich Village and run by the Sisters of Charity. Varela raised the funds for its establishment and operation.[45] It eventually became the Roman Catholic Orphan Asylum, its buildings later integrated into St. Vincent's Hospital.[46] His individual acts of charity became legendary among New York's Catholics.

Part of his obligations as pastor of Transfiguration was to retire the mortgage on the building while also meeting the parish's escalating operating expenses. It was a daunting task that became almost an obsession with him. In 1846 the parish's debt was over $36,000.[47] He raised funds and also borrowed money, eventually taking out another mortgage on the property and contributing whatever personal funds he had left. In 1842 he was taken to court by a Thomas Gorley, who filed suit against Varela and the Corporation of the Transfiguration seeking payment on a loan he allegedly made five years before for the purchase of the church building. Gorman sought payment on the $3,000 principal plus interest of 7 percent, compounded semiannually. Three years later, the Court of Common Appeals ruled in favor of Varela, citing the plaintiff's failure to produce the evidence that the sum was a loan and not a gift.[48]

Varela's residence at 23 Reade Street was the operations center of one of the largest parishes in the diocese. The 1840 U.S. census found him there, as the head of a household consisting of twelve people: six men, four women, and two children.[49] All were probably either parish religious staff or servants and their offspring. One of the characteristics of Transfiguration Church was its multinational staff. The most notable of the various assistant pastors to serve under Varela was Alessandro Muppietti, an Italian Carthusian monk who was also known for his charitable work and became a trusted aide and friend of Varela during the Cuban priest's last years in New York.[50]

Eusebio Guiteras, a Cuban writer who lived in Philadelphia, visited Varela at that time and years later wrote a description of 23 Reade Street. It was a modest two-story brick house with a "poorly furnished living room" and a room on the second story that served as both bedroom and study for Varela, with "a simple bed, a copper-topped writing desk, and several walnut shelves full of books."[51]

Eventually Varela shifted all of his attention to his pastoral work in New York, virtually abandoning the situation in Cuba. He stopped writing essays in Spanish for readers on the island. His priestly duties probably overwhelmed him but gave him a greater sense of purpose in life than trying to influence the destiny of the island. He was convinced that the *Cartas a Elpidio* were not well received there. Furthermore, he may have felt a certain futility about changes in Cuba's political status. Not only were the Spanish intent on maintaining firm control of the island, but many of his fellow Cubans were starting to support annexation to the United States as an alternative to Spanish rule. They included some of his closest New York followers, such as Cristóbal Madan.[52] Despite Varela's fondness for the United States, he could not support annexation. He opted for withdrawing from the scene rather than oppose his friends. One of those friends, Gaspar Betancourt Cisneros, visited him several times at 23 Reade Street in a fruitless effort to get him involved in the growing annexationist movement. His frustrated parting words to Varela after their last meeting in 1849 were, "even if Cuba is no longer yours, you belong to Cuba, and Cuba will not renounce its right to Varela."[53] Betancourt Cisneros later observed to a friend that Varela was "entirely devoted to his Church and his Irishmen."[54]

Despite his separation from the affairs of his homeland, Varela's sentimental attachment to Cuba remained unshakable. When asked why he had not become a U.S. citizen, he replied,

> I am in affection a native of this country, although I am not nor ever will be a citizen, having made a firm resolution to become a citizen of no other country, after the occurrences which have torn me from my own. I never expect to see it again, but I think I owe it a tribute to my love and respect by uniting myself to no other.[55]

His exhausting work regime, the financial problems of the parish, and all those New York winters eventually took their toll on the frail priest. He developed respiratory problems and was advised to go to warmer climates. During the late 1840s he would spend the winters in St. Augustine, Florida, where he had lived for several years as a child and had several acquaintances. His departure from New York before the winter of 1849–1850 was his last. The New York diocese had no facilities to care for ailing priests. He had just turned sixty-one. In April 1850 he deeded the property of Transfiguration Church, which had been in his name, to Bishop John Hughes (who had succeeded DuBois years before).[56]

Varela accepted the hospitality of the pastor of a church in St. Augustine, who gave the ailing priest a small room at the rear of the parish school. It was there on Christmas Day, 1852, that he received the visit from Havana of one of his former students, Lorenzo de Allo, who was shocked to find his revered teacher in such poor health and austere living conditions. Upon Allo's return to Cuba, he wrote a letter about Varela's plight that circulated among the priest's followers. One of them, Gonzalo Alfonso, convened a meeting at his home in Havana to raise funds to send to the priest.[57]

The money collected was sent to St. Augustine with José María Casal, who boarded a steamship for Savannah on February 23, 1853. Because of a storm, the ship could not berth in Savannah and had to continue to Charleston. When Casal finally arrived in St. Augustine on March 3, he learned that Father Varela had died a few days before. He was buried in St. Augustine in a tomb that throughout the rest of the nineteenth century became a place of pilgrimage for many Cubans traveling to the United States. In New York, Bishop Hughes celebrated a Requiem Mass for Varela in the old St. Patrick's Cathedral.[58] Two months later, in May 1853, Transfiguration Parish moved from Chambers Street into yet another former Protestant church building, on Mott and Park Streets, where it now serves a predominantly Chinese congregation with both a church and a school.[59] In 1911 Varela's remains were transferred to Havana and placed in a marble urn on a pedestal in the University of Havana's main assembly hall.

Because of Varela's many contributions to the New York diocese, not the least of which were the founding of two parishes that survive to this day, it can be said that no other Cuban New Yorker has left such an indelible mark on the city as the frail priest who arrived in Manhattan with no intention of staying.

* * *

Father Varela's presence in New York acted as a magnet for other Cuban intellectual and political figures who made the city their permanent or temporary home away from the island. The most prominent one to do so was a young lawyer and philosopher who had replaced Varela on the faculty of the San Carlos Seminary in Havana: José Antonio Saco. Saco arrived in New York on May 22, 1824, aboard the ship *Robert Fulton*.[60] Varela had temporarily relocated to Philadelphia, so Saco followed him there. Since he had not been banished from Cuba, Saco was not an exile and chose to return to the island after a few months in Philadelphia. But in the summer of 1828 he was back in the United States, this time to New York, where Varela had settled. Saco was accompanied on that second trip by José de la Luz y Caballero. Both in their twenties, they had been students of Varela.[61] During almost a year, until May 1829 when de la Luz departed for Paris, New York hosted the three most important Cuban intellectual figures of the time: Varela, Saco, and de la Luz.[62] They were the intellectual pillars in the development of a Cuban national identity and liberal social thought early in the nineteenth century. Saco would eventually be known as a historian and essayist and an early opponent of slavery and of annexation to the United States. He also wrote works in engineering and the natural sciences. His best-known work is a universal history of slavery. De la Luz became a philosopher and educator whose school in Havana trained several generations of Cuba's elite.[63]

Saco remained in New York three years before returning to Havana. During that time he and Varela edited what was arguably the first serial publication edited by Cubans in New York and in the United States, *El Mensajero Semanal*. This publication was different from Varela's *El Habanero* in that it was published with regularity, usually every Saturday. Seventy-six issues appeared between October 18, 1828, and January 29, 1831.[64] *El Mensajero* circulated in Havana, although the Spanish authorities viewed it with suspicion because of its liberal and progressive bent. The publication served to reaffirm New York's position on the Cuban cultural and intellectual map.

* * *

Cristóbal Madan apparently had become the designated greeter of Cubans arriving in New York. A week after Father Varela showed up at the counting house of Jonathan Goodhue, a trio of Cubans also made

Figure 2.2. José María Heredia. Source: "Biografía de José María Heredia," *Pensar y escribir es como vivir* (blog), May 23, 2011, www.letrasporlaweb.blogspot.com.

their way to South Street looking for Madan. It was December 22, 1823, and the three young men had just arrived in New York from Boston on the Post Road stagecoach. They were from Matanzas, where Madan's family owned sugar estates. Of the three, the most remarkable one was a twenty-year-old aspiring poet named José María Heredia.

Like Varela, Heredia arrived in New York after barely escaping the grasp of King Ferdinand, who had been restored to the Spanish throne. Heredia had been accused of taking part in a conspiracy in favor of independence, and an order was issued for his arrest on November 7, 1823.[65] He hid in the home of friends on the outskirts of Matanzas.[66] A week later, disguised as a sailor and having bribed the ship's captain, he boarded the brigantine *Galaxy* in Matanzas Bay, bound for Boston.[67]

Guided by Madan, the three men found lodging at a boardinghouse at 44 Broadway.[68] From the moment he arrived in Manhattan, Heredia was beset by the same banes that afflicted Varela: the climate and the language. In a letter to his family in Matanzas, he justified with these words his plans to take a trip south during the winter: "You may think I am just being silly, but that's because you do not know what a winter is like in this land."[69] He had harsh words for English, a language that frustrated him:

> My soul becomes oppressed and I even want to die when I realize that my only hope rests in living the rest of my life among these people, hearing their horrible language, . . . a language that is all anomalies, and I can hardly understand how such a great people has convinced itself to use such execrable gibberish.[70]

But despite the afflictions he suffered in New York, Heredia came to the same conclusion, and for the same reasons, that Varela reached when he arrived in the city. In the first letter Heredia writes from New York, he tells his mother, "One reason I am inclined to remain here is the constant communication there is with Havana; it is where I can easily and frequently receive news of my family."[71] Trade had turned New York into the closest place to Cuba. The commercial ties and the frequency of the contact served to attract and sustain a growing expatriate community. In the case of Heredia, for example, not long after he arrived in the city he was receiving a monthly stipend of fifty dollars from an account in the counting house of the Howland brothers, who were active in the Cuba Trade and were Moses Taylor's initial employers.[72] The account belonged to Heredia's maternal uncle in Matanzas, who supported the aspiring poet after Heredia's father died in 1820. At first, Heredia received all his correspondence from Cuba through the Howland firm, but eventually he transferred his mailing address to Goodhue's counting house, where Cristóbal Madan collected it for him.[73]

Once, when Heredia was visiting New Haven, he wrote a short whimsical letter to Madan that shows the connection between the counting houses, the influx of Cubans into the city, and Madan's singular role at Goodhue's. Addressing Madan as "My dear Consul," he apologetically asks the young clerk to perform some mailing tasks for him, and ironically tells him that at some point Madan may see himself forced to abandon the laborious and sterile job the Republic has entrusted to you, but which you carry out to the satisfaction of all. You have no one to blame but your own generosity, which makes you suffer from the impertinence of runaways and wanderers.[74]

Runaways from Cuba, such as Varela and Heredia, were flocking into New York, and from Goodhue's counting house, Madan was their unofficial consul.

The monthly stipend from his uncle allowed Heredia to move to a more comfortable boardinghouse at 88 Maiden Lane, which he described as an "inn owned by a Frenchman."[75] He wrote to his uncle that there he paid $6.50 a week for room and board, plus $2.00 weekly in the winter to keep the fireplace going. There were cheaper houses, he wrote, for four or five dollars, but they did not serve "rust-beef" with potatoes at lunch nor codfish and all the bread you can eat for breakfast. It was worth it, he assured his benefactor, although he claimed that the expense practically used up his entire allowance.[76]

Heredia earned extra money giving private lessons in Spanish and French, languages that many New Yorkers wanted to learn.[77] The extra income allowed him to travel regularly. He was especially taken by New Haven, which he visited in the summer of 1824 and found its port reminiscent of Matanzas.[78] There it dawned on him that his problems learning English were due to the lack of practice in New York, where he continually spoke only Spanish within the circle of expatriates. In a place like New Haven one can "make progress in English, speaking nor hearing anything else."[79]

But one trip was to mark his literary career: his voyage to Niagara Falls in June 1824. By that time, the Falls had become a major travel destination for Americans. Writers and artists captured them in their writings and paintings, usually portraying the natural wonder as a symbol of America's promise and virtues as a young nation.[80] At Goat Island, facing the Horseshoe Falls, Heredia wrote "Niágara," the ode that would become his most famous poem.[81] "Its stanzas," wrote a twentieth-century analyst of Heredia's work, "bear the mark of the poet's genius and youth as well as the unequivocal message of a romantic, sentimentally Christian moral age."[82] The emotional descriptions of the torrents of water evoked freedom and a reverence for nature, two basic elements in Heredia's poetry that reflect the influence of Byron, his favorite poet, who had died less than two months before in Greece.[83]

The ode first appeared as part of a collection of Heredia's poems under the title *Poesías*, published in New York in June 1825 by Behr and Kahl, booksellers and publishers located at 129 Broadway.[84] *Poesías* was printed by Gray and Bunce, 347 Pearl Street, the printing house that in the same year produced numbers 5 and 6 of Félix Varela's *El Habanero*.[85]

Almost as soon as it appeared, "Niágara" became a classic of Latin American romanticism. Its themes of freedom, the exile condition, and the yearning for a politically impoverished homeland resonated in a continent shaking off colonialism.[86] For decades thereafter, many Latin American intellectuals and writers felt compelled, whenever traveling to New York, to make a pilgrimage to what became Heredia's waterfall to experience what had inspired the Cuban poet.

New York's weather wore down the poet's resolve to stay in the city. Félix Varela, with his priestly stoicism, had turned down the offer from President Victoria of Mexico to move, under his government's protection, to the safety and warmth of that country. When Victoria made the same offer to Heredia, the poet accepted it. He probably decided to go to Mexico for health reasons. In New York he had already contracted tuberculosis, belying the glowing reports about his health he would send in his letters to his mother.[87]

On August 22, 1825, Heredia boarded the schooner *Chasseur*, bound for Alvarado, Mexico.[88] Although he lived in New York less than two years, Heredia left a mark on the city's literary landscape even after his departure. That he was able to do so despite writing in Spanish is a testament not only to his talent, but also to the city's emerging cosmopolitanism and receptivity to the arts. It was a time when New York started to fulfill its destiny as the nation's cultural capital, acting as a magnet for talented writers and artists, creating arts and literary institutions, and attracting the patronage of the city's merchant elite.[89] James Fenimore Cooper and Washington Irving were at the cusp of their careers (*The Last of the Mohicans* appeared in 1826). From his home in the Catskills the English-born painter Thomas Cole, who founded the Hudson River School of American painting, was creating landscapes with a romantic, even religious, reverence for nature's majesty that paralleled Heredia's "Niágara," including at least one painting of the Falls.[90] Years before inventing the telegraph, Samuel Morse was not only painting, but also was heavily involved in the New York Atheneum, an important institution of civic culture in the city.[91]

In that vibrant cultural and intellectual climate, the works of a Cuban romantic poet, even if he wrote in Spanish, did not go unnoticed. Less than two weeks before Heredia left for Mexico, the newspaper *New-York American* published a two-column review of *Poesías*. What was extraordinary about the review is that it was in Spanish, probably making it, as Ernest Moore noted, "the first review in Spanish of a Spanish American book published in the United States."[92] Furthermore, although the review was unsigned, it is attributed to Father Varela, who praised not only Heredia's poetry, but also his "patriotism."[93]

The publication, in Spanish, of Varela's review of *Poesías* in the *New-York American* was a remarkable development, but even more so was the fact that one of the city's most influential intellectual figures set out to translate and edit Heredia's poems. William Cullen Bryant, a New Englander drawn to New York's intellectual climate, arrived in the city the same year Heredia left it.[94] It is not likely that they ever met.[95] But the young Bryant was one of those New Yorkers with sufficient knowledge of Spanish to notice and appreciate Varela's review of Heredia's work. Romantic reverence for nature was a theme that resonated with Bryant's own work. In 1827 Bryant published a translation of Heredia's poem "En una tempestad" ("The Hurricane") and collaborated in the translation and editing of "Niágara." The latter appeared in Bryant's *United States Review and Literary Gazette*.[96]

Despite his short residence in the city, Heredia left us many glimpses of his particular gaze on the events and places of New York. In his letters back home to his mother and uncle he wrote in great detail about what he saw around him, sometimes with a combination of awe and childlike humor and at other times with puzzlement or vexation. He chronicled his trips on the Hudson, the features and services of the steamboats, and the magnificent view of Manhattan from the river.[97] He was not impressed with the parks and gardens of the city, except for Vauxhall Gardens (he called it Vaushall), where, he wrote, one is charged a dime to get in so as to "dispense with the loafers," but once inside one can get free wine or ice cream. On the days when they have fireworks, he noted, they raise the price to forty cents.[98]

When his mother asks for his advice on whether or not his uncle Domingo should put his money in a bank in the United States, Heredia answers that there is no safer place to save or invest in the world, much safer than having it buried several feet underground in Cuba.[99] It was a conclusion that many Cubans would reach, judging from the growing number opening accounts in counting houses and banks in New York.

Heredia's most interesting New York story is his description of a rally he witnessed in City Hall Park in support of DeWitt Clinton, who had been fired by the state legislature from his position as an unpaid commissioner on the Erie Canal Board.[100] Heredia describes how, despite some scuffles and heated exchanges between the demonstrators and their detractors, the event took place, the Clinton supporters had their say, and then everyone calmly went home with no further consequences. He was surprised that there was no serious violence despite the highly charged climate of the rally, in a society where "invariably they hang someone for grabbing a pointed knife to assault another . . . which is why everywhere the dinner knives are rounded so as to avoid any calamities."[101]

Heredia's observations on New York were among the first texts of what would become, by the end of the nineteenth century, a large body of literature by Cubans on the unfolding spectacle of democracy and modernity they witnessed through their residence or sojourns in the United States, especially New York. Abetted by the burgeoning trade and travel between Manhattan and Cuba, that literature was both a consequence of, and a contributor to, the increasing space New York was occupying in the Cuban consciousness. A contemporary literary critic, Luisa Campuzano, expressed it this way:

> With the configuration, increasingly more precise, in the Cuban social imagination of the United States as an alternative option to Spain as a possible model for future nationhood and as a privileged space in which modernity developed vertiginously, a varied and practically undiscovered *corpus* of texts started taking shape in the 1830s written by Cuban travelers who arrived in the cities because of persecution and banishment and who analyzed, favorably as well as unfavorably, U.S. institutions.[102]

Among the Cuban travelers who recorded observations about New York, not exactly favorable ones, was María de las Mercedes Santa

Figure 2.3. María de las Mercedes de Santa Cruz y Montalvo, Countess Merlin. Source: "Presencia de la mujer en la música," Radio Cadena Habana, February 15, 2014, www.cadenahabana.icrt.cu.

Cruz y Montalvo. Daughter of the third Count of Jaruco, she was a member of one of Cuba's oldest and most prominent families of the sugarocracy. Born in Havana in 1789, Santa Cruz moved to Madrid as a teenager with her family, where she remained with her mother after the sudden death of her father.[103] Her maternal grandfather was the Spanish war minister and ally of Joseph Bonaparte, Napoleon's brother and king of Spain. Santa Cruz met and married one of Joseph's aide-de-camps, General Antoine Christophe Merlin, a French count with a distinguished military record in Napoleon's army.[104] As the Countess Merlin, Santa Cruz became one of the most celebrated *belles-dames* of the Paris cultural scene, hosting in her salon meetings and concerts with the foremost artists and literary figures of the time, including George Sand, Chopin, and Balzac.[105]

An educated and opinionated woman who was exposed to the most important intellectual trends in Europe, the countess wrote several memoirs, most of them travel accounts, which are regarded today as perceptive and colorful chronicles of the time. Perhaps the best known is *La Havane*, a travel diary published in Paris in 1844 as a series of letters written in 1840 during her emotional return to Cuba after her husband's death.[106]

Letters 3 through 7 of *La Havane*, written in May 1840, contain descriptions and commentary on New York, where she waited for several days for the ship that would take her to Cuba after the transatlantic voyage from Bristol. This was Santa Cruz's first visit to the United States, and her observations offer a window on how someone of her social position within Cuba's landed aristocracy, a social class increasingly tied to New York, viewed the spectacle of emerging modernism and democratic urban life. For the Countess Merlin, it was not a pretty sight.

She had difficulty finding lodging in the city, commenting that "this city is a veritable ant colony; the hotels are packed. Here reigns a general and perpetual movement. These people do not live, they rush."[107] She found the influence of classical architecture in Manhattan's buildings to be "pretentious and grotesque."[108]

The countess did praise the stylish dresses of New York's women and the work of philanthropic organizations on behalf of the disadvantaged. But she had harsh words for the American ethos and practice of equality, which she viewed as "a very heavy burden." "To satisfy the demands of all," she wrote, "one must submit to intolerable afflictions."[109] She recounts her train ride to Philadelphia, where she had to travel in the same car with "seventy or eighty individuals who chew tobacco, spit, and smell bad."[110] Attending a performance in Manhattan by the famed Viennese ballet dancer Fanny Elssler, she bemoaned that there were no exclusive seating areas in the hall, forcing one to sit among strangers. And even worse, she writes, upon leaving the performance one had to compete with the unruly throng in the street for an available carriage, without being able to use a servant or tip anyone to go and fetch one, since, of course, "an American must not dedicate himself to serve another."[111] On her first morning in New York, she asked the manager of the hotel to secure for her a carriage and a foot servant to follow her around the city:

He laughed in my face and told me that in New York that does not exist; that the cabs are there for everyone, and that servants never ride in the rear, since each person can easily, upon lowering the window, stretch out a hand, turn the knob, and serve oneself.[112]

For the Countess Merlin, the price of collective liberty was individual enslavement, especially of the rich, who in the United States are "always oppressed by the poor and pushed around by the envy of the masses. Thus, liberty is sacrificed to equality."[113] She did not like what she saw in the democratic and egalitarian culture of New York, but she had the uncomfortable feeling she was looking at the future:

Will these American customs be those of the peoples of the future? Are they the inevitable consequences of democratic principles?[114]

For another Cuban woman writer and New York sojourner, the future did not seem at all bleak. The poet Gertrudis Gómez de Avellaneda was a contemporary and admirer of Heredia. She wrote a moving eulogy upon learning of his death.[115] Not until she was a widow, twenty-five years later, did she finally visit New York and make the pilgrimage to Niagara Falls. By the time Gómez de Avellaneda visited Niagara in 1864, at least three other prominent Cuban intellectuals had already retraced Heredia's steps to the Falls. José de la Luz y Caballero and Domingo del Monte, another of Varela's former students, made the trip during their stay with their teacher in Manhattan in the 1820s. In 1848 José Jacinto Milanés, a prominent Matanzas poet, also stood at Goat Island facing the Falls.[116]

In Niagara, Gómez de Avellaneda composed a new homage to Heredia. It was not, however, simply an incantation to nature, but rather a poem that concluded with praise for the progressive spirit and industrial development of the United States, a "young nation," she wrote, "that astounds the world, which sees it as a giant with institutions established by the liberal mind as a model for the Present."[117] In the poem, Gómez de Avellaneda shifts from admiring nature to eulogizing the imposing railway suspension bridge that spanned the Falls: "aerial, indescribable bridge, work of man, who seeks to emulate the work of God, . . . valiant symbol of industrial progress."[118]

Gómez de Avellaneda's praise for the technology and progressive spirit of the new American nation was influenced by the impressions of the United States, and of the Falls, written by a longtime colleague, Ramón de la Sagra.[119] Born in La Coruña, Spain, de la Sagra moved to Cuba in 1823 to accept a position as director of Havana's Botanical Gardens. A man with a wide range of intellectual interests and abilities, de la Sagra was a prolific writer, producing important scientific works on Cuba's agriculture, demography, economics, history, geography, horticulture, biology, and even climate. In 1835 he spent five months traveling throughout the United States. In his meticulous diary of the trip, published a year later in Paris, he repeatedly expressed his admiration for the technology and material progress he observed. He described in detail transportation networks, factories, businesses, and public institutions he visited, citing figures on costs, production, technical specifications, labor, and profits. He also praised the progressive and liberal spirit of the new republic, especially evident in New York, with its gaslit, crowded streets bustling with commerce.[120]

De la Sagra wrote extensively in his diary about Niagara Falls, where he spent several days. He described his emotions before the natural spectacle and gives minute details about the Falls. He even records his lunch and conversations at the hotel with Daniel Thomas Egerton, the British artist who was painting several scenes of Niagara.[121] But de la Sagra did not make a single allusion to Heredia in his travel diary, despite the fact that he was well acquainted with the Cuban's ode. De la Sagra was a liberal and a progressive, an opponent of slavery and a supporter of enlightened government, but he was also Spanish and a foe of Cuban separatism. The historian Ramiro Guerra y Sánchez noted that when de la Sagra arrived in Cuba he became a paladin of Spanish intellectual superiority, purposely ignoring the contributions that Cubans had made to the arts and to the advancement of science.[122] The growing recognition garnered by exiled intellectuals, such as Varela and Heredia, was irksome to loyalists such as de la Sagra. When Heredia was praised for his poetry in a literary magazine published in London by exiled Spanish writers, de la Sagra was incensed.[123] In the summer of 1829, six years before his trip to the United States, de la Sagra used a journal he had founded in Havana to launch a scathing attack on the quality of Heredia's poems. Faulting the poet for "poor knowledge and use of the Spanish language" and "inattention to proofreading," de la Sagra labels Heredia a "fool who has set out to write verses with few ideas to write about."[124]

By this time, Heredia was already living in Mexico, but some of the poems de la Sagra had criticized had been published in *El Mensajero Semanal*, the journal Saco and Varela were editing in New York. Saco, aware of what was behind de la Sagra's attacks and already resentful of the Spaniard's arrogance toward Cuban intellectuals, rose to Heredia's defense in *El Mensajero Semanal*, characterizing de la Sagra's attacks as cowardly and underhanded.[125] De la Sagra, in turn, replied with attacks on Saco and other "sinister men of bad faith" who seek with their defense of Heredia to boost the circulation of their newspaper in Havana. De la Sagra also made elliptical references to the political context of the controversy.[126] The attacks and counterattacks continued into 1830, most of it in the pages of *El Mensajero Semanal*, since Saco would reprint de la Sagra's response from Havana before proceeding to reply to it.[127] Saco even published several essays questioning de la Sagra's credentials as a scientist and naturalist. Although Saco was careful not to fall into the trap of attacking Spain, the colonial authorities on the island sided, as expected, with de la Sagra. Governor Claudio Martínez de Pinillos, who was a friend of de la Sagra and had sponsored his work in Cuba, prohibited the entry through customs of Saco's writings, including *El Mensajero*.[128] It was one factor that led to the publication's demise in 1831.[129]

The bitter Saco-de la Sagra controversy was obviously not about Heredia, but about what Heredia's life and poetry represented in political terms: freedom and independence. The contemporary writer Antonio Benítez Rojo argued that the controversy represents the first set of texts in Cuban history in which literary criticism becomes part of the discourse of resistance.[130] The conflict garnered a great deal of attention in Havana and New York, because, as the historian Ramiro Guerra y Sánchez noted, it was "understood that the covert hostility between the Cubans and the Spanish was manifesting itself in a new form and in a new arena."[131] As such, the controversy was one of the most important Cuban-Spanish intellectual debates of the nineteenth century, for it was an opening volley in the emerging conflict over the future of the island. Originating with Heredia's ode to Niagara and played out in a Cuban newspaper edited in Manhattan, it represented yet another New York episode in the continuing Cuban struggle to achieve nationhood.

* * *

Father Félix Varela did not return to New York after the winter of 1849–1850, preferring to stay in St. Augustine for the remaining three years of his life. Had he gone back to 23 Reade Street in that spring of 1850, he would have been greeted by some extraordinary news on May 11, a Saturday, as he turned to the large headline of that morning's *New York Sun*: "DEPARTURE OF THE EXPEDITION AGAINST CUBA!" He would have found even more extraordinary an accompanying story that announced that "the flag of free Cuba" would be flown that morning in front of the *Sun*'s offices in Manhattan.[132] Varela would have studied with great curiosity the *Sun*'s sketch and description of the flag. The ailing priest, the most renowned pioneer of Cuban separatism and national identity, had never seen this nor any other piece of cloth identified as a flag of Cuba.

Had Varela been in New York that morning, perhaps his former student, Cristóbal Madan, now some forty-five years old, would have come by 23 Reade Street to pick him up so that the priest could witness that singular event: a Cuban flag flying in the breeze. As he had done nearly thirty years before when he was a teenager accompanying Varela on walks along an iced South Street, Madan would have steadied his ailing mentor as they made their way across Chambers Street and through City Hall Park, down Nassau past Ann Street, where the old Christ Church used to be, to the corner of Nassau and Fulton, the location of the *Sun*. There they would have seen not just a Cuban flag, but *the* Cuban flag, the one that would be adopted by the separatist movement and remains to this day, despite a turbulent history, the flag of Cuba. It was on that day, in New York, that it flew for the first time anywhere, reportedly designed and sewn in a Manhattan boardinghouse.[133]

Varela was not in New York for that milestone, but Madan probably was. The following month, on June 27, 1850, he filed his petition for naturalization as a U.S. citizen in U.S. District Court in Manhattan.[134] Exactly a month later, on July 27, an enumerator assigned to the Eighteenth Ward by the U.S. Census Bureau found him living in the Madison Square area, which was fast becoming the uptown neighborhood of choice for wealthy New Yorkers.[135] The enumerator recorded his name as "Cristover Madden" and indicated that he was

Highly Important Intelligence!

DEPARTURE OF THE EXPEDITION AGAINST CUBA!

Expected News of a Great Battle!

Figure 2.4. The first published depiction of the Cuban flag, appearing in the *New York Sun* on May 11, 1850, the day the flag flew for the first time anywhere, outside the *Sun* building on Nassau and Fulton Streets. Source: "The Flag of Free Cuba," *New York Sun*, May 11, 1850, 2.

forty-five years old, born in Cuba, and a "Gentleman" by occupation. He headed a large household consisting of his wife, six children, and eight other persons not members of the family, presumably servants and their children. All the servants were females ranging in age from fourteen to thirty, and included a black woman born in Cuba, two English women, and three Irish women (one of them, ironically, with Madan's ancestral surname, Madden). All of Madan's children, including the youngest, an infant, were listed as born in Cuba.[136] The four oldest, two boys and two girls, were the teenaged offspring of Madan's deceased first wife, María Casimira Gómez y Pastrana.[137] The youngest two, a girl of four and the infant Julián, were the children of his second wife, Mary, listed in the 1850 census as a thirty-year-old native New Yorker.[138]

Mary's maiden name was O'Sullivan, and she was the sister of John L. O'Sullivan, an influential New York Democrat, the editor of the *New York Morning News* and the monthly *Democratic Review*, and a staunch supporter of U.S. expansionism.[139] In an 1845 editorial in the *Democratic Review* on the annexation of Texas, O'Sullivan coined the term "manifest destiny" to refer to the expansionist sentiment that guided the subsequent acquisition of Oregon and more than half of Mexico's territory.[140]

In 1847 O'Sullivan traveled to Havana with the editor of the *New York Sun*, Moses Yale Beach, with the purpose of meeting secretly with a group of prominent Cubans who had clandestinely formed an organization called El Club de La Habana.[141] Madan was a member and no doubt set up the meeting for his brother-in-law. Held at the sumptuous Aldama Palace, the newly constructed residence of the wealthy planter Domingo Aldama and his son Miguel, it was a gathering of kindred spirits. El Club had been created to advance the cause of Cuban annexation to the United States. In addition to Madan and the Aldamas, El Club included other wealthy Cubans such as José Luis Alfonso and the Count of Pozos Dulces.[142]

Of all the movements that throughout the nineteenth century sought to alter Cuba's colonial status, annexationism was surely the most conflicted. It had its heyday in the 1840s and 1850s; its origins, as well as the motivations of its proponents, were varied and often contradictory. One condition that led to the rise of the movement was Spain's steadfast refusal to relax colonial controls and grant Cubans a role in determining the island's affairs. When in 1837 the elected Cuban representatives to the Spanish legislature were excluded from participating in the assembly, in violation of the Spanish constitution, Spain was sending a clear message that Cuba was not a province, but a colony.[143] From 1834 to 1848 Madrid sent to Havana a succession of autocratic governors who stifled any expression of Cuban separatism, leaving no doubt about Spain's intention to keep the island under its direct control.

Spain's intransigence led some progressive Cubans to regard annexation to the United States as a desired alternative to Spanish rule. Becoming a U.S. state seemed a pragmatic and dignified path for Cuba, especially given the relative autonomy enjoyed by the states in the American federal system and the progressive spirit of the United States. Those who shared this view represented, according to the historian Leví

Marrero, a "liberal" current within the annexationist movement, for they saw annexation as an attainable way to shake Cuba loose from its colonial shackles and move it into the modern era, "to share," as the historian Hugh Thomas put it, "in the vast adventure of North American capitalist enterprise."[144] The "liberal" annexationists included some prominent intellectuals and professionals, such as the poet Juan Clemente Zenea and the writer Cirilo Villaverde.[145]

But for most historians, at the core of the annexationist movement were neither liberals nor progressives, but rather what Marrero kindly labeled "economic annexationists."[146] The historian Philip Foner was much blunter in identifying what he called the "sordid" motive of most annexationists: save slavery.[147] Slavery needed to be saved because it was the basis of the sugar planters' wealth and by the 1840s it was under siege, primarily from British abolitionists. The planters were not confident that the Spanish government, weakened by a liberal reform movement, would long resist the aggressive anti-slavery campaign mounted by the British.[148] Becoming a U.S. slave state seemed to offer the best guarantee for continuing the institution, since at the time the United States had shown itself to be a powerful defender of slavery in its own nation, rebuffing British efforts to end it immediately.[149]

But the annexationists' motives, as well as their stance on slavery, were much more complex. Despite their reliance on slave labor, planters such as the Madans, the Aldamas, and the Alfonsos recognized the long-term danger to their interests of continuing the slave trade. They had been shaken by a series of slave rebellions that culminated in an alleged "conspiracy" in 1844 that resulted in the execution of some 78 slaves and free blacks, the imprisonment of about 1,300 (including 6 whites), and the exile of nearly 500.[150] The planters were also keeping an apprehensive eye on the racial demographics of the sugar boom. The 1841 census showed that whites were now a minority on the island, with the slave population amounting to more than 43 percent, with an additional 15 percent classified as "free colored."[151]

Fears of an "Africanization" of Cuba, as well as the realization that the slave regime could not be sustained forever, led the Cuban planters to a more equivocal, if no less self-serving, position on slavery. While vehemently opposing immediate abolition, they favored the elimination of the slave trade and a very gradual transition to free labor so as to "whiten" the population and stem what they perceived to be the danger of a growing African influence. That scheme, they reasoned, was better served by annexation.[152] Not only was the United States in the best position to defend the continuation of slavery, but it was a model of how slavery could survive the abolition of the slave trade. In short, it was annexation that gave them the greatest security.

Although the annexationists were willing to support military expeditions to Cuba to accomplish their goals, their instincts as property owners also led them to pursue a less destructive alternative: the purchase of Cuba by the U.S. government. That was the purpose of the clandestine meeting El Club de la Habana held at the Aldama Palace with O'Sullivan and Beach.

Both Americans returned from Havana committed to annexing the island. As a newspaperman, Beach chose to make the cause a public one, and the *Sun* became the standard bearer of Cuban annexationism in the United States. O'Sullivan, however, proceeded immediately to use his contacts in Washington to quietly lobby for the purchase of Cuba. He was persistent in his efforts: as a supporter of both expansionism and slavery, O'Sullivan embraced the cause of annexing Cuba as a slave state.[153] He established direct communications on the matter with President James Polk, Secretary of State James Buchanan, and Senator Stephen Douglas, a champion of expansionism.[154] O'Sullivan's efforts culminated in a May 10, 1848, White House meeting with Polk and Douglas in which O'Sullivan laid out the benefits for the United States of annexing Cuba. The president was receptive, but did not commit to any course of action.

In New York, O'Sullivan's brother-in-law and other supporters of annexationism were publicly promoting their cause. Besides Madan, the other important figure of Cuban annexationism in the city was Gaspar Betancourt Cisneros, the same man who nearly three decades before had joined José Aniceto Iznaga in the mission to see Bolívar, and the one who, repeatedly and without success, visited 23 Reade Street to ask Varela to join the annexationist cause. The priest refused because he was in agreement with his former collaborator, José Antonio Saco, by this time living in Paris, who in 1848 wrote an essay opposing annexationism, arguing that Cuba would be absorbed by the United States, destroying Cuban culture and national identity.[155] Furthermore, it was

not likely that Varela would have joined any movement designed to preserve slavery.

Betancourt Cisneros sparred with his friend Saco, taking a pragmatic
position toward the movement: "Annexationism is a calculation, and in
no way a sentiment."[156] Betancourt Cisneros had a long history of activism on behalf of Cuban separatism. He received most of his education in
the United States and moved to New York when the Spanish authorities
exiled him and confiscated his property.[157] In 1847, together with Madan
and his old friend José Aniceto Iznaga, Betancourt Cisneros formed in
New York the Cuban Council to support in the United States the work
of El Club de La Habana.[158]

One of the most notable efforts of the annexationists in New York was
the establishment of a pro-annexation bilingual newspaper, *La Verdad*,
which appeared biweekly from 1848 to 1853. It was printed at the *Sun* and
the editor was one Cora Montgomery, a pseudonym for a relative of Moses
Yale Beach, Mrs. W. L. Cazneau, who also owned the Manhattan boardinghouse where Betancourt Cisneros lived.[159] *La Verdad* had well-defined
goals, outlined in one of its founding documents: (1) a democratic future
for Cuba; (2) the need for annexation to the United States; (3) achieving
annexation preferably through peaceful means by "just and generous indemnification," but if that is not possible, through the use of force; (4) no
discussion of changes in the system of slavery; and (5) the elimination of
the slave trade and the encouragement of white colonization.[160]

La Verdad was clearly a newspaper supported by wealthy annexationists and produced by, and for, elites and intellectuals. It was the voice of
a movement and not a commercial venture, carrying virtually no advertising and distributed free of charge to readers. Typically, *La Verdad*
had four pages plus a supplement in English, all of it crammed with
long pro-annexation tracts printed in small type. The pieces were usually unsigned, probably written by Madan, Cisneros Betancourt, or the
poet Miguel Teurbe Tolón. Most of the articles extolled the advantages
to the United States of Cuban annexation, presenting economic and
geographic information on the island. Other pieces were replies to the
enemies of the cause. In the December 15, 1851, issue, for example, the
entire front page was devoted to one long piece answering an open letter
sent to Cubans by the queen of Spain.[161] In 1852 several issues were primarily dedicated to answering Saco's arguments against annexation.[162]

In the meantime, the lobbying efforts of John O'Sullivan in Washington had paid off. President Polk instructed his ambassador in Madrid to offer the Spanish government $100 million for Cuba. The Spanish foreign minister refused the offer, replying that "sooner than see the island transferred to any power," his government would prefer "to see it sink into the ocean."[163]

The failure to purchase Cuba shifted emphasis to the campaign to forcibly liberate it from Spain. At the center of that movement was a Venezuelan-born Spanish army officer stationed in Cuba by the name of Narciso López, who had connections on the island with many of the wealthy annexationists. In May 1848 López's plans to lead an armed revolt against the Spanish were foiled and he had to flee the island, arriving in New York in July of that year with the intent of raising the necessary resources to stage an armed campaign on the island. Such a campaign, however, would have to be carried out with soldiers of fortune. Cuban annexationists were men of capital, not men of arms. El Club de La Habana pledged 80,000 pesos if López could raise an army of 1,500 men.[164] With the help of Cristóbal Madan, López took advantage of an excellent recruitment pool available in the United States: veterans of the just-concluded Mexican War who were eager to continue the adventure of fulfilling America's "manifest destiny."[165] López offered them their regular U.S. Army pay and a bonus of $1,000 and some land in Cuba after victory was achieved. To lead what was essentially an army of Americans, López tried to recruit two southern generals, veterans of the Mexican War: Jefferson Davis and Robert E. Lee, but they both turned him down.[166]

López ended up taking command of the expedition himself, except that it never made it to Cuba. Its staging area, Round Island in Louisiana, was blockaded by the U.S. Navy and the men who had gathered there were dispersed. In addition, two expeditionary vessels loaded with ordnance and supplies that were docked in Manhattan and Staten Island were confiscated by order of the U.S. attorney in New York.[167] Those preemptive federal actions in September 1849 were the result of an order from Zachary Taylor, the new U.S. president, who despite being a southern slave owner, had no interest in involving the United States in a conflict with Spain.[168] Aware that plans were under way to organize on U.S. soil an expedition of Americans, he issued on August 11 an executive order announcing that U.S. citizens participating in any action that violated U.S. laws and treaty obligations would face severe criminal charges and would lose any rights to have the U.S. government intercede in their behalf to protect them.[169]

López was undaunted. He started planning his next expedition, but he found that by late 1849 the support of many Cuban annexationists for an armed conflict had waned. One factor was President Taylor's stance against any U.S. involvement. But more importantly, political events in Spain made less likely the possibility that slavery would be abolished in its colonies. Progressive domestic movements had been quashed and relations with Britain had improved, virtually eliminating the antislavery pressures on the Madrid government. The Cuban planters could feel more secure that their livelihood would continue to be protected under Spanish rule. As the historian Ramiro Guerra y Sánchez noted, the "conservative spirit of the planters once again prevailed, . . . leading most of them to lay aside the risky recourse of pursuing annexation through violent means."[170] Some in El Club de La Habana even started seeking solutions to Cuba's problems that would not involve separation from Spain.

In that context, López's insistence on organizing yet another expedition led to a rift among New York's annexationists. Supporting López's plan to take a war to Cuba were the writer Cirilo Villaverde, who had recently arrived in New York after escaping from a Cuban prison, Juan Manuel Macías, a young New Yorker from Matanzas who would remain a fixture in New York émigré politics for many years thereafter, and José Sánchez Iznaga, a nephew of José Aniceto Iznaga.[171] Also joining López was Ambrosio José González, who had been dispatched to the United States the year before by El Club de La Habana to promote the military option and had subsequently become a loyal supporter of López.[172] González had received his education in the French Institute in Manhattan, where he was enrolled from 1828 to 1832.[173]

Opposing a new military initiative by López were those who were closely allied with planter interests and El Club de La Habana: Madan, José Aniceto Iznaga, the poet Miguel Teurbe Tolón, and Betancourt Cisneros.[174] They formed a new organization, while the López group formed its own. It was perhaps the first time, but certainly not the last, that Cuban émigrés in New York would splinter into competing factions.

The Madan group focused on a pro-annexation campaign aimed at U.S. public opinion. In addition to editing *La Verdad*, it collaborated with American sympathizers in publishing booklets and broadsides extolling Cuba's rich resources and the advantages the United States would derive from its annexation. One example was the small book entitled *Cuba and the Cubans* written by Richard Burleigh Kimball, published by George Putnam, and printed at the shop of Samuel Hueston at 139 Nassau Street.[175] Kimball, an eclectic and prolific New York writer of travelogues and unremarkable novels, had previously published a Cuban travel diary. In *Cuba and the Cubans* he argues for annexation, primarily for economic reasons, presenting data on the value of Cuba's exports and imports, and concluding that

> the advantages to be obtained by the United States by the annexation
> of Cuba, are incalculable. If annexation was fully and freely established,
> Cuba would be as valuable to this confederacy as New York itself.[176]

Kimball's connection with Madan and his group is clear from the book's appendix, a four-page reply to the anti-annexationist arguments of Saco, penned by one León Fragua de Calvo, a pseudonym used by Cristóbal Madan.

After losing the backing of New York's wealthiest Cubans, Narciso López left the city, accompanied by Ambrosio José González, and went to Washington and then to Louisiana and Mississippi, hoping to drum up support among southerners interested in adding Cuba as a slave state. He was helped in that task by John O'Sullivan, who set up meetings for him with southern politicians and Mexican War veterans. But Cristóbal Madan was covertly using his own contacts to undermine López's efforts. When O'Sullivan learned of it, he felt deeply betrayed by his brother-in-law.[177]

López enlisted the help of Governor John Quitman of Mississippi, a Mexican War veteran who nearly resigned from the statehouse in Jackson to lead the military campaign to Cuba. Through the issuance of bonds and other fundraising efforts among supportive southern gentlemen of means eager to invest in the potentially profitable enterprise of annexing Cuba, López managed to put together enough resources and men to outfit not just one, but two subsequent expeditions.[178] The first one, in May 1850, was the one announced by the *Sun* on that day Moses Yale Beach flew the Cuban flag for the first time outside his newspaper's building. Despite the *Sun's* optimism about the success of the expedition, it failed to dislodge the Spanish from Cuba.[179] López had gone as far as actually capturing the city of Cárdenas, where he landed, but eventually had to leave Cuba when the Spanish sent reinforcements to the city.

As soon as he returned to New Orleans, the indefatigable López started planning his next military campaign. As part of that effort, John O'Sullivan purchased in New York a barely seaworthy streamer named *Cleopatra*, which was to serve as the flagship of the new expedition. The plan was to have two smaller ships leave Manhattan and South Amboy, New Jersey, rendezvous with the *Cleopatra* at Sandy Hook in Lower New York Harbor, and proceed south. Because this expedition was being organized primarily in New York, most of the men recruited for it were European exiles living in the city, especially German and Hungarian veterans. O'Sullivan also recruited for the campaign a young man named Henry Burtnett, who ran a drugstore on the corner of St. Mark's Place and Third Avenue. Burtnett involved himself in all aspects of the operation, including the clandestine meetings and military training sessions held in lower Manhattan.[180]

Burtnett turned out to be an informant; at the critical moment he tipped off both the U.S. and Spanish authorities. On April 24, 1851, federal agents confiscated the vessels while they were still in port, including the *Cleopatra*, which was to have sailed before the others but was delayed because its crew was drunk from a night's outing in the city and demanded to be paid before the ship could leave.[181]

The next day, President Taylor's successor, Millard Fillmore, reaffirmed the White House's policy against American involvement in foreign conflicts, characterizing the expeditions to Cuba as "adventures in larceny and looting," and warning all individuals involved in them that their actions were unlawful, they were subject to prosecution, and the U.S. government would not intervene to protect them.[182]

Based on the Neutrality Act, a federal grand jury in New York issued indictments against O'Sullivan and several of his associates. After a mistrial a year later, all charges were dismissed. The incident ended O'Sullivan's dreams of annexing Cuba. His biographer, Robert

D. Sampson, notes that despite this "brush with disaster and near disgrace," the well-connected New Yorker bounced back immediately, occupying the plum position of vice president of the Broadway Railway Association.[183]

From New Orleans, López organized one last expedition. In early August 1851 he left for Cuba aboard the ship *Pampero* with about four hundred men. Most of them were Americans, with a regiment of Cubans and a smattering of Hungarians and Germans.[184] One artillery regiment of Americans was commanded by Colonel William L. Crittenden, a Kentuckian, West Point graduate, and veteran of the Mexican War who worked at the New Orleans customshouse.[185] After a series of errors and mishaps, the expedition landed along Cuba's northwest coast, where the Spanish forces eventually captured most of it, including López. The Spanish governor, out of patience with López's excursions and emboldened by Fillmore's declaration, ordered the summary execution of López and fifty Americans, including Crittenden.[186]

The executions set off a wave of street protests in various cities across the United States.[187] In New York, a large and vociferous demonstration was held at City Hall Park. The *New York Herald* placed the crowd estimate at over eight thousand.[188] In New Orleans, the Spanish consulate was sacked and burned.[189] Despite the outrage, and even though Crittenden was the nephew of Fillmore's attorney general, the president stood by his original declaration that he would not intervene on behalf of the expeditionaries. A year later, the Spanish government pardoned the 135 members of the expedition who had been imprisoned in Ceuta, a Spanish jail in northern Africa. In exchange, the United States indemnified the Spanish for the losses to its legation in New Orleans.[190]

Ambrosio José Gonzalez, López's loyal aide, had been ill and did not take part in that last fatal expedition. He settled in Charleston, where he married into a prominent Carolinian planter family and later joined the Confederate Army, serving as colonel under the command of an old classmate at the French Institute in Manhattan, General P. T. G. Beauregard.[191] Penniless after the war, he moved to New York and died in 1893 in the Home for Incurables (now St. Barnabas Hospital) in the Bronx.[192] He is buried in Woodlawn Cemetery.

The death of Narciso López did not end the annexationist movement. It continued to thrive for several years thereafter in New York as more

Cubans, persecuted by the repression unleashed by the Spanish, arrived in the city. But it declined around 1855 after many of its proponents realized that the U.S. government was unwilling to risk its relations with Europe to annex Cuba and that it would continue to oppose the launching of expeditions from its own soil.[193] The movement was nonexistent by the time of the U.S. Civil War.

For the rest of the century, New York would be the setting for many other émigré revolutionary activities and movements, most of them pursuing nothing less than total sovereignty and independence for Cuba. Those nationalist revolutionaries, as well as generations of Cuban historians, would look back at the annexationists with contempt because of their willingness to sacrifice independence in the defense of their narrow elite economic interests. It is not an unfair characterization. But the activities of the annexationists in New York marked the beginning of organized efforts on the part of Cubans in the city to effect changes in their homeland.

* * *

The year before the final and ill-fated López expedition, the governor of Cuba, Federico Roncali, Count Alcoy, was trying to keep a watchful eye on troublesome Cubans. The name Cristóbal Madan kept coming up in connection with the annexationist movement, but the count was confused. He knew that a Madan family owned property in Matanzas, but he could not figure out where Cristóbal Madan lived. On March 8, 1850, Alcoy sent a letter to his subordinate, the brigadier general of Matanzas province, asking for any intelligence he might have on the Madans. He specifically asked whether one Don Cristóbal in the United States was related to the ones in Matanzas, "since what date has he been absent and for what reason," and any information on the family, "their occupation, assets, and conduct."[194] The reply from Matanzas provided the count with a detailed history of the Madans, verifying that they owned property in that province but had also established residence in Havana, their relationship through marriage with the Alfonsos of the capital, and vouching for the Madans' "good behavior in conducting their public and private matters."[195] As for Cristóbal, the official in Matanzas claimed ignorance of his whereabouts, adding that if he does reside in the United States, it must be because "he married in second nuptials a widow of that country, or because it suits him to live where he obtained his education."[196]

It is not surprising that the Spanish authorities in Cuba were confused about Madan's whereabouts. The correct answer to the count's inquiry was that in 1850 Cristóbal lived in both New York and Havana, and could probably also be found occasionally in his family's mill in Matanzas. Perhaps it was Madan's discreetness in New York (signing his political tracts with pseudonyms), or his position primarily as a wealthy planter and not a writer, that earned him the privilege of leading a true transnational life, dividing his time between Cuba and his home near Madison Square. Unlike Varela, Heredia, and others who were exiles banished from Cuba, in 1850 Cristóbal Madan could be in New York one day conducting business, furthering the annexationist cause, and filing for U.S. citizenship, and a few days later be in Havana attending the birth or baptism of his son Julián, joining his brother-in-law and other annexationists for a meeting at the home of the Aldamas, or supervising operations at his family's sugar mill in Matanzas.

Cristóbal Madan was not alone. New York started receiving more and more Cubans who were able to live transnational lives, taking advantage of the traffic between South Street and the Cuban ports to cement business, professional, family, and political ties in both places. By the middle of the nineteenth century, New York became a Cuban crossroads, a high-traffic area for transnational elites, political activists, intellectuals, exiles, and sojourners. It had become the largest and most important community of Cubans outside the island.

The annexationist movement was, however, a harbinger of things to come as Cuban New York became more and more impacted by the emerging conflict between Cubans and Spaniards over the future of the island, as other separatist movements arose and Spain countered with greater repression. Even Cristóbal Madan, who tried to keep a low profile, saw his transnational life disrupted in the wake of Spain's response to the annexationist threat. A year after the debacle of the last López expedition, the Spanish government sentenced *in absentia* the leading figures of the annexationist movement in New York, including Gaspar Betancourt Cisneros, Cirilo Villaverde, Juan Manuel Macías, Ambrosio José González, and Madan. Cristóbal was sentenced to ten years of supervised exile in Spain. Joaquín Madan traveled from Matanzas to

Havana to plead with the authorities that the sentence against his son be lifted so that he could return to Cuba. According to one historian, however, the record shows that on March 19, 1852, Cristóbal Madan was arrested in Havana and detained in La Cabaña fortress. Without any regard for Madan's U.S. citizenship, General José de la Concha, the Spanish governor, ratified the sentence on June 5, and the man who had once been the teenaged "unofficial Cuban consul" on South Street, welcoming Varela and Heredia to Manhattan, was banished to Spain.[197]

3

An Emerging Community and a Rising Activism

In Cuba, as far as I know, is where you can find the largest
number of Cubans; but besides Cuba nowhere else are there
more Cubans than on the docks of the *Columbia* or the *Mar-
ion* on sailing days. Someone said that it appears as if New
York is a neighborhood of Havana, and I could not disagree.
—Simón Camacho, *Cosas de los Estados Unidos*, 1864[1]

In the early morning of Monday, February 17, 1845, passersby on Barclay
Street, between Church and West Broadway, heard loud noises from the
rooftop of the boardinghouse at number 58. Looking up, they saw a man
clad in his pantaloons, shirt, and socks, sitting atop a dormer window,
waving his arms wildly and shouting incoherently. Those who lingered
to watch the spectacle stood horrified when the man suddenly threw
himself off the roof of the three-story structure, a distance of sixty feet,
landing headfirst on the curbstone below and dying instantly.[2] The New
York press took an interest in the tragedy when it was learned that the
victim was Gonzalo Aldama, a member of a very wealthy Cuban family,
a young man, observed the *New York Herald*, "with brilliant prospects
before him."[3] His suicide was hard to understand. The initial explanation, put forth by the *Brooklyn Daily Eagle*, was that Gonzalo suffered
from temporary insanity, caused by a lightning bolt that struck very
near to him on Saturday night.[4] In the boardinghouse all day Sunday he
acted erratically, even violently, as other boarders tried to subdue him.
He even attempted to cut his throat with a razor.[5]

Upon further investigation, the *New York Herald* concluded that it
was not lightning, but an impossible love that had fatally struck the
young Aldama.[6] Gonzalo had fallen in love in Havana with a beautiful,
charming, and educated woman somewhat older than he, but below his
family's social status. His father would not entertain the idea of Gonzalo marrying the woman and banished him to New York, ostensibly

to study medicine. By all reports, Gonzalo arrived in the city with the intention of forgetting the woman. He was seen frequenting the theater, the opera, and the ballrooms. But even Manhattan's best amusements failed to make him forget. He wrote repeatedly to his father, pleading for permission to marry the woman. A few days before his suicide, he received his father's irrevocable decision: Gonzalo could not return to Cuba until he renounced his romantic intentions. The *Herald* reporter concluded that the "warm and passionate and impetuous temperament of the Spaniard could no longer suffer and he therefore resolved to end his troubles."[7]

Gonzalo's father was Domingo Aldama y Aréchaga, one of Cuba's wealthiest men.[8] Born in Spain to a family of modest means, he migrated to Cuba determined to succeed in the island's expanding trade business. Eventually he achieved enough success to marry one of the daughters of his employer, Gonzalo Alfonso, an aristocrat, merchant, and sugar mill owner who had befriended the young enterprising immigrant and introduced him into the upper levels of Cuban society.[9] Domingo made the most of his new social position and soon amassed a fortune from the booming business in sugar and slaves. Many of his first investments were in the slave trade, underwriting expeditions to Africa to supply his father-in-law's sugar mills with labor.[10] Eventually, Domingo Aldama acquired his own mills as well as controlling interests in the island's major railroads and insurance firms.[11] He built a palatial home in Havana, the first residence to be built outside the city's walls.[12] The Aldama Palace, as it was called, still stands and is regarded as "the most acclaimed building in nineteenth-century Havana."[13] It was there, two years after Gonzalo's suicide, that Domingo and his other son, Miguel, hosted the meeting between the members of El Club de La Habana and the Americans John O'Sullivan and Moses Yale Beach.

Miguel was anointed the heir to the family fortune. He had been a good student, an obedient son, and a responsible manager, and he married a woman from a prominent family. His brother Gonzalo, on the other hand, was troublesome and rebellious and intent on marrying unwisely. So Gonzalo was sent away; not to Spain, where Domingo was born, nor to France or England, nor even to Mexico or another nearby Latin American country. He was sent to New York, where the Aldamas sold their sugar and bought virtually everything they needed to furnish their new Havana palace.[14] Besides, Gonzalo was already familiar with New York. In 1836, accompanied by his brother Miguel and his cousin Gonzalo Alfonso, all teenagers, he visited Manhattan, arriving on May 24 aboard the *Norman* from Havana.[15]

Gonzalo Aldama's story was repeated throughout the nineteenth century: New York as the place of refuge, exile, banishment, or escape for Cubans. The trade center on the Hudson became that world outside the island where Cubans went to acquire an education, opportunity, and wealth, to start a new life or forget an old one, to evade royal authority, plot a revolution, experience freedom, buy and sell. Many of those stories, like Gonzalo's, ended tragically. Others were steeped in heroism and sacrifice, and yet others in opportunism and mendacity. But they all represent the building blocks of a New York community that by the middle of the nineteenth century was attracting increasing numbers of Cubans as the island tumbled into the tumultuous decades that would close out the century and define Cuban nationhood and identity.

Although by the middle of the nineteenth century New York had become a privileged destination for Cuba's sojourners and émigrés, its resident population of Cubans was still relatively small, even at the height of the annexationist movement. In 1850, the year of the first U.S. decennial census that ascertained place of birth, there were 231 Cuban-born persons living in what are now the five boroughs, with 207 of them in Manhattan.[16] The population born in Spain was slightly higher: 307 in the five boroughs.[17] In that census the Spanish-born and the Cuban-born were by far the two largest groups of Spanish speakers in the city. The 1850 census was the last census in which those born in Spain outnumbered the Cuban-born, with the latter experiencing much faster growth thereafter, tripling their number by the time of the 1860 census and becoming the largest Spanish-speaking group in the city for the rest of the century.

The presence of the Spanish in New York, however, was undoubtedly due largely to the city's connection with Cuba. As indicated in chapter 1, by the 1820s there were more passengers arriving in New York from Cuban ports than from all ports in Latin America and Spain combined. Many of the Spanish living in the city probably arrived there from Cuba, perhaps after years of residence on the island. Furthermore, since Cuba was a colony and there were, *de jure*, no Cubans, distinguishing between Spaniards and Cubans during this early period is problematic. No doubt many of those who indicated to the U.S. census enumerator that they were born in Spain may well have been born in Cuba but considered the island part of Spain. The English-language press in New York frequently referred to persons from Cuba as Spaniards, a label that was not, of course, inaccurate in terms of citizenship.

Not long after Father Félix Varela arrived in Manhattan, New York already had a weekly newspaper printed entirely in Spanish, *El Mercurio de Nueva York*, which first appeared in 1828. Unlike most of the countless New York Spanish-language newspapers that emerged during subsequent decades (many of them short-lived ventures), *El Mercurio* had no evident political agenda, no advocacy role on behalf of émigrés intent on liberating the homeland. It was a commercial venture by Lanuza, Mendia, and Company, a printing house, publishing firm, and bookstore located at 30 Exchange Place, at the corner of William Street. Published on Saturdays, each issue had four tightly packed pages in small print.[18] The first three pages had long articles, usually descriptive reports on political, economic, and social events and trends in Europe, especially Spain, and Latin America. *El Mercurio* had practically no local or national U.S. news, except for occasional notes on the crime rate in the city. Most of the paper's readers (who paid six dollars annually for a subscription) were evidently involved in foreign commerce. It had a section with trade statistics, featuring New York and ports in Latin America: customs data, ship traffic, and the prices of various export and import items.

It is the fourth page of *El Mercurio*, however, that reveals a great deal about the early presence of Spanish and Latin Americans in the city. It was packed with ads for businesses in the city that catered primarily to Spanish-speaking customers. It shows not only the importance of those customers, but also the broad range of commercial establishments that by the 1820s had already been established in New York by its Spanish-speaking residents.

Antonio Pastor, an actual barber from Seville, invited the readers of *El Mercurio* to his shop at 55 Fulton Street, where they could find an excellent selection of "British razors, . . . all types of French pomades, colorful oils and soaps, lavender cologne, and the celebrated almond soap, all of the best quality and at fair prices." Samuel Whitmarsh and Company, tailors and merchants at 116 Broadway, across from the City Hotel, offered "Señores Españoles" a wide selection of men's clothing, private dressing rooms, and the assurance that customers could be served in Spanish. "Señora Cornwell" rented rooms in a boardinghouse at 9 Nassau Street with multilingual attention. In a school directed by José J. Villariño and Carlos Cordet, students could avail themselves of a method of simultaneously learning Spanish, French, and English, as well as classes in Latin, Greek, drawing and painting, music, piano, violin, flute, guitar, dance, fencing, all for $300 a trimester, including, room, board, and general instruction. There were separate fees, however, for stationery, pen, and ink ($8), use of the piano ($12), and a seat in church ($10). Auguste Guigou announced in his ad the establishment of a pasta factory on the road to Bloomingdale, at the corner of Tenth Avenue and 69th Street, turning out pasta in the style of Genoa and Naples, and directing buyers to Mr. Arnaud's shop at 9 Warren Street. Also on Warren Street, at number 22, Mr. Bryan offered clients his "original and superior method" of extracting teeth and replacing them with porcelain ones. Byrne and Company on Walker Street wished the readers of El Mercurio to know that they manufacture, sell, and repair all kinds of carriages.

There are numerous advertisements from the newspaper's publishers, Lanuza and Mendia, who offer books for sale at their store. However, it appears that in 1829 Lanuza and Mendia sold the newspaper to another printer, José Desnoues at 23 Provost Street, who designated Eugenio Bergonzio of 7 Nassau Street as the paper's business agent, responsible for subscriptions and advertisement. With the change in management, the newspaper targeted even more the Spanish-speaking businessman and trade merchant. El Mercurio named agents in Philadelphia and Havana, who submitted commercial news and handled subscriptions in those cities.

Starting in 1829, the advertisements on page 4 reflected an even greater emphasis on business and commerce. In his ad, José Attinelli, of 46 Exchange Place, announced to the public in general and "transient Spanish gentlemen" in particular that he performs any and all services related to customs matters, including the immediate translation of documents into most modern languages. The J. W. Hallett company bills itself as an "American Agency in Territorial Properties, no. 17, Merchants Exchange, Wall Street," offering foreign investors houses and lots in the city and in various places in the United States, with a complete catalog of the properties available in its office for immediate inspection.

Eugenio Bergonzio, *El Mercurio*'s business agent, advertises in the paper that he can perform any service or transaction that may be required by a foreigner, including "the steps that need to be taken so as to obtain whatever is requested from public officials, the easiest way to obtain U.S. citizenship, customs transactions, . . . translations and interpreters, . . . commission sales and purchases, . . . credit collection and the remittance of payments, . . . and providing the most satisfactory advice."[19]

In 1829 *El Mercurio* also started featuring more news from Havana, highlighting the importance of the Cuba Trade in relation to total volume of trade with Spain and the increase in ship traffic with the island.[20] An increasing number of ads offered for sale large lots of imported Havana cigars. In the issue of August 15, for example, Mr. Attinelli advertised that he had twenty-four thousand cigars of "superior quality" for sale that had arrived from Havana on August 1 aboard the brigantine *Mary Jane*.[21]

About twenty years after *El Mercurio* ceased publication, the 1850 U.S. census yielded a profile of the city's Cuban-born population that showed the persistence of what was reflected on the pages of that pioneer newspaper: the importance of trade and commercial activities in shaping the early presence of Cubans in the city. Of the sixty-six Cuban-born men who reported an occupation, twelve were "merchants," five were in marine-related occupations (e.g., captain, sailor, sailmaker), thirteen were craftsmen, and nearly a quarter of the sixty-six were involved in the tobacco industry, either as cigar makers, retailers, or importers. Only a couple reported being employed in an unskilled occupation, and professionals amounted to a mere handful (an engineer, an architect, a chemist, and two teachers).

The place of residence within Manhattan of the 207 Cuban-born persons living there in 1850 showed a concentration either in the areas surrounding the port or in the upcoming elite residential neighborhoods, underscoring the relative importance of port-related activities and the presence of prosperous merchants among the early Cubans in the city. More than half of the Cuban-born population of the city was concentrated in Wards One and Three, at the tip of lower Manhattan,

Figure 3.1. Map of New York City, ca. 1850, showing wards. Source: Lionel Pincus and Princess Firyal Map Division, New York Public Library Digital Collections, www.digitalcollections.nypl.org.

adjacent to the piers, and Wards Nine, Fifteen, and Eighteen. The latter three include Greenwich Village and the area between Madison Square Park and Union Square, regarded as among the most affluent neighborhoods of the time. In the mid-nineteenth century, according to museum curator Jan Seidler Ramírez, Greenwich Village became known as an area where the residents were well-mannered and largely native-born, and was often approvingly called the "American ward."[22] The Madison Square Park area, where Cristóbal Madan lived in 1850, was becoming a choice neighborhood for wealthy New Yorkers, as pointed out in chapter 2.[23] In contrast, very few Cubans lived in what were the low-income and immigrant areas, especially Wards Four, Six, Seven, Ten, Eleven, and Thirteen, the districts along the East River that encompass what are now referred to as the Lower East Side, Chinatown, Five Points, the Bowery, and other areas where by the 1850s the first immigrant tenements in Manhattan started making their appearance and where average real estate assessments were among the lowest in the city.[24] It was the urban settlement pattern one would expect from a group in which commercial elites and skilled craftsmen predominated, and the pattern that Cubans would generally follow during the rest of the century as many more arrived in Manhattan from Cuba.

The Malibrán family, headed by Carlos, thirty-two, a merchant born in Cuba, lived in Ward Fifteen to the east of Washington Square. He and his Cuban-born wife, Isabel, thirty, had four children, ranging in age from four to thirteen, all born in Cuba. The family had enough income to have four servants: two Irish women, a Cuban woman, and a middle-aged Cuban man who was the household's waiter.[25]

The Malibráns and the Madans lived in single-family dwellings, a necessity for large families with servants, but an extravagant luxury for almost everyone else, even if they were well off. In 1850 most Cubans in the city lived in boardinghouses or hotels, especially if they were single or had small families. That was the case with Gaspar Betancourt Cisneros, the prominent annexationist. A member of a wealthy planter family from Camagüey, Betancourt Cisneros was forty-eight years old in 1850 and had not yet married (he would finally do so seven years later in Havana and had a son at age fifty-six).[26] He lived in a large boardinghouse in the Sixth Ward, just north of City Hall. The house was run by a New York native-born family that, in addition to Betancourt Cisneros, boarded families and individuals from Germany, England, Ohio, and Connecticut. It was an upscale house: all the boarders had white-collar occupations.[27]

Other boardinghouses had almost exclusively Cuban boarders. In the Third Ward, Mr. and Mrs. Agramonte and their four young children, all born in Cuba, lived in a large boardinghouse where eight other Cubans, apparently unrelated to them, also lived, including a printer, a daguerreotyper, and a student.[28] An even larger boardinghouse, perhaps a hotel, also in the Third Ward, had nine Cuban residents. It was a fairly heterogeneous place with respect to both nationality and occupation: New Yorkers, Italians, Irish, Canadians, bookkeepers, merchants, cooks, an editor, clerks, and ten Spanish-born actors (nine males and one female).[29]

The 1850 census also reflected the proclivity, noted in chapter 1, of the Cuban planter class to send its children to be educated in New York. A boarding school run by a French headmaster in the Ninth Ward had fourteen Cuban boys in its dormitory, ranging in age from nine to twenty and most of them with last names that were prominent among Cuba's wealthiest families.[30] In the Seventeenth Ward, three Cuban teenaged boys were enrolled in another boarding school with a French headmaster.[31] Three teenaged Cuban girls were receiving their education, perhaps as novices, in the Sacred Heart Convent located in the remote Twelfth Ward.[32] In that same ward, the Angulo sisters, ages eight and four, probably orphans, were under the care of the nuns in the Mount St. Vincent Convent.[33]

Another Cuban interned at an institution in the city was twenty-six-year-old Josephine Goudelo. She was one of twenty-three women living in the New York Magdalen Asylum, the infamous Irish Catholic institution that sought to help prostitutes and other "fallen women" lead a respectable life, usually by confining them indefinitely. In 1850 the asylum had moved to a new location on East 88th Street in the Twelfth Ward.[34]

* * *

In 1856 a New York printing house published the first comprehensive guidebook to the city written in Spanish.[35] Its appearance so early was a testament to the growing Spanish and Latin American presence in the city, both permanent and transient. Featured in its listings were recommendations regarding retail stores, with a comment on what the anonymous author or authors regarded as a New York innovation: luxurious store exteriors designed to catch the eye and tempt the customer to enter the establishment. The guidebook is not as positive about residential buildings, which it regards as being of inferior construction compared to those in Havana, Mexico, "and other countries inhabited by Spaniards and their descendants."[36]

Another Spanish-language guidebook that appeared only seven years later, in 1863, was much more detailed.[37] Written by R. Alvarez and I. G. Grediaga, it contained, along with the usual recommendations on sights and shopping, a directory of "Spanish"-owned businesses. By far the largest category of firms was, as expected, "commission agents and importers." The next largest category was tobacconists.[38]

But what makes the Alvarez and Grediaga guidebook notable is that the authors were straightforward with their observations and practical advice for the visitor, giving us a window into how someone from Spain or Latin America may have viewed the life and culture of New York at that time. Chapter 15, "Special Recommendations for Foreigners," lists several "don'ts" that more than 150 years later remain good pieces of advice for the visitor to New York:

> Do not walk alone at night in deserted streets, do not trust people who offer their services or effusive greetings on the street, do not detain yourself to gawk at sights in high-traffic areas where pickpockets abound, be wary of cab drivers, do not buy theater tickets on the street, be careful of "street sirens," be careful of cheap merchandise (especially jewelry) being passed off as expensive, do not go to places where games of chance or the charms of the fair sex are offered.[39]

But one recommendation is especially interesting in a cross-cultural sense, revealing, at the street level, the literal clash between the pace of modernity and traditional Old World sensibilities such as courtesy and honor:

> Never get upset when someone shoves you in the street. Continue on your way and you do the same to the next person you encounter. Americans are always in a rush, attending to their affairs, and they do not take

care to give satisfaction for what they do, nor to demand it when something is done to them, a trait, by the way, that is extremely laudable and worthy of being imitated, for one can thus avoid infinite aggravations and wasted time.[40]

By the time the 1860 census was taken, the Cuban-born population had tripled to more than six hundred, representing nearly half of all Latin Americans and Spaniards living in the city. It was a growth that brought with it a greater occupational diversity, with more professionals, artists, teachers, small businessmen and retailers, and even laborers and servants. The influx was large and diverse enough to necessitate the formation in New York of a Cuban Benevolent Society "to offer assistance to those natives of Cuba who may find themselves in a state of indigence or distress. . . . A great many of our countrymen, . . . unacquainted with the English language, . . . are unable to get a situation or employment, and earn their livelihood."[41]

Despite the trend toward greater socioeconomic heterogeneity, Cuban New York was still a population disproportionately derived from the island's upper social strata, something evident not only from the occupational profile, but also from their patterns of settlement in Manhattan. In 1860 there were proportionately fewer Cubans than in 1850 living downtown, with many more in the fashionable uptown neighborhoods that were attracting affluent New Yorkers. Greenwich Village and the Madison Park area continued to be important as places of residence for Cubans, in addition to an up-and-coming area, the northern portion of the East Village. The wards that encompassed those neighborhoods, the Fifteenth, Seventeenth, and Eighteenth, contained more than half of all Cubans living in Manhattan. The pattern of 1850 also continued into 1860 with respect to low-income areas, with very few Cubans living on the Lower East Side, the Bowery, and the Five Points.[42] In 1860 Brooklyn started emerging as a place of residence for Cubans, primarily skilled craftsmen and middle-level white-collar Cubans, with machinists, clerks, cigar workers, crafts apprentices, and students making up the bulk of the more than sixty Cubans who had settled just across the East River from Manhattan.[43]

The increase from 1850 to 1860 no doubt reflected the growing supremacy of New York, in relation to other U.S. cities, especially New

Orleans and Philadelphia, as the choice destination for Cubans arriving in the United States. But there were "push" factors from the island as well. In the wake of the failed López expeditions, the island suddenly became a far less hospitable place for Cubans who were active in seeking a change in the island's political status. Starting in 1852 General José de la Concha, the Spanish governor, unleashed a wave of repression throughout the island that gave no quarter to dissidents, without regard for social status or whether they had become U.S. citizens.[44] Cristóbal Madan was one who suffered the consequences of Concha's crackdown when he was captured in Havana, his pending sentence applied, and he was banished to Spain (see chapter 2). Other prominent Cubans implicated in annexationist activities thought it best to seek refuge outside the island, and New York was usually the preferred destination given the already well-established ties with the city.

In the 1860 census we find settled in New York many of the Cubans who had earlier transited through the city as students, sojourners, business travelers, or political activists. The political climate in Cuba convinced them to sink deeper roots in Manhattan, and they became fixtures in the development of Cuban New York, most of them becoming U.S. citizens while still working toward separating Cuba from Spain. That did not deter them, however, from occasionally returning to Cuba and attempting to reestablish their transnational lives whenever the Spanish colonial government relaxed its controls and authorized their return.

Perhaps the best example is Juan Manuel Macías. Born in Matanzas, he left that city at age nineteen aboard the *Flora*, which arrived in New York on July 6, 1846.[45] He eventually became one of Narciso López's closest collaborators and was a member of the first López expedition that briefly occupied the city of Cárdenas in 1850 (see chapter 2). Macías was among those sentenced *in absentia* with Madan in 1852, but there is no evidence that he, unlike Madan, ever gave the Spanish government the opportunity to apply the sentence.[46] That same year, on March 17, he was granted U.S. citizenship in the Common Pleas Court of New York County.[47]

In 1857 Macías took advantage of an easing of political controls on the island to apply for amnesty and for permission to return to the island. His request was granted, and he traveled to Cuba in February of that year to assume control of his family's estate, which had been placed under an embargo by the authorities. During his entire stay in Cuba he was under close surveillance by the police and the political division, who reported his every move to the governor. In late April he returned to New York.[48]

In 1860 Macías was living at 297 West 22nd Street, with an office downtown at 36 Beaver Street, where he conducted business as a merchant.[49] Macías had settled in Manhattan, but he was not giving up his personal and business connections in Cuba or renouncing his political activism. He would remain a resident of the city for the rest of his life, traveling to and from Cuba whenever he could and probably maintaining another home as well as business interests on the island, as Madan had done.

During the 1850s and 1860s many of New York's Cubans were engaged in the same juggling act that Madan had pioneered during the 1840s and which Macías was attempting to replicate: balancing business with separatist politics, and dividing their time between residences and business interests in Cuba and Manhattan. A good example are the Moras, a large clan with sugar estates in Matanzas that throughout the rest of the century would be a constant and growing presence among Cubans in the city. Starting in the 1850s, some Moras started moving to New York to handle the sales of not only their products but those of other Cuban producers, establishing sugar commission businesses near South Street. Because there is no published genealogy of the family, it is difficult to tell exactly what was the relationship between the different nuclear families with that last name that lived in Manhattan well into the twentieth century. They were all, however, undoubtedly related. Not only did they share a common origin in the sugar industry of Matanzas, but many also lived on the same street in Manhattan and eventually ended up in the same place: a large family plot in Green-Wood Cemetery in Brooklyn.

From 1855 to 1858 three Mora family members were doing business in lower Manhattan as "commission merchants" under different and evolving corporate partnerships. Two were brothers: José María Mora and Antonio Máximo Mora, and the other was the son of José María, José Antonio. They were involved in partnerships with José F. Navarro, Pedro Bombalier, and Frederico Fernández Lanz. By 1859 they were joined by three other Moras who figure in the list of partners engaged in commission sales: Pedro Mora, Mariano Mora, and Fausto Mora.[50] That same year, Fausto became a U.S. citizen, joining two other Moras who had already done so.[51]

Although they maintained properties and other interests in Matanzas, the Moras quickly sank roots into their new city. While most Cuban New Yorkers kept their assets liquid, depositing their proceeds from the sale of sugar in investment accounts with counting houses such as Moses Taylor's, the Moras immediately invested at least part of their capital in Manhattan real estate. As early as 1856 Antonio Máximo Mora owned five properties on the southern side of West 28th Street, between Ninth and Tenth Avenues. The properties were detailed in a suit brought by the trustees of the Scotch Presbyterian Church against Antonio Máximo for failing to pay a loan from the church using those properties as collateral.[52]

The Moras also invested heavily in numerous properties in and around East 13th Street, between Second and Fourth Avenues, and it was in that area where various members of the clan lived. Fausto Mora's 1859 application for U.S. citizenship listed his address as 139 East 13th Street, the same address given by one Máximo Mora on his application in 1864. When Antonio Máximo Mora became a U.S. citizen in 1869, his address was listed as 235 East 13th Street.[53] The 1860 census found a Manuel Mora, fifty-six years old, living with his wife, María, their four children, and an English servant at 124 East 13th Street.[54] Their next-door neighbor, Orlando Moore, a New York-born broker with a wife, four children, and two servants, was ordered in 1861 by the New York Court of Common Pleas to pay the firm of Mora Brothers $223.94 for rent owed on a property at 120 East 13th Street.[55]

Those two blocks of East 13th Street, between Second and Fourth Avenues, were apparently crowded with Cuban families in 1860. It may have been that the Moras bought most of the property on that street and then rented to their compatriots, or perhaps they bought into an area where many Cubans already lived.

Manuel Trujillo, a forty-five-year-old merchant, lived on the other (northern) side of 13th Street from Manuel Mora and Orlando Moore, at number 125. No related adult female is listed in the household, but Manuel lived there with his four children and three servants. On either side of Trujillo were two Cuban families headed by retired merchants. One was the family of Juan Bautista Ponce de León y Espinosa, a man who belonged to one of the oldest families in Cuba. Earlier in his life he was a jurist who had served as the secretary of the Royal Council and had been named Gentleman in the prestigious Spanish Order of Isabel la Católica.[56] For reasons that are unclear, he moved his family to New York and in 1860, at age sixty-six, was living on East 13th Street with his wife, six children, a son-in-law (a New York-born physician), an infant grandchild, and three servants (two Cubans and one Irish). The family on the other side of Trujillo, whose last name is not legible in the census form, had six members, all born in Cuba, as well as three servants, all Irish women. There were also three adult Cubans unrelated to them in the household, perhaps boarders: an elderly male teacher and his son and Fernando Agüero, a twenty-nine-year-old druggist.[57] In subsequent decades, as more Moras arrived in New York, many of them would live in the Cuban neighborhood they helped to create around East 13th Street.

Not all affluent Cuban families lived on 13th Street with the Moras. Mateo Rodríguez, thirty years old, headed a large household that lived in the outskirts of the city at West 140th Street and Twelfth Avenue. In addition to his wife, Rufina, twenty-nine, Mateo had four young children, all born in Cuba, and two Irish female servants, a black Cuban-born male servant, and an Irish coachman. He listed his occupation as "Gentleman" and indicated that the value of his personal estate was $600,000.[58] Francisco Yzquierdo, a merchant, lived in a single-family house in the West Village at 118 West 10th Street with his wife, six children, and two Irish servants.[59]

One of the most interesting and perhaps visible of all Cuban families in New York were the Apezteguías, who in 1860 occupied the home prominently located at 1 Washington Square North. An interesting feature of the household is that the oldest member of the family, as recorded by the census, was twenty-three-year-old Amelia Apezteguía. The rest of the Apezteguías, five males and two females, ranged in age from one to twenty-one, all born in Cuba, even the baby. But these children were not living by themselves. They were taken care of by six servants, almost all of them Irish women, in addition to a waiter, a coachman, and an Italian cook.[60] It appears from their names and ages that at least three of them, Adela, Inés, and Julio, were the children of Martín Felipe Apezteguía, a Spanish immigrant to Cuba, and his second wife, the Cuban-born Josefa Mariana Tarafa. The other children may have been their nephews, since Martín had three brothers who migrated to Cuba with him from their native Navarra. In Cuba, the Apezteguías had enough wealth and prestige to be granted (or to have purchased) the title of marquis.[61] This family does not appear in any subsequent census of New York. It is likely that this arrangement was a way to get the children educated in New York, a sort of swank private dormitory with its own support staff.

The Apezteguía household was not the only one that may have been established in New York for the purpose of serving as a place for students to live while they received an education in the city. Also living in the Washington Square area, for example, were seven Cuban students, all males ranging in age from seventeen to twenty-two, probably students at New York University. They lived by themselves in one house, but with the support of three female servants, two of them Irish and the other a native New Yorker.[62] Next door, there were four other college-age Cuban students living in a boardinghouse run by a New York couple and with students from other nations.[63]

The number of Cuban students who were interns at private schools continued to increase in the 1850s. In one boarding school in the Twenty-First Ward, in the West 30s, almost all the students boarded there in 1860 were Cuban boys and girls, a total of sixteen, ranging from eight to eighteen years of age.[64] In a large French boarding school in the Eighteenth Ward, nine teenaged Cuban girls were enrolled.[65] Almost every private or Catholic boarding school in Manhattan had at least one Cuban student.

* * *

If the New Yorkers of the mid-nineteenth century had formulated a stereotypical image of Cubans, a generalized construct of Cuban national characteristics, it was probably an image shaped primarily by such upper-class families as the Apezteguías, the Moras, the Yzquierdos, the Madans, and others who lived in comfortable homes, even mansions,

with servants and carriages. It was an image of opulence and even nobility rooted in what Cuba represented for New York: a booming trade with
a Spanish colony that was producing agricultural commodities that fed
the city's commercial juggernaut. For New Yorkers, the typical Cuban
was a planter or merchant whose vast estates and commercial operations brought him to New York to do business, shop, vacation, educate
his children in the best schools, and even to live in a style that could
be ostentatious but that also had a whiff of Old World noblesse attributed to elites of a society that was still a European colony. Prosperous
Cubans even made their presence felt in Saratoga Springs, which by the
1850s had become the foremost summer playground for wealthy New
Yorkers. The elegant United States Hotel in Saratoga, "the nation's most
brilliantly fashionable resort," offered the men liquor and gambling while
the women organized lavish dress balls.[66] In a story about the balls and
other amusements in Saratoga, the *New York Tribune* noted the presence
of Cubans:

> Here, as everywhere in Saratoga, one notices the great number of Cu-
> bans. . . . These Cubans, with their yellow-brown complexions, their
> slumberous eyes, and old, sad faces, would seem out of place at revels,
> if the glitter of their unnumbered jewels and their lithe, swaying, pas-
> sionate dancing did not contradict the promise of their somber presence.
> There are two sisters at the ball, in robes of yellow gossamer, with scarlet
> blossoms in their black hair, and on their tiny feet slippers of scarlet satin
> smaller than Cinderella's. Flashing down the long hall in the gallop, these
> gorgeous creatures look like the incarnate tropics.[67]

The Venezuelan Simón Camacho visited Saratoga and in his chronicle of
life in New York he wrote about constantly hearing the cadence of Cuban
Spanish in "the most fashionable place in the United States. . . . All of
Saratoga is today Cuban."[68] As noted in chapter 1, it was in Saratoga,
mixing business with pleasure, that Henry Coit, Moses Taylor's right-
hand man, connected sugar producers with New York buyers.

If the temporary or permanent presence in the city of wealthy Cubans
and their vacations in fashionable Saratoga were not enough to associate
Cubans with opulence in the minds of many New Yorkers, then surely
one singular social event in 1859 served to cement that stereotype:

Mr. & Mrs. Bartlett
Request the pleasure of your company at the marriage ceremony of their
daughter Frances Amelia, with Don Esteban Santa Cruz de Oviedo, *On
Thursday, the 13th of October*[69]

"The nuptials," wrote the chronicler of the *New York Times*, "mark indeed an epoch in our social history."[70] It was 1859, and New York had not
yet entered the Gilded Age with its excesses of public consumption.[71]
New Yorkers were not sure how to react to such an unabashed display
of luxury and ostentation. It was an event, the *New York Daily Tribune*
commented, "toward which all minds had turned for months expect-
ant. . . . Society has seldom been more deeply moved."[72] The *New York
Times* was more critical, describing it as "a bridal ceremony conducted
with a sumptuous disregard of conventional rules."[73]

The wedding was viewed by many as a crass public demonstration of
what unlimited wealth could buy, and New Yorkers followed in the press
every detail of the courtship and the preparations with a vicarious curiosity and a tinge of resentment. A very rich foreign man was flaunting his
ability to afford not only an indecently extravagant wedding, but also a
young and fair American bride, the daughter of a distinguished ex-officer
of the U.S. Navy. The *New York Times'* report on the ceremony was written in an almost mocking tone, with allusions to the tale of "Noureddin
and the Fair Persian, whom he bought for an incredible price and loved
without any assignable limit."[74] Indeed, contrasting skin tones and ages
were at the heart of the descriptions of the groom and the bride.

Her fair blonde shone somewhat more luminously by contrast with the
more somber complexion of Don Esteban. Tall and dignified, though
young her mien indicates eighteen years.[75]

Don Esteban, continued the *Daily Tribune*,

is some inches shorter than the lady, darkishly disposed in the matter
of complexion, with heavy half-curled black whiskers and mustache to
match.[76]

Harper's Weekly added one important detail, Don Esteban's age:

He is fifty-five years old, and of short stature, somewhat shorter than his bride. . . . The deep Castilian tinge of his countenance finely relieves the blonde purity of her complexion.[77]

No one knew precisely the extent of the groom's wealth, but each new guess seemed higher than the last, into the millions. "Don Esteban," wrote *Harper's Weekly*, "is the possessor of some of the most valuable estates in Cuba."[78] The *Daily Tribune* indicated that Don Esteban "is a Cuban gentleman of large possessions valued at many millions of dollars, so many that critical closeness as to the precise number is quite out of the question."[79] The *New York Times* reported that he was the owner of "large sugar and coffee plantations in Cuba, and Negroes without number."[80]

The estimates of Santa Cruz de Oviedo's wealth were not entirely exaggerations. He owned the La Santísima Trinidad sugar plantation in the Matanzas region, with nearly 1,800 acres and a technically advanced processing plant with steam-driven grinders. The property had its own aqueduct and was regarded as one of the most picturesque plantations in Cuba, with beautiful landscaping. Don Esteban was not the typical absentee Cuban planter. He managed the plantation himself, tending to every administrative detail. He also protected his investments. The pattern in most Cuban sugar mills was to mercilessly squeeze the labor out of the slaves until they died, buying more to replace them. Santa Cruz de Oviedo believed in reproducing his own. Of the one thousand slaves in his plantation, about a third were born in Cuba. There were about thirty births a year among the Trinidad's slaves, the highest birth rate among all plantations on the island. He took care to give them a relatively good diet: three meals a day of cornmeal, beans, rice, and frequent servings of beef and pork. It was apparently a profitable strategy: in just one year, 1855, the Trinidad produced 1,667 metric tons of sugar, which were shipped through the port of Matanzas.[81]

There was, however, more to the story of Santa Cruz de Oviedo that did not appear in the New York newspapers. Despite his age and wealth, the wealthy plantation owner had never married. But he did have offspring, at least twenty-six of them, all of them the children of several of his female slaves. Santa Cruz had over the years handpicked from each new group of slaves arriving at his plantation any young woman who struck his fancy. He placed them in the main house, sparing them the

Figure 3.2 The Santa Cruz de Oviedo-Bartlett wedding, (Old) St. Patrick's Cathedral, October 13, 1859. Source: Art and Picture Collection, New York Public Library, Astor, Lenox and Tilden Foundations.

usual life of a slave, in effect creating a harem to provide him with sex, company, and children. While never recognizing the children as heirs, he provided them with a privileged education, even sending some of them to study in New York.[82]

Santa Cruz y Oviedo could well pay to celebrate his (official) first nuptials with an extravagant wedding.[83] The bridal gown cost $5,000, along with four alternate gowns of $3,000 each and a trousseau of some seventy-five dresses, all presented to the bride by Don Esteban. The dresses were designed and made by the prominent fashion designer J. N. Genin from the finest silk and linen purchased at A. T. Stewart's "Marble Palace" on Broadway. The necklace, bracelet, brooch, and earrings worn by the bride were festooned with pearls and diamonds and manufactured under special order by Tiffany and Company.

The press reported the details of how the couple met that same year in January, when Santa Cruz de Oviedo, in the city on a business trip, attended a social gathering at the home of a friend of Miss Bartlett. He was reportedly quite taken with her when he discovered he did not need his translator to introduce himself, since she spoke Spanish fluently. Later, when he fell ill and was confined to his room at the St. Nicholas Hotel, she helped to nurse him back to health.

The ceremony was officiated by Archbishop John Hughes at the old St. Patrick's Cathedral on Mott and Prince Streets. There was no need, as originally planned, for a second ceremony at Grace Episcopal Church. The bride obligingly converted to Catholicism. Two separate invitations were issued to guests. One, a blue elegant invitation, went to "intimates," who were to enter the private Mulberry Street entrance to the vestry and assume the comfortable reserved pews in the front. The rest of the guest list, with red invitations, had to enter through the public entrance on Mott and take whatever seats they found or stand behind balustrades. A total of two thousand invitations were sent out, more than the modest church could comfortably accommodate. At ten in the morning the doors of the Mott Street entrance were flung open and in just a few minutes the church was filled entirely in "wild struggles and a furious rush."[84] The ceremony was not due to start until noon.

Outside, it was bedlam on the narrow streets that surrounded the church. The police superintendent personally took charge of attempting to enforce order in a crowd that the *New York Times*, in a hyperbole appropriate to the occasion, estimated at one hundred thousand.[85] The regular weekday traffic was rerouted to Broadway so as to accommodate the flow of carriages to and from the cathedral. The wedding party itself was transported in eight carriages.

The ceremony lasted less than thirty minutes, which was just as well. The bustle and clamor in the cathedral, the "rustling masses of humanity writhing in sinuous motion,"[86] the crowd jostling for a better look, and the occasional fainting lady—all drowned out the voice of the archbishop, who delivered a combative sermon against those two defilers of Catholic marriage: Henry VIII and Napoleon I. As soon as the bride signaled the end by facing the crowd and kissing her bridesmaids, the throng rushed out to get a glimpse of the procession of carriages headed to the reception at the home of the bride's family, 39 West 14th Street. The police had to then deal with the congestion and disruption that ensued along both Broadway and 14th Street. The family had private security to keep the crowd back from their home.

The public attention did not end with the ceremony. Immediately the finger pointing started on how a wedding had been turned into such a public spectacle, something that violated social convention of the time. The New York press was chastised by a Philadelphia newspaper for sensationalizing the event, something, argued the newspaper, which would not have happened in genteel Philadelphia. The *New York Times* responded that the parties themselves encouraged the attention by announcing the engagement and being indiscreet about the preparations, even sending invitations to the press.[87] The bride's father wrote a letter to the *Times* replying that it was not his family nor Mr. Santa Cruz de Oviedo who had made public the details of the wedding and that members of the press were invited as "gentlemen," not as reporters.[88]

It was not the first time Lieutenant Washington Bartlett had to write a letter defending his family. When the *Daily Tribune* wrote about how his daughter had ministered to Don Esteban while he was ill and confined to the St. Nicholas Hotel, the lieutenant considered the story's tone insinuative and wrote a letter to that paper clarifying that Miss Bartlett was properly accompanied when she visited her fiancé at the hotel.[89]

One consequence of the wedding was to reaffirm the image of Cubans as the prototype of the wealthy foreigner of the day. Camacho, the Venezuelan writer who lived in New York, devoted an entire chronicle to the wedding. He concluded it by reporting a conversation near Gramercy Park with a lady who, upon learning that Camacho was Latin American and clarifying that her sister was single, asked him, "Do you know a Cuban like Mr. Oviedo?"[90]

* * *

Not all Cuban New Yorkers, however, were fabulously rich planters. By 1860, as noted earlier, some class diversity was already evident within the Cuban-born population of the city. The city's many boardinghouses were increasingly taking in a greater number of Cubans who were artists, small businessmen, professionals, craftsmen, and laborers. Some boardinghouses had almost exclusively Cuban guests. In others, Cubans represented one of many groups sharing living quarters with boarders from Europe and throughout the United States. Cubans were accepted in such multinational houses as long, of course, as they were white. In nineteenth-century New York, neighborhoods were not always racially segregated, but boardinghouses almost always were.

In the Fifteenth Ward, for example, there were four unrelated Cuban white males in their twenties living in one huge house with more than a hundred other boarders and fourteen female Irish servants. The boarders, all white, with some families as well as single men and women, were from Germany, Spain, Ireland, Puerto Rico, England, Poland, and virtually every state in the Northeast and the Midwest.[91] In a smaller house also in the Fifteenth Ward, Emily West, a fifty-year-old English lady, had eight Cuban boarders, including two families, as well as boarders from England, Germany, and Scotland.[92] An engineer and a clerk were among the twelve Cuban boarders at a house in the Seventeenth Ward.[93]

Francis Bowman, a twenty-four-year-old woman born in Cuba, ran a boardinghouse in the Eighth Ward, what is now SoHo, with the help of her New York-born younger sister Elizabeth and three German servants. It must have been an interesting place. There were twenty-four boarders, all single white males between twenty and fifty-four and most engaged in creative occupations. A majority were Cubans, including two photographers, a sculptor, a flower arranger, and a picture frame maker. The rest were from Spain, Portugal, Germany, France, and New York and included a hatter, a watch case maker, a silversmith, a marble cutter, a chair maker, and a jeweler.[94]

A young Cuban physician by the name of Augusto Arango, who was active in émigré revolutionary politics, took in three boarders in the Greenwich Village house where he lived with his wife and three children. Arango's boarders were businessmen and professionals from Ireland, Germany, and England (a broker, an importer, and an "artiste"). The Arango house was located at 24 West 11th Street. The family that lived next door also took in boarders and was headed by Charles Scribner, who listed his occupation as "publisher" and whose sons John, Charles, and Arthur also lived there but were not yet old enough in 1860 to have entered the family business.

Although merchants, professionals, craftsmen, artists, clerks, and students tended to predominate among Cubans in New York, there were Cubans engaged in a wide range of pursuits and in very diverse housing arrangements throughout the city. Two New York Cubans were grocers, two were coopers, one a butcher, and another a brewer. There were ten Cubans in Manhattan who responded "gentleman" to the occupational question, but only one Cuban "gentleman" in Brooklyn. Five of the nuns and teachers at the large Academy of the Sacred Heart in Bloomingdale (Twelfth Ward) were Cubans.[95] In that same part of the city, the Bloomingdale Lunatic Asylum had three Cuban inmates in 1860.[96] There were three Cuban men in the Tombs, the city prison in the Sixth Ward, and one in the penitentiary at Blackwell's (now Roosevelt) Island. Francisco Beauvais, twenty-two years old, was living in a "poor house" in Queens County. Luis Fernández was a young staff physician at Bellevue Hospital.[97] A seventeen-year-old dental apprentice lived with his Louisiana-born master and his family in the Fifteenth Ward. In that same ward, Eugenia Fernández was a sixteen-year-old servant at the Astor Place Hotel. In addition to Eugenia, twelve Cuban women listed an occupation in 1860: six teachers, two seamstresses, one milliner, one dressmaker, one who did "days work," and one baker (this last one in Brooklyn). Nineteen-year-old Anne (no last name) was the only Cuban woman in a house with seven other white women younger than twenty-eight. The house, in the Fourteenth Ward (what is now NoLita), had four African American women as servants, and was headed by "Madam Parker," a thirty-five-year-old white Virginian who indicated that she ran a boardinghouse. No occupation is listed for any of Madam Parker's "boarders."

By 1860 cigar manufacturing had started its ascendancy as a major occupation among Cuban New Yorkers. Twenty-four Cubans in Manhattan and five in Brooklyn declared that as their occupation. Those numbers are relatively small compared to what would be registered in subsequent decades as New York developed a cigar manufacturing industry that used leaves, as well as workers, from Cuba. While the manufactured Cuban cigar had long been imported into New York, the importation of Cuban tobacco leaves for manufacture in the city was a phenomenon that started largely in the 1850s. It was not until that decade that "Clear Havana" leaves became popular in the U.S. market, increasing the consumption of cigars in the United States.[98]

Clear Havana leaves were actually not from Havana, but it was the term used to refer to the light-colored tobacco leaves from the region of Vuelta Abajo in western Cuba.[99] Cigars manufactured in the United States from Clear Havana leaves came to be regarded as the best and most expensive smokes.[100]

In 1851 the *Tobacco Circular*, a monthly trade newsletter published in New York, started keeping track of the amount of leaf tobacco imported into the city from Cuba. It divided those figures into Cuban tobacco and Clear Havana leaves. The former were usually of inferior quality and were processed for use in a variety of tobacco products, whereas the Havana leaves were of the quality used in the manufacture of cigars. At the beginning of the decade, only one bale of Clear Havana was imported for every three bales of imported Cuban leaves. The actual figures in 1851, for example, were 14,185 bales of Cuban and 5,229 of Havana. Starting in 1855, however, the number of Havana bales imported start outnumbering the Cuban bales by almost two to one (22,920 Havana and 12,073 Cuban), signaling the rise of a cigar-making industry in New York using Cuban leaves.[101] As with sugar, it was yet another case of New York turning a good profit by the further elaboration of an imported agricultural product from the island. Many of those Havana leaves were turned into cigars by European immigrants, especially Germans,[102] but by 1860 there is the beginning of the entry of Cuban craftsmen in that industry, as well as Cuban importers and tobacconists.

Most of the Cuban cigar workers lived in boardinghouses, either as single males or with their families, in working-class areas of the city. Some pooled their resources and shared a dwelling. José Millián, a twenty-eight-year-old cigar worker, his wife, and infant daughter shared their living quarters in the Tenth Ward with two other Cuban cigar workers, the Lara brothers. The same was true of Miguel Delgado, a thirty-six-year-old cigar maker. He and his wife lived with the family of another cigar maker in the Seventeenth Ward. In addition to cigar workers, there were ten Cubans in the city who were tobacco importers or tobacconists. José Xiqués was one of the first Cubans to have a cigar store in Manhattan. It was located at 372 Canal.[103] By age thirty-five Ramón Latorre, who was born in Spain, had a thriving business at 187 Pearl importing Cuban cigars. In 1860 he listed his assets as $20,000 and owned a home valued at $12,000 in the West 30s, where he lived with his Irish-born wife, Eleanor, his three New York-born small children, and two Irish servants.[104]

Although greater class diversity was starting to show among Cubans in New York, the same was not yet true of racial diversity. Of the more than six hundred Cubans who lived in New York City in 1860 in what are now the five boroughs, only sixteen were classified as either "black" or "mulatto." Many of them had English or French last names, an indication that while they were born in Cuba, they may have been of West Indian origin. Only a few were cigar makers, the occupation that in later years would account for a substantial number of nonwhite Cubans in New York. Afro-Cubans who were already living in New York in 1860 were employed, with few exceptions, in low-paying and unskilled occupations: porter, waiter, day worker, servant, and so forth. Aside from the handful of nonwhite cigar makers, the only other skilled nonwhite Cuban who appears in the 1860 census is a fifty-year-old ship carpenter who lived in the Eighth Ward. A majority of Cuban nonwhites indicated to the census taker that they did not know how to read or write. Marie Ann Wales, for example, a Cuban-born "mulatto" woman who lived in the Twentieth Ward with her husband, a "mulatto" tailor born in South Carolina, indicated that neither she nor her husband was literate. But Genora Simonson, a twenty-three-year-old nonwhite Cuban woman who did "general housework" in Staten Island, declared that she did know how to read and write.

Given the small number of Afro-Cubans in New York in 1860, it is not likely that they posed any challenge to the image New Yorkers had at the time of Cubans as white rich planters and merchants, an image reinforced by the Santa Cruz de Oviedo-Bartlett wedding. Yet the same year as the wedding, 1859, another event involving a Cuban in New York served to let New Yorkers know that there were also poor Afro-Cubans living in the city. The case of Félix Sánchez involved an unfamiliar intersection of race and nationality, and the New York press seemed confounded by the concept of a black Cuban in their city.

* * *

Félix Sánchez was one of three Cubans the 1860 census found imprisoned in the Tombs, the popular name for the city prison on Centre Street. How he got there is a story of domestic violence, justice, slavery, and racial and ethnic identity in antebellum New York. It started in the early morning of January 6, 1859, when police from the Eighth Precinct arrived at a house in the rear of 154 Sullivan Street, just south of Houston, to find a bloody crime scene.[105] Herman Carnon, "a colored man," was found stabbed through the heart with a sword. His wife and daughter were injured in the attack, carried out by the man who had married Mr. Carnon's daughter only a few weeks before. The alleged perpetrator, Félix Sánchez, twenty-one years old, had lived in the city for two years, taking on a succession of jobs, including hotel waiter, and had developed a reputation, according to the New York Times, for "vicious inclinations and a malignant and revengeful spirit."[106] The victim, "a respectable and industrious man," was advised by friends not to allow his daughter Sarah Jane to marry Sánchez, but Carnon disregarded the warnings and the wedding took place. Sánchez moved in with his new wife's family. Almost immediately he became consumed by jealousy, convinced that Sarah Jane, described by the New York Daily Tribune as a "sprightly colored girl," was being unfaithful to him.[107] The morning of the murder, Sánchez armed himself with a sword and in a rampage tried to kill his wife, but it was Carnon who ended up dead when he interceded to protect his daughter. Sánchez fled before the police arrived at the scene.

The initial stories in the New York Times, the New York Herald, and the New York Daily Tribune described Sánchez as a "young Spaniard." The Times later expanded that description to "a short, dark-haired, dark-eyed, swarthy and good-looking young Spaniard."[108]

Despite an all-city manhunt, Sánchez was not apprehended. He was last seen in the vicinity of Fulton Street, near the ferry landing. Police searched everywhere, including, the Times reported, the "tenements of the Spanish population."[109] The Times story also gave details about the fugitive's background.[110] Sánchez had been born in Trinidad, a town in southern Cuba, the son of a wealthy Cuban planter and one of his female slaves. The father recognized paternity and gave his son his own last name as well as his freedom. Sanchez's father relocated to New York and eventually had his son join him there, putting him up in a boardinghouse and securing for him a position as a tailor's apprentice. Sánchez had a volatile temperament and little patience for the craft, and he eventually abandoned that pursuit and became estranged from his father. He married Sarah Jane Carnon on Thanksgiving Day, 1858.

In May 1859, four months after the murder, Félix Sánchez surfaced in New Orleans. He had fled from Manhattan to Mobile with the help of a Cuban friend who, once there, betrayed him and sold him into slavery, believing that Sánchez would stay quiet because of the arrest warrant pending against him. But as soon as Sánchez arrived manacled in New Orleans to be sold, he declared to the authorities that he was a free Cuban and a New Yorker, which led them to establish his identity and trace him to the crime in New York. Sánchez was quoted as saying that "he would rather have a short life at hanging, than a long one at picking cotton."[111]

Sánchez's return to New York under the custody of Sergeant Lent of the Eighth Precinct was widely covered by the New York press. Given what they now knew about the murderer's family background and his temporary enslavement in the South, the label "swarthy Spaniard" no longer seemed appropriate, and the newspapers in unison agreed that Sánchez was a "Cuban mulatto."[112] The reporter for the *Daily Tribune*, after seeing the prisoner arrive at the Tombs, was still unclear about Sánchez's race, noting that "he is slender in form and rather good-looking, displaying more of the Spaniard than the negro."[113] The *New York Herald* reporter echoed that judgment when he wrote during the trial that "the prisoner is a good looking young man, and would be mistaken by many for a Spaniard."[114] The New York press, and probably most New Yorkers following this story, evidently had some difficulty categorizing foreigners of mixed racial ancestry, especially Cubans, who, after all, were supposed to be white "Spaniards."

Less than twelve days after his return to New York, Sánchez's trial was under way at the Court of General Sessions in Manhattan.[115] It lasted only two days and the verdict, as well as the sentence, were handed down immediately: guilty and death by hanging.[116] In subsequent newspaper stories about the case, another verdict was rendered by the press: now that he was a convicted murderer, Sánchez was definitely a "Cuban negro."[117] But even a year after his sentencing, the *Brooklyn Daily Eagle*, in a follow-up story, still grappled with Sánchez's identity: "he is almost as black as an African."[118]

Sánchez's legal appeals kept the executioner away for several years, even as he made his case for clemency more difficult by being a very troublesome prisoner at the Tombs. He was involved in an escape attempt in 1860, he assaulted a prison employee in 1861, and in 1862 he attacked and almost killed a fellow inmate.[119]

No existing record attests to why Félix Sánchez was never executed. Perhaps the Civil War intervened or perhaps, given his behavior in prison, it was decided that, contrary to the expert testimony presented at his trial, he was, after all, insane. In December 1870 a census enumerator assigned to the Thirteenth District of the Nineteenth Ward found one "Felix Sanches," a Cuban-born man in his thirties, in the Blackwell's Island Lunatic Asylum. When asked his occupation, the inmate gave the answer that many Cubans in New York, including his white father, would have given: "merchant." The census enumerator entered his race as "colored."[120]

* * *

The growth and increasing heterogeneity of the Cuban population in New York during the 1850s and 1860s helped to usher in a new era in the development of émigré political activism. The annexationist movement did not die with the failure of the last López expedition in 1851, but it would not have long to live. After 1855 the center of gravity of the separatist movement in New York shifted away from the economic interests of the elite toward a more broad-based and self-reliant revolutionary movement that had Cuban sovereignty as its goal.[121] With the rise of merchants, shopkeepers, craftsmen, and professionals among Cuban New Yorkers, the separatist movement took a more popular and nationalistic turn and was no longer under the exclusive control of planters with transnational economic interests and powerful connections who favored annexation. Furthermore, the possibilities of annexing Cuba through a sale or negotiation became progressively less likely.

The Spanish steadfastly refused to sell Cuba no matter what price the United States offered. Purchasing Cuba was the only means by which the United States was willing to acquire it in response to Southern interest in annexing the island. No matter how much concern there was about the "Africanization" of Cuba through the continuing slave trade and the benefits that might accrue to the United States in annexing it, successive U.S. administrations did not want to risk entering into a conflict with Spain by supporting armed excursions into the island.

The election of Franklin Pierce to the White House in 1852 gave renewed hope, if only ephemeral, to annexationists that the United States would once again pursue the purchase of Cuba. Pierce, a pro-expansionism Democrat, gave every indication that he had an earnest interest in acquiring the island. His secretary of state was a committed expansionist, William L. Marcy, a former U.S. senator and governor of New York. Marcy named as ambassador to Madrid the French expatriate and Louisiana senator Pierre Soulé, an outspoken advocate of annexing the island.[122] In August 1853, when Soulé stopped in New York on his way to assume his post in Madrid, he was hailed as a hero by many Cubans in the city, who paraded and gave speeches in front of the New York Hotel, on Broadway, where the ambassador was staying.[123] The following year, Pierce authorized Soulé to offer the Spanish $130 million for the purchase of Cuba, more than Polk had offered in 1848.[124] In response, the Spanish foreign minister publicly rejected any possibility of selling Cuba, calling the decision a question of honor.[125] That essentially ended the U.S. efforts to annex Cuba, especially since Pierce reaffirmed long-standing U.S. policy that the island would not be acquired by supporting violent or extralegal means.

Even before Pierce's attempt to buy the island was dashed by Spanish pride, many prominent New York émigrés, most of them annexationists, decided that they could not count on the United States and had to take matters into their own hands to oust the Spanish from Cuba. It was the beginning of a period of émigré activism that would span roughly from 1852 to 1867 and was characterized by shifting and diverse ideological currents that had in common only the desire of Cubans to be free to determine the island's destiny, whatever that determination might be.

In the early 1850s some elites continued to embrace annexation as a desirable outcome. But most separatists were willing to forgo the discussion of Cuba's future until after the Spanish were forced to leave. This brought together men with diverse ideological and economic positions who were willing to cooperate toward the common goal of ending Spanish rule on the island.

The organization of clandestine expeditions characterized much of émigré activism in the 1850s. As we saw in chapter 2, this was an insurgent tactic inaugurated by the annexationists, especially López and O'Sullivan, but one that took on even more urgency in the 1850s as the prospects for a U.S. purchase or a negotiated resolution of the Cuban question were dimmed.

Many émigrés identified with a term for the expeditions that in the United States was largely disparaging: filibustering. Rodrigo Lazo argues that in the antebellum period an entire culture of filibustering pervaded Cuban émigré activism, extending beyond the expeditions themselves to literature and newspapers.[126]

Lazo explains the origin of the term and its application in the antebellum United States:

> From the Dutch *vrijbuiter*, or "freebooter," modified into the French *filibustier*, the Spanish *filibustero* became common in the seventeenth century as an epithet for pirates who plundered the Spanish West Indies. This sense of the filibuster as a criminal adventurer, one who seizes objects by force, infused the English "filibuster."[127]

In the 1850s the term was applied to the soldiers of fortune who largely constituted the many expeditions that set out from the United States to capture regions of Latin America. The López expeditions were frequently referred to as filibustering expeditions because they did indeed include many European and American mercenaries. The New York newspapers critical of the expeditions, especially the *New York Times*, started using the term to refer to all Cuban activists, even those, for example, who gathered on Broadway to honor Minister Soulé while he was in New York.[128] But because the term had a romantic connotation, linked to a history of challenging Spanish authority in the Caribbean, the Cubans embraced the term. One newspaper founded by Cubans in New York in 1853 was called *El Filibustero*.[129]

After the López expeditions, the first concerted effort to launch a *filibustero* movement in New York was organized on October 19, 1852, at the Apollo Hall on Broadway.[130] The meeting was called by annexationists who had previously been divided over their support for López. The newly elected junta members were a fairly diverse group of men, including the perennial activist and annexationist Gaspar Betancourt Cisneros, Porfirio Valiente (who had just fled Cuba after being implicated in a conspiracy), Ambrosio José González (López's loyal follower and future Confederate colonel), Juan Manuel Macías (discussed earlier in this chapter), Cirilo Villaverde (the writer), Miguel Teurbe Tolón (the poet and a co-creator, with López, of the Cuban flag), and the ubiquitous John L. O'Sullivan.[131] Elected as treasurer of the junta was Domingo de Goicouría. Of all those men, Goicouría was the most emblematic activist figure of this period. He started out as an annexationist who hired others to do the fighting against Spain, but evolved into a supporter of independence willing, and eager, to risk his own life on the battlefield. As such, he personified the evolution of the separatist movement during the 1850s and 1860s. Goicouría was also a man with a checkered history who embodied not only the heroic and noble aspects of this period, but also its darker side.

* * *

Domingo de Goicouría y Cabrera was born in Havana to Spanish immigrants who had acquired various titles of nobility in their native Basque region.[132] Unlike most of the wealthy separatists, especially the annexationists, Goicouría did not have his origins in the *criollo* sugarocracy, but in the capital's Spanish commercial class. Although the family was wealthy, Goicouría and his brothers, Gonzalo and Felipe, did not sit on their inherited wealth, proving to be very successful merchants in their own right, doing quite a bit of business from Havana with commission agents in New York. In 1858, for example, the Goicouría brothers filed a suit in New York Superior Court against Emilio Sánchez y Dolz, a Cuban merchant in Manhattan, alleging that they were shortchanged for commissions on a shipment of 310,000 cigars and a consignment of hides. The court ordered Sánchez y Dolz to pay the brothers $1,525.81.[133]

Unlike many other émigré separatists, Goicouría was not an intellectual or a writer, although he did receive a privileged education, attending elite schools in Havana and in Bilbao and La Coruña in Spain. Early in his life he also lived for a time in England and Philadelphia, where he was exposed to democratic ideals and developed an impassioned intolerance for Spanish autocracy.

Throughout his life, Goicouría demonstrated an uncanny ability for business, several times emerging out of financial ruin by creating profitable business ventures that enabled him to contribute sizable amounts of money to the Cuban separatist cause. He was elected treasurer of the junta largely because he was expected to underwrite with his own money much of the cost of the planned expedition. In Cuba he built a substantial personal fortune not only by forming part of his family's commercial ventures, but also by striking out on his own in a wide variety of business pursuits, including a contract to build a railroad line from Havana to Cárdenas, raising horses, growing coffee, and building the island's first nail factory.[134]

Goicouría was an opponent of slavery and actively promoted free white migration to the island, personally recruiting more than two thousand laborers in Spain to work in Cuba.[135] Goicouría Brothers was also active in promoting, as a business, the importation of laborers from Yucatán, in Mexico, to work in Cuban sugar plantations under indentured servitude arrangements. After bringing in about four hundred *yucatecos* in 1855, the project was abandoned.[136]

When not in Cuba or in Spain, Goicouría resided in New York. Not only did he do business there, but he was married to Carlota Mora, a sister of José María and Antonio Máximo, discussed earlier as New York businessmen who were among the first of the Mora clan to move to the city. Goicouría educated his three children in Manhattan and became a collaborator of *La Verdad*, the annexationist newspaper.[137] He provided most of the funding for one of the López expeditions and he happened to be in Havana when it failed. The Spanish learned of his role, imprisoned him, and deported him to Spain. He returned to New York shortly thereafter, but the experience made him a committed revolutionary, and he would thereafter apply to his separatist activities the same penchant for adventurism that he had displayed in business matters. That emboldened disposition would eventually bring him into conflict with a junta dominated by cautious businessmen, property owners, and intellectuals.

The historian Ramiro Guerra y Sánchez, writing about the 1852 New York junta, bemoaned the "inferiority complex that made a majority of Cubans mistrust their own capacity for action and force sufficient to defeat Spain militarily."[138] This tendency, argued Guerra y Sánchez, combined with the interest of property owners in avoiding a long conflict and the evident lack of military experience among Cubans, made the junta follow the worn strategy of the old annexationist Club de La Habana:

Recruit and organize in the United States a sizable military contingent, place it under the orders of an experienced and renowned general, disembark on the island, and then support the invading force with a general uprising on the island.[139]

The junta hired someone they knew to head the military effort: General John Quitman, former governor of Mississippi, the same one who almost accepted a similar offer from Narciso López a few years before. Goicouría was not convinced about the choice, largely because of Quitman's pro-slavery credentials. Since he was putting up part of the money, Goicouría insisted on going down to Natchez to meet the general. The meeting convinced Goicouría that Quitman was, according to one historian, a "phoney."[140] But Goicouría relented when a majority of the junta decided to put their faith in the southerner and gave him the half a million dollars they had raised.[141] Quitman was expected to recruit some five thousand men for the expedition.

After more than a year, Quitman had made little progress in readying the expedition. Goicouría clashed with a majority in the junta when he demanded the firing of Quitman. The junta decided to be patient with the American general. In the end, Goicouría was proved right in his judgment of Quitman. The general was summoned to Washington by Secretary of State Marcy, who voiced the administration's strong objections to the planned expedition, urging Quitman to abandon it. Quitman did so, leaving the junta without its expedition and without its money.

No doubt expressing the opinion of many New Yorkers, the *New York Times* voiced little sympathy over the collapse of the entire enterprise. Calling Quitman the "Lieutenant General of the Filibusteros," the newspaper reserved its harshest criticism for what it viewed as the junta's attempts to portray itself as a victim clamoring for an accounting of its lost money:

> They should talk only of folly—their own folly. . . . In this City there were wary men, some of them slave traders, . . . who put up a larger share of the funds invested, and lost in the venture. The venture was one of American blood, . . . American youth who were assuredly doomed had the expedition sailed, . . . while the reckless contrivers of the plot, losing nothing but money they are better without, would live on undisturbed by the catastrophe. . . . To sympathy they have no rational claim.[142]

In August 1855 the junta officially folded, declaring an end to its campaign by issuing a statement placing the blame for its failure on successive U.S. administrations that acted as the "foremost adversaries of Cuban revolutionaries," through the "confiscations of our means of action, constant espionage, and serving as informants of our movements."[143] Goicouría, however, sought to disassociate himself from the junta's failure by issuing in New York a lengthy "I told you so" statement vindicating his actions. The real reason for the disaster, he argued, was the conservative nature of the junta, which caused it to defend Quitman: "I was not as blind as my colleagues, and had the good fortune to recognize in time that we had made a mistake with General Quitman."[144] The junta, he concluded, denied him the opportunity to fulfill "my ardent wish to shed my blood."[145]

The junta was finished, but Goicouría was not. If the Cubans in New York could not be decisive in putting together an expedition, then he would join forces with a proven man of action, someone with a successful filibustering record. In 1856 the most notorious filibusterer was a native Tennessean and New Orleans lawyer by the name of William Walker, who led a mercenary expedition to Central America so that he could become the ruler of Nicaragua. In January 1856 Goicouría struck a deal with Walker: Goicouría would organize an expedition to Central America and help Walker assume power in Nicaragua. Once that was accomplished, Walker would help Goicouría oust the Spanish from Cuba.[146] The deal satisfied Goicouría's need for adventurism and military involvement, as well as the possibility of renewing the fight against Spanish colonialism in Cuba. Walker even stroked his ego by giving him the title of "brigadier general."[147] Collaborating with Walker, however, was a move that even Goicouría's admiring biographer was at a loss to justify, regarding it as his greatest error.[148] Nicaraguan historians have been relentless in their criticism of the role of Goicouría in bringing their nation under foreign control.[149] In effect, his alliance with Walker betrayed the very principles of his struggle against the Spanish in Cuba.

Goicouría kept up his end of the bargain with Walker. In May 1856 he arrived in Nicaragua with about 250 men, and Walker dispatched him to the Chontales region, where Nicaraguan rebels had taken up arms to oppose Walker's takeover of the country.[150] Goicouría and his men were involved in numerous battles; he was wounded in one skirmish, and was responsible for the summary execution of a number of rebel leaders. One Nicaraguan historian wrote that Goicouría "planted terror in the region and like a tiger left a trail of blood behind him."[151] The Nicaraguans gave him the nickname Barba Blanca (White Beard). Although he was only forty-six his beard was prematurely gray, and he was determined not to trim it until Cuba was free from Spanish control. It already covered his chest.[152]

After installing himself as president of Nicaragua, Walker named Goicouría emissary to Europe to gain support there for the new government. Goicouría stopped in New York on his way to the Continent to meet with Commodore Cornelius Vanderbilt. Walker had earlier annulled the monopoly that Vanderbilt had been granted for operating a profitable waterway transportation system through Nicaragua that linked the Atlantic states and California, awarding the contract instead to two of Vanderbilt's rivals in the shipping business.[153] Vanderbilt had funded Goicouría's expedition to Nicaragua, and the Cuban felt that Walker made a mistake alienating the powerful American magnate.[154] Goicouría tried to make amends with Vanderbilt, but Walker promptly repudiated that conciliatory effort, writing to Goicouría that he was not authorized to negotiate with Vanderbilt.[155] That action, of course, upset Goicouría, but not as much as the next bit of news he received from Nicaragua: Walker declared his intention to institute slavery in that country.[156] With that, Goicouría broke all ties with Walker. In a lengthy letter to various New York newspapers, Goicouría denounced Walker, claiming that the Tennessean planned to extend his rule to all of Central America, reinstate slavery, and thereby create a "Southern despotism as a counterbalance to the United States."[157] After signing the letter, Goicouría provided his New York address: 122 East 13th Street (between Third and Fourth Avenues), the Manhattan block that was largely owned by his in-laws, the Moras.

After a few months he moved to New Orleans, where he lived for a few years and rebuilt his fortune.[158] While there, he made an attempt to broker yet another unsuccessful deal to free Cuba, this time with Benito Juárez of Mexico.[159] The Civil War had disastrous consequences for his shipping business in New Orleans, so he moved back to New York, where he was granted U.S. citizenship by the Common Pleas Court of New York County on June 12, 1865. He gave as his address 127 East 12th Street, in the same neighborhood as his in-laws.[160]

In 1867 Goicouría moved with his family to Rio de Janeiro, where one of his married daughters lived.[161] He was already fifty-seven years old, so one might think that this retreat to Brazil is the end of his story. But Domingo de Goicouría will reappear only a year later in New York to become involved in a new chapter of separatist activism. He had not yet fulfilled the prediction his father Valentín made years before when Domingo became obsessed with liberating Cuba from Spain: "The Spanish hate you, and one day they will hang you."[162]

* * *

After 1857 neither Goicouría nor the junta were players on the New York activist stage. But with the continued growth of the Cuban community, the manifestations of a separatist spirit among the émigrés also grew. The proliferation of political newspapers was perhaps the most evident of those manifestations. Prior to 1850 only three politically oriented newspapers had been established by Cubans in New York: Varela's *El Habanero*, Saco and Varela's *El Mensajero Semanal*, and the annexation-ists' *La Verdad*. The historian Enrique López Mesa has documented the appearance, from 1850 to 1867, of sixteen titles.[163] Most were short-lived and published weekly, biweekly, or monthly. They usually arose as the official publications of émigré organizations or movements that lasted for a limited amount of time and had specific political objectives. Some also had literary content. But these were not the newspapers of an ethnic or immigrant community. They were not about life in a new country; they were not about the world of Cuban New York. They were the newspapers of émigrés intent on determining the future of their homeland. As Rodrigo Lazo notes, these periodicals were transnational texts, in both their content and their circulation.[164] The émigrés were writing to Cuba, so these were the print versions of the filibuster movement. The expeditions were intended to take the armed struggle to the island. The newspapers were printed and circulated so as to take to Cuba denunciations of Spanish rule, calls for revolution, and ideas such as self-determination, democracy, independence, freedom, and progress.

Not that there was uniformity in the expression of those ideas. Some of the newspapers, if not most, represented elite interests, which meant, for example, that in the 1850s the concept of freedom was not, explicitly or implicitly, extended to slaves. On the other hand, at least one Cuban

New York newspaper of that decade, *El Mulato*, which had a run of only thirteen issues in 1854, was devoted to the cause of abolition both in the United States and in Cuba, criticizing the alliance of many émigrés with pro-slavery forces in the South.[165] Abolitionists were responsible for the publication of *El Mulato*, most notably Lorenzo Allo, the former student of Varela who had visited his dying teacher in St. Augustine.[166] When it first came out, *El Mulato* was publicly repudiated by many Cubans in New York. There was even a public meeting to denounce it. The trend, however, was toward greater support among Cubans for abolition. By the 1860s, abolition had become part of the Cuban separatist agenda, especially in New York.[167]

The newspapers were outlets for the intellectual and literary figures who were gathering in New York and devoting their pens to the Cuban cause. Miguel Teurbe Tolón, the poet and writer who had collaborated with *La Verdad* and with Narciso López, was responsible for publishing four different newspapers during the 1850s. Cirilo Villaverde, a writer and exile who years later, in New York, would write the most important Cuban novel of the nineteenth century, also collaborated with several newspapers during the antebellum period.[168]

Teurbe Tolón and Lorenzo Allo were involved in the founding in 1853 of what may be regarded as the first Cuban cultural institution in New York, the Cuban Democratic Atheneum, housed in the Assembly Rooms at 600 Broadway.[169] Courses were offered there on such subjects as Cuban history, political economy, and U.S. constitutional law.

Leaving aside the exceptional work in New York of Father Varela, none of the first organizations and publications established by Cubans in New York were centered on Catholicism. For a number of reasons, primarily Cuba's development as a port colony, the Church never had the influence on the island that it had in the rest of Latin America. Cuba has traditionally been a secular society.[170] This was especially true among Cubans in New York. A priest was usually asked to give an invocation at meetings in New York, as a Father Valdés did at the founding meeting of the 1852 junta, but there is no evidence that during this period there were any Catholic-based organizations or publications. Cubans in New York were influenced by the city's modern and progressive culture, and émigrés tended to reject many of Spain's traditional institutions. As we saw in chapter 1, even plantation owners thought of themselves as enlightened.

It is therefore fitting that the only religiously based organization established by a Cuban in New York during the antebellum period was Fraternal Lodge No. 387, the first Spanish-language Masonic lodge in the United States. It was founded in 1855 by Andrés Cassard, who arrived in New York as a political exile from Cuba in 1852 and became a Freemason a year later.[171] Lodge No. 387 was the beginning of the long and important story of Freemasonry among Cuban New Yorkers. In 1865 Cassard established a newspaper, *El Espejo Masónico*.[172]

Newspapers and cultural institutions were not, of course, the only vehicles for the expression of émigré activism in New York. The period from 1855 to 1867 also saw the celebration of meetings and rallies, fundraising, the creation of political organizations, and even the actual launching or near-launching of an expedition or two.

Juan Manuel Macías, the supporter of López who became a New York merchant, was one of the most politically active figures in the 1860s. He was largely responsible for the establishment of two organizations devoted to bringing together Latin Americans in New York committed to "liberty and independence for all peoples in the New World": the Democratic Society of Friends of America in 1864 and in 1865 the Republican Society of Cuba and Puerto Rico.[173] Macías also served as the editor of the two publications affiliated with those organizations.[174] Early in 1868 Macías traveled to the Dominican Republic to meet with the Puerto Rican Ramón Emeterio Betances and the Dominican José María Cabral to discuss a plan Betances had proposed many years before: the creation of a federation of the Spanish-speaking Antilles. The initiative did not go beyond the discussion stage.[175]

From 1865 to 1867 Cuban separatism was briefly distracted by an initiative launched by a new and liberal administration in Madrid. The Spanish held out the possibility of instituting reforms that would give Cubans some relief from oppressive fiscal and tax measures as well as a measure of home rule. They convened in Madrid an assembly of sixteen elected representatives from Cuba and four from Puerto Rico to present a list of proposed reforms. Many elites enthusiastically embraced this reformist initiative, hoping that Spain would give Cubans enough autonomy to govern their own affairs while maintaining economic continuity and avoiding violence.

Among the elected commissioners of the assembly, called the Junta de Información, was José Antonio Saco, anti-annexationist and collaborator of Varela nearly forty years before in New York. Saco accepted his post with considerable reluctance because of his reservations about the reformist plan. Another one of the commissioners was Moses Taylor's foremost client, Tomás Terry, elected from the Cienfuegos area. The Spanish government named its own representatives to the assembly. Among them was Saco's old rival in the 1829 controversy over Heredia in the pages of *El Mensajero Semanal*: the Spanish scientist Ramón de la Sagra.[176]

The junta was aggressive in its proposals and contentious in its debates on abolition. But in the end, it did not matter. The liberal government had in the meantime fallen from power, and on April 16, 1867, while the junta was still in session, a royal decree was issued terminating its work.[177] The commissioners left Madrid the same way Varela left it in 1823 when he went there to push for reforms before the Spanish parliament: empty-handed and frustrated. In forty-four years, little had changed in the Spanish government's disposition toward Cuban demands for changes in the colonial regime.

* * *

Annexation and reformism failed for reasons that originated not in New York or in Havana, but in Washington and Madrid. President James Buchanan made one last try in 1860 to buy Cuba, but could not get Congress to appropriate the money.[178] As historian Gerald Poyo noted, "sectional politics in the United States with regard to slavery made the acquisition of Cuba virtually impossible."[179] In Madrid, the Spanish government not only steadfastly refused to sell Cuba but also stubbornly rejected any attempts to give an iota of self-rule to the Cubans.

With annexation and reformism discredited, the movement for Cuban self-determination was inexorably headed in a popular, progressive, and nationalist direction, settling for nothing but total independence.[180] A growing and more diverse Cuban community in New York, no longer dominated by elite planter interests, embraced that direction. But Cuban New Yorkers knew, as did all Cubans, that unlike annexation and reformism, which could have been accomplished through negotiation, independence could be attained only through violence. Resorting to violence was certainly not something new for Cuban separatists. But what erupted in October 1868 was indeed something new. In its intensity and scope it was unlike anything that had been experienced before through conspiracies, expeditions, and local insurrections.

It was war. It came unexpectedly, literally out of nowhere, for it did not originate in the usual places. It was not hatched in the meeting halls or newspaper offices of émigrés in New York, nor in the sugar plantations of Matanzas, and not even in the Havana homes of impatient intellectuals or merchants. It came from the backwater that was eastern Cuba, spearheaded by long-neglected and resentful landowners, most of whom were virtually unknown in Havana or Matanzas or New York. But in 1868, when those easterners decided they had had enough of Spanish rule and were willing to risk everything to end it, Cuba and its émigré community in New York would not be the same again.

PART II

War: 1868–1895

4

War and Exodus

The situation in Cuba was grievous and inconsolable. The war dominated everything. . . . Onto the tranquility of old, the sweet serenity of the countryside, so pleasant in Cuba, had erupted the horrible tempest of passions.
—Emilio Soulere, *Historia de la insurrección de Cuba*, Barcelona, 1879[1]

With deep sorrow we left the country of our birth, and we said a last farewell with tears in our eyes and an ache in our heart. The valuable possessions we left behind, our beloved mother, our dear family, lifelong friends, all remained on the island that had become so embittered by great upheavals and bloody cataclysms.
—Carlos de Sedano, *Cuba: Estudios políticos*, Madrid, 1873[2]

As José Manuel Mestre made his way through the bustling streets of Havana to the Palace of the Captain Generals, he was wondering why he had been summoned there for a meeting with the military governor. He was hopeful, however, that the governor would be announcing the beginning of a new era in Spain's relationship with its colony.[3] Such an announcement, Mestre felt, was exactly what was needed. It was October 24, 1868, and he sensed that the political situation on the island was at a critical moment, "on the road to desperation," he wrote to a friend, "and it is to be feared that everything will end gravely and in a decisive schism."[4]

Mestre was thirty-six years old and a prominent Havana lawyer and professor. His rise to Havana's upper classes had been anything but typical. Mestre's father, born in Spain's Catalunya region, was neither a planter nor a merchant, but a chocolatier, owner of a modest factory and shop on Ricla (now Muralla) Street, in the heart of Havana.[5] When

José Manuel was only twelve years old his father died, leaving a widow and four children. The tragedy, however, expanded Mestre's opportunities considerably beyond chocolate making. His maternal aunt had married a rich man and they had no children, so they took financial responsibility for the education of the Mestre children, placing them in the best schools in the city. Eventually, José Manuel enrolled at the University of Havana, pursuing degrees in philosophy and jurisprudence and graduating with honors. He was able to count among his professors and fellow students the most prominent thinkers and writers in Havana at the time, such as Felipe Poey, Antonio Bachiller y Morales, José Ignacio Rodríguez, Nicolás Azcárate, Enrique Piñeyro, Francisco Fesser, and Nestor Ponce de León.[6] He developed a reputation as both a lawyer and an academic, successfully trying some high-profile criminal cases, handling the legal matters of many of the city's richest families, and teaching philosophy at the university.

In 1856 Mestre married into the Alfonso-Aldama-Madan clan. His wife, Paulina Alfonso, was the granddaughter of Gonzalo Alfonso, Domingo Aldama's father-in-law, and therefore she was a first cousin of Miguel Aldama.[7] Mestre's biographer and lifelong friend, José Ignacio Rodríguez, claimed that while Mestre's marriage greatly helped his law practice, it did not pull him into the sugar business of his wife's family, nor did it sway him from his opposition to slavery. Mestre remained a lawyer and an academic as well as an abolitionist. Rodríguez recalled Mestre's fascination with *Uncle Tom's Cabin* and his interest in seeing the publication of a loose translation adapted to a Cuban setting.[8]

Mestre's first dabble with politics was during the reformist experiment of 1867. He actively supported the work of the Junta de Información, which had been formed to try to extract from Madrid some measure of home rule and fiscal reform for Cuba and Puerto Rico. José Morales Lemus, Nicolás Azcárate, and José Antonio Echeverría, three of his closest friends, were commissioners in the junta. The work of the junta was frustrated by the fall of the liberal government in Spain, but in September 1868 a revolution dethroned the queen, bringing to power another liberal government that promised to extend rights and liberties to all Spaniards, giving renewed hope to Cuban reformists.[9]

For many in Havana, like Mestre, the new Madrid government represented the last hope of avoiding the "decisive schism" that loomed on the eastern horizon. On October 10, the landowners in the valley of the Cauto River, centered on the cities of Bayamo and Manzanillo, declared independence, freed their slaves, and formed an army and a government. A war had started. Although he had not been told the purpose of the October 24 meeting with the governor, Mestre was hoping that in response to that threat the governor would be announcing to prominent members of Havana's society the Spanish government's intention to extend its liberal reforms to the island.

Mestre was not the only one who did not know the purpose of the meeting with the governor. The host, Governor Francisco Lersundi, also did not know why he was being asked to meet with a group of Havana residents. And he certainly had neither orders nor intentions to announce any reforms in how Cuba was governed. Lersundi was loyal to the deposed queen. In fact, he had been named to the top Havana post only a year before by Her Majesty's government precisely to quell any manifestations of reformism or separatism among the Cubans. He was expecting the new liberal government to recall him at any moment, and that was fine with him. He had no interest in implementing a reform plan to relax colonial rule. Reformists like Mestre were hoping that the governor would be sent packing to Madrid. It would be a signal that Spain's new liberalism was about to be extended to Cuba. Besides, Lersundi was disliked in the colony. He was a man with an authoritarian disposition and brusque demeanor who was intolerant of any discussion of the island's colonial status.

Governor Lersundi lived and worked in the same beautiful colonial building that for nearly a century had housed his predecessors. It was known then, and even today, as the Palace of the Captain Generals, for that was the official title of Spain's colonial governors. The governorship was a military post, reflecting the manner in which the Spanish ran their colony.

As the governor walked to the meeting along the open arched corridor that surrounds the palace's courtyard, his mind was no doubt on extinguishing the insurgency in the east. A meeting with residents of Havana was the last thing he needed that Saturday evening. He was therefore very displeased when he walked into the room and instead of the handful of visitors he was expecting, there were more than fifty people waiting for him.[10] Word had spread in Havana that the governor was holding a political meeting and all prominent residents were invited. The principal organizer of the event, Apolinar del Rato, a Spaniard, a royalist, and a supporter of Lersundi, had thought the meeting would be a good opportunity for the governor to mend fences with the locals, perhaps on the assumption that the Havana *criollos* such as Mestre were not supporting their eastern compatriots. Witnesses recalled seeing Lersundi's face contort into an angry expression. He immediately told the visitors that he was not expecting such a large gathering and that he was not pleased. There was an uncomfortable silence as it became obvious that the governor had nothing to say to the group. Del Rato tried to salvage the situation by saying that all of those people had gathered at such a difficult time to express their solidarity with the governor's policies and actions.

Mestre had gone to the meeting to listen and not to speak, but he could not abide del Rato's gross misrepresentation of his position. He asked to speak, and after expressing the appropriate respects to the governor, Mestre firmly voiced his hope that the freedoms that the new Madrid government had promised would be extended to Cubans and that such an action would be the only way to guarantee the future peace and prosperity of the island. Only one other person spoke after Mestre, Juan Modet, a Spanish colonel in the colonial army's engineer corps, who expressed his support for Mestre's words. But he did not get to finish. Lersundi had heard enough. He interrupted Modet and declared the meeting over, but not before saying that he had felt "ambushed" that evening and that the views he had heard expressed were no different than the motives of the eastern insurrectionists. Furthermore, he said that the time for talk was over, and that his administration had the means necessary to punish the "rebels and agitators" and suppress the uprising.

There were no immediate consequences for Mestre or for the other attendees, with the exception of Colonel Modet. The Spanish had a very small degree of tolerance for rebellious Cubans, but apparently none at all for one of their own. Modet was immediately shipped off to Spain, his career finished. Lersundi stayed on as governor for nearly three more months, replaced in the end not because he was not a liberal, but because he failed to quell the rebellion. There were no reforms.

The brief meeting of October 24, 1868, was a turning point, or more accurately, a point of no return for Cubans such as José Manuel Mestre. After that, as one historian noted, he "submitted to the inevitable,"[11] and actively supported the armed movement started by the easterners, most of whom he did not know personally. The "decisive schism" he had feared would soon envelop the island, and it would take Mestre, and many other Cubans, to New York.

Eastern Cuba was not blessed, or cursed, with the sugar revolution that had swept the western portion of the island in the nineteenth century. Sugar mills in the easternmost province of Oriente tended to be small operations, many of them still grinding with animal power and with few slaves.[12] In 1868 the wealthiest man in the entire eastern region was probably Francisco Vicente Aguilera, who owned three modest sugar mills that altogether had only five hundred slaves. In Oriente, he could not have amassed his capital, estimated at over $3 million, had he depended solely on sugar and slavery. He owned more than 331,000 acres of land devoted to coffee, tobacco, and grazing some 35,000 head of cattle and 4,000 horses. He also owned numerous buildings and lots in the various towns in the region, including a theater and dry goods warehouse in Bayamo, where he was born.[13]

Aguilera was in many ways typical of the landowners in eastern Cuba. Unlike their western counterparts, the landed elite of Oriente and Camagüey provinces were far removed from their Spanish roots. They were the descendants of Spanish settlers who had arrived in Cuba in the sixteenth or seventeenth centuries as part of the original colonization of the island by Spain. They established themselves on large pastoral estates, and eventually the island's development bypassed them when the center of the colony's economic activity shifted to Havana. The port on the northwestern coast became the hub of Spanish trade in the New World and eventually, as we saw in chapter 1, it evolved into the center of a sugar revolution that brought unprecedented wealth to the island. The trade and sugar boom created new elites in Havana, such as the Madans, the Aldamas, and the Alfonsos, most of whom arrived in the late eighteenth or early nineteenth century.

The eastern elites remained stuck in a more modest and diversified agricultural economy that emphasized cattle production, especially in the Cauto Valley, surrounding the towns of Bayamo, Manzanillo, and Tunas, and also in the plains of Camagüey, a vast and scarcely populated region in east central Cuba that had as its center the city of Puerto

Príncipe, a curious name for an inland settlement. These easterners had lived in relative isolation for generations, intermarrying, and developing an economy that depended little on Spain, selling their cured beef to the English and the French who had many slaves to feed in their sugar colonies throughout the Caribbean. Furthermore, the diversified estates of the east used some free labor and were therefore less reliant on slaves than those in the west.[14]

Aguilera, born in 1821, was a fifth-generation Cuban whose ancestors had arrived in Bayamo from the Canary Islands in the seventeenth century.[15] The Puerto Príncipe families, such as the Agramontes, the Mirandas, and the Varonas, had even longer histories in Cuba, arriving in the sixteenth century.

The eastern elites had endured generations of neglect from colonial authorities. They had few sentimental or economic ties to Spain. To them, colonial rule meant only oppression and taxes. Without a great dependence on slavery and sugar and therefore devoid of an economic stake in the continuation of the colonial or slave regime, eastern patricians such as Aguilera had no use for annexationist or reformist formulas.[16] The only thing that made sense to them was independence, and unlike their cautious Havana compatriots, who feared the consequences of violence for their economic interests, the easterners had relatively little to lose and were willing to risk all of it. The desire for freedom and independence was stoked by the privileged education that Aguilera and his eastern peers received, including boarding schools in Havana, and trips to Europe and the United States, where they were exposed to liberal and democratic ideals.[17] Unlike the Havana sugarocracy, who were residents of the capital and only visitors to their estates, the eastern elites lived primarily on their rural properties, so they were experienced in handling horses, guns, and swords and were therefore more likely, and prepared, to resort to an armed conflict than their western counterparts, whose separatist activism had always been limited to reformist initiatives or paying for expeditions in which others did the fighting. Aguilera and his contemporaries in the east were therefore men of action, and by the late 1860s they were more than ready to act decisively upon their grievances with Spain.

The vehicles for organizing the rebellion were the Masonic lodges in Bayamo, Manzanillo, and Puerto Príncipe. Freemasonry provided an attractive alternative to liberal Cubans who regarded the Catholic Church as an ally of the Spanish. The secretive lodges were also an excellent cover for clandestine meetings that forged the unity of various centers of unrest in the region into a revolutionary movement.[18] Aguilera, already in his forties, was the Venerable Master of the Tropical Star No. 19 Lodge in Bayamo. Another native of Bayamo, Carlos Manuel de Céspedes, headed the Good Faith Lodge in Manzanillo. In Puerto Príncipe the Tínima Lodge No. 16 (named after a river in the area) brought together some of the most prominent figures of Camagüey society, including Salvador Cisneros Betancourt, Bernabé Varona, and Ignacio Agramonte.[19]

It was Céspedes who provided the spark for the armed rebellion. A lawyer who had acquired a modest sugar mill from his brother, Céspedes headed most of the clandestine meetings leading to the uprising. A man with an impulsive personality and an excellent horseman and fencer, Céspedes had studied in Havana, Spain, Germany, and Italy. Back in Bayamo, he was imprisoned several times for his known opposition to Spanish rule, and he was eventually expelled from the city and settled in nearby Manzanillo.[20]

Because of his impatient nature, or perhaps because he feared that the Spanish were about to uncover the conspiracy, Céspedes declared the beginning of the war before Aguilera and the others were ready. On October 10, 1868, at his sugar mill, he freed his slaves and proclaimed the start of a war that would last ten years. All the other centers of opposition were forced into action. Céspedes issued a manifesto that had been drafted jointly with the other leaders, declaring independence and naming himself the chief military officer.[21]

At first, the Spanish authorities in Havana played down the rebellion. The pro-Spanish *Diario de la Marina* characterized the insurrection as an "insignificant gang," "outlaws whose actions are as ridiculous as they are unwise and criminal."[22] But Céspedes's forces were growing rapidly, swelled by white farmers, as well as slaves and free blacks.[23] They lacked uniforms and proper weapons, but they scored some early victories, mostly notably the capture of Bayamo, which surrendered to rebel forces on October 22.[24] By the end of the month Céspedes had nearly ten thousand men under his command.[25] The uprising spread further as the Camagüeyanos, headed by Ignacio Agramonte and Salvador Cisneros Betancourt, joined the uprising in November.

Governor Lersundi and his military government were unprepared to deal with the rebellion. There were only about seven thousand regular Spanish troops on the island.[26] The governor quickly moved to activate and expand the number of *voluntarios*, a paramilitary corps of loyalists who were ready to fiercely defend Spanish-owned properties, ruthlessly assert colonial control, and put the rebellious Cubans in their place. With the financial support of some of the wealthy Spaniards on the island, more *voluntarios* were recruited in Spain, with promises of bonuses once the rebellion was defeated.[27] But by December, the rebellion was still raging and Lersundi was finally recalled to Madrid. One of Lersundi's legacies was to leave a force of at least thirty-five thousand *voluntarios* throughout the island.[28] It was a lamentable legacy. The new recruits tended to be young, poor, uneducated, and imbued with a zealous patriotism and a hatred of rebellious Cubans. They were an "antisocial and *provocateur* element," according to one historian.[29]

The first to reap Lersundi's legacy was his replacement, General Domingo Dulce, a man close to the new liberal government in Madrid. He was sent to Cuba with instructions to try a conciliatory approach to the rebellion. When he arrived in Havana on January 4, 1869, he received a cold reception from the *voluntarios* and other loyalist elements in the city. Dulce immediately issued two proclamations that were met with vehement opposition from those who favored a tough crackdown on the insurgents. In one he proclaimed freedom of expression and the press, except on the topics of the Church and slavery. The second offered a general amnesty to the rebels, pardoning any crimes against life and property if they disarmed within forty days.[30]

The reaction to the conciliatory measures was swift and uncompromising. A group of prominent Spanish citizens of Santiago de Cuba, in Oriente, sent a blistering letter to the governor, demanding "extreme measures, . . . heroic remedies, not palliatives nor any considerations," arguing that the government "cannot make concessions . . . with the larcenists and arsonists that infest so much of eastern Cuba."[31] Emilio Soulere, a career Spanish diplomat in Havana who supported Dulce's measures, noted in his memoirs that never before had anyone questioned the authority of a captain general with such "inconvenient language."[32]

The *voluntarios* ran amok, provoking various violent episodes in Havana against perceived sympathizers of the insurrectionists and unleashing a wave of terrorism throughout the city that cost the lives of even women and children.[33] Their supporters among the Spanish elite in the city carried out a virulent press campaign intended to discredit Dulce, and many wealthy loyalists financed the recruitment and wages of more *voluntarios*.[34] With *voluntarios* outnumbering regular troops, the beleaguered governor was in effect under siege in his own palace. His situation became untenable when Céspedes rejected the amnesty offer, vowing to fight on.

Rebuffed by the insurgents, Dulce had no choice but to do an about-face and appease the *voluntarios* and their supporters. Madrid authorized him to issue two repressive edicts on February 12. One reinstated controls on political expression, especially the press. The other spelled out what would henceforth be considered treasonous acts, to be judged by military tribunals. These included rebellion, conspiracy, sedition, harboring or supporting rebels and criminals, subversive expressions of any form, political assembly or association, and alterations of the public order.[35] The repressive measures spiraled upwards on both sides of the conflict. On the battlefields, the order was given to carry out executions without trials. In his memoirs, the Spanish general Antonio Peláez recalled the orders he received directly from Dulce:

> Any ringleader caught: executed. . . . Any person supporting the insurrection in any way: executed. . . . I was verbally ordered to shoot on the spot any medical doctor, lawyer, teacher caught with the insurgents. . . . I gave orders to shoot any rebel taken prisoner in the course of battle.[36]

As the president of the newly proclaimed Cuban Republic-in-Arms, Céspedes countered with his own orders, issued as an edict from his general headquarters:

> All prisoners who have taken up arms as volunteers against the Republic will be, without exception, executed. . . . Among civilians there are no neutrals in this conflict, so those who are not with us are against us and will be judged and punished accordingly. . . . All those voluntarily rendering any service to the Spanish government will be shot immediately after their capture.[37]

In Havana and other cities, the *voluntarios* zealously went about applying the new repressive measures. Two hundred and fifty men, most of them professionals and members of the upper and middle classes, were rounded up and imprisoned. Dulce was authorized by Madrid to deport them to the Spanish colony of Fernando Póo, a small island on the Gulf of Guinea that is now called Bioko, off the coast of present-day Cameroon in West Africa. The 250 were banished from Cuba on the same day, creating a dramatic scene that was probably intended to strike fear into the residents of Havana. The men had been imprisoned in the

Figure 4.1. Prisoners escorted from La Cabaña fortress to the ship *San Francisco de Borja* on Havana Bay for deportation to the island colony of Fernando Póo. Source: *Harper's Weekly*, April 10, 1869, 225.

Figure 4.2. "Scene on the house-tops of Havana during the embarkation" of the deportees to Fernando Póo. Source: *Harper's Weekly*, April 10, 1869, 232.

Cabaña fortress, located on a bluff directly across the bay from the city. On March 21, 1869, they were marched down the outdoor walkway that spiraled from the fortress to the bay, in plain view of the crowd that had gathered on the other side of the bay at the edge of the city's waterfront or on the rooftops of buildings.[38] Many in the crowd were the families of the prisoners, hoping to get a last glimpse of their loved ones before they were placed aboard the *San Francisco de Borja* for the long voyage to Fernando Póo.

The entire scene was captured by an artist in two drawings published in *Harper's Weekly*.[39] The prisoners and the onlookers are depicted as very well attired. The women have fine dresses, hats, and parasols. It may not have been an exaggeration of the artist. Among the prisoners were seventeen property holders, fifty-two clerks, nine lawyers, three brokers, two bankers, seven sugar plantation administrators, three dentists, seven teachers, four druggists, four engineers, three justices of the peace, six physicians, an architect, five sugar masters, four surveyors, the president of a gas company, and even "a painter of history."[40]

Believing that the insurrection was financially supported by many affluent Cubans, on April 1 Dulce decreed an embargo of all the property and assets of Cubans who were rebels, deportees, or exiles, extending it later to just about any property owner whose allegiances were suspect and who was not living on his estate. The embargo made it impossible for property owners to live from assets they had on the island. A commission was established to implement the edict and identify those Cubans who would be subject to its provisions. Eventually, nearly four thousand Cubans had their properties embargoed. The historian Leví Marrero identified by name more than two thousand.[41] The original edict in April named sixteen, among them José María Mora and two other Moras. Also on the original list: José Manuel Mestre.[42]

The decisive schism that Mestre feared had now come to pass, with a swiftness and intensity no one could have anticipated. Up until that time, Cubans had formed part of Spanish colonial society despite the broken promises of greater autonomy, the festering resentments, the conflicts, the expeditions, and the conspiracies that had created tensions between Cubans and Spaniards since Father Varela's time. Cubans had even occupied administrative positions in the colonial government. When prominent members of Havana's society were summoned to the Palace of the Captain Generals, as they were on that October 24, 1868, Cubans such as Mestre were part of the gathering. But in the few months that followed that meeting, everything changed, and the schism of 1868–1869 would have consequences that would last the rest of the century, consequences that helped to shape Cuban New York.

The most evident impact for New York of the events of 1868–1869 was an exodus of elites and professionals that dwarfed the earlier migrations of Cubans to the city. Entire families were leaving the island without knowing when, and whether, they would ever return again.

The schism of 1868–1869 also served to heighten New York's role as the most important setting for émigré separatist activism. With a war raging in Cuba, that activism took on a greater urgency, as external support for the rebels became a critical factor in the struggle. The volume and intensity of Cuban émigré activities in New York were turned up substantially and became more visible elements in the city's landscape.

The schism left another less evident but profound legacy. The events of 1868–1869 served to ensconce in Cuban political culture the value and practice of intransigence. The inability or refusal to consider a mutually beneficial agreement, to compromise, is usually considered a negative, or at least impractical, cultural trait in societies with civilian and democratic, especially parliamentary, political systems. However, up to at least 1868 the Spanish carried the burden of a centuries-old political culture shaped by a virtually uninterrupted history of absolutism in which intransigence became part of the style of governance and political discourse.[43]

Far from being regarded as a negative trait, intransigence became a virtue in Spanish political culture. Negotiation, dialogue, and yielding to any demands by the opposition were seen as signs of weakness and dishonor. In dealing with the threat posed by Cuban insurgents, those who sought to preserve "national integrity" explicitly embraced intransigence. In a book published in Madrid in 1872 advocating a hard line in dealing with the rebellion, Brigadier José María Velasco of the Spanish army was unapologetic about his intransigence:

> We gladly accept the label of intransigents if anyone wants to call us that, because in effect we are just that in our opposition to the effort to separate or dismember any part of our national territory.[44]

Brigadier Velasco goes on to reveal one of the corollaries of intransigence: intolerance for those within one's own camp who favor anything less than inflexibility and a firm hand in dealing with the enemy. Referring to those Spaniards "who criticize the defenders of national integrity," Velasco argues that those who see the rebels as anything other than murderers and thieves "give us the right to suspect them . . . and demand that they be considered as accomplices in the treachery and judged as such."[45]

Juan de Almansa y Tavira, a Spanish loyalist in Havana, penned a pamphlet that he dedicated to one of the leaders of the *voluntarios*. Brushing aside what he called the "inevitable criticisms of the renegades and traitors," and after a stern warning to those who consent to such treachery, Almansa made a frightful threat:

> Spaniards in Cuba will never be defeated, ceded, or sold. Cuba will remain Spanish or we will leave it in ashes.[46]

By February 1869 intransigence and intolerance had come to dominate the political climate on both sides of the schism. Spaniards in Cuba
who were appalled by the repression and the zealotry of the *voluntarios*
found it increasingly difficult to have a political space in which to influence what they saw as a disastrous setback for the best interests of Spain.
Even the governor was pressured to yield to the forces of extremism.
Soulere, the Spanish diplomat, wrote that those who represented "a regular government, an established order, an administration, a disciplined
army" could not descend to the level of those who were "impatient and
who through excesses had compromised our cause."[47]

On the Cuban side, prominent figures such as José Manuel Mestre,
who even at the eleventh hour had hoped to avoid violence, were forced
to cross the Rubicon and support the rebellion. Decades of pleadings
and demands by generations of Cubans, starting with Varela's failed mission to the Spanish Cortes in 1823, had not resulted in any change in Cuba's colonial status. Peaceful solutions, including buying the island, were
indignantly rebuffed by the Spanish government without the slightest
consideration. The terrorism of the *voluntarios*, the mass detentions and
deportations, and the embargo of properties finally nailed the coffin on
any attempts to peacefully resolve the status of the island. Among Cubans, there would henceforth be little tolerance for those who favored
negotiation or appeasement. The approach of the eastern landowners
became the only game, even for the cautious *habaneros*: it was independence or nothing, and independence had to be wrested from the
Spanish. Intransigence and intolerance had now become Cuban virtues.

The importance of those two traits in shaping the development of
Cuban émigré activism through the rest of the century cannot be underestimated. Cubans in New York became known for their uncompromising and unrelenting struggle for independence. We shall see how
intolerance led to bitter political divisions among Cuban New Yorkers.

* * *

Justo Zaragoza was one Spanish colonial official who bemoaned the
abuses and "lamentable indiscretions" committed against Cubans due
to "zealotry or lack of intelligence on the part of lower-level officers."[48]
In his memoirs he observed that in those first few weeks of 1869 the

most evident result of the terrorism of the *voluntarios* and the repressive measures of the Dulce administration was

> the spectacle of an emigration so numerous and vertiginous that there were days in which ship tickets were violently disputed and even the cargo holds of ships leaving Havana were filled with passengers.[49]

Families from throughout the island, according to Zaragoza, arrived in Havana prepared to sail on the next ship out. He estimated that from February to September 1869, two to three thousand families left every month.[50] As secretary to the colonial government, he was in a position to know: his office was responsible for issuing passports. During the last week of January 1869 he personally signed passports for 299 families.[51]

People were leaving to wherever they could book passage, but no doubt New York was the preferred destination. The developments in Cuba, especially the deportations and the embargo, had targeted elite families, many of whom, as has been shown, had previous trade and financial connections to New York and who were likely to have visited or even lived in the city previously. Furthermore, it was in New York where many of those families had accounts with counting houses, a critical consideration if their properties in Cuba had been embargoed. Those who did not have such accounts quickly sought to establish them. On February 13, 1869, Antonio de la Fuente wrote from Havana to Moses Taylor and Company on behalf of a friend, a Manuel B. Moré, who "wished to place in the control of a totally trustworthy house some funds to attend to the expenses of his family in the event that the abnormal circumstances on this island make it advisable to leave here temporarily." De la Fuente, presumably a client of Taylor, indicated that Moré was not fortunate to have any relations or connections in New York.[52]

Passenger ships from Havana to New York that for years carried Americans as well as Cubans were now arriving in Manhattan's piers filled to capacity entirely with Cuban families. The year 1869 set a record in the number of Cuban and Spanish passengers disembarking in New York from ports on the island.[53] March was the busiest month. It was on the fourth of that month that the ship *Eagle* arrived from Havana carrying 171 passengers, the largest single shipload of passengers from

Cuba that year. The *Eagle*, which for years made regular biweekly runs to Havana, normally carried some fifty passengers.

Some of the entries in the *Eagle*'s manifest were already familiar names among Cuban New Yorkers.[54] There were, for example, seven Moras on board, including Fausto, the same individual who in 1859 had become a U.S. citizen, lived with his kin on 13th Street, and had joined the family's downtown merchant firm. The transnational nature of many elites meant that they were once again traveling to New York, as they had done many times before. This time, however, they were departing the island essentially as political refugees with no idea of when, or whether, they would be able to return.

One family on the *Eagle* was not planning on returning. Carlos de Sedano, his wife, Teresa, and their three young children were not staying long in New York. They were sailing on to Spain. Sedano was emblematic of the complex allegiances and identities at the time of the 1868–1869 schism. He was born in Cuba to a family that had established itself on the island in the middle of the eighteenth century.[55] Yet the Sedanos apparently never abandoned their identity as Spaniards. "We have always loved the country of our birth and our Spanish nationality," he wrote.[56] He was one of the influential voices arguing for reforms in Cuba, from the perspective of a Spaniard who supported the liberal movement and wanted the freedoms instituted by the new Madrid government to be extended to the island.[57] He also saw the reforms as a way to avoid separatist movements, which he opposed. To Sedano, insurrection and intransigence were devastating developments that caused him to abandon Cuba and flee to what he considered to be his true home:

> We resolved to not concern ourselves further with Cuban matters.... Ours had been a stance of peace and conciliation, of unity and moderation, which could not find an echo among the intransigents of either side who wanted to solve everything with hatred and bloodshed. . . . Far from that climate of passions and hate . . . we will live in Spain, proudly calling ourselves Spaniards, which is what we have always been and will be forever.[58]

He and his family stayed in New York just long enough before sailing to Spain to observe that the intransigence and intolerance that he had left in Cuba were echoed in New York among the émigrés. Dismayed that Cubans in New York had "openly declared their hostility to Spain," Sedano wrote about "the unseemly attitude of political men who call themselves liberals . . . who imagine themselves capable of imposing their politics on all their compatriots."[59] Sedano claimed that in New York he was urged to join the separatist movement with approaches that ranged from entreaties to threats and provocations.

The *Eagle* also brought to New York about a dozen members of the Valdés-Fauli family, headed by José Valdés-Fauli, a lawyer who months before had taken part in meetings with Mestre and others to further the reformist agenda in Havana.[60] Valdés-Fauli had served not only as director of the Sociedad Económica de Amigos del País, one of the most important cultural organizations of the island, but also as president of the University of Havana.[61] The Valdés-Fauli family aboard the *Eagle* also included members of José's second wife's family, the Chappotins.[62] As Zaragoza noted, large extended families filled out most of the ships leaving Havana.[63] The Valdés-Faulis were typical of the social class origins of many of the emigrants: upper-class Cubans active in the academic, intellectual, and professional circles that formed the core of the Havana reformist movement and were therefore exposed and targeted by the repression.

Another family that arrived in New York exactly one month before the Valdés-Faulis provides the best example of how the climate on the island impacted the Cuban intelligentsia. In 1868 there were probably few intellectual and academic figures in Cuba of the stature of Antonio Bachiller y Morales. Already fifty-six years of age, he was a senior professor at the University of Havana and dean of its philosophy department.[64] Trained as a lawyer, he taught and wrote on a broad range of topics, from law and philosophy to agriculture and archaeology. Bachiller also occupied a number of positions in the public sector, including Havana city councilman, at a time when Cubans were involved in the colonial government.[65] He helped establish a number of academic journals and was active in virtually every intellectual organization on the island, including the Sociedad Económica de Amigos del País directed by José Valdés-Fauli. In 1847, while still living in Havana, he became a member of the New York Historical Society.[66]

Figure 4.3. Antonio Bachiller y Morales. Source: Cuban Heritage Collection, University of Miami Library Digital Collections, www.merrick.library.miami.edu.

Generationally he bridged the early intellectuals such as Varela, Saco, and Luz y Caballero and a younger generation of thinkers, such as José Manuel Mestre, who were enrolled at the University of Havana in the 1840s. He was mentor to many students who would form the core of Havana's reformist movement. It was Bachiller who exposed Mestre and the others to the latest currents of thought in European, especially German, philosophy. He had a tradition of hosting intellectual and political soirees at his home in San Miguel Street in Havana, and this raised the suspicions of the *voluntarios*, who on occasion would shout threats from the street and pound on his door. Tipped off that his arrest was imminent, he rushed to leave the country.[67]

On February 4, 1869, Bachiller y Morales arrived in New York aboard the *Columbia*.[68] He was accompanied by his wife and five of his six surviving children, ranging in age from twenty to twenty-seven, a son-in-law, three grandchildren, and four nephews. The nephews were the children of his brother Gabriel, who had died four years earlier.[69]

That voyage of the *Columbia* also took to New York another prominent figure of Cuban reformism who, like Mestre, was left with little choice but to support the rebellion. José Morales Lemus had been one of the most active members of the ill-fated Junta de Información that met in Madrid in 1867. The following year he turned sixty years of age. Most of his life had been dedicated to the legal profession, first as a clerk and then as a lawyer in Havana.[70] He helped his younger colleague, Mestre, establish his own practice. Both were men of humble origins who had risen to the top of the city's legal and intellectual circles through a combination of hard work and sheer luck. Unlike many of their associates, they were not born into privilege. This was especially true of Morales Lemus, who was born in the small coastal village of Gibara in eastern Cuba to a woman from the Canary Islands whose husband abandoned her shortly after giving birth. As also happened to Mestre, a relative of means took responsibility for his upbringing and moved the family to Havana, where Morales Lemus received an excellent education. Years later, good fortune smiled on him again when a wealthy man who had no family, and for whom the young Morales Lemus served as assistant, died and named him sole heir. That windfall enabled him to complete his legal studies, start a family, and establish a very successful law practice.

Aside from his participation in the Junta de Información, Morales Lemus's most important political contribution in Cuba was the central role he played in the founding in 1863 of *El Siglo*, a Havana newspaper that despite the constant vigilance of Spanish censors managed to establish itself as the reasoned voice of the reformists, printing the views of some of the leading Cuban intellectuals of the day.

Morales Lemus attended the fateful meeting with Governor Lersundi.[71] After that, as happened with all prominent Cubans with a history of activism on behalf of changing the colonial regime, his life took a dramatic turn. The constant harassment by the *voluntarios* and the possibility of imprisonment and deportation prompted him to board the *Columbia*. One month later, his friend and protégé José Manuel Mestre joined him in New York.[72] José Morales Lemus's name was among the sixteen listed in Dulce's edict of April 1 embargoing the properties of enemies of the Spanish state, as was Mestre's. In fact, the name José Morales Lemus was the first one on that list.[73]

The list of affluent families and prominent individuals who appear on the manifests of ships leaving Cuban ports for New York during 1869 is endless.[74] More members of the Mora clan arrived in New York in two separate sailings of the *Morro Castle* during July and August. The large Angarica-de la Rua family, leading Freemasons, came in two groups, one disembarking in New York from the *Morro Castle* on March 13 and the other aboard the *Columbia* on April 27. A week earlier, on April 21, the *Morro Castle* took to New York seven members of the Madan family, as well as nine members of the Govín family. The head of the Govín family, Félix, had already arrived with his wife on April 15 on the *Eagle*. More members of the Govín family traveled months later, in August, aboard the *Missouri*. The manifest of the *Columbia*, which reached New York on September 2, listed three large families headed by merchants. The next sailing of the *Columbia* from Havana, which arrived in Manhattan on September 25, carried a large contingent of the Socarrás-Duque de Estrada family of Puerto Príncipe, most of them women and children, as well as several servants.[75] The following month the *Morro Castle* took to New York the noted educator and writer Francisco Calcagno.[76]

Families were not choosy about the ships they boarded, sailing on whatever vessel would take them out of Cuba. Those departing from port cities other than Havana frequently had to book passage on cargo ships that had only limited accommodations for passengers. Members of the Portuondo family, for example, were among the thirteen passengers arriving in New York on May 6 aboard the *Burnbrae* from Santiago de Cuba. The following day, the Boitel family disembarked in lower Manhattan from the *Lizzie* with only ten passengers, most of them members of the family. A young Fidel Pierra, who would later play a role in émigré politics, was among the ten passengers who arrived on April 16 aboard the *Blanche* from Guantánamo.

Many individuals and families who eventually settled in New York did not necessarily arrive there directly from Cuba. This was true, of course, of many of the prisoners deported to Fernando Póo aboard the *San Francisco de Borja*. They did not stay long in the small island in the Gulf of Guinea. It was not a penal colony, so the deportees were not confined, and once there, they made arrangements for transportation to Europe and the United States.[77] The bulk of them left Fernando Póo on a ship chartered by the Spanish government, which, bowing to international criticism of the deportation, pardoned the prisoners and transported them to Spain.[78]

From Europe some of the deportees made their way to New York. Among them was Carlos del Castillo, a sixty-one-year-old banker from eastern Cuba who in the 1850s was director of a savings institution in Havana and had creatively arranged for the financing of various rebellions and conspiracies against the Spanish.[79] Del Castillo played a major role in émigré separatist politics for years thereafter. Like many other Cubans who were arriving in the city, he lived comfortably in New York on the nest egg he had prudently built for years through remittances to Moses Taylor and Company. Despite the loss of their property in Cuba, many New York Cubans were far from being penniless exiles.

Moses Taylor and Company also had an account for Miguel Aldama. By 1868 Aldama, at the age of forty-eight, had become one of the wealthiest and most influential men in Cuba. More than twenty years had passed since the suicide of his brother Gonzalo in New York, and almost that many years since he and his father hosted in the Aldama Palace the meeting of the annexationist Club de La Habana with John L. O'Sullivan and Moses Yale Beach (see chapter 2).

Miguel had taken over the family business operations from his aging father, Don Domingo, the astute immigrant who had married the daughter of his boss, Gonzalo Alfonso. The Aldamas were sole owners of two sugar mills, the Armonía and the Santa Rosa, in addition to being part owners of several others.[80] It was in the Santa Rosa where Miguel liked to spend his time when he was not in Havana or New York. He purchased the latest technology for his mills and introduced in Cuba a steam-driven plow.[81] Together with the Alfonsos, the Aldamas owned one of the biggest sugar warehouses in the port of Matanzas.[82] The Alfonso-Aldama clan also owned numerous other agricultural properties devoted primarily to cattle production and had controlling interests in major railroads in western Cuba.[83] Miguel himself managed one of the biggest, the Camino de Hierros de La Habana. The family also had investments in financial institutions and insurance companies.[84]

While much of Miguel's wealth had been made by Don Domingo, who got his start by capitalizing on his father-in-law's resources and contacts, Miguel greatly expanded his business interests by also taking advantage of family connections, integrating further his father's wealth with that of his mother's family. Miguel emerged as the most important figure of the Alfonso-Aldama clan, a position reinforced by a series of intermarriages that were typical of elite families of the time.[85] One of Miguel's sisters, María de los Dolores (Lola), married one of her first cousins, José Luis Alfonso y García, a nephew of her (and Miguel's) mother. Later, one of Miguel's daughters, Florinda, married another Alfonso, Cristóbal Alfonso y Madan, a relative of Cristóbal Madan, and another nephew of Miguel's mother. Florinda, in other words, married a first cousin of her father, Miguel. That marriage represented yet another link between the three wealthy families, the Alfonsos, Aldamas, and Madans.

Another one of Miguel Aldama's sisters, Rosa, married Domingo del Monte y Aponte. Del Monte, a native of Venezuela, was a principal officer of the Cárdenas railroad and was instrumental in expanding the control of the Alfonso-Aldama family over the western railroads.[86] Del Monte, however, is remembered primarily for his literary career.[87] Domingo and Rosa's son, Leonardo del Monte, married one of Miguel Aldama's daughters in yet another first-cousin marriage. That daughter had been named after her aunt Rosa, who became her mother-in-law. Leonardo del Monte followed in his father's footsteps, pursuing a literary and academic career. He formed part of the Havana intellectual circles that included Bachiller y Morales, Valdés-Fauli, Morales Lemus, Mestre, and others. Through Leonardo and Mestre, Aldama maintained a close relationship with those Cuban academics and intellectuals who had formed the nucleus of the reformist movement. As noted earlier, Miguel's first cousin Paulina Alfonso y Poey had married José Manuel Mestre. In addition, one of Aldama's closest friends was José Antonio Echeverría, a poet and educator from Matanzas who had served as a member of the Junta de Información and was a member of the Sociedad Económica de Amigos del País. Aldama was also a longtime friend of José Antonio Saco.[88]

In 1868, therefore, there were few Cubans as prominent as Miguel Aldama. He led one of the island's wealthiest families and also exerted influence over the group of Havana intellectuals and academics that led the reformist movement, occasionally helping to finance some of their activities, including the establishment of the reformist newspaper *El Siglo*, to which he was the principal financial contributor.[89] Yet despite his wealth and influence, Miguel Aldama was powerless to avert the crisis of 1868–1869. Like most Cubans, he was swept up in its wake.

During the summer of 1868, when Céspedes and the other easterners were planning their armed rebellion, Aldama was vacationing in
Saratoga. He and most of his family, including his father, Domingo, his
unmarried daughter Leonor, his son-in-law (and nephew) Leonardo del
Monte, and Leonardo's small children arrived in Manhattan on August
11 aboard the *Columbia*.[90] On August 26 he wrote a note to Moses Taylor
and Company informing the South Street counting house that in a few
days he would be leaving Saratoga for Niagara Falls and asking that any
correspondence arriving from Havana, as well as $400 from his account,
be sent to him before his departure.[91]

From New York Aldama traveled to Europe.[92] If his friends and associates among the Havana elite had little idea of what was about to happen in eastern Cuba, Aldama was even more clueless. When Céspedes
declared the start of the war on October 10, Aldama was probably on a
ship in the Atlantic returning to New York. After his return to Manhattan he received a letter from his relative José Manuel Mestre in Havana,
dated October 24, the same day as the meeting with Governor Lersundi
at the palace. If Aldama had underestimated the seriousness of the situation on the island, Mestre's letter must have given him some concern:

> A deaf discontent reigns in this country, and never have we been closer to
> a social and socialist revolution. . . . This government has done everything
> possible to make the country understand that it should expect nothing
> from the freedoms in Spain and that we are to continue under the omi-
> nous tutelage of the Holy Ghost of the metropolis.[93]

Mestre went on to characterize the eastern insurgents as those who are
"impatient because they suspect another deception." When he wrote the
letter, hours away from the meeting at the palace, Mestre still harbored
hope that the easterners had indeed been impatient and that violence
could be avoided, as he wrote to Aldama: "Lersundi has summoned several 'friends' to a meeting at his house tonight. Let's see what comes out
of it. I will let you know."[94]

As we already know, the meeting dashed all hope for peace, and Aldama hurried his return to Havana. No sooner had he arrived than he
received a letter from none other than Don Carlos de Borbón, the Carl-
ist pretender to the Spanish throne who took advantage of the destitu-

tion of Queen Isabel to act as monarch during the liberal regime. In the letter, dated October 31, Don Carlos addressed Aldama with a familiar tone and offered him the position of civil governor of Cuba, "to help General Lersundi with your influence, your contacts, . . . to develop the wealth and moral welfare of that country for the benefit of the metropolis."[95] It was an attempt to recruit Aldama into a figurehead role as part of the effort to appease the country. Aldama was so taken aback by the letter that he went to see Lersundi to verify its authenticity. The governor confirmed it.

Aldama's reply to Don Carlos spoke volumes about that critical historical moment. Only a few weeks before, Aldama may have welcomed the opportunity to try to influence Madrid to reform its relationship with the island and avoid violence, his long-standing goal and that of the Havana elites close to him. But he turned down Don Carlos's offer in a letter, dated December 7, that showed just how much the reformists had been pushed into accepting the inevitability of the easterners' solution:

> Your offer . . . may have been well received before now by a people that have always aspired to the autonomy of the country as a way to harmonize the union with the metropolis and its own survival and prosperity. *Unfortunately, the circumstances have changed.* Some are fatigued, others are disillusioned, many are exasperated, and all are dissatisfied, and a considerable portion of our inhabitants has thrown itself into a fight, looking to have firearms succeed in the search for liberties and guarantees that could not be attained after thirty years of resigned suffering.[96]

Aldama ended the letter saying that he was fulfilling his duty "not to conceal the truth, at a time when one's country [*la patria*] *expects all its children to proclaim it.*"[97]

All of Havana learned of Aldama's refusal and of the content and tone of his letter. The pro-Spanish forces, especially Lersundi, were not pleased.[98] Unlike some of the largest landowners in Cuba, Aldama had taken himself out of the loyalist camp.

Aldama proceeded with his life and business as usual, while at the same time preparing for the inevitable. A few days after the letter to Don Carlos he wrote to Moses Taylor and Company, thanking them for "not losing sight of my interests," and inquiring about the "placement" of some of his funds. He also let them know that he found the situation on the island much worse than he had expected, but that the sugar harvest was under way, although he could not predict, given the circumstances, whether the entire crop would be harvested.[99] The day after Christmas he wrote again to Taylor on behalf of his friend José Antonio Echeverría, the poet and former member of the Junta de Información, indicating that Echeverría "wished to place some funds" in New York, funds that were being remitted to the firm on the same sailing as the letter. Aldama asked the firm to give the money whatever use Taylor and Company deemed "safe and convenient." As reference, Aldama mentioned that Echeverría had accompanied him to New York on his summer trip and that he had personally introduced Echeverría to Moses Taylor.[100] Aldama and his friends were not wasting time arranging their exit to New York.

Aldama no doubt welcomed the arrival in January 1869 of Domingo Dulce as military governor. He knew Dulce well from the general's previous tenure as governor, when he earned a reputation as a liberal administrator. As we have seen, however, Dulce had little control over the *voluntarios*, who were eager to demonstrate their defiance of the governor's initial appeasement policies. Aldama was a perfect target: a powerful friend of Dulce who had publicly criticized Spanish policies and refused to join the government. On January 24, less than a month after Dulce arrived, *voluntarios* belonging to the Third and Fifth Battalions forced their way into the Aldama Palace and ransacked and looted it, slashing paintings with their swords, breaking mirrors, damaging furniture, tearing curtains, and breaking into armoires and taking the valuables inside. They were eventually dispersed by regular troops dispatched by General Dulce. The family was not at home, since it was a Sunday and they were spending the weekend at the Santa Rosa sugar mill.[101]

Although Dulce advised Aldama to leave Cuba, he stayed on the island for several months, longer than most of his colleagues, apparently because his wife, Hilaria Fonts, had suffered a stroke and could not travel.[102] Perhaps because of Aldama's prominence and his relationship with the governor, he was not among those arrested and deported to Fernando Póo. But Dulce himself would not be staying long in Havana. In poor health and still unpopular with the loyalists, he was replaced as governor and on June 2 departed for Madrid, where he died not long after.

Aldama left Havana a month earlier than Dulce aboard the *Morro Castle*, which arrived in New York on May 10. It is likely he left clandestinely, because his name does not appear on the passenger manifest, which does list most of his family, including his daughters, his father, Domingo, and his son-in-law and nephew Leonardo del Monte.[103]

Once Aldama departed, the Spanish government promptly embargoed all his property in accordance with the decree that had been issued in April by Governor Dulce. Given the extent of his holdings in Cuba, it was a severe economic blow, but Aldama had anticipated this contingency. One historian, citing a source close to Aldama, indicated he may have had as much as $700,000 in assets in New York at the time of his migration.[104] An 1872 ledger sheet in the Moses Taylor Papers has an entry of $100,000 in the name of Miguel Aldama.[105]

* * *

There is no better summary of the consequences of the 1868–1869 crisis than the sentence handed down by a Spanish military tribunal in 1870.[106] More than fifty Cubans were sentenced to be executed by public garroting for their role in the rebellion, including those who supported it from abroad. Very few of the sentences could be immediately applied, since virtually none of the condemned were living in Havana or any other city or town in Cuba where the Spanish could apprehend them. Most on the list were on the battlefields on the island, and it seemed as if the rest were in New York. Miguel Aldama, Leonardo del Monte, José Manuel Mestre, José Morales Lemus, José María Mora, Antonio Mora, and Carlos del Castillo were just a few of the New Yorkers due to have their necks squeezed by a tourniquet if they set foot in Cuba. There were no activists or reformists left in Havana. The economic, intellectual, and academic elites that had long formed the core of the push for annexation, autonomy, or self-determination were now in New York.

The war would last until 1878. During those years, many more Cubans would seek refuge in New York, including some of the easterners who had been on the battlefield, or their widows and children. The year 1870 opened the most tumultuous decade in the history of Cuban New York, as the war in Cuba resonated in the streets of the city.

5

Cuban New York in the 1870s

> Those fleeing Cuba grouped themselves in different localities. . . . New York was the most important one, not only because it had the largest number of émigrés, but also because there you could find those with the most capital and political importance.
>
> —Enrique Collazo, *Desde Yara hasta el Zanjón*, 1893[1]

J. W. Robertson, a U.S. census enumerator assigned to Manhattan's Seventeenth Ward, was conducting a fairly routine canvass of the household of José María Mora on June 24, 1870, until he reached the occupation question. The response he got was anything but routine and probably not one Robertson had heard before: "Cuban refugee," answered the fifty-eight-year-old man sitting across from him.[2]

José María Mora had not always thought of himself as a refugee. As early as 1859 (see chapter 3), he and his brother Antonio Máximo and son José Antonio were doing business in lower Manhattan as commission merchants. Those were the days when many Cuban New Yorkers traveled freely between the piers of Manhattan and Havana, attending to their businesses, educating their children and shopping in New York, and even maintaining residences in both cities. By 1860 the Moras had made significant investments in Manhattan real estate and were renting out homes to their compatriots, creating a Cuban neighborhood in and around 12th and 13th Streets, between Second and Third Avenues.

But by the time Robertson went to the neighborhood to do his job for the census on that Friday in 1870, everything had changed for the Moras. José María and his brother Antonio Máximo were among those whose property and assets in Cuba were embargoed by the Spanish authorities, and both brothers were also on the list of those sentenced *in absentia* to be executed if they returned to the island.[3] José María Mora had returned to being a New York merchant and investor, but when the

enumerator asked him his occupation, he gave his identity, not his occupation, an identity that had now overtaken him, forged by war and
banishment: refugee.

* * *

José María Mora was joined in New York by many others of his social
class who had been in one way or another active in separatist or reformist circles, especially in Havana or Matanzas. In 1870 most of the
pro-independence easterners were on the battlefield. But, as we saw in
the previous chapter, in the west, and especially Havana, the reformist
elite that had been dragged into the conflict had no alternative but to
leave. They were planters, merchants, intellectuals, lawyers, and professionals who were suddenly in danger from the repressive measures of
the Spanish colonial government and the terrorism unleashed by the
voluntarios in the capital. Some were even taken from their homes and
forcibly shipped off to Fernando Póo. As was the case with Mora, the
preferred destination was New York, a city many had frequented over
the years and where they had established homes and squirreled away
assets.

The 1870 U.S. census captured the flight of the most prominent members of the Havana reformist elite and those who gravitated around the
financial interests of western Cuba, especially sugar and railroads. Table
5.1 lists those prominent Cubans enumerated in Manhattan and Brooklyn in 1870.

Virtually all of the planters, business elites, reformists, and activists
discussed in chapters 3 and 4 found their way to New York by 1870 and
were enumerated in that year's census: Miguel Aldama and his nephew
and son-in-law Leonardo del Monte, José Morales Lemus, José Manuel
Mestre, Carlos del Castillo, Antonio Bachiller y Morales, Félix Govín,
the Moras, and Juan Manuel Macías.

The table also lists other names, among them Enrique Piñeyro, a
young writer and educator who had been a student of José de la Luz
y Caballero and of Mestre and formed part of the intellectual circle of
the Havana reformist elite.[4] The son of a Spanish-born literature professor and Latinist at the University of Havana, Piñeyro published in the
newspaper *El Siglo*, the principal voice of the reformists, as well as in *La
Revista Habanera*, established by the poet Juan Clemente Zenea.[5] These

TABLE 5.1 Prominent Cubans Residing in New York City, 1870

Name	Age	Address
Enrique Piñeyro	28	9th Ward, 9th District (160 W. 14th St., corner of 7th)
Carlos del Castillo	68	15th Ward, 8th District
Juan Manuel Macías	40	15th Ward, 10th District
Francisco Fesser	34	16th Ward, 7th District
Hilario Cisneros Francisco Javier Cisneros	44 34	16th Ward, 13th District (406 W. 22nd St., between 9th and 10th)
José Manuel Mestre	38	16th Ward, 13th District (135 W. 21st St., between 6th and 7th)
José María Mora	58	17th Ward, 4th District (217 E. 12th St., between 2nd and 3rd)
Antonio Máximo Mora	50	17th Ward, 4th District (220 E. 12th St., between 2nd and 3rd)
José Antonio Mora	38	17th Ward, 4th District (235 E. 13th St., between 2nd and 3rd)
Cristóbal Madan	60	18th Ward, 22nd District (234 Fourth Avenue)
Miguel Aldama	50	19th Ward, 7th District (43 W. 47th St.)
Leonardo del Monte	31	19th Ward, 7th District (31 W. 47th St.)
Juan Jová	35	19th Ward, 13th District
Joaquín G. de Angarica José G. de Angarica	80 72	20th Ward, 9th District (308 W. 27th St.).
Félix Fuentes	36	20th Ward, 12th District (316 W. 27th St.)
Félix Govín	55	21st Ward, 14th District (54 W. 37th St.)
José R. Simoni Amalia Simoni [de Agramonte] Matilde Simoni [de Agramonte]	60 25 24	22nd Ward, 8th District
José Morales Lemus	60	Brooklyn, 21st Ward
Antonio Bachiller y Morales	59	Brooklyn, 21st Ward
Nestor Ponce de León	33	Brooklyn, 21st Ward
José Gabriel del Castillo	46	Brooklyn, 7th Ward

Sources: Names, ages, ward, and district are all derived from the U.S. Bureau of the Census, *1870 United States Federal Census, New York City and Kings County*, accessed through www.ancestry.com. Some addresses are derived from the census in those cases in which the enumerator noted the address on the margins of the schedule. Other addresses were taken from *Trow's New York City Directory, 1870–71* (New York: Trow City Directory Company, 1871), but only in those cases in which the Trow entry was consistent with the census record's ward and district entry.

associations and activities made him a target of the Spanish authorities, and he left for New York in 1869. His name was subsequently added to the list of Cubans whose properties were embargoed.[6]

In the city Piñeyro moved into the same boardinghouse where Luis Felipe Mantilla, a colleague and former student of his father, lived.[7] Mantilla, thirty-seven, listed his occupation as "Professor of Languages," while Piñeyro gave his occupation as "Secretary, Cuban Legation," the position to which he had been appointed by Morales Lemus, who at the time was in charge of representing the Céspedes government in the United States.[8] The boardinghouse, at the corner of 14th Street and Seventh Avenue, was run by an Italian woman, Emilia Cuppia. It was an upscale boardinghouse with a staff of five servants, all Irish-born women. In addition to Piñeyro, Mantilla, and Cuppia's family, there were ten other guests, all Latin Americans, including four merchants (two Cubans, a Peruvian, and a Venezuelan), and one Antonio Hernández, who lists his occupation as "Minister of Venezuela." Also living in the boardinghouse was Simón Camacho and his family. Camacho was the Venezuelan-born writer who years earlier chronicled the Santa Cruz de Oviedo-Bartlett wedding as well as other New York happenings for Latin American readers. In the 1870 census Camacho listed his occupation as "Consul of Honduras."

Francisco Fesser, a member of a prominent Havana banking family, is also listed in table 5.1.[9] He was part of the inner circle of Havana reformists, taking part in meetings as far back as 1866 in preparation for the work of the Junta de Información.[10] That activism earned him a place not only on the list of Cubans whose properties and assets were embargoed, but also on the list of those condemned to death *in absentia*.[11] In 1870 Fesser lived with his wife, Rosa, in the West 20s and was one of the few Cubans in New York who divulged income figures to the enumerator, declaring his real estate assets to be $50,000 and setting his personal estate at $3,000, apparently enough to have two Irish servants.[12]

The Cisneros brothers, Hilario and Francisco Javier, lived on West 22nd Street in Manhattan, near the Mestre family. Hilario's wife, Mariana, and their young daughter María Concepción lived with them, as well as their brother Juan (a physician), several other family members, and five domestic servants.[13] Although Hilario had practiced law in Havana and had become part of the city's reformist network through his colleagues Mestre and Morales Lemus, the Cisneros were born in Santiago de Cuba, where their family had lived since the middle of the seventeenth century and where their father had occupied several important positions in the local judiciary system.[14]

Hilario attended the infamous and decisive meeting of October 24, 1868, with Captain General Lersundi that sealed the fate of the reformists.[15] He embraced independence after that and the Spanish took due note of it, embargoing his property and condemning him to death.[16] The same fate befell Francisco Javier, except that being prone to action, he made a more compelling case for the penalties than his older brother. Francisco Javier was an organizer, in November 1868, of an aborted attempt at armed insurrection in western Cuba in support of the eastern uprising.[17] Faced with imprisonment or worse, Francisco Javier Cisneros left for New York, where he became the point man in the émigrés' efforts to organize expeditions destined to take men and weapons to Céspedes in Cuba. From December 1868 to July 9, 1870, the date the census enumerator found him at the home of his brother, he had organized five expeditions, most of which failed to reach the island. The most successful one, however, was the one that he led aboard the *Perrit*, a ship purchased by José María Mora, which left for the Bay of Nipe, on the northeastern coast of Cuba, in May 1869 with 250 men and a substantial cache of arms and ammunition, which Cisneros personally delivered to the army of the Cuban Republic.[18]

Unlike most other Cubans in New York, Juan Jacinto Jová was neither from Havana nor from the east, but rather from the central region of the island. The Jovás were of Catalonian origins and although in Cuba they originally settled in Santa Clara, where Juan Jacinto was born in 1837, their sugar estates were in Cienfuegos, on the south-central coast.[19] As a young man, Juan Jacinto traveled extensively in Europe and the United States, eventually graduating as civil engineer from Columbia University's School of Mines. He stayed in New York to act as his family's business representative, importing sugar and selling it in the city, and also buying the latest equipment for the family's sugar operations in Cienfuegos. Marriage and the 1868 war made him stay in New York permanently. That year he married Marie Gabrielle Vatable at St. Vincent de Paul Church in Manhattan. Marie Gabrielle was from a prominent French family that had settled in New York after leaving

Guadeloupe when slavery was abolished. In New York the Vatables were engaged in the sugar trade, which is how Juan Jacinto became acquainted with the family and with Marie Gabrielle. Although Juan Jacinto Jová had not been previously involved in separatist activities, he would eventually become active in émigré politics. In 1870 he and Marie Gabrielle already had an infant daughter and were living in the Nineteenth Ward with two Irish domestic servants. Jová declared his occupation as "shipping merchant" and gave the enumerator the figure of $100,000 as the value of his real estate holdings and $6,000 as the worth of his personal estate.

Félix Fuentes was not a prominent activist in Havana, but he was nevertheless taken from his home in March 1869 and ceremoniously deported to Fernando Póo along with 250 other residents of the capital.[20] He was able to escape from that island and settle in New York, where he undoubtedly had placed substantial funds. Although his property and assets in Cuba were subjected to the Spanish embargo, by the time the enumerator found him, barely a year after his deportation, he had made a nice recovery, living in the West 20s with his wife, three children, and several domestic servants, and with an office at 75 Broadway.[21]

Brooklyn's Twenty-First Ward, the northern portion of what is now Bedford-Stuyvesant, was the home in 1870 of two of the most prominent and senior members of the Havana reformist group: José Morales Lemus and Antonio Bachiller y Morales.[22] Morales Lemus lived there with his wife, several relatives, and two servants. Bachiller y Morales settled temporarily in Brooklyn surrounded by his large family. In his house lived his wife, Carlota Govín, and his unmarried daughters, María de Jesús, twenty-four, and Adela, twenty-one, as well as his daughter Carlota and her husband, José Morales, a lawyer, and Carlota and José's three-month-old daughter, María. Next door lived a physician, Juan Landeta, and Landeta's mother and sister. Landeta would soon marry Bachiller's daughter Adela. On the same Brooklyn street lived another of Bachiller's daughters, Antonia, who was married to Nestor Ponce de León, a lawyer. They had four young children between two and eight years of age. Bachiller y Morales's oldest daughter, María Teresa, also lived in Brooklyn with her husband, José Gabriel del Castillo, and their four children, not too far from the rest of the family, in the Seventh Ward, the area now known as Clinton Hill, near the Pratt Institute.[23]

Antonio Bachiller y Morales had placed funds in New York with Moses Taylor prior to arriving in the city. Bachiller y Morales's future son-in-law, Dr. Landeta, had also placed money with Moses Taylor. All four Bachiller households in Brooklyn had a combined total of ten servants, six of whom were Cuban-born blacks, including Ambrosio Aguirre, a teenaged servant who had been born in the Bachiller household in Havana and who, according to one source, Mrs. Bachiller "could not bear to leave behind" when they left the island. He remained with the Bachiller family until his death in 1895.[24]

Bachiller's son-in-law Nestor Ponce de León had been an active member of the reformist group in Havana not only because of his father-in-law, but also through his connections as a lawyer with Mestre and Morales Lemus. Nestor, his father-in-law, and his brother-in-law, José Gabriel del Castillo, all had their properties embargoed, but of the three only Nestor merited the death penalty as well.[25] Although in 1870 he told the census enumerator that he was a lawyer, Nestor did not practice law in New York, but rather made a living from his true vocation: bibliophile. He opened a bookstore and stationery store on Broadway that remained a fixture in the city's émigré community for many years.

The Bachiller y Morales Brooklyn clan would have been even larger had it not been for circumstances that no doubt weighed heavily on the patriarch as he adjusted to life in a new country. In addition to five daughters, Antonio Bachiller y Morales had two sons. The eldest, Alfredo, died in 1867 of tuberculosis at the age of twenty-five, not long before the family left the island.[26] His other son, Antonio, left Cuba with the family aboard the *Columbia* in February 1869, but only three months later joined an expedition to the island, where he became a captain in the army of the Republic of Cuba and was not in Brooklyn in July 1870 to be included in the family's census record.[27]

In Manhattan, the lives of the Aldamas paralleled those of the Bachiller y Morales clan in Brooklyn. Miguel Aldama was living on West 47th Street, just west of Fifth Avenue (now the heart of the diamond and jewelry district), surrounded by three of his married daughters and their families. Sharing a house with him and his wife, Hilaria Fonts, were his daughter María de los Dolores and her husband, Isaac Carrillo, a lawyer and educator. On the same block lived Leonardo del Monte and his wife, Rosa, Miguel's daughter. As noted in chapter 4, Leonardo was not only

Miguel's son-in-law but also his nephew. Also on that block lived another daughter of the Aldamas, Florinda, who was married to Miguel's cousin Cristóbal Alfonso y Madan. The Aldama clan had a fairly large retinue of servants, and although some were Cuban blacks, most were Irish women. Like Antonio Bachiller y Morales, Miguel Aldama also carried the burden of grief. Four years before, in 1864, his only son, Domingo, had died.

Although in 1870 the Havana elites, especially the reformist group, tended to predominate among the prominent Cubans in New York, the census that year also captured the beginnings of what would be a growing phenomenon during the remaining years of the war: the arrival in the city of eastern families whose men were on the battlefields or, in some cases, had already been killed. The most dramatic example was the family of José Ramón Simoni, a sixty-year-old physician the census found living in the Twenty-Second Ward, on Sixth Avenue, just south of Central Park.[28] Simoni was from Puerto Príncipe (Camagüey), where the landed aristocracy had joined their neighbors to the east in the uprising of October 1868. Living with Dr. Simoni in New York were his wife, Manuela, fifty, their son José Ramón Jr., twenty-two, and Manuela's niece Victoria Ginferrer, sixteen. Also in the household were the Simonis' two married daughters with their children. The oldest, Amalia, twenty-five years old, had an infant son, Ignacio Ernesto, and was pregnant with a second. The other daughter, Matilde, was twenty-four and had a two-year-old son, Arístides.[29] Both of Dr. Simoni's sons-in-law were in Cuba. Amalia was married to Ignacio Agramonte, a young patrician, not yet thirty years old, who had led the Camagüeyanos into the war and with the rank of major general was their foremost military leader. A member of one of Camagüey's oldest and most respected families, Ignacio had been educated in Europe and earned a law degree at the University of Havana. He was one of the authors of the constitution of the government-in-arms. Dr. Simoni's other daughter, Matilde, was married to Ignacio's cousin Eduardo Agramonte, also a combatant in Camagüey and a member of the Céspedes cabinet.[30] Needless to say, the Agramonte cousins were near the top of the list of those to be executed in the event of their capture.[31] Dr. Simoni was not on any list, but no doubt he left Cuba fearing for the safety of his daughters and grandchildren.

The Simonis were not the only members of Ignacio Agramonte's family who felt compelled to take refuge in New York. The 1870 census found his mother, María Filomena Loynaz, forty-six, living with her sister-in-law and Ignacio's aunt Mercedes Agramonte, forty-five, and with Ignacio's brother, Enrique, twenty-five, at 104 West 20th Street, between Sixth and Seventh Avenues, in the Sixteenth Ward. There were also four teenagers in the household, probably nephews and nieces of María Filomena.[32]

The Simoni and Agramonte households in New York were emblematic of the very different financial conditions of the eastern elites in the city in contrast with their western compatriots. As has been pointed out repeatedly, the latter had long-standing business and personal connections with New York, stemming from the trade that developed with the boom in sugar production in the western provinces of Havana and Matanzas. In contrast, the wealth of the eastern landed aristocracy, such as the Agramontes, was based on a more diversified agricultural economy rooted in cattle production and therefore not likely to be engaged in trade with New York. Economically and geographically, they were isolated and outside the flow of that trade. It was not until the beginning of the twentieth century, for example, that a railroad line was built linking the eastern and western halves of the island. The easterners did not have money waiting for them in New York when they felt compelled to leave the island. None of the well-known eastern families, for example, had accounts with Moses Taylor and Company.[33] Although the prominent families from the west almost without exception had domestic servants in the city, either black Cubans or Irish women, the Simonis and the Agramontes lived in what appear to be boardinghouses with no domestic servants.

The 1870 census records the reappearance in New York of Cristóbal Madan. The longtime New Yorker and annexationist, the teenager who in 1823 greeted Varela and Heredia when they arrived in New York, was already in his sixties when the 1870 census enumerator found him and his son Cristóbal Jr., thirty-five, living in the Eighteenth Ward.[34] In 1850, the last time the U.S. census enumerated him, Madan also lived in the Eighteenth Ward, in a house near Madison Square large and sumptuous enough to accommodate his six children, his second wife, Mary O'Sullivan, and a contingent of servants and their children (see chapter 2).

It is not clear what happened to Madan in the years after 1852, when he was sentenced to a forced exile in Spain for his role in the annexationist movement. Neither he nor any member of his immediate family was counted in New York in the 1860 census. His wife, Mary O'Sullivan, died in 1867.[35] At some point he must have secured a pardon and returned to Cuba from Spain to take control of his family's sugar estates in Matanzas and to open a law office in Havana. We know of the law office because early in 1869 he hired as a clerk in that office a sixteen-year-old boy who was getting himself into trouble with the authorities for writing rebellious tracts: José Martí.[36]

On April 21, 1869, seven Madans arrived in New York on the *Morro Castle* from Havana, including Cristóbal Jr., but the senior Madan was not on the passenger list.[37] Although there is no record of it, it is likely that Cristóbal left Cuba about that same time, fleeing from the terror and persecution led by Dulce and the *voluntarios*. By May 12 he was definitely in New York when his daughter with Mary O'Sullivan, María de los Dolores, married a Spanish marquis, José Francisco Pedroso, in St. Francis Xavier Church on West 16th Street.[38]

Less than three months after the wedding, Governor Dulce embargoed Madan's properties and assets. Madan protested, claiming that he had done nothing to deserve the penalties; as a U.S. citizen, he appealed to Washington to intercede in his behalf with the Spanish government, to no avail.[39] As unlikely as it may seem for a longtime New Yorker, Madan apparently did not have substantial funds in the city. Since he had not been politically active, he had not anticipated the sanctions. But living abroad and having questionable associations were grounds enough to warrant application of the embargo. Perhaps it was punishment for his past political transgressions, or perhaps it was just capriciousness. After all, more than four thousand Cubans eventually had their properties embargoed, most on flimsy pretexts. Historians have argued that what started as a wartime strategic measure quickly degenerated into abuses, graft, and a massive theft of properties on the part of the Spanish.[40]

The embargo apparently had a drastic effect on Madan's finances. The conditions in which Cristobal and his son lived in 1870 were very different from the very comfortable living arrangements recorded in the 1850 census. In July 1870 he and Cristóbal Jr. were residing in the home of

General Zachariah Deas and his wife. General Deas was a South Carolinian who had served in the Confederate Army. After the Civil War
Deas settled in New York and returned, very successfully, to the same
occupation he had in Mobile before the war: cotton broker.[41] Only five
months after being enumerated at the Deas household, the Madans were
included in the census recount and were found living at a boardinghouse at 234 Fourth Avenue, in the Twenty-Second District of the Eighteenth Ward. Father and son were joined there by Julián, twenty-five,
one of Madan's two children with Mary O'Sullivan. It appears that it was
a modest boardinghouse, with relatively few servants.[42]

For years thereafter Madan dedicated himself to recuperating his embargoed properties, pursuing legal action and taking his case before an
arbitration commission established by the United States to adjudicate
claims filed by U.S. citizens against Spain.[43] Perhaps for that reason, he
did not become involved in émigré revolutionary politics in New York,
despite his many personal connections with the Havana elite residing in
the city. This is evident from Madan's correspondence, starting in 1869
and lasting until 1871, with his friend and fellow New Yorker José Manuel
Mestre, about matters unrelated to Mestre's political activities on behalf
of Cuban independence.[44] Rather, the letters deal with Mestre's requests
that Madan use his contacts with city officials and with the New York
diocese to solve the problems of several needy Cubans in the city. In one
case, Mestre brought to Madan's attention the plight of an abandoned
Cuban girl in Westchester County, and Madan immediately requested
the help of the president of the Society for the Protection of Destitute
Roman Catholic Children and also of the director of the Sacred Heart
School in Manhattan. On November 20, 1871, Madan was living at yet
another address, 30 West 47th Street, when he wrote a letter in English
to an acquaintance of his, J. Nicholson, commissioner of public charities,
requesting an appointment for Ana Betancourt de González, "a sorrow-
fully tried lady," wrote Madan, "brought to this country by the ruin of
Puerto Príncipe on the island of Cuba." He goes on to explain that

she has placed her daughters where they honestly earn a living and she is
the person of who I spoke to you yesterday desiring to send her ungov-
ernable boy to an institution where he may be closely kept and improve
on as economical terms and her circumstances demand.[45]

In a separate letter Madan notified Mrs. Betancourt of her appointment with Nicholson at the office of Public Charities at 11th Street and Third Avenue, and advised her that the best option for her son, twelve years old, was the "children's school" in Randalls Island, a reference no doubt to the House of Refuge, a public reformatory located there.[46]

Half a century had passed since Madan first served as New York's unofficial "consul of the Republic," as Heredia called him, the teenager who received the mail and secured accommodations in downtown Manhattan for the poet as well as for Father Varela. Despite the passage of nearly five decades, his forced exile in Spain, and the prospect of economic ruin, Cristóbal Madan evidently remained the most informed and well-connected Cuban in New York, the person newcomers from Cuba would go to for help as they made their way in a new and daunting city. And there were more and more Cuban newcomers in New York.

The well-known Cubans listed in table 5.1 brought from Cuba their prominence in political and intellectual matters and became visible in the city during the 1870s for their activism on behalf of the war in Cuba. But those prominent elites represented only a fraction of all Cubans living in New York. By the time the 1870 census was taken, the Cuban-born population in what are now the five boroughs had surpassed 2,700 persons, more than quadrupling its size since the 1860 census.[47] About 88 percent lived in Manhattan. Most of those nearly three thousand Cuban New Yorkers are unknown to history. They were men, women, and children who for a myriad of reasons left Cuba and in New York concerned themselves not so much with abstract concepts of independence and sovereignty as with shaping their lives in a city they now called home, a place that could be promising, exciting, and frightening.

The outbreak of the war in 1868 was responsible for accelerating the decades-old pattern of Cuban migration to New York. Wealthy landowners, prosperous merchants, progressive professionals, and liberal intellectuals were not the only ones caught up in the wave of abuses, violence, and lawlessness that started sweeping Cuba in 1868. It was a war in which everyone was forced to choose sides, and one did not have to be sentenced to death or have one's property embargoed to feel threatened by the scope and intensity of the forces that had been unleashed on the island.

One measure of the war's effects was the significant presence of women and children among Cubans in New York. Political upheavals

that compel people to leave their countries generally result in migration flows with a fairly large number of families, compared with labor
migrations, which usually consist almost entirely of single men. In 1870
slightly more than 40 percent of all Cuban-born New Yorkers were female, and children under eighteen represented more than a fourth of the
population, a fairly high proportion considering it includes only Cuban-
born children and not those born in New York to Cuban parents.

But the war was not solely responsible for the rapid growth of New
York's Cuban population. During the 1860s the trend that had started
in the previous decade, described in chapter 3, was in full swing: New
York as a center for the manufacture of cigars made from Clear Havana
leaves. The growing popularity of the Cuban leaves helped to greatly
expand the city's cigar industry. In the 1860s and 1870s New York had by
far the largest number of tobacco-related establishments of any city in
the United States, becoming, as Burrows and Wallace noted, "the capital
of the North American cigar industry."[48] An 1867 directory of manufacturers, importers, and dealers in tobacco listed 1,309 entries for Manhattan and 166 for Brooklyn.[49]

Another directory published that same year had similar, but more
specific, data for Manhattan: 899 cigar dealers and manufacturers, 170
warehouses and commission merchants, and an additional 206 identified more broadly as tobacco dealers and manufacturers. There were
also a number of ancillary industries, such as the manufacture of cigar
boxes, tobacco tin-foil, and the new presses and other machinery used
to make cigars.[50]

By 1870 New York's cigar industry was in the midst of a boom, as
cigar establishments in the city multiplied.[51] A detailed tobacco industry
directory published in 1872 listed 1,486 cigar manufacturers (excluding
dealers and importers) in Manhattan and 406 in Brooklyn. Cigars were
also being produced in Astoria, Jamaica, and Long Island City.[52]

One estimate placed the number of cigar workers in the city at 2,800,
most of them German Jewish immigrants, the group most responsible
for the growth of New York's cigar industry.[53] Germans, Czechs, and
Hungarians had been behind the establishment of the Cigar Makers International Union in 1864.[54] The expanding industry, however, started
attracting cigar makers from Cuba, especially as conditions on the island
deteriorated rapidly with the advent of the war. Furthermore, Cuban

cigar makers enjoyed a certain cachet as the cigars made from Clear Havana leaves became the priciest and most sought-after cigars in the city. Thomas J. Rayner, for example, the owner of the Smoke cigar factory at 102 Liberty Street, advertised that his cigars were "manufactured by CUBAN workmen of ALL HAVANA TOBACCO equal in quality, style, and fragrance" to the cigars manufactured in Havana but at more reasonable prices than the imported product.[55]

Cachet, of course, did not necessarily translate into good pay, especially since Cuban cigar makers in New York were, at least initially, not part of the organized labor movement started by their European colleagues. But what is certain is that more and more Cuban cigar makers were arriving in New York.

Table 5.2 presents the occupations of the 913 Cubans in the city who declared an occupation in 1870. More than one-third reported that they were engaged in a tobacco-related occupation, most of them as cigar makers. Overall, tobacco-related occupations represented the largest occupational group among Cubans in what are now the five boroughs, and even that figure could well underestimate the importance of tobacco-related employment in that it includes only those who explicitly reported to be engaged in such an occupation. Others who simply reported "merchant" or "sales" may have also been engaged in the cigar business but were not specific in their response.

Overall, the data in table 5.2 point to a dichotomously stratified community. Cigar makers, as skilled craftsmen, represented the only numerically significant middle category. It is telling that the two largest categories after the cigar makers were, at one end, professionals and merchants (tobacco and non-tobacco combined), and, at the other end, the unskilled, a category in which domestic servants predominated. In fact, there were more domestic servants than there were persons in the entire clerical and sales category. The figures in table 5.2 no doubt underestimate the number of Cubans in the upper socioeconomic levels, since many of those self-employed in commerce or with substantial financial accounts were less likely to report an occupation. Among the Cubans listed in table 5.1, Aldama, the Mora brothers, and Carlos del Castillo, to name a few, did not report an occupation and are therefore not included in this table.

TABLE 5.2. Reported Occupations of the Cuban-Born Population of New York City, 1870

Occupation	Number	Percent
Total reporting an occupation	913	100.0
Merchants, except tobacco (e.g., wholesalers, importers)	72	7.9
Financial agents and brokers (e.g., insurance, real estate, stocks)	19	2.1
Professionals	116	12.7
physicians	*41*	
lawyers	*19*	
Artists	13	1.4
Clerical and sales, except tobacco	96	10.5
Craftsmen and semi-skilled, except tobacco	78	8.6
Tobacco-related occupations	308	33.7
cigar makers and cigar packers	*230*	
cigar trade, wholesale and retail	*78*	
Lodging, restaurant, and personal services	53	5.8
waiters and cooks	*33*	
Unskilled	118	12.9
domestic servants	*96*	
Miscellaneous	40	4.4

Source: U.S. Bureau of the Census, *1870 United States Federal Census, New York City and Kings County*, accessed through www.ancestry.com.

The stratified nature of the community is made clearer when we look at gender and race. Although women, as noted previously, are well represented among Cubans in New York in 1870, the same cannot be said for nonwhites. Less than 9 percent of the Cuban-born population of the five boroughs was classified in the census as either "black," "mulatto," or "colored." Among nonwhites, there are almost as many females as males. Males and females, whites and nonwhites, however, are not evenly divided among the different occupational categories. White males accounted almost exclusively for those in the professional, business, white collar, craftsmen (including cigar makers), and even the semi-skilled occupations. In contrast, nonwhite males represented 85 percent of all waiters and cooks, while females of both races accounted for more than three-fourths of all domestic servants.

Nonwhite females were almost exclusively found in the low-skilled service occupations, with more than 94 percent of them employed as either domestic servants or laundry washers. Only two nonwhite Cuban-born women in New York were not in the unskilled category: a seamstress and a hairdresser. The bulk of nonwhite males were employed as waiters, cooks, domestic servants, white washers, coachmen, laborers, and porters. There were a few nonwhite male craftsmen: eight cigar makers, two coopers, a shoemaker, and a carpenter. There were also four nonwhite Cuban-born sailors living in the Sixth Ward, two of them in the "Colored Seamans Boardinghouse." The only white professional women were two teachers. Three white women were clerks or salespersons and eight were seamstresses.

That women and nonwhites were at the bottom of Cuban New York's occupational distribution should not be surprising, especially among migrants from a Spanish colony where, in 1870, slavery was still practiced. The community's social structure, however, had implications for the settlement patterns of Cubans in the city. Domestic servants, laundry washers, coachmen, waiters, and cooks lived, of course, not only in the same areas of the city, but usually in the same homes, as the social classes they served. Given the relatively large number of elites, merchants, and professionals among Cubans, it is not surprising that the fairly large categories at both ends of the occupational structure lived in the city's upscale areas. There was a concentration of Cubans in what at the time were the most fashionable uptown neighborhoods. The wards with the most Cubans were the Fifteenth and Seventeenth, where more than one-fourth of the city's Cubans lived. The former surrounds Washington Square and the latter is just east of that, from Fourth (Lafayette) Avenue to Tompkins Square. An additional 35 percent of all Cubans lived just north of those two wards, in the Sixteenth, Eighteenth, Twentieth, and Twenty-First, the four wards that encompass all of Manhattan between 14th and 40th Streets. Some Cubans also started settling in what were the new outlying elite areas north of 40th, especially in the Nineteenth Ward, along Fifth Avenue, the area that would become the Upper East Side.

In contrast to the settlement patterns of the elites and their servants, Cuban cigar makers tended to live where they worked, that is, somewhat further downtown, conforming to the pattern of working-class

New Yorkers. As historians Burrows and Wallace point out, "The bulk of the working class—still unable to afford public transportation—had to live near their jobs."[56] In fact, cigar makers tended to work at home, as Burrows and Wallace also point out.[57]

Only 31 (less than 15 percent) of the 209 Cuban-born cigar makers who lived in Manhattan resided north of 14th Street. None lived in the Sixteenth Ward, where many prominent Cubans had settled. The wards with the highest concentrations of cigar makers were the Eighth, the Fourteenth, and the southern portions of the Fifteenth and Seventeenth Wards, essentially the central and western portions of Manhattan immediately surrounding Houston Street and south to Canal Street, areas now known as SoHo, Little Italy, NoLita, the Bowery, and the area of the Village directly south of Washington Square. It was there that many of the city's tobacco-related businesses were located.[58]

One household of Cuban cigar makers in the Eighth Ward (now SoHo) was the exception to the pattern of racial and gender stratification. Although 96 percent of all Cuban cigar makers in the city were white males, the house at 102 Prince Street, between Mercer and Green, contained a family of black Cuban cigar workers, including one woman, forty years of age, who indicated that she was employed in that occupation. What is also noteworthy about this family is that they were apparently boarders in a house with white European immigrants, probably Jews. One family was headed by a German dressmaker, Charles Haupt, and another family in the house was that of Max Goldstine, a Polish tailor, and his German wife, Anna. That the house was racially integrated must have struck the census enumerator as highly unusual, for not only did he clearly write "C" in the race column for the Cubans, but also scribbled "(Negro)" diagonally in front of their names, perhaps to make sure his supervisor did not think he had made a careless mistake in recording race.[59]

Many Cuban cigar makers were no doubt employed in cigar factories that boasted of producing cigars made by Cuban craftsmen. But many were also self-employed, setting up shop right where they lived, with several members of a family, or even unrelated individuals, engaged in the craft, while still others were involved in selling the product. A household-based cigar manufacturing business was a tradition among Germans, Czechs, and Hungarians in New York, largely because it required virtually no capital to start it. In his memoirs, Morton R. Edwin, who spent a lifetime in the tobacco business in New York, recalled how his family prospered when, with $125 that they had managed to cobble together, they purchased a small retail store and factory, where the family lived, made cigars, and sold them.[60]

A logical extension of the concept of the small home-based cigar factory was the tenement factory, a larger operation where a sizable number of cigar workers lived and plied their craft. The usual arrangement was for a manufacturer to let or sublet apartments in a building to cigar makers and their families. The landlord would provide the tobacco leaves and the workers would make the cigars in their apartments and then sell them to the landlord for a fixed price that was well below what regular factory workers received.[61] These tenement factories did not become widespread in the city until the late 1870s, at which time their abolishment became a priority of the Cigar Makers International Union.[62]

The 1870 census shows that tenement employment was, at least at that time, rare among Cuban cigar makers, who tended to live either in relatively small households where they probably had a family-based factory, or in boardinghouses that were mixed in terms of their occupational composition, which meant that those workers were likely to be employed in regular factories outside their dwellings. One possible exception, and a rather extraordinary one, was a large boardinghouse in the Eighth District of the Fifteenth Ward. The keepers of the house were three men and a woman who were apparently related to each other. Two of the men were brothers from Belgium and the other man was French. The woman was Swiss and was related to the brothers. Almost all of the boarders (with the exception of just a handful of Europeans) were white Cuban-born males, a total of thirty-two, all of them in tobacco-related occupations. Seventeen were cigar makers, and the rest indicated that they were either "tobacco dealers" or simply "in the tobacco business." This particular house had every appearance of being a diversified factory tenement with not only cigar makers, but also those engaged in procuring the leaves and in selling the finished product, probably as street peddlers. Further evidence that it was tenement and not a proper boardinghouse was that for such a large house it had only two live-in Irish servants, far less than the number necessary to provide so many boarders with personal housekeeping services.

Affluent Cubans, however, like all affluent New Yorkers, did not have to live where they worked. They could afford the cab rides and personal carriages that would take them to and from their downtown businesses to residences in the tonier neighborhoods above 14th Street, where their servants, usually Irish women or black Cubans, lived with them.

The Moras were the best example. While they had their mercantile offices downtown (Fausto Mora at 50 Exchange Place and José Antonio Mora at 29 Broadway), all of the Moras lived in the uptown neighborhood where they had been making real estate investments since the 1850s. As noted earlier, their ownership of a substantial number of properties in and around 12th and 13th Streets, between Second and Fourth Avenues, led to the settlement of many members of their extended family in that area, as well as other Cubans who rented from them or who may have taken their lead and also bought property there. By 1870 the influence of the Moras in creating a sort of Cuban enclave in that neighborhood was evident. Those city blocks formed part of the Fourth and Eleventh Enumeration Districts of the Seventeenth Ward, precisely the two districts that in 1870 had the largest number of Cuban-born persons in the entire city. And those Cubans were at both ends of the occupational scale: merchants and other elites and their servants. The Mora households (and there were several) typified that dichotomy, since they brought with them the servants they had in Cuba, many of whom no doubt had been house slaves.

Antonio Máximo Mora's home at 220 East 12th Street, between Second and Third Avenues, contained, in addition to the family, two domestic servants, both "colored," and both with the same last name as the family: Victoriana Mora, thirty, born in Cuba, and Julio Mora, forty-five, whose birthplace is listed as "Africa." At 235 East 13th Street, in a house that may have shared the backyard with Antonio Máximo's house on 12th, José Antonio Mora, his wife, Josefa, and their six children were served by three Irish women and by Pancho Mora, a "colored" domestic servant, twenty-seven, born in Cuba.

José María Mora's household at 217 East 12th Street, just across the street from the home of his brother Antonio Máximo, had two male domestic servants in their twenties, Federico (a cook) and Felipe, both born in China. Starting in 1847 Chinese laborers started arriving in Cuba under "coolie" contracts to augment the declining African slave trade.[63]

By 1870 more than 107,000 Chinese had arrived in Cuba through Havana and sold as indentured servants.[64] Typically, they adopted or were given Spanish first names and the last names of their employers. Although the Moras' Chinese servants were employed as domestics, most Chinese in Cuba worked in agriculture in conditions not very different from those of the African slaves. A royal decree of 1860 mandated that after the expiration of their contract, Chinese laborers either had to renew it or leave the island within two months.[65] Given the level of ship traffic between Havana and Manhattan, many of those who chose to leave Cuba probably did so through New York. On July 5, 1870, for example, the steamship *De Soto* arrived in the city from Havana with twelve men in their twenties traveling in steerage who had Spanish names but who declared China as both their country of origin and their country of intended final destination.[66] It is impossible to know just how many Chinese from Cuba may have stayed in New York as free laborers, since they would appear in the census as born in China, indistinguishable from other Chinese immigrants in the city. We know about Federico and Felipe Mora because they were part of José María Mora's household. It is interesting, however, that when the Mora family was enumerated again in January 1871 in the census recount, Felipe no longer appears in the household, perhaps after having explored more attractive employment options in the city.

The Moras were certainly not alone among elite families in bringing house servants from Cuba. As noted previously, the Bachiller clan in Brooklyn had six Cuban-born black servants living in their homes. Also in Brooklyn, José Morales Lemus had a twenty-two-year-old Cuban-born black male listed as a domestic servant in his household. Although Miguel Aldama had only Irish servants in his household, down the block on 47th Street his daughter Rosa and her husband, Leonardo del Monte, had, in addition to Irish and English servants, a black Cuban woman and a Chinese-born male waiter. In the Twenty-First Ward, Félix Govín employed Manuela Díaz, a nineteen-year-old black Cuban woman.

In the Fifteenth Ward in Manhattan, José and Josefina Reyes and their six children counted on the services of two Cuban-born black women in their twenties. Evaristo and Teresa Ramírez, Martín Cárdenas, and Pucha Socorro were all Cuban-born black servants at the home of Hilario and Francisco Javier Cisneros on West 22nd Street, in the Sixteenth

Ward. On Fourth Avenue, a block away from the Moras' enclave in the Seventeenth Ward, Fernando Romero, a sixty-year-old Cuban-born white man, ran an all-Cuban boardinghouse that included a physician and his family. He had the help of two black compatriots in their fifties, Agustina Romero and María Escavel.[67] In the Nineteenth Ward a large multi-family Cuban household with a cigar dealer, a physician, their wives, and eight children also included five Cuban-born black servants who are identified in the census only by their first names.[68] Juan Toscano, his wife, and six grown children, all of whom were born in Cuba and lived on 45th Street between Second and Third Avenues, were served by Dolores (no last name), a black woman thirty-five years of age also born in Cuba, and by Joaquín (also no last name), a native of China. There were three black Cuban-born children ranging in age from four to ten in the household, presumably Dolores's offspring. Félix Fuentes, the merchant who had been deported to Fernando Póo, had three black Cuban women born in Havana working as servants in his house, in addition to a twenty-five-year-old Chinese-born man named Domingo (no last name).

The most evident example of the transplantation to New York from Cuba of the legacy of slavery was the household of Ricardo del Prado, a thirty-three-year-old sugar broker who lived in the Thirteenth District of the Twenty-Second Ward with his twenty-year-old wife, Carolina, both born in Cuba. In addition to having two U.S.-born domestic servants, the del Prado household included Ela Elavonda, a twenty-five-year-old black Cuban woman whose occupation is listed as "nurse." The del Prados had two children, also born in Cuba: Carolina, two years old, and América, an infant two months of age. In post–Civil War Manhattan, there was still at least one black woman serving as a wet nurse to a white child.

Although the bulk of Cuban nonwhites who were servants in New York probably arrived in the city with their employers or former masters, many of them no doubt did what Felipe Mora did after arriving with the Moras: in effect "emancipated" themselves, seeking positions in which they were treated, and paid, as free laborers, without employment conditions that had been established under slavery or indentured servitude. Mrs. A. J. Black, a white woman from Massachusetts, employed two black Cuban men, a waiter and a cook, as well as two black Cuban women as servants in her boardinghouse in the Eighteenth Ward. The boardinghouse catered primarily to Cuban boarders and included a lawyer, a physician, and the families of two brothers, Rafael and Juan Zayas, who gave their occupation as "farmers." Emilia Rodríguez and Jane Cardoso, black Cuban-born women in their twenties, were employed as domestic servants in the home of the painter Thomas Hicks, forty-six, and his wife, Angie, thirty-five. The Pennsylvania-born Hicks was best known for his portraits and was a member of the National Academy of Design in Manhattan. James Watson Webb, a sixty-eight-year-old New York newspaper publisher and former U.S. minister to Brazil, employed a sixteen-year-old black Cuban male as his coachman.

There are various examples in the 1870 census of Cuban-born blacks who may have left domestic service in favor of self-employment. Two black Cuban women in the Twenty-Second Ward (their names are illegible) shared their own household and made a living by taking in laundry. On West 30th Street, three black Cuban seamstresses, all related, lived in a multi-family household with U.S.-born blacks who had occupations such as laundress, waiter, and chimneysweep.

The conflict on the island brought more than just Cubans to Manhattan. Foreign residents of Cuba also joined the migration stream to New York. It is difficult to estimate their numbers, since they would appear in the U.S. census as persons born in their respective countries, as was the case with Chinese laborers in Cuba. William Adams and his wife, Carmen, are one clear example, however, of how the flow of people from Cuba increased the city's population beyond the Cuban-born. Carmen was Venezuelan and William was a sugar merchant born in Virginia. But their seven children, ranging in age from six to twenty, were all born in Cuba. In 1870 their house in Brooklyn's Ninth Ward, the area directly north and east of Prospect Park, also included three Cuban-born black domestic servants, two women and one man.

One single household accounted for more than half of the thirty Cuban-born residents of Staten Island in 1870. Esteban Rodríguez and his wife, Dolores, both forty-nine years old and born in Cuba, lived in Castleton with their twelve children, all Cuban-born and ranging in age from five to twenty-three. Also in the household were two black Cuban domestic servants, Felipa Díaz, fifty, and Margarita Rodríguez, twenty-five, as well as Margarita's three-year-old daughter Catalina. Rodríguez gave his occupation as "painter," but he was either a house painter or an artist whose work has yet to be discovered.

That was not true of other Cuban painters who lived in New York. Some of Cuba's best-known artists were part of the exodus that followed the outbreak of war. Foremost among them was the painter Federico Martínez, a native of Santiago de Cuba, who at age forty-two was already one of Cuba's best-known portraitists. At the time of the 1870 census he lived by himself in a multi-family dwelling at 82 Fifth Avenue (corner of 14th Street). He listed his occupation as "artist in oil painting," as did three other non-Cuban residents of the house. Martínez had made provisions for his migration to New York: he had an account with Moses Taylor and Company.[69] Three of his portraits currently hang in the permanent Cuban collection of the Museo de Bellas Artes in Havana. One of them was painted in New York in 1881, a portrait of the girl María Wilson y Mijares.[70]

Less known than Martínez was the landscape painter Louis Boudat, thirty-five, also born in Santiago de Cuba. In 1870 he lived with his wife, Lucinda, born in South America, and their young daughters, Hortense and Aletha, in a boardinghouse at 7 Bank Street, in the West Village. Unlike Martínez, Boudat did not stay long in New York. He moved to Peru, where he spent the rest of his life.[71]

Another painter born in Santiago de Cuba, Guillermo Collazo, much younger than Martínez and Boudat, reputedly lived in New York, where as a teenager he was sent by his father in 1869 to avoid imprisonment in Cuba for his activism against Spanish rule on the island.[72] Collazo was a student of Martínez in Santiago de Cuba, and would later become known for his interiors, portraits, and dreamy landscapes. He does not, however, appear in the 1870 census, despite evidence that he lived in New York before returning to Cuba in the mid-1880s. One of his paintings is in the Museo de Bellas Artes in Havana. He died in Paris in 1896.[73]

There were two Cuban musicians who arrived in New York as part of the 1868–1869 exodus, Emilio Agramonte and Pablo Desvernine. Both remained in the city for many years and developed most of their careers there. Agramonte, the younger of the two, was from Camagüey but was not related to the Agramontes, Ignacio and Eduardo, who were on the battlefield. Emilio was educated as a lawyer in Spain, but studied voice and piano in Italy.[74] In New York he was primarily a music educator and organizer of concerts and chorales under various musical organizations he established in the city. In 1870, at age twenty-five, he lived in the Fifteenth Ward with his wife and three young daughters in a boardinghouse that also included other Agramonte family members and José Godoy and his family, all born in Cuba. Both Emilio Agramonte and Godoy listed their occupation as "pianist." Pablo Desvernine had ancestral ties to music and to New York. His mother was Adelaida Victoria Legrás y Menard, a pianist who had been born in New York and in 1820 married in Havana a French immigrant named Pierre Desvernine, a mathematician and chemist from Bordeaux.[75] By the time their son Pablo arrived in New York from his native Havana, he was in his forties and had studied and toured in Europe, where he won acclaim as a concert pianist.[76] In New York he not only performed, but also gave private piano lessons. One of his students was a young Edward MacDowell, who went on to become one of the most gifted and representative American pianists of his generation.[77] In 1870 Desvernine and his wife, Liboria Carolina, lived on 33rd Street between Second and Third Avenues with their six children. Also in the household were Pablo's younger brother Pedro Eugenio, his wife, Elena, their five children, and four Irish female domestic servants. Neither Pablo nor his brother reported an occupation.

At least one prominent Cuban scientist was living in New York in 1870. Andrés Poey had followed in the footsteps of his father, Felipe Poey, a naturalist with an international reputation as a zoologist who studied Cuba's fauna, especially unique species of fish and butterflies. Andrés, however, was a physicist, a meteorologist, and a geographer who left behind an eclectic body of work. He wrote on the history of hurricanes in the Caribbean and North Atlantic, published the first atlas for use in Cuban primary schools, created a nomenclature of clouds, was responsible for establishing Cuba's first meteorological observatory, and even dabbled in archaeology and in the application of electricity to medicine.[78] Although most of his time outside Cuba was spent in Paris, he occasionally collaborated with colleagues and taught classes in New York, where the 1870 census found him living by himself in an upscale boardinghouse in the Seventeenth Ward with U.S.-born professionals and merchants. He declared his occupation as "astronomer." He was probably in New York temporarily on matters related to his profession, since Poey had a wife and two children in Havana.[79] Not all Cubans in

New York were exiles banned from the island. The ship traffic between Manhattan and Cuban ports continued in the years after 1868 despite the war, and those persons who were not under threat of persecution on the island came and went freely, as so many Cubans had done for decades.

The 1870 census revealed an intensification of the long-standing trend of educating Cuban children in New York boarding schools. The crisis in Cuba and the exodus of families multiplied the number of Cubans boarding in private schools in the city. By far the school with the largest number of Cuban students was the Academy of the Sacred Heart in the Twelfth Ward, around West 130th Street in what was then the bucolic village of Manhattanville. The Sacred Heart of Jesus was an order established in France by Sister Madeleine Sophie Barat dedicated primarily to educating upper-class young women. The New York school was the first Sacred Heart school established in the Western Hemisphere. In 1870 there were twenty-six Cuban-born girls ranging in age from ten to twenty enrolled and boarded at the school. The Sacred Heart also had four Cuban nuns in its convent.

The large Cuban presence at this Manhattanville school was a result of the Sacred Heart's ties with Cuba, a further example of the many connections between Cuba and New York that had been built over decades and that brought so many Cubans to the city's doorstep, especially during the 1868 war. The Sacred Heart school in Havana had been founded in 1858 by sisters from the Manhattanville school, who had traveled to the island from New York under instructions from Sister Barat to establish a school there.[80] The school in Havana formed part of the order's North American vicariate, or province, which had New York as its seat and administrative center. Sister Aloysa Hardey, the Maryland-born Mother Superior in New York, founded the Havana school and had oversight responsibility for it.

In 1860, with the Havana school up and running with nearly one hundred students, there were only three Cuban students in the New York school. But the 1868 conflict changed everything. The exodus of the Havana elite to New York meant that the school in Manhattanville started enrolling and boarding the displaced Havana students. Among the twenty-six Cuban girls in the school in 1870, there were many with prominent last names, including two Madans. The Manhattanville convent also received Cuban nuns who were compelled to leave. The

Spanish authorities, and even the Church hierarchy, considered the Sacred Heart nuns a "foreign order." An orphanage and asylum the order ran in Sancti Spíritus closed. The 1870 census found a former director of the Havana school, Sister Rosa de Abreu, among the nuns living in Manhattanville.

The Sacred Heart was not the only boarding school in the Twelfth Ward, a rural area at the time and a popular place to locate schools. Almost all of the schools there had Cuban students. Two schools that were both named the French School each had eleven Cuban-born students. One of those schools, in the Eighteenth District, had exclusively teenaged boys; the other, in the First District, was coeducational and had students ranging in age from five to nineteen, and one Cuban-born teacher, Inés Socarrás. Near the Sacred Heart, the Christian Brothers School had a fourteen-year-old male Cuban student among its boarding pupils.

There were other types of "boarding" institutions in the Twelfth Ward with Cuban guests. Six-year-old Felipe Rosable was among the children in the New York Colored Asylum, which had relocated to 143rd Street and Amsterdam Avenue after it was burned down during the 1863 draft riots.[81] Three men and two women, all Cuban-born and most in their thirties, were inmates at the Bloomingdale Insane Asylum. Also in the Twelfth Ward, there were two Cubans, a man and a woman, interned in the complex of city hospitals and asylums on Ward's Island.

Other asylums throughout Manhattan also housed Cubans. Carmen Suárez, thirteen, was living in the Roman Catholic Orphan Asylum in the Fourteenth Ward. The Arteaga sisters, Consuelo, eight, and Clementa, five, were at the Protestant Episcopal Orphan Asylum in the Upper East Side. In that same ward, at Blackwell's (now Roosevelt) Island, six Cubans were patients in the charity hospital, two Cubans were house physicians, and another was an orderly. In the Lunatic Asylum at Blackwell's there were six Cubans, including Félix Sánchez, condemned eleven years earlier for the murder of his father-in-law (see chapter 3). Also interned in the Lunatic Asylum was a twenty-five-year-old Cuban-born white male whose name appears as "John Doe."

Like many New Yorkers, middle- and working-class Cubans, especially those without families, tended to live in boardinghouses. Many houses were small and others very large, with accommodations and services that varied greatly according to cost and hence socioeconomic level. Some were close to being comfortable residential hotels while, at the other end, some were only slightly better than tenements. They were not necessarily segregated by national origins. Some boardinghouses had almost exclusively Cuban boarders, while in others Cubans shared quarters with persons from a variety of nationalities. Almost without exception, however, the boardinghouses were racially segregated. The boardinghouse owned by the Pierce family, native New Yorkers, on 12th Street between Broadway and University Place was apparently a fairly upscale house. Eleven Cubans, all single white males, including a civil engineer, a shipping merchant, and an office clerk, lived in the house with at least twenty other boarders, most of them U.S.-born white males. They were served by six female Irish servants.

Further downtown, in what is now SoHo, Sarah Mann, an African American widow from Tennessee, ran a boardinghouse at 103 Laurens (now West Broadway) with twenty-three boarders, all blacks and most of them U.S.-born single males unrelated to each other. There were only five women, three of them seamstresses. The men also had semi-skilled occupations, such as plasterer, seaman, and cook. There were four Cubans: a cigar maker, a waiter, and two coopers. The house apparently had no servants.

Also in SoHo, in the Third District of the Eighth Ward, was a house run by a forty-four-year-old Prussian-born woman, Sophia Bloom, who gave her occupation as "keeps house" and indicated that the value of her personal estate amounted to $1,500. Her five boarders were all white women in their early twenties, born in England, Massachusetts, the West Indies, New York, and one, Emma Deveau, born in Cuba. In the space for "occupation" the enumerator placed only a capital *P* for each of the young women, information he must have deduced, for it is not likely that Madame Bloom's "boarders" declared an occupation.

* * *

The results of the 1870 U.S. census draw a picture of Cuban New York at a critical moment in its development. The war in Cuba had started barely a year before, yet in that short period of time New York had seen a flow of people from the island unprecedented in the already long history of Cuban migration to the city. It was just the beginning. The war in Cuba became a protracted conflict that would last until 1878, when the insurgents and the Spanish government reached an agreement to put an end to it. During the years the war dragged on, New York received the casualties of the conflict: veterans fresh off the battlefields, the widows and children of those who left their lives on those battlefields, those at risk of being executed or imprisoned, and many others who simply found it difficult to live in a country torn apart by war, its economy in ruins and its future uncertain. And there were also those who were not so compelled to leave the island, but who simply sought to expand their horizons in a modern city. For cigar makers, employment prospects were better in downtown Manhattan than in a war-ravaged island.

It was in the mid-1870s that Cuban New York would reach its demographic apex in the nineteenth century. Those were also the years, as we shall see in the next chapter, of the most intense activism on behalf of Cuban separatism. All of this occurring within the broader context of post–Civil War New York, the period that catapulted the city to the forefront of the modern era.

The end of the Cuban war in 1878 made it possible for many to return to the island, since the agreement that ended the conflict promised amnesty for those who had been convicted since 1868 of "political crimes."[82] As we shall see, the 1880 census shows slightly fewer Cuban-born persons in the city than the number enumerated in 1870. The 1870s was therefore the decade in which Cuban New York reached a crescendo, demographically, economically, and, especially, politically. Not even in the decade preceding independence, the 1890s, would there be in New York such a concentration of Cuba's economic, intellectual, and political elites, nor would separatist activism reach the intensity and acrimony that were evident among the émigrés during the 1868–1878 war.

The economic vitality of the Cuban community was no doubt hampered by the Panic of 1873, which forced businesses and banks to close and raised unemployment in the city.[83] Even so, Cuban New York showed signs of vitality. The magazine *El Ateneo*, started in 1874 by the Cuban writer and literary critic Juan Ignacio de Armas y Céspedes, was full of advertising aimed at Spanish-speaking consumers in the city and throughout the Americas. With offices and printing facilities located at 31 Park Row, the magazine stayed away from political topics, billing itself as an "illustrated Spanish monthly of popular literature, art and science circulating in Mexico, Central America, West Indies, California, New Mexico and the principal cities in the United States." Promising advertisers that El Ateneo "supplies a want long felt by the Spanish-American population of this continent," the publisher "shall gladly give any desired information concerning the Spanish American markets, free of charge." It also offered that "advertisements will be translated without extra charge, a proper translation in all cases being guaranteed."[84]

Many New York businesses, suffering from a slump in sales during the depression, apparently felt it was worthwhile to try to reach the Spanish American market. Manufacturers of billiard tables, coffee makers, sewing machines, steam engines, printing presses, hair tonic, saddles, iron safes, Colt revolvers, carriages, even locomotives, placed ads (in Spanish) in El Ateneo, as did banks, life insurance companies, hotels, steamship lines, lard refiners, and retailers of ladies' shoes, men's hats, textbooks, encyclopedias, and stationery.

Spanish- and Cuban-owned businesses in the city were also advertisers in El Ateneo. The Ambos Mundos Restaurant, owned by F. Pont, at 13 Cedar Street (previously at 4 Liberty Street), promised patrons superior service and a richly varied menu of Spanish dishes "in the style of Cuba."[85] Nestor Ponce de León, Antonio Bachiller y Morales's son-in-law, advertised his bookstore at 40–42 Broadway with a listing of the best-selling titles.[86] Also in El Ateneo, Luis Felipe Mantilla, mentioned earlier in this chapter as a fellow boarder of Simón Camacho and Enrique Piñeyro, advertised several Spanish-language textbooks he authored or edited. The Cuban-born Mantilla, who identified himself in the ad as a professor of Spanish language and literature at New York University, cites in the ad several favorable reviews of his books and refers interested buyers to the offices of his printer at 140 Grand Street.[87] José María Mora's son, also named José María, in his twenties and an aspiring portrait photographer, advertised his studio, located at 707 Broadway, on the magazine's back cover.[88] The St. Louis School on West 42nd Street advertised itself in El Ateneo as "El Colegio de San Luis," claiming to be the only "select French Catholic school in the city exclusively for Catholic families." Founded in 1869, it offered instruction at the elementary level in English, French, German, and Latin, and a special class especially for children from Spanish-speaking homes.[89]

Besides ads there were, of course, articles in *El Ateneo*, most of them probably written by De Armas himself, who was thirty-three years old and came from a prominent Camagüeyano family.[90] With a growing reputation as a man of letters, De Armas would regularly give his readers advice on the principal works of world literature they should be reading, and he also published original poetry and fiction from contributors.[91] But most of his articles were essays of literary and artistic criticism focused on the New York cultural scene, undermining a bit his claim to advertisers that his readership spanned the hemisphere. In the September 1876 issue he noted, for example, William Cullen Bryant's poetic descriptions of New York's dreary fall weather, adding that autumn is nevertheless a relief from the city's insufferably hot summers.[92] De Armas bemoans what he believes to be the sorry state into which the dramatic arts had fallen "in the premier city of the American continent." Case in point, he argued, is the work playing at the Booth Theater, *Sardanapalus*, a tragedy by Byron ("as a poet admirable," writes De Armas, "but as a playwright, detestable") that was, in his opinion, poorly acted and badly staged. He leveled equally critical reviews at the works playing at Niblo's Garden and the Fifth Avenue Theater.[93]

In the December 1875 issue of *El Ateneo*, De Armas included a small biography and drawing of Ignacio Cervantes, the young Cuban pianist and composer who, jointly with José White, a violinist who was also a composer, had just finished a much-acclaimed concert tour of the United States. In New York, Cervantes and White gave two concerts at Steinway Hall on October 19 and 21, 1875.[94] Cervantes has been described by one writer as "the most important Cuban composer of the nineteenth century."[95] Both he and White had to leave Cuba when it was discovered that the proceeds of one of their concerts on the island had been donated to the cause of independence.[96] Although Cervantes stayed in New York for four years, White went on to Paris, but not before performing twice during the 1875–1876 season as a guest soloist with the New York Philharmonic under the direction of Theodore Thomas.[97] Born in Matanzas in 1835 and of African descent, White had studied in Paris as a young man at the urging of American pianist and composer Louis Moreau Gottschalk. The two met in Matanzas at White's first public concert in 1854.[98] White is best known for composing "La bella cubana," an *habanera* that has remained one of the most emblematic compositions of nineteenth-century Cuba.

In the September 1876 issue of *El Ateneo* De Armas ridiculed all the nervous predictions in the press about an impending cataclysm as the U.S. Army Corps of Engineers prepared to blast away the underwater rocks that threatened shipping at Hell Gate, the strait between Astoria and Ward's Island.[99] "Almost a third of the city witnessed the explosion, which was heard by no one," wrote De Armas.[100]

That same year, two statues were unveiled in the city, and De Armas reviewed them. One, of "medium merit," was the statue of Lafayette in Union Square by Bertholdi, "facing that of Washington, in the same square, as if offering him his sword."[101] De Armas is more enthusiastic about the sculptor's pending project, the colossus on the bay that will let New Yorkers take pride in having one of the "great marvels of the modern world." The other statue unveiled that year was the one of William Seward at Madison Square, which added, De Armas noted, "to the small number of monuments this city possesses."[102]

The Seward statue was also the subject of an essay by Enrique Piñeyro, another Cuban New Yorker who wrote on what he saw in the city during the 1870s. From an artistic point of view, the statue, wrote Piñeyro, is "bad, very bad. . . . If the seated figure stood up it would easily be thirteen feet tall." Piñeyro also found unusual that the sculptor chose to have Seward with legs crossed, an unflattering pose, in his view. Accustomed to marble sculptures in Europe and in Cuba, Piñeyro remarked that bronze is used in all statues in New York because it is cheaper than marble and because it is better suited to the character of the "metal age."[103]

But Piñeyro devoted most of the essay to Seward's life, which gave him the opportunity to comment on the political institutions of the United States in the post–Civil War era. He criticized the nominating conventions of the political parties, an informal process "not envisioned by the founders of the Republic" and which in Chicago in 1860 served to deny Seward the Republican nomination in favor of Abraham Lincoln.[104] The Seward article is part of an entire book of essays by Piñeyro on the United States in the 1870s, inspired, he wrote in the prologue, by a pleasant autumn walk in Brooklyn's Green-Wood Cemetery. The book was printed in 1880 in the shop of Thompson and Moreau at 51–53 Maiden Lane. In the central article of the work, "The United States in 1875," Piñeyro recounted his far-ranging observations during a trip taken that year throughout the country. He bemoaned the tragedy of the Civil War and what he viewed as the disastrous legacy of Reconstruction, but in the end he praised the affirmation of the principle of equality.[105] He noted the plight of Native Americans and the dismal treatment of Chinese laborers in the West, and was unreserved in his criticism of Mormonism, calling Joseph Smith "a charlatan," questioning the justification for establishing of such a "sect," and assailing its acceptance of polygamy.[106] In the end he praises the United States, labeling it a "triumphant" nation, and lays out the reasons why the American system is successful and worthy of being imitated.[107]

* * *

By 1874 Antonio Bachiller y Morales and his family had relocated from Brooklyn to Manhattan. When Antonio and his wife, Carlota Govín, became U.S. citizens on April 22 of that year, they listed their address as 275 West 22nd Street, in the same ward and district as José Manuel Mestre and the Cisneros brothers.[108] His married daughters and sons-in-law lived nearby.[109] It was in their Manhattan home that the Bachiller family hosted a dinner for Guillermo Prieto, a Mexican intellectual, writer, and longtime friend of Antonio.[110] In his three-volume published diary of the trip he took throughout the United States in the mid-1870s, Prieto described the dinner at the Bachillers' home, a family affair attended by several of Antonio's daughters and two of his sons-in-law, Dr. Juan Landeta, the physician, and Nestor Ponce de León, the bookstore owner.[111] It was an elegant evening, Prieto recalls warmly, with Bachiller y Morales graciously leading an animated conversation over a dinner of soup, a roast, and two desserts: a flaming sweet omelette and a sugar tart. Fine burgundy was also served.

Prieto found noteworthy that in the Bachiller household the women were as likely as the men to express their views at the dinner table. The topics ranged from New York ladies (they are likely to be out and about all day and not at home, which is why they spend all their money on their wardrobe and not on their households), American husbands (drunks excluded, they tend to be faithful, dedicated to their families, and patient with their children), the almighty dollar (Americans worship it and they not only know how to make it, but also know how to spend it), the American family (it is not necessarily a bad thing that the U.S. legal system, unlike Spanish law, allows one to disinherit one's children), and the curious customs of the wealthy vacationers in Saratoga (the mineral springs are not as popular as the social events in the hotels). The evening concluded with a precocious young girl (probably one of Bachiller's granddaughters) reciting the long poem "El desterrado" ("The Exile" or "The Uprooted"), written in 1855 in New York by a poet from Santiago de Cuba, Pedro Santacilia.[112] The poem had become a sort of lyric anthem for the exiles of the war. A forlorn and nostalgic poem, the last stanza tells how a Cuban exile, remembering the Cauto River of his native island, cried as he contemplated one afternoon the "clear waters" of the Hudson.[113] The evening ended on a silent and somber note, wrote Prieto, "as the memory of the homeland sobbed in our souls."[114]

Antonio Bachiller y Morales was well into his sixties in 1874. He had an account with Moses Taylor and his daughters had married successful professionals. Exiled, and having lost his law practice, his teaching position, his ample home and excellent library, he might have easily slipped into retirement in his new English-speaking city. But Bachiller was a restless intellectual. In the 1880s, when José Martí frequented the Astor Library on Lafayette Place, he was told of the "Cuban gentleman" who a decade earlier could always be found on the same leather chair in the reading room, earnestly consulting the library's holdings.[115]

A great deal of the research Bachiller y Morales conducted at the Astor Library was for a guidebook he was writing of New York and its surroundings. *Guía de la ciudad de Nueva York y sus alrededores* was published in 1876 by his son-in-law Nestor Ponce de León.[116] Unlike some of its predecessors, this is not a whimsical guidebook. It does not dispense lighthearted practical advice to tourists. In fact, it is not really a guidebook at all. It is a detailed description of the New York area written by an intellectual, intended for the Spanish-language visitor or resident interested in the city's history, culture, and institutions. Its 238 pages are full of observations, facts, figures, and illustrations. Although, of course, Bachiller y Morales borrowed heavily from published sources in English, especially for the data he presented on the city's demographics and infrastructure, the scope, depth, and detail of what he compiled and de-

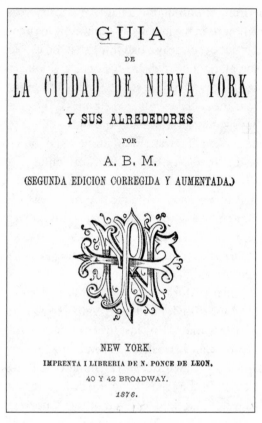

Figure 5.1. The cover of Antonio Bachiller y Morales's 1876 guide to New York City. Source: Photographed from the book in the New York Public Library collection.

scribed in this book may well have surpassed any other book about New York that appeared during this period, in any language. He wove the facts and figures into a text that shows a command of the city's history and its importance. He started the book, appropriately, with the Hudson River, drawing a parallel between the sailing of the *Half Moon* into the bay and another transcendent voyage on the Hudson, that of "Fulton's Folly," the steamboat *Clermont*, "which made wind unnecessary for navigation."[117] After a brief history of the city, Bachiller y Morales described each landmark and neighborhood in detail. He noted, for example, the infamous history of the Five Points, which gave him the opportunity to mention Father Varela's work decades before among the poor, especially the Irish. He predicted that before the end of the century the entire island of Manhattan would be blanketed with buildings and that it would expand further with bridges and ferries.

Bachiller y Morales devoted an entire chapter to Central Park, praising its democratic nature by attracting families from all social classes: "Just as one finds magnificent carriages, . . . one also finds those who go on foot."[118] After describing each of the city's parks, he devoted a good portion of the book to the city's charitable societies and institutions, which he argued were some of New York's most unique and laudable features: "It is not possible that in any other part of the world there are more beneficent institutions."[119] He attributed this to the city's ethnic and religious diversity, since each group or creed seeks to establish centers for assisting its own members, in addition to the public institutions available to all. He also described every church, temple, museum, and financial institution. Bachiller y Morales included an extensive index for easy reference and inserted at the end (without attribution) a translated version of "Wilson's Street and Avenue Directory of the City of New York," which annually appeared as an appendix to *Trow's New York City Directory*.[120] More than a guidebook, *Guía de la ciudad de Nueva York* is an inventory, with commentary, of the city in the mid-1870s.

* * *

The war in Cuba did not interrupt the flow of people and goods to and from the island. While many exiles faced grave consequences if they returned to their country and therefore had no choice but to remain in New York, others were free to come and go, as Cubans had long done aboard the many ships that regularly provided service between Cuban ports and Manhattan's wharfs. The historic transnational ties that bound together Cuba and New York remained largely intact despite the conflict raging on the island. There is no better example of the continued strength of those transnational ties than the bizarre caper of the "kidnapping" of José Holgado y Cruces and the Havana lottery tickets.

The story begins on March 8, 1876, with the apparent disappearance of Señor Holgado from the corner of 4th Street and Lafayette Place. The police were alerted to the disappearance by the Spanish vice-consul in the city, Daniel de Rafarte, who went to police headquarters to report what he had been told by some associates of Holgado, that is, that the victim had been standing at the corner when two English-speaking men forced him into a carriage and sped away. Holgado allegedly had about $30,000 in Spanish gold coins in his possession at the time, all of which he had brought from Cuba only a few days before.[121]

As soon as the press started reporting the story, it was evident to New Yorkers that there was some mystery or even deception behind Holgado's disappearance. Things were not what they appeared. The day after the initial press stories about the incident, it came out that Holgado was not wealthy and that what he had in his pockets was not money at all, but a large cache of Havana lottery tickets "of a red color." Furthermore, one of Holgado's associates, a Mr. Moren, who was first reported to be his cousin, was not related to him.[122] Reports started surfacing that Holgado was last seen walking off on his own accord in the company of some Spanish-speaking men in the vicinity of the Hotel Español, 21 East 4th Street, where he was reported to have been staying.[123] The Spanish consulate engaged a private investigator and offered a reward, widely disseminating the information that Holgado's associates had provided, including the detail that Holgado had in his possession a large number of Havana lottery tickets "of a red color."[124]

Almost a week after his "disappearance," Holgado was found at a downtown hotel. He was identified from the press reports by James Betts, the proprietor of the Eastern Hotel, on the corner of Whitehall and South, who indicated that Holgado and two associates had been staying there under fictitious names since two days before the alleged disappearance. Betts also reported that Holgado had sequestered himself in the hotel the day his supposed kidnapping was first reported in the press. Since he hoped to claim the reward, Betts had summoned officials of the Spanish consulate, and not the police. The officials arrived at the Eastern Hotel and whisked Holgado away before the police and the press arrived.[125]

After questioning Holgado and ascertaining that he was safe, the Spanish vice-consul emphatically distanced himself from the entire matter, ending the consulate's involvement. Holgado rejoined his associates in the city while police looked further into the mystery and the press was left wondering what had happened.[126] Less than a week later, New York police arrested Augusto Moren, one of Holgado's associates, on a warrant from Havana, where he was accused of swindling a Gerona Fernández out of $31,000 she gave him for the purpose of buying lottery tickets. Holgado was believed to be implicated in the swindle, but he had apparently already left the city.[127]

The explanation of the affair provided to baffled New Yorkers by the *New York Times* spoke volumes about the ties between the city and Cuba, underscoring that those ties did not always involve legitimate commerce or scrupulous merchants:

> Everybody knows that there is a Government lottery regularly drawn at frequent intervals in Havana, and that tickets purporting to be issued by the managers of this lottery are offered for sale in this City.[128]

The *Times* went on to note that counterfeit tickets were printed in New York and offered "for sale as genuine tickets imported from Havana," leading to a "sad lack of public confidence in the alleged Havana Lottery tickets on sale in this City."[129] Given that lack of confidence, concluded the *Times*,

> if a Spaniard with a large quantity of Havana Lottery tickets—of a red color—were to land in the City; if intelligent kidnappers were to certify to the genuineness of those tickets by abducting the Spaniard in order to rob him of them; and if the tickets should afterward be recovered and offered for sale, they would be bought with a good degree of confidence.[130]

The *Times* felt duped into acting as an unwitting accomplice to the entire scheme and drew this lesson from it:

> The press, the Police, and the City authorities can hardly be made to advertise the Havana Lottery business a second time, and the chief result of the Holgado affair will be a total refusal on the part of everybody to take the slightest interest in the fate of the next Spaniard or Cuban who may vanish from Fourth Street or any other street with Havana Lottery tickets of a red color in his pocket.[131]

Months later, Betts, the proprietor of the Eastern Hotel who had identified Holgado as one of his guests, filed a suit in U.S. district court against the government of Spain, alleging that its New York consulate had failed to pay him the entire reward ($2,000 in gold) it had offered for information on the whereabouts of Holgado.[132]

* * *

The schemes of Havana con men were part of the textured landscape of Cuban New York in the 1870s, the decade during which the number of Cubans in the city grew dramatically. There were elites and intellectuals, exiles, immigrants, and sojourners. There were artists painting their canvases and musicians playing their instruments. There were white Cubans, Afro-Cubans, and Chinese Cubans, men and women. There were cigar makers plying their trade and house slaves who in a new country were still serving their white masters in uptown mansions. Some Cuban New Yorkers, such as Bachiller y Morales, were engaged in intellectual pursuits, others busied themselves with making money honestly through their labor or acumen, and yet others, like Holgado, were engaged in mendacious schemes.

But throughout most of the decade, Cuban New York was dominated by the pall of war. The war was in Cuba, but it was also in New York, where families grieved for their lost or missing loved ones and where the intensity of émigré separatist activities reached a fever pitch, resulting, most prominently, in deep and acrimonious fissures within the community that would prove fatal to the cause of independence.

6

Waging a War in Cuba . . . and in New York

January 15, 1872

Mr. José Manuel Mestre

Dear Sir and Cherished Compatriot,
I am going to Cuba. My request of you is a Remington
carbine with an ammunition belt and five hundred bullets. If it is within your will and possibilities to give me
more, my gratitude will be even greater. Please let me
know on what day this week, the place, and the time I
should go and pick up these items from you.
—Melchor Agüero
41 W. 16th St.[1]

J. FUSSELL & CO., Wholesale and Retail Ice Cream Dealers, 284 Fulton Street. Cuba must be ours. We want cheap
sugar. What say you, Mr. Grant?
—Advertisement, *Brooklyn Daily Eagle*, 1869[2]

New Yorkers who happened to be in the vicinity of City Hall Park on the
afternoon of October 11, 1869, must have wondered what all the commo-
tion was about. A volley of gunfire saluted the hoisting of an unfamiliar
flag atop the park's flagpole. More of the flags were unfurled from the
sides of a City Hall balcony packed with dignitaries as a brass cannon
fired one hundred rounds and a band struck up "Hail Columbia."[3] The
scene turned grisly as the cannon discharged prematurely and one of the
men loading it, Theodore Munn, had his right arm blown off.[4] Munn,
who resided at Goerick and 3rd Street and was probably Irish, was sar-
castically hailed by the *New York Herald* as a "Cuban martyr."[5]

Those were Cuban flags that were unfurled at City Hall Park that day.
The unfortunate man had lost his arm during the celebration of what the

New York Times called "the anniversary of the Cuban Fourth of July."[6] It was an event organized by city officials to demonstrate the support the Cuban cause enjoyed among New York's leaders, including Mayor Oakey Hall.

One tumultuous year had elapsed since that October day in 1868 when Carlos Manuel de Céspedes issued the call for independence that started the war. The first anniversary of the exact date, October 10, fell on a Sunday, so the Manhattan festivities were scheduled for the following day. The ceremony was scheduled in the late afternoon out of respect for the funeral that morning in New Hampshire of former president Franklin Pierce.

That evening a large audience filled the Cooper Institute to hear several speakers, Cuban and American, support independence for Cuba. The hall was festooned with U.S. and Cuban flags and the images of the principal leaders of the revolution: Céspedes, Aguilera, and Agramonte.[7] The emotional speeches were punctuated by frequent and enthusiastic applause, and the *New York Herald* characterized the event as a "brilliant affair."[8]

Nowhere else was the first anniversary of the start of the Cuban war celebrated with more fanfare than in New York. So many prominent Cubans were now living in the city. And there was the appropriateness of the Cuban flag returning home to Manhattan. Twenty years had passed since the original of the flags that were unfurled during that anniversary celebration was designed and sewn in a downtown boardinghouse and flown for the first time at Nassau and Fulton, literally only a stone's throw from City Hall Park (see chapter 2). It was (and still is) a red, white, and blue lone star flag, a symbol and product of the annexationist era, when Cuban émigrés tried, among other things, to persuade U.S. presidents to buy Cuba from Spain. President Pierce, whose funeral was held the same day as the anniversary celebration, had actually made an offer that was flatly declined by Madrid (see chapter 3). In a twist of fate, that New York-made annexationist flag was adopted as the symbol of the belligerent independence movement launched by Céspedes.[9] It was a movement that had started with all the fervor that came from the conviction that decades of frustration and unmet aspirations were nearing their end. But on that first anniversary in 1869, the movement for independence was at a critical crossroads and the end of the struggle for Cuban nationhood was nowhere in sight.

* * *

No one was more acutely aware of the challenges facing the Cubans' push for independence than the man who presided over the speeches at the Cooper Institute: José Morales Lemus. The past two years had been the most eventful, possibly frustrating, and certainly dangerous period of his life. Already in his sixties, he had served in Havana as the editor of the reformist newspaper *El Siglo* and had led the Cuban delegation to the meetings of the Junta de Información in Madrid, placing, to no avail, the concerns of Havana's reformist elite before the Crown. Once war broke out in eastern Cuba he was among those who walked away from the meeting with General Lersundi convinced that supporting the rebellion was the only remaining option. He headed the newly formed Revolutionary Junta of Havana, established by what had been the reformist elite with the purpose of supporting the insurgency. On January 24, 1869, Morales Lemus's house was raided and looted by the *voluntarios*.[10] The following week he left clandestinely for New York aboard the *Columbia*.

Morales Lemus arrived in New York to find the city's Cuban émigrés already active on behalf of the revolution. Less than a month after Céspedes's uprising, a group of Cubans met at 54 Bond Street to form a committee to raise funds and procure weapons to send to the insurgents on the island.[11] The committee consisted in part of Cuban residents of New York who had been living there since the annexationist period, but it also counted on the participation of more recent arrivals, such as the language professor Luis Mantilla, who was elected secretary of the group. Many of its members, including the Puerto Rican José Bassora, had formed part of the Republican Society of Cuba and Puerto Rico established years earlier in New York by Juan Manuel Macías (see chapter 3).

The New York committee quickly established ties with the Revolutionary Junta of Havana, the group headed by Morales Lemus in the weeks before his departure from the island. By December 1868, Francisco Javier Cisneros, Hilario's brother, had arrived in the city as an envoy from the Havana group to help organize the work of the New York committee.[12] Francisco Javier had acquired a reputation as a man of action after his daring but unsuccessful attempt to lead an uprising in western Cuba in support of the eastern insurgents. His instructions from the Havana junta were to "buy arms and everything else needed, on a grand scale, so that you will be able to direct there all operations."[13] There was no doubt as to Cisneros's mission: to outfit expeditions of men and arms and have them reach Céspedes's army. Cisneros could count on hefty remittances from the Havana group through the same conduit its members had used for decades to send money to New York: Moses Taylor and Company.[14] In yet another chapter in its long history in the Cuba Trade, the South Street counting house had become the bank for the insurgents' money in New York.

Cisneros did not waste time. Only three days after Morales Lemus's arrival in New York on February 4, 1869, the first of five expeditions organized by Cisneros was launched with the departure of the steamer *Henry Burden* from Jacksonville. In Rum Key in the Bahamas it was joined by another ship, the *Mary Lowell*, which was loaded with ordnance, and then both proceeded to Ragged Key, one of the Bahamas islands closest to Cuba. Mechanical problems stalled the mission, and two Spanish ships captured the *Mary Lowell* before she could reach Cuba, although Cisneros was able to salvage and store most of its cargo.

Two months later, on May 4, Cisneros launched his most successful expedition with the voyage of the *Perrit*, a ship chartered in New York by José María Mora that landed at the bay of Nipe on the northeast coast of Cuba, unloading both men and arms. The *Perrit* carried nearly two hundred men, a majority of them Cuban, including Antonio Bachiller y Govín, Bachiller y Morales's only surviving son, and also Federico Mora, a younger member of the Mora family.[15] That Cubans were in a majority in the *Perrit*'s expeditionary force marked a departure from the pattern established years before when Narciso López organized expeditions that were financially supported by Cuban and southern U.S. annexationists and consisted primarily of mercenaries and adventurers, many of them U.S. veterans from the Mexican War as well as European émigrés living in New York.

But the revolution that Céspedes launched in 1868 had a much broader base of support among Cubans than the annexationist movement ever had. As the exodus from the island swelled the Cuban communities in the United States, especially in New York, there were now Cubans available and willing to join expeditions to fight in Cuba. Still, nearly eighty of the expeditionaries aboard the *Perrit* were not Cuban, most of them Americans, men ready to take part in the adventure of helping the Cuban cause against the Spanish. The most prominent among them was General Thomas Jordan, a Virginian and West Point graduate who had distinguished himself in the Battle of Shiloh and had served as chief of staff to General P. G. T. Beauregard.[16]

Cisneros not only landed and unloaded the *Perrit*, but continued inland with the expedition until he personally delivered the men and the munitions to the insurgent headquarters at Guáimaro.[17] After leaving General Jordan in command, Cisneros returned to New York, via Jamaica, to organize other expeditions.

Morales Lemus arrived in New York with a mission. Only a couple of weeks before his departure from the island, the junta he headed in Havana sent a communication to the committee in New York informing it that Morales Lemus would be leaving Havana for that city and that on his arrival the committee should give him leadership of the group.[18] The Havana junta was making plans for its inevitable relocation to New York, given the persecution it was facing in Cuba. José Valiente, a member of the New York committee and longtime resident of the city, replied on behalf of his group that they would be very pleased to place themselves under the direction of the representative from Havana.[19]

The Havana junta also sought authorization from Céspedes to represent the movement in the United States. Although until that point Valiente had been entrusted with that role, Céspedes viewed Morales Lemus and his collaborators as best equipped, because of their social position and experience, to further the cause of the revolution internationally. He immediately granted the representation of the movement in the United States to the Havana group.

Since, ultimately, Céspedes was the legitimate leader of the movement, and since the New York committee had already been receiving material support from the Havana junta, channeled through Cisneros, for the work of organizing expeditions, it is not surprising that Valiente and his committee did not hesitate to subordinate themselves to the newly arrived Morales Lemus. It was the first step in a takeover of New York's émigré leadership by the Havana group, as more and more of its members arrived in the city. The reformist elite in Havana managed to transform itself in New York into the representatives of the armed revolution initiated by the easterners, a revolution the reformists had long tried to avoid but were forced to embrace as the only option. There were those in New York who from the outset did not trust Morales Lemus's leadership, for they suspected that the Havana group was still reformist at heart and driven by its economic interests, uncommitted to the armed struggle for total independence and ready to strike a deal with the Spanish that would betray the goals of the uprising led by Céspedes. The initial actions by Morales Lemus in New York seemed to confirm their suspicions.

Immediately after his arrival in the city, Morales Lemus started a process of institutionalizing the émigré leadership in such a way that placed his newly arrived Havana collaborators in key positions while eventually excluding those Cuban New Yorkers who had a longer history of émigré activism in the city. By the middle of 1869, Morales Lemus had reorganized the émigrés into what became known as the Central Republican Junta of Cuba and Puerto Rico, evoking the name of the old New York group, but leaving out many of those who had been its members, notably José Valiente, José María Mora, Plutarco González, and Agustín Arango. Instead, the junta that Morales Lemus now headed included his protégée José Manuel Mestre, Francisco Fesser, Hilario Cisneros, Nestor Ponce de León (Antonio Bachiller y Morales's son-in-law), and other members of the Havana group who had arrived in New York only within the preceding few months.[20] Eventually other members of that group, and close friends of Morales Lemus, such as José Antonio Echeverría and Enrique Piñeyro, were also placed in leadership positions, the latter as secretary.[21] The junta established its headquarters at 71 Broadway.

Although the takeover of the émigré leadership by the Havana group was criticized by many, Morales Lemus was invested with the mantle of legitimacy by Céspedes, especially after April 1869, when the insurgents constituted themselves into a government, with a constitution and with Céspedes as president. The new insurgent government then proceeded to give Morales Lemus the title of "envoy extraordinary and plenipotentiary minister of the Republic of Cuba to the United States," charged with the responsibility of "securing not only recognition for the independence of the island, but also all moral and material assistance that would lead to freeing Cuba from Spanish control and the swift end to the war."[22]

Sending men and armaments to Cuba was no doubt an important function of the newly formed New York junta, and Morales Lemus continued to facilitate the work of Cisneros in outfitting expeditions. But giving Morales Lemus a high-sounding title as representative of the insurgent government in the United States was a clear signal from the Céspedes government that Morales Lemus's priority should be enlisting Washington's support.[23] There is no other explanation for Céspedes favoring Morales Lemus and his group as leaders of the émigrés. They were not men with a history of recruiting soldiers, buying guns, and organizing military ventures. They were landowners, lawyers, merchants, and investors in railroads who had long tried, albeit unsuccessfully, to engage the Spanish government in negotiations to liberalize the colonial regime. And Morales Lemus was probably the most experienced of the group in those negotiations, serving as the point man for the Cuban side in the ill-fated Junta de Información in 1867, the swan song of the reformists. From the outset of the rebellion, Céspedes had placed a great emphasis on obtaining the support of the United States for the cause of Cuban independence.[24]

In the spring of 1869 the prospects for that support appeared excellent. In March, Ulysses S. Grant was inaugurated president of the United States, and his new secretary of war was a well-known supporter of the Cuban cause, Grant's friend and former aide-de-camp, John Rawlins.[25] Grant and Rawlins, as military men and Civil War veterans, were predisposed to supporting the Cuban rebels, especially as a way of settling the score with the Spanish government for its support of the Confederacy during the war.[26]

Even before his official diplomatic appointment by the new Céspedes government, Morales Lemus approached the Grant administration. According to Morales Lemus's secretary, Enrique Piñeyro, Grant received Morales Lemus at the White House and communicated to the Cuban an unmistakable message of hope for U.S. support: "Hold on a bit longer," he reportedly told Morales Lemus, "and you will obtain more than you expected."[27] Encouragement also came from Capitol Hill. On April 9, the day before the Cuban rebels promulgated their constitution at Guáimaro, the U.S. House of Representatives passed a resolution, by a vote of 98 to 25, recognizing the independence of the island and calling on the U.S. government to provide moral and material support to free Cuba from Spanish control.[28] But not everyone in Washington was convinced that the United States should support the rebels. Morales Lemus found

Grant's new secretary of state reticent to have his government recognize and assist the Cuban rebellion against Spain.

* * *

Hamilton Fish was born on Stuyvesant Street in Manhattan, a descendant, on his mother's side, of Peter Stuyvesant.[29] In 1869, when Grant offered him the top job at the State Department, Fish was already sixty and had served as congressman, senator, and governor of New York. He was the president of the New York Historical Society and was looking ahead to a quiet retirement in the estate he had acquired in Garrison-on-Hudson, across the river from West Point.[30] A man tempered by his experience in public service, especially the debates and compromises of the antebellum Congresses, he had a conciliatory and cautious nature well suited for diplomacy and represented a well-reasoned voice in Grant's cabinet. Very early in his tenure as secretary of state, Fish realized that one of his most important roles in the new administration was to balance what he regarded as Grant's impulsiveness.[31]

Of all the problems Fish faced as secretary of state, the "most exigent and disturbing," according to his biographer Allan Nevins, was Cuba.[32] American public opinion and the press were sympathetic to the rebel cause. Fish's experience, however, predisposed him to oppose any U.S. involvement in Cuba. In 1855, when he was in the U.S. Senate, he took a trip to the island and although he was quite taken by its beauty and charm, he concluded that Cuba was a thoroughly foreign place with an entrenched landed elite, a people that could never be absorbed into the United States. When he became a member of the Senate Foreign Relations Committee he discouraged any proposal to acquire Cuba by wresting it from Spanish control.[33] Furthermore, Fish had misgivings about the New York émigré leaders, doubting their disposition to truly sacrifice for their cause, given their elite origins and the style in which many of them lived in the city. Nevins, his biographer, put it this way:

Fish was decidedly suspicious of the New York Junta. He knew that these Cuban officers—some careful to keep a thousand miles from the battle-front, and to meet the hated Spaniard in Union Square, with a tailor in one flank, a washerwoman on the other, and Delmonico's in the rear—were constantly plotting to violate our neutrality laws.[34]

Even if as secretary of state Fish had placed aside his biases regarding U.S. involvement in Cuba, the fact was that recognizing and supporting Cuban belligerency would have placed the United States in an untenable position. The Cubans were indeed violating U.S. neutrality laws. Furthermore, for Fish the question of Cuba was enmeshed in a much broader, and far more important, set of issues involving the relationship of the United States with Europe in the post–Civil War period. A sunken Confederate warship was at the heart of those issues and became the principal concern for Fish as soon as he took office.

The *Alabama* was a steamer built in Liverpool and launched on July 29, 1862. It had been commissioned by the Confederate States of America and secretly delivered to its navy over Washington's strong objections to the British government. The *Alabama* went on to inflict significant losses to Union shipping. In its first year alone it captured forty-eight Northern merchant ships. It was finally sunk by the U.S.S. *Kearsarge* off the coast of Cherbourg on June 19, 1864.[35]

After the war, the losses caused by the *Alabama* became the flash point of U.S. claims and recriminations against the British for the many ways they helped to arm and support the Confederacy. The prevailing opinion in the United States was that Britain's actions had prolonged the war. As the historian Adrian Cook noted, "America felt betrayed, insulted, and injured. At no time since the close of the War of 1812 had Anglo-American relations been worse than they were at the end of the Civil War."[36]

The Grant administration aggressively pursued reparations with the London government for the losses caused by the *Alabama* and other Confederate vessels built in Britain. It was a priority for Fish, and the resulting Treaty of Washington, signed in 1871, which provided for the settlement of the claims by an international tribunal of arbitration, was considered a triumph of diplomacy and perhaps his greatest achievement as secretary of state.[37] Not only did London end up paying $15.5 million in gold as reparations, but the treaty led to an improvement in relations with Great Britain, an important goal for Fish. In that context, recognizing the Cuban insurgent government and providing it with material support seemed to Fish to be a glaring contradiction that would have undermined U.S. claims against the British.[38] The United States maintained good relations with Spain, and supporting the Cuban rebels was viewed by Fish as akin to the British support of the Confederacy. On March 24, 1869, when he met with Morales Lemus in Washington, Fish kept the Cuban at arm's length, insisting that the meeting was unofficial (a conversation between gentlemen), and he refused to accept any document that Morales Lemus offered to him, lest it be interpreted as a signal that the United States was willing to recognize the Céspedes government.[39] Fish wrote in his diary that he told Morales Lemus that "whatever might be our sympathies with a people . . . struggling for a more liberal government, we should not depart from our duty to other friendly governments."[40]

Despite Grant's predisposition to help the rebels and Rawlins's insistence on it, Fish was able to prevail upon the president to look at the larger picture and abandon his support for the Cuban insurgents. At one point Grant had even signed a proclamation officially recognizing the Cubans' right to belligerence, forwarding it on to Fish, who simply shelved it and let it die without ever releasing it.[41]

On June 20, 1869, Fish summoned Morales Lemus to his home in Washington and informed him that there would be no recognition of the Céspedes government or of the Cubans' right to belligerence and therefore no support for the insurgency. But he had an alternative plan he presented to Morales Lemus, one that had already been approved by Grant and the cabinet.[42] The plan was to have the United States enter into negotiations with Spain for the purpose of securing Cuban independence. The specifics were (1) Spanish recognition of the independence of Cuba; (2) Cuban payment to Spain of an indemnity for the loss of revenue associated with abandoning the island (a figure later set at $100 million, the same figure President Polk had offered years before, with payment guaranteed by the U.S. government); (3) the abolition of slavery; and (4) an armistice during the negotiations.[43] Morales Lemus was disappointed, but signed off on the proposal.[44] The old reformist, who had failed to extract any concessions from the Spanish only two years before during the meetings of the Junta de Información in Madrid, was skeptical of the success of a plan to negotiate with the Madrid government over the future of Cuba.[45]

Morales Lemus's skepticism turned out to be justified. The Spanish government initially voiced interest in the proposal, but dragged out the negotiations over three months and finally formulated a response that in both content and language was unacceptable to Fish.[46] It was, according to Piñeyro, "an insulting and sarcastic" response, which, among other things, called upon the United States to show its "sympathy and good faith to Spain" by "advising the members of the Cuban Junta of New York, who are totally unworthy of the hospitality they receive, to cease fomenting insurrection."[47] On September 28 Fish withdrew his offer of negotiation.[48] The only proposal Fish had been willing to make for a U.S. role in changing the status of the island had failed. Morales Lemus's mission in Washington had already suffered a setback a couple of weeks before with the death of Rawlins, the émigrés' strongest ally in the Grant cabinet.

The failure of Morales Lemus's lobbying efforts was a turning point in émigré activism on behalf of the Cuban insurgents. Without prospects for U.S. support, the lobbying effort was abandoned and the New Yorkers' role was reduced to supporting the military effort in Cuba through fundraising and the shipment of arms and men to the island. That purpose favored men of action, not well-connected elites, so the legitimacy of Morales Lemus and his group as leaders of the émigré movement was now questionable. The backing of Céspedes for Morales Lemus and his group had been based on their value as representatives in Washington. Those in New York who had resented their takeover of the émigré leadership now intensified their criticisms, especially since the old reformists had in effect confirmed the worst suspicions about them when they bought in to Fish's plan to negotiate with Spain. Any negotiation was perceived by Morales Lemus's critics as a willingness to settle for something less than what the rebellion was all about: total independence.

Morales Lemus was still reeling from the failure of his diplomatic mission when he presided over the anniversary event at the Cooper Institute the evening of October 11. Less than a month later he resigned from the top post of the New York junta, turning it over to the man who, because of his economic influence, was the natural leader of the Havana reformist elite: Miguel Aldama.[49] Morales Lemus remained active in émigré activities, especially through meetings and correspondence with friends such as José Manuel Mestre.[50] But a chronic intestinal ailment eventually confined him to his home at 369 Bedford Avenue in Brooklyn.[51] On June 28, 1870, three weeks after he was enumerated by the U.S. census, Morales Lemus died at the age of sixty-two. He is buried in Green-Wood Cemetery.

* * *

Miguel Aldama had arrived in New York in May 1869, somewhat later than the rest of the Havana group (see chapter 4). Prior to Morales Lemus's resignation he had not assumed a position in the junta, perhaps preferring not to become involved in the diplomatic effort that was already under way.

Aldama's rise to the presidency of a newly restructured junta in November 1869 did little to bridge the growing divisions among Cuban New Yorkers—quite the contrary. His wealth and aristocratic demeanor provided a bigger target than Morales Lemus for those in New York who mistrusted the actions and motives of the reformist group. Furthermore, the new junta under Aldama was still dominated by the newly arrived Havana group that Morales Lemus had placed in key positions. José Manuel Mestre, Aldama's relative and Morales Lemus's protégé, was assigned the diplomatic functions that Morales Lemus had once exercised

Figure 6.1. Miguel Aldama. Source: *Harper's Weekly*, December 4, 1869, 769.

Figure 6.2. Cirilo Villaverde. Source: Roberto Méndez Martínez, "La casa de dementes vista por Cirilo Villaverde," *Hotel Telégrafo* (blog), January 14, 2016, www.hoteltelegrafo. blogspot.com.

as minister in the United States, but with the title of "commissioner of the Republic."[52] José Antonio Echeverría was also given that title, to act, if necessary, in Mestre's stead. Aldama, as the leader, had the title of "agent general of the Cuban Republic." The reformists in New York would henceforth be referred to by both contemporaries and historians as the *aldamistas*.

Spearheading the attacks on the *aldamistas* was a married couple who had resided in New York since the days of Narciso López and the annexationists: Cirilo Villaverde and Emilia Casanova. Villaverde was a writer and educator, a native of Pinar del Río, historically a backwater province west of Havana. In 1848 he was imprisoned for collaborating with the López expeditions, and the following year he escaped to New York, where he served as secretary to Narciso López and wrote for *La Verdad*, the annexationist newspaper. Villaverde lived for a while in Philadelphia, where in 1854 at the age of forty-two he married Emilia Casanova, who was twenty years younger than he, the daughter of a Spanish-born landowner from Cárdenas, a port city in the Matanzas region. The following year the couple moved to New York, where Villaverde taught Spanish in private schools and also gave private lessons. For a few years starting in 1864 they operated a school across the Hudson in Weehawken, New Jersey, while becoming active in separatist activities.[53]

In July 1869 Villaverde drafted a lengthy and carefully annotated tract entitled *Cuba's Revolution as Seen from New York*, intended as an unsolicited report to Céspedes on what was happening among émigrés in the city, especially what Villaverde regarded as the misdeeds and missteps of Morales Lemus's junta. In November of that year, after the resignation of Morales Lemus and the ascension of Aldama to the presidency of the junta, Villaverde had a revised version of his report printed and distributed widely among Cubans in New York.[54] It contained a litany of accusations against Morales Lemus and the junta, starting with the manner in which the group, in Villaverde's view, usurped the leadership role among the émigrés by falsely claiming to represent the Céspedes government before such representation was granted by the Assembly in Cuba. Noting that almost all members of the junta were Havana lawyers, Villaverde argued that others with a longer history of separatist activism in the United States were pushed aside in favor of those with little political experience: "Friendship brought them together in Havana and kept them together here. . . . Birds of a feather flock together."[55] Villaverde also claimed that the new group from Havana attempted to control and monopolize all revolutionary activities in New York, and then proceeded to botch everything up through its incompetency and lack of dedication. Morales Lemus was especially criticized for agreeing to Fish's proposal to negotiate with Spain, which, Villaverde argued, was something that Morales Lemus was not authorized to do and that responded to the eagerness of the Havana group to negotiate away Cuban independence and place the island's destiny in the hands of the Grant administration.[56]

The report was one of the first of many bitter salvos that would be leveled at the *aldamistas* by fellow Cuban New Yorkers. Villaverde's attacks were scathing enough, but the truly acerbic pen in the Villaverde-Casanova marriage was not his.

Figure 6.3. Emilia Casanova. Source: *Apuntes biográficos de Emilia Casanova de Villaverde, escritos por un contemporáneo* (New York, 1874), General Research Division, New York Public Library, Astor, Lenox and Tilden Foundations.

Emilia Casanova was one of sixteen children born to a Cuban woman, Petronia Rodríguez, and an immigrant from the Canary Islands, Inocencio Casanova.[57] Inocencio owned considerable land in Matanzas, but suffered heavy losses when a hurricane struck the area. When Emilia was very young, the Casanova family relocated to Cárdenas. There she gave evidence very early of what one of her biographers called a "willful character."[58] The Casanova household was frequently thrown into disarray because of her obstinacies in pursuing her projects and whims. Her personality was matched by her appearance. By age twelve she had, according to one biographer, the physical development of a young woman of fifteen, and her athleticism gave her a vigorous presence that matched her headstrong behavior.[59]

Emilia Casanova's life-defining moment came on May 19, 1850, when she opened her bedroom window to see, for the first time ever, the

Cuban flag, which had been raised over Cárdenas's main square by Narciso López during his brief occupation of the city.[60] The López expedition eventually failed, but it marked Emilia Casanova for life. At age eighteen she had a found a purpose to her life and a channel for her passion and energy: Cuban independence. Young Emilia's epiphany would prove a huge headache for her father, who despite not being a supporter of Cuban separatism, found that his family came under increasing scrutiny from the authorities for his daughter's public criticisms of Spanish rule.

In the summer of 1852, Inocencio Casanova decided it was best to temporarily relocate his family to the United States, where, after visiting New York, Niagara Falls, Saratoga, and Albany, they settled in Philadelphia.[61] It was there in 1854 that the twenty-two-year-old Emilia Casanova met and married Villaverde, who impressed her with his résumé of sacrifice on behalf of Cuban separatism. Emilia and Cirilo stayed in the United States and moved to New York when her family returned to Cuba. Eventually they had three children, although their only daughter died before her seventh birthday.[62]

Throughout the 1860s, the couple remained active in New York émigré politics. They were involved in 1866 in the creation of the Junta Republicana de Cuba y Puerto Rico.[63] In 1867 Emilia, anticipating the coming war, prevailed upon her father to liquidate his assets in Cuba and move permanently to New York. For $150,000 Inocencio bought the old Leggett mansion on Oak Point, in what is now the Hunts Point area in the Bronx.[64] Originally part of the estate of the family of writer and political reformist William Leggett, the house had been totally renovated by a wealthy New York grocer named Benjamin Whitlock, who built vaults underneath the house to store wine. Whitlock lost most of his fortune with the decline in the cotton trade during the Civil War, and the house was shuttered when the Casanovas bought it in November 1867.[65] When the war broke out the following year, the house became a hotbed of militant activity in the New York area. Favoring action over negotiation, Emilia Casanova helped to organize more than a few expeditions to take men and arms to Céspedes, to whom she was fervently loyal. The mansion's vaults were converted into storehouses for guns, rifles, powder, and ammunition. Its relatively isolated location near the coast made it ideal for discreetly smuggling ordnance out to the East River or to the

Long Island Sound for shipment to Cuba.[66] The neighbors were well aware of the secret activities going on, and years later, after the Casanovas moved out and it stood deserted, the house retained a mysterious reputation. As Stephen Jenkins, a historian of the Bronx, wrote in 1912,

> The visits of the dark-skinned, mysterious-looking men ceased, and the house was deserted; while whispers of murdered Spanish spies and of ghosts and strange and unaccountable noises in the vacant house filled the neighborhood. . . . So many weird tales were told about the old mansion that its demolition was watched with intense interest.[67]

In addition to helping outfit expeditions from the Bronx, Casanova traveled to Manhattan almost daily organizing fundraising events. In January 1869 she established the organization La Liga de las Hijas de Cuba (League of Cuba's Daughters) as a way of organizing the Cuban ladies of the city on behalf of the insurgents. It also served as her political platform. The League was the first ever political association organized by a Cuban woman.[68] In March, the League sponsored a theatrical performance that raised nearly $4,000 for the Cuban cause.[69] Casanova was also a prolific letter writer, staying in touch with Cubans, especially ladies, living in different parts of the world, corresponding even with Cuban generals on the battlefield, and soliciting support for the cause of independence from members of the U.S. Congress and from world leaders, including Giuseppe Garibaldi (who actually replied with a cordial letter supporting the oppressed everywhere).[70] She reportedly met with Grant and Fish on more than one occasion.[71]

From the beginning, however, Emilia Casanova and Cirilo Villaverde were at odds with Morales Lemus and the junta. The conflict, at least initially, stemmed from the resentment that Casanova and Villaverde must have felt from being overlooked, after years of activism in New York, by the newly arrived Havana group as it attempted to monopolize all émigré political activities in the city. In his report to Céspedes, Villaverde maintained that Morales Lemus did everything possible to control the leadership and finances of the League of Cuba's Daughters, to the point of encouraging the creation of a rival women's group subordinated to the junta.[72] In that same report, Villaverde also mentioned that he had addressed a letter to Morales Lemus pointing out the need to name a representative of the insurgents to London and that he was soliciting the appointment. Villaverde never received a response.[73]

Villaverde and Casanova were not the junta's only detractors. Carlos del Castillo, the Havana banker and Moses Taylor client who had been deported to Fernando Póo, was also a critic of the *aldamistas*.[74] In 1870 his cousin, José Gabriel del Castillo, started publishing in New York the newspaper *El Demócrata*, which was usually filled with tracts against the junta. The *aldamistas* had earlier established their own newspaper, *La Revolución*, also printed in New York and directed by Nestor Ponce de León and Enrique Piñeyro.[75]

Two events in 1870 served to bitterly and definitively widen the breach between the *aldamistas* and their detractors in New York. The first involved a deposed Cuban general; the second, a poet.

* * *

General Manuel de Quesada y Loynaz was from a Camagüeyano family that had first established itself on the island in the early seventeenth century.[76] In April 1869, with the adoption of a constitution and the establishment of the Cuban Republic, the Cuban Assembly (the new government's legislative body) elected Céspedes as president and named Quesada commander-in-chief of the army.[77] Almost immediately thereafter the relations between the Assembly and its chief military officer began to sour. General Quesada had an authoritarian character and rejected any oversight by the Assembly over his command.[78] The Assembly perceived that he was acting as a military dictator without accountability to the government, and on December 22, 1869, it relieved him of his duties and in his place named General Thomas Jordan, the former Confederate who had arrived in Cuba in the *Perrit* expedition.[79]

The Assembly's removal of Quesada from his command placed President Céspedes in an awkward position. Only a few weeks before, on November 4, Céspedes, a widower, had married Quesada's sister Ana in Camagüey.[80] After Quesada's dismissal, Céspedes, without consulting the Assembly or even his own cabinet, gave his brother-in-law the assignment of going to New York and raising funds in support of the revolution. The move did not sit well with the Assembly and marked the beginning of a deterioration in the relationship between Céspedes and the legislative body of the insurgents.[81]

Quesada arrived in New York on March 1, 1870, with instructions from Céspedes to raise money and organize expeditions. Because Céspedes had named him without the approval of the Assembly, Quesada was not the official representative of the Cuban Republic in the United States. That designation still belonged to Aldama. The arrival of Quesada in New York was not viewed favorably by the *aldamistas*, who saw the general's assignment as an indication that Céspedes no longer had full confidence in them. The Havana group had not only failed in its diplomatic mission, but it had not been very successful in organizing expeditions. Céspedes may well have started listening to the criticisms of the junta's detractors. Those detractors, especially Emilia Casanova, welcomed the arrival of Quesada with open arms, and saw the general as a man of action who had been sent by Céspedes to put the *aldamistas* in their place and provide effective leadership to the émigrés.

As soon as he arrived in New York, Quesada met with Aldama, Mestre, and Echeverría and presented to them an ambitious plan to raise money and organize a large expeditionary force. The junta's mistrust of Quesada's mission, as well as reports that reached them from members of the Assembly about the general's authoritarian character, predisposed the *aldamistas* to withhold any support for the plan.[82] The junta's reticence prompted Quesada to proceed on his own, even setting up an account with Moses Taylor, managed by Carlos del Castillo, to collect funds and buy armaments.[83] Contrary to the wishes of Céspedes, Quesada and the junta went their separate ways.

The division in the émigré ranks was made worse when Aldama, possibly as a snub to Quesada, organized a collection to buy an engraved sword as a token of appreciation for General Jordan, Quesada's replacement in Cuba.[84] Emilia Casanova was outraged. She mobilized the League of Cuba's Daughters to buy Quesada his own engraved sword, which she presented to him at an event she organized at Irving Hall on June 29, 1870.[85]

Thereafter, the faction opposed to the *aldamistas* would be known as the *quesadistas*. Rival engraved swords were drawn, emblematic of the drawing of battle lines between the two émigré factions in New York.

* * *

But nothing aroused more passion and recriminations among the émigrés than the ill-fated mission to the island of a highly regarded poet who lived in New York, Juan Clemente Zenea. Zenea was a committed revolutionary with a long history of militant activism against Spanish rule in Cuba, and in the late 1850s he was forced to flee the island for New York. In 1859 he published a book about his experiences as an exile with the title *Far from the Homeland: Memoirs of a Young Poet,* followed two years later by a far-ranging essay on trends in U.S. literature.[86] He also dedicated a poem to Green-Wood Cemetery, where, he wrote, he wished "to rest in peace."[87]

Zenea's tragic story begins in early August 1870, with the arrival in New York from Madrid of his friend Nicolás Azcárate, a man with a full pedigree as a member of the Havana reformist group. An affable lawyer with a distinguished presence, he had collaborated with *El Siglo,* had served in the Junta de Información, and had married into the Fesser banking family.[88] Unlike his colleagues, however, Azcárate remained an unabashed reformist who opposed the war. Even so, his support for reforms made him the target of the *voluntarios* and he fled to Spain. In Madrid he founded a newspaper in which he argued for the abolition of slavery, an end to hostilities on the island, and the implementation of the liberal reforms he had always advocated so that Cuba would be granted self-rule while remaining part of Spain.[89] Obviously, his position made him the target of virulent attacks from both extremes: Spanish hardliners and Cuban revolutionaries.[90]

Given his political agenda and his personal connections at the highest levels of the Spanish government, Azcárate's arrival in New York was greeted with the rumor that he was the bearer of an offer of negotiation from the Spanish government for Céspedes. The rumors even made it into the New York press, and Azcárate was compelled to send a note to the New York Associated Press flatly denying that his trip had any political purpose: "While, as a Cuban, I deplore that a misunderstanding between many of my countrymen and modern Spain should keep up in Cuba a cruel and ruinous war, . . . I am not the bearer of any mission whatever."[91]

But he was. Azcárate met with Aldama, Mestre, and Echeverría to elicit their collaboration in communicating to Céspedes an offer from the Spanish government that had three major points: (1) an immediate ceasefire, (2) the disbanding of the *voluntarios*, and (3) autonomy (not independence) for the island.[92] Zenea agreed to go to Cuba and personally present the offer to Céspedes. The poet carried with him a document signed by the Spanish minister in Washington, Mauricio López Roberts, guaranteeing him safe passage through Spanish-held areas of the island so that he could meet with Céspedes.[93]

Zenea reached Céspedes's camp. There is no reliable record of what the two men talked about.[94] The only known result of the meeting is that Céspedes asked Zenea to escort his wife out of Cuba and to New York for her safety. Zenea, of course, agreed, but before he and Ana de Quesada could leave the island they were intercepted near the coast by a Spanish troop, which took them to Havana under custody. Ana de Quesada was released shortly thereafter and allowed to leave for New York. But Zenea was imprisoned, accused of treason, and eventually executed in La Cabaña fortress.[95] He was unable to fulfill his desire to be buried at Green-Wood.

We do not know what message, if any, Zenea was carrying back from Céspedes, nor do we know for certain why Zenea's guarantee of safe passage was not honored by the Spanish.[96] What we do know is that once the entire plan became known, it landed like a bombshell among Cuban New Yorkers. As far as the *quesadistas* were concerned, the *aldamistas* had been caught red-handed doing what they were always suspected of favoring: negotiating to end the war and continue Spanish rule in Cuba so that their properties on the island would be spared.

Leading the outcry, of course, was Emilia Casanova. *El Demócrata* printed a statement signed by her on behalf of the League of Cuba's Daughters in which Zenea was pronounced a traitor for having been commissioned by Azcárate to carry out a mission with the "purpose of deceiving President Céspedes and disheartening the patriots there and discredit those here . . . so as to make them desist from their determination to liberate Cuba by the force of arms."[97] Casanova went on, in what the historian Juan Casasús called "an explosion of indescribable rage," to call upon all Cubans to condemn Zenea to "perpetual infamy and the execration of mankind" and to regard Aldama and Mestre as "principal accomplices in Zenea's dark treason . . . and as accomplices do not deserve the trust of Cuban patriots."[98]

Although in the past the junta had refrained from replying to Casanova's attacks, the virulence of the accusations prompted Aldama, Mestre, and Echeverría to issue a reply in the form of a thirteen-page printed document entitled "The Commissioners and the Agent General of the Republic of Cuba in the United States, to all Cubans."[99] While admitting that they had knowledge of Azcárate's mission and had contact with Zenea regarding his trip to Cuba, the junta members denied having supported the negotiation initiative, producing as evidence a document in which they had communicated to Azcárate that the Spanish proposal did not contain anything new beyond what had already been rejected numerous times by the Madrid government and that the possibility of negotiating for anything short of independence was unacceptable.[100] Aldama and his colleagues also addressed, with more than a tinge of sexism, the source of the "bastard insinuations" against them:

> To make even more painful the wound, the weapon has been placed in hands that, given the sex to which they belong, should more readily be used to pour ointment on the sores of the homeland than to deliver disastrous blows.[101]

Emilia Casanova's blows had indeed struck deep. Despite the junta's disavowals, most Cuban New Yorkers probably found unconvincing the *aldamistas'* protestations that while having knowledge of the Zenea mission they did not support it. The Zenea debacle came at a particularly difficult time in Aldama's life. Only a few months before, his father, Domingo, who had accompanied him to New York, had died. Miguel's wife, Hilaria Fonts, remained ill after suffering a stroke, and she died in April 1871.[102] Aldama buried both of them in a mausoleum he purchased near the main entrance to Green-Wood Cemetery in Brooklyn.

Miguel Aldama eventually tendered his resignation to Céspedes as the agent general of the Republic. In effect, the junta ceased to exist. This, however, was not enough to satisfy Casanova, who for years thereafter continued to rail against the *aldamistas*, accusing them of having a hand in just about every setback suffered by the revolution. Even her adulatory biographer recognized that she committed "errors because of that trait that situated her at the extremes. . . . Her temperament dragged her through the turbulent path of partiality."[103] She was not above using sarcasm and ridicule. She always referred to Aldama as *el benemérito* (the worthy one). In one especially inflammatory printed tract from the League of Cuba's Daughters, written in 1874 and signed by her, she refers to the "notorious ineptitude of *el benemérito*" and labels his service to the cause of independence "an absurd pretension." She goes on: "If *el benemérito* Aldama does not want, can, nor knows how to be useful to the homeland, he should step aside and not be a hindrance. . . . He not only fails to do anything useful, but keeps others from doing so."[104]

Many *quesadistas* shared the intense personal dislike that Casanova evidently had for Aldama and his group, a dislike that went beyond simple political rivalries. The papers of Carlos del Castillo, which form part of the archives of Moses Taylor and Company, contain some of the internal correspondence of the *quesadista* group as well as printed ephemera the group distributed among Cubans in New York.[105] Some of the correspondence and tracts were unsigned and even in code, using sequences of numbers to mask the names of collaborators.[106] But there was no caution at all in the language and tone used in the references to the *aldamistas*. In one anonymous letter, written in a very small and careful handwriting, references are made to Aldama, "that trader in Chinese laborers, a mannequin without a mind"; and to Mestre, "social climber par excellence, consummate schemer." Not even the deceased Morales Lemus was spared: "M. Lemus . . . went down the drain and died of diarrhea when his ineptitude became evident."[107]

To be sure, resentment toward the *aldamistas* was well justified on several grounds: their high-handed takeover of the leadership in New York, their refusal to cooperate with General Quesada, their presumptive role in the Zenea affair, and their failure at both diplomacy and the outfitting of expeditions. But the level of invectiveness directed at them by Casanova and her associates had a more profound cause, and direct clues to the cause can be found throughout the writings of the *quesadista* group. In a letter written by José Gabriel del Castillo to his cousin Carlos del Castillo we find the following description:

Those who constitute the Junta, men who believe themselves to be representatives of Cuba and pretend to govern us because they see themselves as worthier than us, . . . those who live in abundance and have fortunes

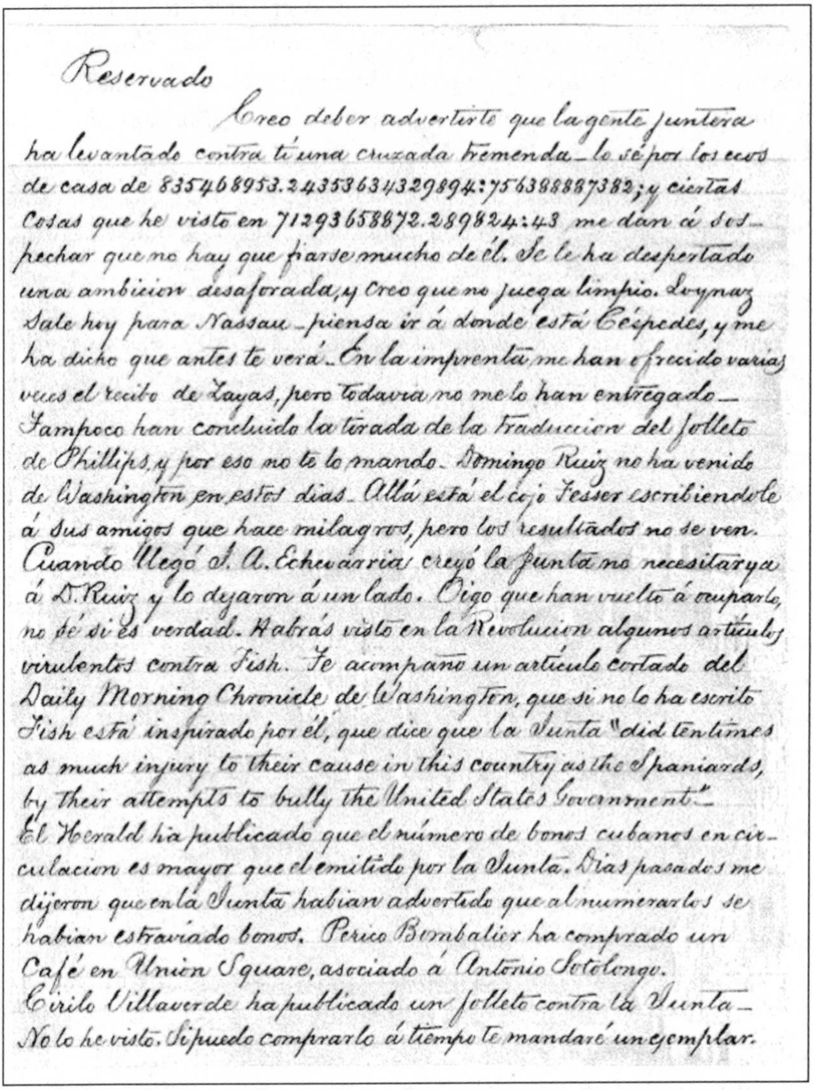

Reservado

Creo deber advertirte que la gente juntera
ha levantado contra ti una cruzada tremenda – lo sé por los ecos
de casa de 835468953.24353634329894:7563888887383; y ciertas
cosas que he visto en 71293658872.289824:43, me dan á sos-
pechar que no hay que fiarse mucho de él. Se le ha despertado
una ambición desaforada, y creo que no juega limpio. Loynaz
sale hoy para Nassau – piensa ir á donde está Céspedes, y me
ha dicho que antes te verá. En la imprenta me han ofrecido varias
veces el recibo de Zayas, pero todavía no me lo han entregado –
Tampoco han concluido la tirada de la traducción del folleto
de Phillips, y por eso no te lo mando. Domingo Ruiz no ha venido
de Washington en estos días. Allá está el ojo Tesser escribiéndole
á sus amigos que hace milagros, pero los resultados no se ven.
Cuando llegó J. A. Echevarría creyó la junta no necesitarya
á D. Ruiz y lo dejaron á un lado. Oigo que han vuelto á ocuparle,
no sé si es verdad. Habrás visto en la Revolución algunos artículos
virulentos contra Fish. Te acompaño un artículo cortado del
Daily Morning Chronicle de Washington, que si no lo ha escrito
Fish está inspirado por él, que dice que la Junta "did ten times
as much injury to their cause in this country as the Spaniards,
by their attempts to bully the United States Government"–
El Herald ha publicado que el número de bonos cubanos en cir-
culación es mayor que el emitido por la Junta. Días pasados me
dijeron que en la Junta habían advertido que al numerarlos se
habían estraviado bonos. Perico Bombalier ha comprado un
Café en Union Square, asociado á Antonio Sotolongo.
Cirilo Villaverde ha publicado un folleto contra la Junta –
No lo he visto. Si puedo comprarlo á tiempo te mandaré un ejemplar.

Figure 6.4. Message written partly in code sent from one *quesadista* to another in New York, underscoring the degree of mistrust that existed among the émigrés. Source: Moses Taylor Papers, Manuscripts and Archives Division, New York Public Library.

deposited in banks, who ride around in carriages and make ostentatious displays of luxury during vacations in Saratoga without ever remembering the sufferings of those who are fighting for their liberty.[108]

In a letter to a friend in Charleston, South Carolina, Emilia Casanova, as she did on numerous occasions, also expressed that same class-based view:

> You ask me who is Aldama, and I answer simply that he is not one of us. Firstly, because of his fortune he belongs to the moneyed aristocracy, and secondly, because of his upbringing, habits, and close contact with the conservative faction, which he accepts, he does not want revolution, because he is sure that with its triumph, democracy, the people, will rule in a free and independent Cuba.[109]

Casanova was fond of using yet another sarcastic nickname, this one mocking the lifestyle of the *aldamistas*: *pasteleros*, that is, those who eat fancy pastries, or *pasteles*, which is what they allegedly did as they took drives around the city in their carriages.[110]

As we saw in previous chapters, the members of the Havana group had long sold their sugar in New York and maintained sizable accounts in the city with financial firms such as Moses Taylor, making it possible for them to enjoy a luxurious exile, even bringing their former house slaves and indentured servants to help them maintain a style not usually associated with refugees. But for others, such as the Villaverde-Casanovas, who were longtime residents of the city but were never wealthy enough to outlast the war's economic effects and the separation from their sources of income on the island, their life in New York was usually a hardship. So too it was for the easterners who started arriving from the war zone without any previous financial connection to New York and therefore with no appreciable source of funds awaiting them in the city.

These stark economic differences naturally led to deep resentments, especially since the *aldamistas*, who presumed to be the leaders of the émigrés and the representatives of the insurgent Republic, were not doing what the easterners and others had done: risking their lives and sacrificing everything to attain Cuban independence. This reinforced the suspicion that the members of the Havana group remained reform-

ists and not fully committed to the success of the revolution, always pro-
tecting their economic interests. One historian, Dionisio Poey Baró, has
even suggested that the *aldamistas* were less than enthusiastic in supporting the armed struggle on the island because they did not want the
war to spread to the west, where their embargoed properties, which they
hoped to recover, were located.[111] José Gabriel del Castillo said as much
in a letter to his cousin Carlos:

> When the leaders of the insurrection threw themselves into battle, risking
> life, family, and everything they owned, the social climbers of Havana,
> who are the ones that make up the New York Junta, did everything they
> could to prevent an uprising in the Western Department.[112]

It was inevitable that the factionalism in New York would take on the
character of a class-based conflict as the Havana group was increasingly
challenged by longtime revolutionary émigrés and the newly arrived
easterners from the battle zones.[113]

Whatever their motives, there is no question that the *aldamistas*,
especially their leader, did not set an example of self-sacrifice for the
cause. While serving as agent general of the Republic, Aldama was busy
investing a fortune in the construction of a huge sugar refinery on the
Brooklyn waterfront.[114] Named after Aldama's embargoed sugar mill in
Cuba, the Santa Rosa sugar refinery was built in 1873 and towered over
all the other buildings in the Red Hook area. It had a chimney 140 feet
in height, surrounded by a complex of buildings, of which the tallest was
the filter house, which rose ten stories, or 120 feet. The entire property
occupied a lot 200 by 125 feet with direct access to the Atlantic Basin
and on to the Buttermilk Channel and New York Harbor. The cost of its
construction was estimated at half a million dollars.[115] After its comple-
tion, the *Brooklyn Daily Eagle* hailed it as "one of the largest and finest
sugar refineries" in Brooklyn and Manhattan."[116] Aldama was making
this very visible investment at a time when the money to outfit expeditions was increasingly scarce.

Emilia Casanova did not let Aldama's priorities go unnoticed:

> The much-touted patriotism of *el benemérito* Aldama is so small, living,
> as he does, in opulence, he does not make the least sacrifice to remedy

the needs of the soldiers of the homeland, who lack even the basics. . . . If he wishes to maintain himself in the prominent position in which, to our misfortune, he has placed himself, he should contribute amply with his money, the only thing that can be expected of him.[117]

Although the bitter division between *aldamistas* and *quesadistas* hampered the effectiveness of the community in supporting the war in Cuba, it also meant there was a decentralization, or fragmentation, in the various separatist efforts, with a resulting proliferation in the number and types of activities carried out in New York on behalf of Cuban independence. There were rival newspapers representing the different factions, even a pro-Spanish one, *La Crónica*, and they continually sparred with each other.[118] There were fundraising events, such as bazaars and concerts, held by competing organizations. In just two months of 1869, for example, three separate benefits were held in Manhattan for the Cuban cause. One was the concert on March 9 organized by Emilia Casanova and the League of Cuba's Daughters.[119] Another benefit concert, "for the relief of the sick and wounded of the patriot army of Cuba," was held at Irving Hall on March 20 before a "large and fashionable audience" and featured music performances, poetry recitations, and an emotive patriotic speech by a Mr. R. J. De Córdova.[120] In April, a three-day bazaar was organized in Apollo Hall, at Broadway and 28th Street, to sell donated jewelry, art pieces, home furnishings, and even a horse. It was sponsored by the Patriotic Junta of Cuban Women, a rival organization to Casanova's League.[121]

Rallies featuring fiery speeches on behalf of the Cuban cause raised money by charging admission or taking up collections. Some of these events were organized by Cubans, others by sympathetic Americans, but their principal function was to demonstrate that many prominent New Yorkers supported a greater U.S. role in helping the rebels. One event, on March 25, 1869, at Steinway Hall, included such New York luminaries as the writer and poet William Cullen Bryant, Charles Dana of the *New York Sun*, Henry Ward Beecher, brother of Harriet and a Presbyterian minister and abolitionist, James Gordon Bennett of the *New York Herald*, the prominent trial lawyer John K. Porter, the founder of *Harper's Weekly* and Harper Brothers, Fletcher Harper Jr., and Simeon Leland, the Manhattan hotelier.[122] Only a month later, many of those same persons held yet another "mass meeting," as it was called, at the Cooper Institute to "give expression of their sympathy for the patriotic Cubans now struggling heroically against Spanish oppression and barbarity."[123] They were joined on that occasion by Mayor Oakey Hall. Only a few days before, the New York City Board of Aldermen had passed a resolution instructing the mayor to "memoralize [sic] the Government of the United States, in behalf of the Corporation of the City of New York, to render all the assistance in its power to the patriots' cause in Cuba."[124]

Many Cubans in New York busied themselves in 1869 and 1870 garnering such support from prominent Americans on behalf of a favorable U.S. policy toward the revolution. Juan Manuel Macías, apparently acting independently of the junta, assembled a long list of governors, members of Congress, and other prominent Americans and formed an organization called the Cuban League of the United States, with an executive committee composed primarily of former Civil War generals.[125] José Manuel Mestre became a member of the American Foreign Anti-Slavery Society, headed by the Reverend Henry Highland Garnet, with offices at 102 West 3rd Street.[126]

The post–Civil War movement to abolish slavery in other countries represented a fertile ground for eliciting support for the Cuban cause, given the expectation that a victory for the rebels would lead to the abolition of slavery on the island. A meeting of African Americans held at the Cooper Institute on December 13, 1872, in support of Cuban independence was covered by almost all of New York's daily newspapers, which in unison echoed the New York Sun's praise for the willingness of the city's "colored residents" to "at last . . . take up the burden of their brothers in Cuba."[127] The New York Herald noted the presence in the meeting of some Cubans "from which we may infer that they are at the bottom of this movement."[128] A Spanish sympathizer, José Ferrer de Couto, editor of El Cronista, handed out leaflets at the meeting pointing out that many of the members of the Cuban junta were slave owners. The speakers at the meeting responded that El Cronista, which circulated in Cuba, ran ads for the sales of slaves.[129] Many of those attending the meeting subsequently formed the Cuban Anti-Slavery Committee, with offices at 62 Bowery, and issued a printed report that included the texts of the speeches delivered at the event as well as the group's declaration, condemning Spanish rule in Cuba and calling upon the U.S. government to give favorable recognition to the Cuban insurrection.[130] The report of the Cuban Anti-Slavery Committee was just one of many documents printed in English that appeared in New York with the purpose of establishing a climate favorable to Cuban independence. The campaign to win over the hearts and minds of Americans to the insurgents' side kept the city's printing presses busy. In 1870, for example, the Cuban junta produced a thirty-one-page booklet entitled "Facts about Cuba," which gave a statistical summary of Cuba's resources and infrastructure, its commerce with the United States, the damages caused by the war, and the alleged plunder of the island by the Spanish. The booklet also gave a favorable account of the advances of the revolutionaries on the battlefield and the obstinacy of the Spanish in defending their colony, and even included a copy of the constitution adopted by the rebels at Guáimaro. It was printed at the *Sun*'s printing office on Printing House Square.[131]

José de Armas y Céspedes, the brother of the publisher of *El Ateneo*, Juan Ignacio (see chapter 5), wrote several political tracts that he had printed in New York criticizing the hesitancy of the Grant administration to recognize and support the insurgents. In one of them, written in 1869 in the form of a diary, he assailed the logic that pursuing the *Alabama* claims against Britain prevented the Americans from recognizing "the patriots of Cuba . . . although they profess the same ideas and principles upheld by the United States."[132] In a subsequent essay, also printed in New York in English, de Armas made the argument that the insurrection and the government it represented fulfilled all the requirements for U.S. recognition.[133]

But perhaps the most persuasive, and certainly the most dramatic, of all the tracts printed in New York on behalf of the Cuban cause was *The Book of Blood*. Published anonymously, but primarily the work of José Ignacio Rodríguez, the first (1871) edition was printed (with the title in red letters) by "M. M. Zarzamendi, Translator & Printer, 40 & 42 Broadway."[134] It is an inventory of crimes committed by the Spanish in Cuba, chronologically arranged day by day, between October 1868 and December 1870. It lists 1,828 names of persons executed, murdered, disappeared, and arrested. There is also a list of 2,650 prisoners and another list of those deported from the island. A subsequent edition, printed in

1873 by the New York bookstore and publishing firm of Nestor Ponce de León, updated the figures to November 10, 1873.[135] The number of deaths, disappearances, and arrests rose to nearly 3,000 and the prisoner count to more than 4,500.

The Book of Blood was one of the highlights of émigré activism during this period. The Cuban community in New York during the 1870s was rich, not only in terms of wealth, but also in its intellectual resources. Publications such as The Book of Blood were the result of the best application of those resources to the struggle to influence American public opinion on behalf of the Cuban cause. The tragedy it so eloquently portrayed, the debacle of the war in Cuba, contrasted starkly with the petty and destructive factionalism that served to undermine the best efforts of Cuban New Yorkers to do something about the situation in their homeland.

These activities by Cuban émigrés and their sympathizers served to give the Cuban cause a visibility that was difficult to ignore. The New York press, especially the Herald, followed closely all Cuba-related events. Residents of the city were kept well informed of the progress of the war as well as the developments in Washington regarding the conflict and the statements and actions by the émigrés in New York. While they were designed to raise money and to pressure the Grant administration into supporting the revolution, the mass meetings, speeches, bazaars, publications, and press stories were not illegal activities. But organizing and outfitting expeditions and training men to fight in Cuba were indeed against the law, and yet, in the early days of the war these activities were carried out in New York as visibly as the rallies and fund-raisers. Reports of impending departures of men and ships for Cuba were carried by the press. Groups of armed Cubans would march in the city as part of parades or processions. In one large march, held in memory of the leaders of the Paris Commune and featuring Garibaldi Guards and a "colored section," all wearing red scarves, there were about twenty Cubans with "their national flag and the standards of The Lancers of Camaguey" marching from the Cooper Institute down the Bowery.[136] A group calling itself the Battalion of Hatuey's Hunters (Hatuey was an Indian chieftain who had rebelled against Spanish colonization of the island) marched on several occasions in 1869 from Washington Square up Fifth Avenue, then over to Fourth Avenue until they reached Union Square,

Figure 6.5. "Cuban Drill-Room in New York City." Source: *Harper's Weekly*, April 24, 1869, 269.

all the time in military formation with their leader shouting marching commands in Spanish. They were greeted by sympathizers and also by those who jeered at them, mocking and ridiculing their martial stride.[137] *Harper's* published a sketch that showed nearly fifty men carrying arms and in formation in a large room festooned with Cuban flags, with the caption "Cuban Drill-Room in New York City."[138]

Those very public displays of Cuban paramilitary activities in the largest city in the United States served to raise the ire of the Spanish minister in Washington, Mauricio López Roberts, who was constantly calling on Secretary of State Fish, demanding that the United States live up to its treaty obligations with Spain and fully enforce its neutrality laws to prevent such activities by the émigrés. To be sure, the United States was not cracking down on these activities during the first two years of the war, no doubt because of the popularity of the Cuban cause among Americans. In June 1869, José Morales Lemus, José Bassora, José María Mora, Francisco Fesser, and three others were arrested in Manhattan with a warrant issued by a federal judge in response to a complaint filed by López Roberts alleging violations of U.S. neutrality laws. But after posting bail, the Cubans were released and the case never went to trial.[139]

In battling Cuban activists in New York, Minister López Roberts was not just relying on the visibility of their activities. The Spanish government had retained the services of the Pinkerton Detective Agency, which in turn recruited informants within the community. Nestor Ponce de León, the bookseller and Antonio Bachiller y Morales's son-in-law, left a diary detailing the covert activities that came to the attention of the Cuban junta from October to December of 1870. According to the entries in the diary, the junta learned of some of those activities because two of the Pinkertons were selling to Aldama and Echeverría the intelligence they were gathering for the Spanish. The diary, which was not published until 1985 in Havana, provides a fascinating glimpse into the intrigues, dangers, and even banalities of international espionage on the streets of New York.[140]

It is not clear how much the intelligence the Spanish were gathering actually hurt the military campaigns of the Cubans. The expeditions to the island faced so many obstacles to their success that only a fraction of them actually reached the island and fulfilled their mission. The divisions within the émigré ranks precluded the launching of one large, well-equipped expedition. Each group, or even individual, relied on limited resources. Since the important investment had to be made on the cargo, which, after all, was the contribution to the war effort on the island, corners were cut in chartering the ships. Consequently, expeditions usually set out in old or rickety vessels, and many had mechanical problems before reaching the island. The ships were also vulnerable to the weather as well as to being captured by swifter Spanish naval vessels as they approached Cuba. U.S. Navy ships occasionally boarded and confiscated the vessels, especially near the U.S. coastline, probably acting upon demands, and intelligence, from the Spanish government.

Of the five expeditions organized by Francisco Javier Cisneros on behalf of the junta in 1869 and 1870, only one, the *Perrit*, reached Cuba.[141] But Cisneros was not the only one organizing expeditions during the first two years of the war. Others, including Emilia Casanova from her home in the Bronx, as well as General Manuel de Quesada, were also active in recruiting men, purchasing arms, and chartering boats. Although many failed, those that did succeed represented the most successful actions by Cuban exiles in support of the insurgency. During the early years of the war those expeditions provided valuable infusions of men and supplies in a military campaign that depended heavily on material support from abroad. The *Perrit* alone took to Cuba four thousand Springfield rifles, hundreds of Remington rifles and carbines, thousands of rounds of ammunition, as well as revolvers and holsters, cannon percussion caps, time grenades, machetes and swords, and many other types of ordnance.[142] One historian estimated that during the first three years of the war the émigrés sent to Cuba more than 24,000 weapons, many cannons, and millions of rounds of ammunition.[143]

Cuban activists in New York had little trouble procuring those supplies. In post–Civil War Manhattan one could stock an arsenal with what was publicly and openly available for sale. The principal supplier, who was more than glad to do business with any of the different exile factions, was Charles H. Pond, whose store at 179 Broadway featured "Remington's breech loaders, Winchester repeaters, Gatling guns, ammunition, equipment, and ordnance."[144] Cisneros was one of his customers, although not always a satisfied one. In an accounting report to the junta he noted that in one shipment from Pond there were eleven missing Spencer revolvers and that Pond charged eighty cents for each holster, much more than the thirty-five cents Cisneros had previously paid elsewhere.[145] Nevertheless, Pond's store on Broadway continued to supply expeditions to Cuba throughout the war. As one of Pond's invoices shows, General Manuel de Quesada made one purchase on December 20, 1871, totaling nearly $10,000 for two thousand Enfield rifles, as well as cartridge boxes, bayonets, and ammunition. The invoice was paid from the account Carlos del Castillo managed for Quesada at the Moses Taylor firm.[146] Pond also did business with the junta. In June 1869 Francisco Fesser, on behalf of the junta, purchased guns and ammunition from Pond totaling $30,000. Half of that amount was to be paid to Pond in four months and the other half in six months, all at no interest.[147]

José María Mora was one wealthy Cuban New Yorker who generously contributed to the outfitting of expeditions. Sometimes acting in concert with the junta, and at other times independently, he took on the role of chartering many of the ships that took the men and arms to Cuba. But of all the expeditions he helped to finance, the best-known one was the voyage of the *Lillian*, an expedition that typified the tribulations of the military ventures launched to Cuba by the New York émigrés.

Recruiting men for the *Lillian* began with the following note in the June 18, 1869, issue of the *New York Times* under the heading "Recruiting for Cubans in Brooklyn":

> An office has been opened at No. 347 Fulton Street, opposite the City Hall, where a large number of recruits for Cuba are being daily enlisted. The company is being raised by a gentleman of military experience, who was also in the Nicaragua expedition under Walker, and will probably be ready to leave by Sunday, when some 200 men will have been enlisted.[148]

There was no mistaking the identity of the gentleman: Domingo de Goicouría was back. At fifty-nine years of age, and with the long beard he had pledged not to trim until Cuba was free of Spanish control, he left his daughter's home in Brazil as soon as he received the news that the war had broken out. Accompanied by his son Valentín, Goicouría arrived in New York ready to take command of the expedition that Mora, his brother-in-law, was organizing.[149]

It took a few months to finalize all the arrangements for the departure of the *Lillian*. In the meantime, Valentín left on the *Perrit* as an aide to General Jordan.[150] Finally, one night in September 1869, some four hundred men gathered at a pier on the Hudson, at 33rd Street, to board a large steamship named, coincidentally, the *Alabama*. It was all done under the cloak of darkness as the men were huddled into the cargo hold in an attempt to keep the entire operation a secret. One participant noted, however, that it was far from a secret and that the New York Police Department had deployed several officers to the pier, some of whom gave helpful directions to those would-be revolutionaries who had lost their way to the ship on the streets of the West Side of Manhattan.[151]

The *Alabama* sailed to Fernandina Beach, just north of Jacksonville, Florida, where the men disembarked and were placed on a train to Cedar Key, on Florida's Gulf Coast. After several days Domingo de Goicouría arrived at the Key with his staff, which included foreign officers, some of them Polish. Not long thereafter, the *Lillian* sailed into the harbor at Cedar Key, with a cargo of four thousand rifles and ammunition. The 407 men who waited there, including Goicouría, boarded the ship and it left for Cuba.[152] Despite such detailed and careful planning, the ship did not carry enough coal to make it to the northeastern coast of Cuba and had to be docked in the Bahamas, where the British authorities confiscated the ship and detained the men.[153] The expedition of the *Lillian*, like so many others, was finished before ever touching Cuban soil. Goicouría was freed by the British after a few days and in Nassau he boarded the *Columbia*, which stopped there after leaving from Havana on its way to New York. He arrived in the city on December 17. The passenger list of the Columbia listed him as "Gnrl. Goicuira."[154]

In New York Goicouría received the news that his son Valentín had been killed in combat. More resolute than ever to enter the fight, and with his penchant for boldness, he assembled thirty-three men and sailed for Cuba in a schooner. This time he did land in Cuba and went inland to meet with Céspedes, who gave him the mission of enlisting the support of Benito Juárez in Mexico, whom Goicouría knew well. He set to sea again bound for the Mexican coast when a Spanish gunboat intercepted him, took him prisoner, and transported him to Havana. He was given a summary trial and sentenced to death.[155]

Goicouría was reportedly defiant to the end, as if embracing his fate and fulfilling the prediction his father had made many years before that the Spanish hated him and would someday hang him. But they were not going to put him to death by hanging, but rather with the brutal garrote. Goicouría demanded that he be executed by a firing squad as befitted a prisoner of war, but the Spanish authorities refused.[156] On May 7, 1870, he was garroted in the Príncipe fortress in Havana. His execution was widely reported in the New York press.[157]

Hamilton Fish lamented the execution of Goicouría, who was a naturalized U.S. citizen. He had cautioned Minister López Roberts that when it came to the loss of American lives the Spanish government had to "tread carefully."[158] No matter what their outcome, the expeditions to Cuba were a serious problem for the U.S. secretary of state, especially given the brazen manner in which they were organized on U.S. soil. If the forays into Cuba were successful in helping the rebels, then they were clear violations of U.S. law and intensified Spanish pressure on Washington. If, on the other hand, they failed and the Spanish were successful in quashing them, there was the loss of lives, including American lives, to contend with. It was a no-win situation that Fish was eager to resolve.

Figure 6.6. Execution of Goicouría, Havana, May 7, 1870. Source: Art and Picture Collection, New York Public Library, Astor, Lenox and Tilden Foundations.

Once his offer of negotiation with the Spanish failed and the Cubans' greatest ally in the cabinet, War Secretary Rawlins, died, Fish gave full rein to his efforts to keep the Cuban situation from jeopardizing broader and, from his perspective, more important foreign policy objectives than Cuban sovereignty. Despite the popularity of the Cuban cause among many Americans, including leading members of Congress, Fish was even more determined than ever to avoid picking a fight with Spain. Not only were the *Alabama* claims still pending, but a conflict with Spain could have had consequences for the lives and properties of Americans in Cuba as well as for U.S. shipping. He was also interested in encouraging the reform movement in Spain, especially since the liberal government there was considering the gradual emancipation of slaves, at least in Puerto Rico.[159] Furthermore, as Fish's diary shows, the Spanish minister in Washington, Mauricio López Roberts, was practically a fixture in Fish's office, constantly providing evidence of, and protesting, the actions of Cuban émigrés who were violating U.S. neutrality laws by organizing and launching expeditions from this country.[160] Fish had to convince Grant that non-interference in the Cuban conflict was not enough, and that the U.S. government needed to distance itself more explicitly from the Cuban rebels and clamp down on expeditions organized from U.S. territory.

The result of Fish's efforts was the strongly worded message that the president sent to Congress on June 13, 1870. According to the historian Allan Nevins, the message, which was written by Fish, was "one of the ablest . . . of all state papers signed by Grant during his Presidency."[161] It was elegantly written, comprehensive, grounded in history, unequivocal, and bad news for the Cuban insurgents. After lamenting the "barbarity" of the acts committed by both sides in the conflict, the president argued that there was no basis under international law for recognizing the belligerency of the rebels, since the conflict in Cuba "seems confined to an irregular system of hostilities" that could not be called a war, and the insurgents did not hold a town or city and had no "organization for collecting and receiving revenue."[162] Under such conditions, recognition of the belligerent rights of the insurgents "is a gratuitous demonstration of moral support to the rebellion" that could have consequences for U.S. commerce.[163]

The president's message had profound implications for the cause of Cuban independence. One was to put the brakes on what had been up to that point a growing movement in Congress favoring intervention in Cuba. In fact, the message was intended as a response to that movement. Only three days after Congress received Grant's statement, and largely as a result of its persuasiveness, the House of Representatives overwhelmingly defeated a resolution urging the granting of belligerent rights to the Cubans.[164]

Secondly, the president's words represented a blow to the ability of the Cuban émigrés to raise funds in the United States, especially through the sale of bonds that Morales Lemus had issued in 1869 on behalf of Carlos Manuel de Céspedes and the Cuban Republic. Printed in New York in several denominations, the bonds would start paying a 7 percent interest, accruing semiannually, after one of the following conditions was met: the ratification of a peace treaty between the Cuban Republic and the government of Spain, the overthrow of Spanish authority on the island, or the recognition by the government of the United States of the political independence of Cuba.[165] The president's statement made it less likely that any of those conditions might be met, making the bonds a very risky investment.

Most of the bonds, however, were not sold, but actually given away by the junta to persons in positions to influence Cuba policy, including

ALAS! POOR CUBA!

Messrs. Fish and Sumner. "Let her stay out in the cold."

Figure 6.7. Cartoon depicting Secretary of State Hamilton Fish (*right*) and Senator Charles Sumner after refusing to support the insurgency against the Spanish, leaving "Poor Cuba" out in the cold. Source: Print Collection, Miriam and Ira D. Wallach Division of Art, Prints and Photographs, New York Public Library, Astor, Lenox and Tilden Foundations.

members of Congress. The discovery that even Secretary of War Rawlins, a staunch supporter of the Cubans, had received such bonds created a scandal. The use of bonds essentially as bribes was a source of considerable irritation to Fish and no doubt served to increase his antipathy toward the New York junta. At one point Fish urged the Department of Justice to consider indicting Morales Lemus and other Cubans on bribery charges.[166] The corrupting influence of the bonds was mentioned in the president's message of June 13: "The object of making their value entirely contingent upon the action of this Government is a subject for serious reflection."[167] Such attention to the issue served to taint the bonds and make them less desirable for investors.

But perhaps the greatest impact of the president's statement was in unequivocally affirming the U.S. government's opposition to the organization of armed expeditions to Cuba on U.S. soil by both Americans and Cubans:

Misguided individual citizens cannot be tolerated in making war according to their own caprice, passions and interests, or foreign sympathies; . . . the agents of foreign governments, recognized or unrecognized, can-

Figure 6.8. A 500-peso bond issued by the Agency of the Cuban Republic in New York in 1869, signed by José Morales Lemus, José Bassora, and Francisco Fesser. Source: José Ignacio Rodríguez Papers, Manuscript Division, Library of Congress.

not be permitted to abuse our hospitality by usurping the function of enlisting or equipping military or naval forces within our territory.[168]

In the wording of the statement, Fish's credentials as a historian showed. He couched the unambiguous opposition to such private military ventures in a tradition of neutrality that had been consistently reaffirmed, he argued, by all U.S. presidents since Thomas Jefferson's tenure as secretary of state. There would henceforth be little tolerance for paramilitary ventures launched from the United States. In a subsequent executive order, Grant called upon all agencies of the U.S. government, civilian or military, to imprison, judge, and punish anyone found in violation of U.S. neutrality laws.[169]

The fortunes of the émigré cause in Washington had obviously fallen far and fast since the inauguration of President Grant, when U.S. support seemed assured. In that June 13, 1870, presidential message, Fish reserved the harshest words for the émigré leadership:

> Remarkable exhibition has been made of large numbers of Cubans escaping from the island and avoiding the risks of war, congregating in this country at a safe distance from the scene of danger, and endeavoring to make war from our own shores, to urge our people into the fight which they avoid, and to embroil this Government in complications and possible hostilities with Spain.[170]

Those words were issued exactly two weeks before the death of José Morales Lemus, for whom they must have been a bitter capstone to his failed mission to win U.S. support. As Carlos Ripoll wrote a century later, "What need did the U.S. government have to insult the Cubans?"[171] In the context of a presidential message to Congress, those were indeed gratuitous words, especially on the heels of the execution of Goicouría, who had provided an example of how at least some Cubans in the United States were willing to sacrifice their lives on the island's battlefields. Given Fish's moderate and conciliatory disposition, one can only assume that the U.S. secretary of state had reached the end of his patience with the activities of the Cuban émigrés, activities he considered contrary to the interests of the United States.[172]

The implementation of a U.S. policy hostile to the interests of the revolutionaries was a defining setback for the cause of Cuban independence. By 1871, following President Grant's message of June 13, 1870, and his subsequent executive order, the number of expeditions started declining as the U.S. government became more aggressive in its enforcement. Potential financial backers in the United States shied away from putting money into military ventures that would henceforth be persecuted and prosecuted by the Grant administration. Adding to this deteriorating picture was the bitter acrimony between the *aldamistas* and *quesadistas*. Disunity diminished the capacity of the émigré community to raise funds and outfit expeditions. The class-based tensions between the exiled factions were heightened by the setbacks the revolution started encountering in 1870, which led to the realization among the émigrés that the war would not be easily or promptly won. Those setbacks occurred on the Cuban battlefields, in New York, and in Washington and had the effect of replacing the initial enthusiasm that had greeted Céspedes's declaration of independence with a sense of frustration. After repeated failures, the expeditions started exhausting the funds of the most committed supporters within Cuban New York. For José María Mora, for example, the *Lillian* marked the end of his backing for expeditions as he teetered on the edge of bankruptcy. In one of his letters to his daughter Amalia, written before setting sail for Cuba for the last time, Domingo de Goicouría shared with her the fate that had befallen her mother's family, the Moras:

> It will be horrible what will happen to the family in New York, because José María, Antonio and others will not be left with enough to live even in a "tenement-house." The first one sells his jewels to subsist, but that will not last another six months. Fausto and Arango are ruined.[173]

The Goicouría-Mora family was at least one family of Cuban New Yorkers who put everything on the line for the revolution. Although many in the community did not make such sacrifices, staying well away from the battlefields, making investments in Manhattan real estate and Brooklyn sugar refineries, and engaging in bitter and destructive infighting, clearly Fish had unfairly generalized in his characterization of Cuban émigré activists.

In the summer of 1871, in the midst of the émigrés' deteriorating political fortunes, New York would witness the arrival from Cuba of a man who would exemplify the ideal of self-sacrifice for the homeland.

* * *

Notwithstanding the increasing hostility of Washington toward the Cuban cause and despite the acrimony that prevailed in New York among the different exile factions, Céspedes continued to believe in the importance of the émigré community's support for the insurgency and hence persisted in having his government maintain official representation in New York after the resignation of Aldama, Mestre, and Echeverría from their respective posts in the Agency of the Cuban Republic. To that end, and in an effort to stay above the bitter factionalism of the exiles, Céspedes sent to New York as his government's representative a man of unimpeachable credentials who was highly respected by all: the vice president of the Republic, Francisco Vicente Aguilera.

Aguilera was the leader of the insurgents in Bayamo and one of the original organizers of the 1868 uprising. He was probably the wealthiest man in all of eastern Cuba. In the war he lost everything, and at age fifty, after almost three years on the battlefield, he was entrusted by Céspedes with the delicate mission of picking up the pieces left by the brawl between the *aldamistas* and the *quesadistas* and restoring vitality and effectiveness to the émigrés' support for the revolution. In his decree naming Aguilera and the Republic's foreign minister, Ramón Céspedes, as the representatives of the insurgent government, President Céspedes noted "the inexplicable divisions" among the New York émigrés "that have brought to the homeland a harm of tremendous transcendence," and specifically charged Aguilera and Ramón Céspedes to "employ conciliatory means to harmonize the spirits and wills of Cubans residing in the United States so that in concert they will dedicate themselves to the happy and prompt success of the revolution."[174] Furthermore, the new representatives were specifically charged with channeling that harmony into effective fundraising.[175]

Although Aguilera's arrival in Manhattan on August 12, 1871, breathed fresh air into the stale atmosphere of New York émigré politics, he was well aware that "harmonizing spirits and wills of Cubans residing in the United States" was nothing less than a daunting task. His son, Eladio,

Figure 6.9. Francisco Vicente Aguilera. Source: Cuban Heritage Collection, University of Miami Library Digital Collections, www.merrick.library.miami.edu.

who accompanied him to New York, wrote years later in a biography of his father what was facing Aguilera upon his arrival in the city:

If in Cuba a war of annihilation raged between Cubans and Spaniards, another, no less ferocious and bloody, raged overseas between Cubans. . . . In Cuba it took four centuries of tyranny, oppression, and humiliation to engender a sentiment of hatred toward the oppressor; abroad, it took little more than a year of ambitions in the managing of affairs of the homeland, of rivalries for recognition, of petty disputes, and of arrogance to develop that same hatred among Cubans.[176]

Unlike General Manuel de Quesada, who contributed to the schisms within the community, Aguilera managed to stay above the fray, focused on his mission. Given that he was one of the founders of the revolution with experience on the battlefield, Cuban New Yorkers greeted him reverentially and Emilia Casanova and her fellow *quesadistas* had no choice but to respect Aguilera and defer to him. Still licking their wounds from the bitter attacks that caused them to resign, the *aldamistas* no doubt welcomed Aguilera's arrival and leadership, despite the fact that it might have been expected that it was with this group that Aguilera would clash most. After sacrificing his wealth and way of life to the revolution and finding himself living austerely in New York, Aguilera could have reacted resentfully, as did Casanova and her group, to how Aldama and the others kept their wealth, the style with which they lived in the city, and the meager results of their tenure as official agents of the Republic.

But Aguilera did not have a resentful nature, and he knew all too well that too much had been sacrificed already, especially on the battlefield, to compromise his mission in New York with pettiness. That mission was to unite the émigrés and raise money, not to add to the divisions. Furthermore, at a personal level the Havana-educated patrician from Bayamo no doubt found more in common with the elites who made up the *aldamista* group than with the somewhat less-genteel folk who made up the quarrelsome *quesadista* faction, which acted with such an appalling lack of civility in its public discourse.

The transition between the incoming and outgoing representatives of the Cuban Republic was, on the surface, seamless and courteous. In a meeting held on October 12 at the home of Leonardo del Monte on West 47th Street, Aldama and Mestre met with Aguilera and Ramón Céspedes and turned over to them all the files of the Cuban Republic in the United States, including the records of nearly $10 million in bonds of the Republic, of which only $1.4 million had actually been issued and about $1.2 million were still in the hands of sellers. Aguilera and Ramón Céspedes outwardly found everything in good order and acknowledged receipt of the files and bonds.[177] In reality, Aguilera was shocked to find that there was literally no accounting of the funds of the agency and asked for such an accounting from Aldama, who resented the request. This served to cool the relations between the two, but it was a dispute that took place discreetly in the correspondence between the two men.[178]

Despite Aguilera's cordial relations with the *aldamistas* during the rest of his years in New York, he became increasingly aware that the group of elite *habaneros* lacked the will to sacrifice everything, as he had done, for the cause of an independent Cuba. Years later, in 1875, Aguilera wrote to a fellow easterner, Tomás Estrada Palma, this forlorn conclusion: "Our absolute lack of understanding of the men of the West has caused great and irreparable harm to our Revolution."[179]

As for the *quesadistas*, Aguilera rebuffed their repeated attempts to draw him into the factionalism of New York émigré politics. José Gabriel del Castillo, for example, wrote a long and rambling letter in which he laid out for Aguilera a litany of accusations and grievances against the *aldamistas*.[180] Aguilera was not going to be distracted and ignored it. He found it much more challenging, however, to ignore the irascible Emilia Casanova, as is most evident in an incident in 1872 that is recounted both in his son's biography of him and in the diary Aguilera kept during his years in New York.

It seems that Casanova had gathered a number of Cuban ladies at the Manhattan home she shared with her husband, Cirilo Villaverde, and issued an urgent invitation to Aguilera to join them. Aguilera was at a critical moment in his handling of the financial mess he had inherited from Aldama and Mestre, and he perceived that Casanova was luring him into a meeting designed to influence his decisions on the matter. He repeatedly declined the invitation, even feigning illness, but Casanova persisted, to the point of offering to send a cab to pick him up. After he adamantly refused, his son Eladio summed up his father's assessment of the refusal: "Aguilera, aware of the nervous temperament of Mrs. Villaverde, said that the incident would upset the lady and lead her to judge us unjustly."[181] But in his dairy, Aguilera expressed that sentiment in a more picturesque language: "Imagine the toads and snakes that lady will heap upon us."[182]

Aguilera plunged into his work in New York, soliciting contributions personally and through an extensive correspondence with potential donors throughout the United States, planning expeditions, granting interviews, and issuing statements to the press.[183] On October 10, 1871, on the occasion of the third anniversary of Céspedes's uprising, he issued a "Declaration of Independence" addressed to the people of the United States asking for their support of Cuban independence.[184] Less than two months later, Aguilera and Ramón Céspedes printed and circulated in New York a fifty-four-page document in English calling the attention of the American people to the pro-abolition provisions of the Cuban constitution, the progress of the war in Cuba and the hardships faced by the rebel forces, and the terror and anarchy fomented by the *voluntarios* in Cuba. The document ended with a call for the "hand of friendship" of the people "of this great Union" for a people who aspire "to a place among the free peoples of America."[185] Aguilera carried out all of this activity while living in New York on a meager allowance from his account as agent of the Republic.[186]

Despite his steadfast dedication to fulfilling his mission, Aguilera had arrived in New York too late to be effective. The U.S. government was already firmly set against any recognition of Cuban belligerency and was earnestly pursuing violations of the neutrality laws by exiles organizing expeditions. The treasury of the Cuban agency in the United States was depleted, and the prospects for replenishing it were grim. The sources of funds were drying up. As Aguilera wrote to a friend from New York, "There are no offerings of money from those who up to now have been accustomed to giving them."[187] And he did not make any progress at all in reconciling the different factions, which remained as bitterly divided as ever. On the contrary, eventually Aguilera himself fell victim to the infighting of Cuban New York. General Quesada, through his sister Ana, who was by now living in the city, was undermining Aguilera's standing with Ana's husband, President Céspedes.

Frustrated with the situation in New York, Aguilera scraped together the money to go to Paris on a fundraising mission among Cubans who lived there. After some vicissitudes, including running out of money to pay for his hotel room, he did garner some substantial contributions that he planned to put into the expedition he had long been organizing.[188]

* * *

Aguilera was still in Paris at the start of 1873, the year that sealed the fate of the Cuban revolution. The most tragic and devastating of the events of that year was the death in May of Major General Ignacio Agramonte, killed by a bullet to his head in the midst of a battle in the plains of his native Camagüey.[189] His widow, Amalia Simoni, received the news at her home in Mérida, Mexico. Her father, Dr. José Ramón Simoni, had relocated his family there from New York, where they had lived after leaving Cuba (see chapter 5).[190] At the time of her husband's death,

Amalia's two children, Ignacio Ernesto and Herminia, were four and two years of age, respectively. Also living in Mérida with Dr. Simoni were his other daughter, Matilde, and her five-year-old son Arístides. Matilde had married Ignacio's cousin Eduardo, also a combatant in Camagüey.

Five months after Ignacio Agramonte's death, Carlos del Castillo, who at the time was serving as a representative of the Cuban Republic in New York, received a letter from Dr. Simoni in Mérida, thanking del Castillo for sending him the official dispatch from General Manuel Sanguily that detailed the circumstances of the death of Ignacio. It was much appreciated by the widow, Simoni wrote. In a chilling postscript to the letter, Simoni requests from del Castillo the dispatch from the battle of San José del Chorrillo, which took place in 1872. "It is anxiously awaited by the widow of Eduardo Agramonte," he wrote.[191] The tragic consequences of the war in Cuba devastated a family in Mérida, where Dr. Simoni found himself with two widowed daughters and three fatherless grandchildren.

* * *

By the time Aguilera returned to New York aboard the steamer *St. Laurent* from Le Havre on March 26, 1873, he was no longer the agent general of the Cuban Republic.[192] General Quesada's intrigues with the president had borne fruit and Céspedes abolished the General Agency that Aguilera represented, establishing in its place something called a "Confidential Agency." The move was ostensibly done to shift the agency's emphasis away from what had clearly become a futile endeavor, lobbying Washington, to the more covert mission of outfitting expeditions. The new "confidential" agents appointed were General Quesada, his sympathizer Carlos del Castillo, and the New York real estate investor Félix Govín.[193]

Aguilera's son Eladio, who served as his secretary, wrote years later that his father was not so much disappointed with his removal as astounded by the sheer folly of Céspedes's move. "Aguilera thought that Céspedes had lost his mind," wrote Eladio.[194] The appointments were likely to stoke further the flames of disunity in New York; moreover, Aguilera reasoned, the move placed Céspedes in a precarious political position given the Assembly's antipathy toward Quesada. That Céspedes was indeed in political trouble became clear when in May Aguilera received a letter from Salvador Cisneros Betancourt, the head of the Assembly of the Cuban Republic, urging him to return immediately to Cuba, in case, "as vice president, it becomes necessary for you to occupy the presidency of the Republic."[195] Aguilera declined, saying that he had made commitments to arrange the outfitting of an expedition, but urged Cisneros Betancourt and the Assembly to follow their conscience and act in the best interests of the future of Cuba.[196] Apparently even Aguilera had found it difficult to defend Céspedes. The president had lost the confidence of many of his generals, including Calixto García and Máximo Gómez, and the Assembly viewed him as dictatorial and arbitrary in his decisions. The appointment of his brother-in-law to the Confidential Agency was the last straw. Even so, given Céspedes's stature as the founder of the revolution, the Assembly struggled for months with the problem, until October 28, 1873, when it unanimously voted to remove the president from office.[197]

In the absence of Aguilera, Cisneros Betancourt, as head of the Assembly, assumed the presidency of the Republic. Barely a month later, the new president sent a letter to José Manuel Mestre in New York announcing the elimination of the Confidential Agency and the appointments of Aldama, Mestre, and Echeverría to their old posts, the first as general agent and the last two as diplomatic commissioners, thus "returning matters to their original state," wrote Cisneros Betancourt, "before the ill-conceived Confidential Agency."[198] Mestre declined the appointment, but Aldama and Echeverría accepted.

Needless to say, the move precipitated yet another storm of invectives from Emilia Casanova, who labeled the removal of Céspedes a "grotesque farce" by the Assembly. She renewed with even greater fervor her attacks on the *aldamistas*.[199]

As 1873 neared its end, the Cuban revolution inside and outside the island was in total disarray, its fate virtually sealed. The three men who had been revered as the founders of the revolution were in effect no longer in the picture: Céspedes deposed, Agramonte dead, and Aguilera in New York. The government of the Republic fell largely in the hands of ciphers, men without the legitimacy of battlefield experience. The army lacked central direction, with each military leader operating as a chieftain in his own region of operations. The highly divided émigré leadership resembled a game of musical chairs with few prospects for doing anything to help the rebels. And the fateful year 1873 was not over yet.

* * *

On October 31, somewhere in the waters between Jamaica and southeastern Cuba, the Spanish warship *Tornado*, after a long pursuit, overtook and boarded the *Virginius*, a side-wheel steamer. Both ships had been built in 1864 in the same Scottish shipyard for the same customer: the Confederate Navy. Of the two only the *Virginius*, originally named the *Virgin*, saw any action during the Civil War as a blockade runner, making trips between Mobile and Havana. While the *Tornado*, a corvette, was acquired by the Spanish Navy after the war, the *Virgin* went through several U.S. owners before it was purchased in 1870 at the Washington Navy Yard by one John F. Patterson, who was in reality a front man for General Manuel de Quesada and José María Mora. The $9,800 used to purchase it came from funds raised in New York by Cuban émigrés, especially Mora.[200]

After a name change and an overhaul in New York harbor, the *Virginius* was once again engaged in a sort of blockade running, illegally carrying men and armaments to Cuba. It had acquired enough of a reputation with the Spanish as an "outlaw" ship that it even came up in the complaints Spanish Minister López Roberts made to Hamilton Fish.

On the voyage to Cuba in which the *Tornado* overtook it, the *Virginius* had made stops in Kingston and Port-au-Prince, where the ship took on men and supplies that arrived from vessels sent from New York. The commander of the troops on board was General Bernabé Varona (alias Bembeta), a rash young man who despite his age had already accumulated many distinctions on the battlefield. Also on board were Agustín Santa Rosa, a New York resident, Pedro de Céspedes, the president's brother, and William Ryan, an Irish-born veteran of the Civil War who rose to the rank of lieutenant in a New York infantry regiment but who promoted himself to general when he signed up for the adventure of liberating Cuba. The crew was headed by Captain Joseph Fry, also an adventurer and a graduate of the U.S. Naval Academy who joined the Confederacy and after the war was unable to receive a commission in the merchant marine. The *Virginius* was carrying a total of 155 men to Cuba and flying the flag of the United States.[201]

By the time it sailed from Haiti to Cuba, the Spanish were well aware of the *Virginius*'s whereabouts. After its capture by the *Tornado*, and the trampling of the U.S. flag on the *Virginius*'s quarterdeck, both the ship and the men aboard were taken to Santiago de Cuba. Within five days, and despite the frantic efforts of the U.S. vice-consul in that city, who was doing his best in the absence of the consul, Varona, Pedro de Céspedes, Ryan, and Jesús del Sol, also a veteran of the Cuban conflict, were blindfolded, made to kneel, and executed by a firing squad. Three days later, after a summary trial by a naval court, Captain Fry and thirty-five crew members were executed, almost all of them Americans or British subjects. On November 8, twelve more men were put to death, bringing the massacre's total to fifty-two.[202] The number would have been even higher if not for the intervention of various European consuls in the city, especially the British one, who stepped in when he learned that a number of the prisoners were British subjects.

The outcry in the United States over the *Virginius* massacre and the desecration of the U.S. flag made Hamilton Fish face, as never before, the very real prospect of war with Spain. Mass meetings were held in New York, at the Masonic Hall and at the Cooper Union, as well as in other U.S. cities, to express indignation for the killings, denounce Spain, and call for an appropriate U.S. response.[203] In the end, the furor died down, especially after the finding that the *Virginius* was not legally flying the U.S. flag. Fish negotiated an agreement that called on Spain to return the imprisoned survivors and the ship itself, as well as pay reparations, the amount to be negotiated at a later date.[204] In the end, the press hailed Fish's handling of the crisis and the secretary congratulated himself on having averted a war.[205]

The survivors of the *Virginius* were taken directly from Santiago to New York aboard the U.S. ship *Juniata*, which arrived at the Castle Garden wharf in the Battery on December 28. The *Times* reported that most of the 103 survivors were very young men, a mixture of Cubans, Americans, and Brits, and there was a mixture of blacks and whites. The following day, to celebrate their safe arrival, members of the New York Cuban community, led by Hilario Cisneros, took them to dinner at a Cuban restaurant at 76 Pine Street.[206]

On December 26, as the damaged *Virginius* was returning to New York, it foundered just off Cape Fear in North Carolina and sank to the bottom of the Atlantic. It was a fitting end to a year that had brought disaster to the cause of Cuban independence. The *Virginius* was the last expedition of any consequence to be sent to aid the Cuban insurgents during the Ten Years' War. Its tragic outcome accelerated the decline in the number of such ventures that were subsequently organized and dispatched by émigrés in New York. The *Virginius* affair nearly swept the United States into a war. From Hamilton Fish's perspective, the Cubans had once again proven to be a troublesome, even dangerous, impediment to peaceful relations with Spain. The Cuban cause now had truly nothing to expect from Washington in terms of support.[207]

The war dragged on until 1878. Its last years proved to be a dreary and mournful time for Cubans in New York, a period of interminable bad news.

* * *

For Ana de Quesada, New York was a bitter chalice. She had wanted to stay in Cuba to accompany her husband, President Céspedes, but for her safety he asked her to leave for New York with the poet Zenea. She endured the ordeal of being detained and questioned in Havana before being allowed to board the *City of Merida* for New York, where she arrived on January 16, 1871.[208] Seven months later she gave birth in the city to twins, a boy and a girl, Carlos Manuel and Gloria.[209]

One of her first addresses in New York was 113 East 14th Street. She lived in the city on an allowance from the Republic of Cuba, an allowance that was either irregular in its disbursement or insufficient, for in April 1872 she informed Aguilera, in his capacity as representative of her husband's government, that her landlady was demanding that she move from the two rooms she was renting unless she came up with two hundred dollars. Aguilera somehow came up with the money.[210] Eventually, however, the turnovers in the émigré leadership put an end to the allowance, and Mrs. Céspedes came to depend on the generosity of Carlos del Castillo, who was a distant relative and close friend of President Céspedes and was named by her as godfather to her son Carlos Manuel. The support from del Castillo was disbursed through his account with Moses Taylor.[211] Ana would correspond with del Castillo about her difficulties adjusting to life in New York with scarce resources. She could not afford a private school, she wrote, and so she schooled Gloria at home because "the public school nearby is attended by the worst class of children, dirty, with bad manners, foul language, and, not surprisingly, sickly."[212]

Figure 6.10. Ana de Quesada. Source: Cuban Heritage Collection, University of Miami Library Digital Collections, www.merrick.library.miami.edu.

As if her economic problems were not enough, Mrs. Céspedes faced constant pressures to take sides in the ongoing disputes between the different émigré factions. Her version of what transpired during Zenea's mission was used by the *quesadistas* to attack the role played by *aldamistas* in the affair and was a major consideration leading to the resignations of Aldama, Mestre, and Echeverría. Her brother, General Quesada, as noted earlier, later used her influence and correspondence with her husband to undermine Aguilera's position in New York.

The twins were not yet three years old when Ana de Quesada received the devastating news that her husband had been killed in Cuba. It was especially hard to accept the circumstances under which he met his death. Once he was deposed by the Assembly, he became a private citizen and no provision was made to protect him. He was not assigned a command or provided a security detail. He retreated with some friends and relatives to an isolated hamlet in the mountains of eastern Cuba while he waited for the opportunity to leave the country and join his wife in New York.[213] Given the symbolic value of his capture or death, the Spanish were looking for him, and it did not take them long to learn of his whereabouts. On February 27, 1874, a Spanish troop descended on the hideaway. Céspedes was reportedly killed after discharging his revolver at the oncoming soldiers.[214]

* * *

Bad news also overtook the family of Antonio Bachiller y Morales in New York. Antonio Jr., who had left the family home in Brooklyn to go to Cuba in the *Perrit* expedition, was killed in a surprise attack by the Spanish on a rebel medical facility. He had been Antonio's last surviving son. Years before, his other son, Alfredo, had died in Cuba of tuberculosis.[215] The Bachiller y Morales family remained in New York for the duration of the war, years during which Antonio Sr. wrote his guide to New York City (see chapter 5).

* * *

Francisco Vicente Aguilera remained in New York, persistent in his efforts to send help to the rebels in Cuba. He did everything he could to raise money, even organizing a benefit billiards exhibition at Tammany Hall featuring the city's best players.[216] He made excellent contacts with New York's elites and the press sought him out for comments on Cuba-related events.[217] He organized and led several expeditions, but none of them were successful and he was forced to return to New York.[218] The expeditions weakened him considerably, largely because he suffered from extreme seasickness. The general endured financial hardships in the city, the cold weather did not suit him, and he had recurrent bouts of fever. In 1876 Aguilera was diagnosed with throat cancer. By that time he lived at 223 West 30th Street with most of his ten offspring, who had managed to leave Cuba.[219] It was there that he died on February 22, 1877, at age fifty-five. The *Times, Herald, Sun, World, Tribune,* and *Evening Post* all ran lengthy obituaries.[220] Both the *Herald* and the *Tribune* provided details on the rather gruesome circumstances of his death. It seems that in the final stages of his illness Aguilera was unable to breathe while in a sitting or reclining position so that until the very end he was standing and pacing around his room when he finally collapsed dead in the arms of his daughters.

Francisco Aguilera's funeral was the most elaborate and well-attended of all obsequies held in Cuban New York before or since. It resembled a state funeral and was a testament not only to the respect Aguilera evoked and the relations he developed in the city, but also to the popularity the Cuban cause still enjoyed in New York, regardless of Washington's policies. After the body was laid out in a coffin in the parlor of the 30th Street house so that friends could pay their respects, it was transferred to the Governor's Room at City Hall. There it was placed in a silver-mounted rosewood casket atop a catafalque of black velvet, where it lay in state all day. According to the New York World, "thousands of Cubans, Spaniards, and people of other nationalities" filed past the casket.[221] The New York Herald noted that it was "the first time on record that the body of a foreigner has ever been allowed to be in state in New York City Hall and the compliment to the struggling Republic of Cuba is no small one."[222]

Both the Cuban and U.S. flags flew at half-mast from atop the building's cupola.[223] It was a very different mood from that other occasion, nearly seven years earlier, when the Cuban flag flew over City Hall in celebration for the first anniversary of the revolution, when there was still optimism for the cause of Cuba.

The following morning the casket was placed on a hearse and followed by a cortege of carriages, some of them carrying the mayor and other city dignitaries, that made its way up Broadway, west on Canal Street, and eventually up Fifth Avenue to St. Francis Xavier Church, a Jesuit church that still stands on 16th Street between Fifth and Sixth Avenues.[224] After the celebration of a high requiem Mass, as the casket was being taken out of the church to the waiting hearse, two separate bands of musicians, one Cuban and the other Mexican, offered to play funeral dirges during the procession to the cemetery. Juan Manuel Macías, who was in charge of the funeral arrangements, politely declined.[225] But Macías did agree to another request: "A very large group of Cuban colored men, some of them formerly slaves, insisted on their privilege and right to carry the body on their shoulders to the cemetery."[226] The men proceeded to hoist on their shoulders the casket of the man who had freed his slaves in Cuba. They led the procession, now without a hearse, and Aguilera's body was carried all the way to the East Village, slowly winding its way on 14th Street to Second Avenue and then down to 2nd Street to a temporary vault at the Marble Cemetery, where the body was "to remain until it can be taken to Cuba," the *Evening Post* reported.[227] One can only imagine the curiosity that the procession must have aroused among New Yorkers along the way when they saw passing by a casket borne by a contingent of black men and followed by carriages filled with city dignitaries and other finely dressed white people.

Miguel Aldama and José Antonio Echeverría, who were still officially the agents of the Cuban Republic, served as pallbearers and were conspicuously present during all of the funeral events. Also in attendance were Nestor Ponce de León, Hilario Cisneros, and many other Cuban activists. Americans attending included Charles Dana, the editor of the *Sun*, and Generals Charles K. Graham and Martin T. McMahon and Colonel Ethan Allen, Civil War veterans from New York who had become friends with Aguilera. Ana de Quesada headed a delegation of women who presented a large crown of white flowers.[228] Various organizations, such as the Cuban League of the United States, sent delegations. The League of Cuba's Daughters, however, was not among those organizations, nor did Emilia Casanova, Cirilo Villaverde, Carlos del Castillo, José Gabriel del Castillo, or Félix Govín appear on any of the lists of attendees included in the lengthy press reports on the funeral.

* * *

On February 10, 1878, almost a year to the day after the death of Aguilera, representatives of the Cuban insurgents and the Spanish government met on an abandoned farm in Camagüey to sign an agreement to officially end the war.[229] Fighting continued for several more weeks as several rebel commanders refused to acknowledge the agreement. The war that had lasted ten years, cost countless lives, and had represented the long-postponed aspirations of the Cubans to free themselves from Spanish rule had ended without accomplishing its purpose.

Known as the Pact of Zanjón, the agreement contained few significant concessions from the Spanish. It was accepted by the Cubans because, as the historian Louis A. Pérez Jr. noted, it was "the most honorable agreement through which to extricate themselves from a cause hopelessly doomed to failure."[230] As part of the agreement the Spanish promised to institute a number of reforms in how the island was governed and to pardon anyone who had committed political crimes since 1868 or been sentenced for such crimes, regardless of whether they lived inside or outside the island. The pact also guaranteed freedom to all slaves and indentured laborers who had joined the rebel army.[231]

The granting of amnesty by the Spanish meant that Cuban New Yorkers could return to the island, and many did. Although the Pact of Zanjón made no mention of the disposition of embargoed properties, many of those who returned were doing so with the hope of recovering what they had lost. But for those Cuban New Yorkers who were laborers, cigar workers, former slaves and indentured servants, domestic workers, and even some real estate investors and professionals, life in New York had meant new opportunities to improve their lives. They had nothing to recover and nothing to gain by returning to a Cuba ravaged by war.

Still others did not return because they could not bear to do so. Those who had suffered great personal losses for the ideal of a free Cuba could not bring themselves to once again live under Spanish rule as if nothing had happened, as if ten years of devastating tragedies had not taken place. That was the case with the widow of Carlos Manuel de Céspedes, who one month after the pact was signed wrote the following in a letter to Carlos del Castillo:

> As for me, I am already resigned to everything that could happen to me, but submit the children of Carlos Manuel de Céspedes to the yoke of the Spanish and the treachery and infamy of the Cubans, *never*! We will first die in poverty in a strange country than live with every comfort (as has recently been proposed to me) in a land where so many crimes have been committed. No, one thousand times no! My soul is too strong to debase itself and stain the name of the great man of Cuba—great for his *idea* and great for his *martyrdom*.[232]

Ana de Quesada stayed in New York, where she raised her two children. She remained convinced that her husband had been a victim not of the Spanish, but of those she regarded as ungrateful Cubans who betrayed him and then abandoned him to be killed.[233] Her bitter words stand as a somber epitaph for a war that had seemingly accomplished nothing except leave a trail of casualties and scars not just in Cuba, but also in New York:

> And although I feel an unheard-of contempt for the majority of Cubans and an irreconcilable hatred for almost all of them, . . . it is my destiny to be the wife and widow of he who sacrificed himself for the most wretched people on earth.[234]

7

The Aftermath of War and a Changed Community

The Cuban feudal *señores* who threw themselves into the uncertain adventure of securing independence from Spanish
despotism not only saw their ideals frustrated in 1878, but
also found themselves completely deprived of their preemi-
nent economic position, displaced as landowners, some of
them dead, and all of them ruined.
—Emilio Roig de Leuchsenring, *13 conclusiones fundamentales sobre la guerra libertadora cubana de 1895*, 1945[1]

"Gossip says," reported the *New York Times*, "that the presents were
many and valuable, but they were not on exhibition."[2] What was on exhibition, however, at the wedding of Leonor Aldama in a spring afternoon
of 1879 was the social position of her family after a decade of continuous
residence in New York. During that decade a war had been fought and
lost for Cuban independence. But barely a year after the Pact of Zanjón
had sealed the fate of that long and bitter conflict, the standing of the
Aldama-Alfonso-del Monte clan in New York society gave every appearance of being undiminished.

Leonor, Miguel Aldama's youngest daughter, married Joaquín Mier, a
Colombian diplomat. The wedding took place in a packed St. Stephen's
Catholic Church, on 28th Street between Lexington and Third.[3] It was
officiated by Cardinal John McCloskey and a retinue of more than a
dozen priests and assisted by five bridesmaids and eight ushers. Among
them were María Mestre, the daughter of José Manuel Mestre, and the
teenager Leonardo del Monte Jr., the bride's nephew. Miguel Aldama,
a widower by this time, gave away the bride and hosted a reception
after the wedding for some four hundred guests at his home on West
47th Street. The house, reported the *Times*, "was a bower of flowers and
ferns."[4] A few days later the newlyweds left for a honeymoon in Europe
aboard a White Star steamer.

Despite appearances, however, Miguel Aldama struggled to pay for the expenses of his daughter's wedding and honeymoon. His finances had been in a tailspin for several years. When the war ended in 1878 he could have returned to Cuba, as did many of his compatriots, to attempt to recover his embargoed properties. But instead he decided to stay in New York to try to revive his Brooklyn sugar refinery and his fortunes there.

The construction of the Santa Rosa sugar refinery in Brooklyn had used up most of the money he had taken out of Cuba and deposited in his account with Moses Taylor. With his properties on the island embargoed by the Spanish at the outset of the war, it was impossible for him to replenish that capital. The refinery never became fully operational, for it required further investments he could not afford.[5] By February 1875 the idle refinery had already accumulated a debt in excess of $120,000. Aldama had used up all his credit to buy turbines from a Philadelphia manufacturer in a futile effort to put the refinery into production. Even Moses Taylor was hesitant to extend any further credit to him. The grocery business that his nephew and son-in-law, Leonardo del Monte, had established in New York, with a $100,000 investment from Miguel, went bankrupt.[6]

Aldama's financial situation was so critical that one of his sons-in-law, Isaac Carrillo, a lawyer who also lived in New York and was married to Miguel's second daughter, María de los Dolores (Lola), took steps to secure his wife's "position" by claiming a portion of what had been the family's wealth at the time of the death of Aldama's wife, Hilaria Fonts, who had passed away a few years before. In claiming that the money, about $6,000, was Lola's rightful inheritance, Carrillo gave rise to a bitter conflict with his father-in-law, greatly distressing Aldama, who feared that the dispute might become public and threaten the family's social position, something Miguel wanted desperately to maintain. Born into wealth, the scion of the fabulously rich Alfonso-Aldama clan in Cuba, Miguel could simply not adjust to a life of financial hardship and did what he could to maintain a social calendar in New York. Spending what little he had left on his daughter's wedding was no doubt important in keeping up the appearance of prosperity. He even hosted a lavish banquet in the city in honor of General Antonio Maceo, who had finally laid down his arms in Cuba after protesting the Treaty of Zanjón. But he had to renege on a pledge of $15,000 he made to Maceo as a contribution to a renewal of the war effort.[7]

By 1885, six years after the wedding, Miguel Aldama was literally penniless. Returning to the island to lay claim to his embargoed estates was his only recourse. But given the experience of other Cuban New Yorkers of his social class who did return immediately after the war to try to recover their properties, Aldama's chances of rebuilding his fortune in Cuba were slim. Their wealth rooted in sugar and railroads, the old Havana reformists who had fled to New York at the start of the war had also seen their financial accounts in the city dwindle during the conflict. They harbored the illusion that with the end of the conflict their embargoed properties would be returned to them by the Spanish, or at the very least, they would receive compensation for them. But that did not happen. The Pact of Zanjón provided amnesty for returning exiles, not redress from the embargo, so Spain did not see itself committed to returning assets to those it viewed as the enemies of colonial rule. The reparations that were made were limited and selective. Some planters, Cristóbal Madan and Máximo Mora among them, would spend the rest of their lives and whatever money they had left in protracted litigation seeking compensation from Spain.

Even if they had recovered their estates, the planter class would have faced immense challenges in making them productive again. The war had caused widespread destruction on the island, the infrastructure was in shambles, and Spain sought to ease its war debt by increasing taxes on just about everything, including land, sales, and imported food and manufactured goods.[8] And that was not the worst of it for the planters. In 1884 sugar prices fell to a historic low, in part because of the depression that had started the year before, but also because of the advent of large-scale production of beet sugar in Europe. Two years later, a final blow to the planters was dealt by a royal decree abolishing slavery.

The demise of the sugar planter class had a lasting impact on Cuban New York. The very origins of the community, as we have seen, were tied to the sugar trade, and those who sold their sugar in the city featured prominently among New York's Cuban residents or sojourners. The constant flow of elites between the island and the city, as sugar planters and merchants went to New York to live, to vacation, and to spend the money they had deposited in their accounts with the counting houses served to create the image of Cubans as prosperous—even aristocratic—foreigners among most New Yorkers.

That changed after 1878, as Cuban New York acquired a more proletarian character with the return to the island of many elites and the dwindling fortunes of the sugar trade. The return flow to the island was not limited to planters eager to claim their property. There were some, intellectuals such as Antonio Bachiller y Morales, who owned no sugar estates, but simply took advantage of the amnesty provision of the Pact of Zanjón to go back and spend the rest of their lives in their native country.

Not all elites, of course, returned. Generally, those who had invested in New York the money they had brought from Cuba stayed in the city. We shall see in this chapter two prominent families, the Govíns and the Angaricas, who remained in New York and lived from their substantial real estate investments in Manhattan.

Also remaining in New York were the many working-class and poor Cubans who had left a country torn by war and found a better life in New York. This was certainly true of the servants and former slaves who had migrated with their employers and masters. And it was also true of craftsmen and laborers, especially the cigar makers, who had few opportunities waiting for them back home.

The results of the 1880 U.S. decennial census reflect the return of many Cubans to the island and the beginning of the trend toward a more proletarian Cuban New York. The total number of Cuban-born persons enumerated in what are now the five boroughs was about 2,100, a decline of more than 600 persons from the 1870 census. While the total number of Cuban professionals in the city dropped by more than 20 percent, the number of cigar makers increased from 226 in 1870 to nearly 400. There were also increases in the categories of craftsmen, semi-skilled, and clerical workers.

The trend toward a more proletarian Cuban New York was also manifested in an increase in the nonwhite population. While the number of white Cubans in the city declined, the number of nonwhites increased slightly. In 1870 nonwhites were only about 9 percent of all Cubans in New York, but by 1880 that proportion rose to 12 percent. The increase, however, was much more noticeable among cigar workers. In 1870 there were only nine Cuban nonwhites listed as cigar makers, barely 4 percent of all Cubans in that occupation. A decade later, however, one in five Cuban cigar makers was nonwhite, their numbers rising to seventy-six.

The nonwhite cigar makers tended to live in racially segregated households concentrated in certain sections of the city, unlike the residential pattern of nonwhites who were waiters, cooks, laundresses, and servants, and who lived in the households or in the neighborhoods throughout the city where they provided those services. One notable cluster of Afro-Cubans, most of them cigar workers, was in the city block bounded by Minetta Lane, West 3rd Street, Sixth Avenue, and MacDougal Street. On that city block alone lived seventeen nonwhite Cubans in seven different boardinghouses, most of them on Minetta. Eleven of the Cubans were cigar makers, nine men and two women. Almost all of the seven boardinghouses had only nonwhite residents (Cuban and non-Cuban), with one exception: a predominantly white U.S.-born family boardinghouse at 122 West 3rd Street where a married couple of Cuban-born "mulattoes," a waiter and a cook, lived with their New York-born young children and the man's Cuban-born mother. That racially mixed boardinghouse, however, was the exception. The other houses on that block were exclusively white, indicating the continuation of the pattern observed in chapter 5 regarding race and residence in New York: while many neighborhoods were not segregated, individual boardinghouses almost always were racially homogeneous. This meant that working-class Cubans in New York were more likely to live with those of their own race than with fellow Cubans of a different race.

Another example of how Cubans generally conformed to the norms of racial segregation in the city was the black enclave located on 32nd and 33rd Streets between Sixth and Seventh Avenues. Fifteen nonwhite Cubans lived in what was almost exclusively a black neighborhood. Among the Cubans there were four cigar makers, three servants, a tailor, two laundresses, and a confectioner. No white Cubans lived in that neighborhood.

Cigar makers, seamstresses, and coopers represented the top rung of the occupational ladder of nonwhite Cuban New Yorkers. The pattern of racial stratification noted for 1870 continued in 1880. Only a handful of nonwhites were in a professional, commercial, or white-collar occupation. Most nonwhites were servants, laundresses, cooks, waiters, and porters. There was even a sixteen-year-old Cuban-born "mulatto" in the Newsboys Lodging House at 9 Duane Street, which housed more than a hundred homeless boys, most of them white.[9] The Cuban youngster, however, was not a newsboy, but a "bootblack."

The 1880 census found two of the black Cubans who three years before carried Aguilera's coffin from the funeral mass to Marble Cemetery. Both were cigar makers. Ramón Romay, thirty-five, lived with his non-Cuban wife, Sarah, in the West 40s, while Antonio Vidal, forty, lived with his wife, Cecilia, in a boardinghouse at 127 West 27th Street.[10] That boardinghouse was another exception to the pattern of racial segregation. The Vidals and another nonwhite Cuban cigar maker and his family lived with several working-class non-Cuban families, all white.

Across West 27th Street from the Vidals, at number 128, stood a boardinghouse that was the scene of a murder that in many ways echoed the case of Félix Sánchez twenty-five years earlier. As with Sánchez's crime, the murder on 27th Street brought out New York City's uneasy intersections of race, nationality, crime, and justice.

* * *

Sometime after ten o'clock on the night of June 20, 1884, many of the residents of the crowded and predominantly black tenement house at 128 West 27th Street rushed up the stairs of the building after hearing a succession of gunshots coming from the fourth floor. They saw what the *New York Herald* described as a "bareheaded mulatto" carrying a pistol and shouting in a foreign language. The man ran down the stairway past the crowd and onto the street, where he disappeared. Upstairs in a bedroom lay the body of a "pretty, colored woman" named María Williams, whose husband, Munroe Williams, was standing over her, trembling. She had been shot through the heart.[11]

Later that night, Detective James Price of the Twenty-Ninth Precinct, acting on information he obtained from Mrs. Williams's neighbors, was staking out a "Cuban lodging-house" at 70 Spring Street when his suspect entered the building. He followed him in, but did not find him on the top floor, where there were several Cubans playing cards. The detective climbed through an open dormer window, and there on the roof was the man he was looking for, trying to escape. After slipping on the tiled roof and nearly falling off the building, Price apprehended the man and took him to the precinct station, where he was locked up until his arraignment the following day at the Jefferson Market Police Court.[12]

The murder suspect was identified as Miguel Chacón, a twenty-year-old Cuban cigar worker who had been living in the city for three years. The press reports quickly rectified the earlier description of him as a "mulatto." The New York Times described Chacón as being "of medium build . . . and black as ebony," while the New York Herald reporter found him to be "powerful . . . and very dark."[13] Subsequent press stories described Chacón as "a coal-black darky," "a full-bodied Ethiopian," and having a complexion "of the blackest possible description."[14]

The victim, María Williams, was a "colored" Cuban woman who was married to a non-Cuban "colored" waiter by the name of Munroe Williams.[15] The Williamses had been married for nearly seven years when they separated and the husband took various temporary jobs out of town, mostly in Virginia and Connecticut. At the time of their separation, nearly six months before the murder, the Williamses leased the entire fourth floor of the house on 27th Street and lived in one of the rooms and rented out the other six to boarders. María continued to operate the boarding business after her husband's departure.[16]

One of the boarders was Miguel Chacón, and he and María became romantically involved, eventually living together as a couple in the boardinghouse; Chacón even bought furnishings for the rooms and kitchen. Six months after the separation, and without having sent any money to his wife during his absence, Munroe Williams decided to return, and María asked Miguel to move out.

The day of the murder, Chacón returned several times to the boardinghouse to pick up his belongings. At the trial, all of the witnesses testified that it was a tense day. Munroe Williams had already moved in and the two men quarreled in the kitchen. Chacón maintained at his trial that the husband had threatened him with a knife. When the Cuban returned for the last time that night, he had a gun. In the hallway of the fourth floor he and Munroe quarreled again and Chacón fired three shots in the direction of where Munroe and María stood. One of the shots went through María's heart, killing her instantly.

Because Chacón had taken a gun to the boardinghouse, the district attorney charged him with first-degree murder. Five months later, Chacón was tried in the New York Court of General Sessions. The trial was covered by every major newspaper in the city. A romantic triangle that resulted in the death of the woman was a sensational story, made even more compelling by a certain sympathy that emerged for the accused. During the trial, the husband, who had abandoned his wife for months, appeared to be aloof and uncaring in reciting the details of the crime. Chacón, on the other hand, had been financially supporting the victim during those months, and during the trial he appeared distraught and remorseful. At one point in his testimony, his attorney asked him whether he had the intention of shooting María when he went back to the boardinghouse, to which he answered through an interpreter, "No sir; I loved her."[17]

The trial lasted three days, and after three hours of deliberations the jury returned a guilty verdict. The *New York Times* reporter noted that Chacón "took the result coolly, and did not seem to care which way the verdict went."[18] The *Herald* reporter observed that the convicted man was "unmoved."[19] Just three days later, the sentence was handed down: death by hanging. The prisoner was remanded to the Tombs, where, the *New York Herald* noted, he was placed in the same cell that four years before had been occupied by Pietro Balbo, a young Italian immigrant executed for murdering his wife in a fit of jealousy, a case that also caught the attention of New Yorkers.[20]

The execution was delayed by appeals. Some two hundred citizens, headed by one Antonio González, sent a petition to Governor David Hill asking that the sentence be commuted to life in prison, adducing that the murder had been an accident, the result of a quarrel between rivals and not a premeditated crime that merited execution.[21] The petition was rejected, as well as all legal appeals, and the hanging was set for July 9, 1886, two years after the murder of María Williams.[22]

The press coverage in the days leading to the execution was overtly sympathetic to Chacón and critical of the death sentence. Extensive coverage was given to Chacón's attempt on June 30 to cut his wrists with a pen knife and the subsequent suicide watch imposed by prison officials. "Knife Better Than the Rope" was the *Herald*'s headline.[23] The *New York Times* published a detailed report on the case based on interviews with Chacón, the warden, and attorneys involved in the case.[24] The article repeated Chacón's claim that he felt threatened by Maria's husband and had acted in self-defense, but that at the last instant María stepped into the line of fire. Attorneys interviewed by the *Times* expressed their "great astonishment" at the outcome of the trial. The *Times* writer argued that "Chacon's inability to grapple with the English language and the fact that he had no friends to intercede for him weighed heavily against him on his trial." Warden Finn of the Tombs offered that "Chacon has never given him or any of the keepers any trouble, but has behaved himself as a well-meaning, bright young man should do."[25] The warden went even further in his support of Chacón when he told the *Times* that "the fact that he is a friendless foreigner is the reason he cannot be saved. A man of influence . . . could certainly have had his sentence commuted if all the facts were known."[26] Warden Finn, according to the *Times*, "is not anxious to see the gallows erected."[27]

The *Daily Tribune* also ran a piece sympathetic to Chacón, repeating his explanation for the crime and even noting that Detective Price, who originally arrested Chacón, had paid a visit to the prisoner.[28] Other visitors to the condemned man's cell included reporters, a priest who said mass and gave Chacón communion, two nuns, and Ramón Rubiera, identified as the editor of the Spanish paper *La República* and secretary of the National Confederation of Cuban Cigar Makers.[29] There was no hope now for Chacón: the governor had already announced that he would not intervene to spare his life.[30] All of the major newspapers in the city chronicled in detail the prisoner's activities and moods in the twenty-four hours leading to the execution, with the *New York Sun* placing the story on its front page.[31]

There were fourteen reporters present on the morning of July 9, 1886, when Chacón, in a prison-issue black suit, white shirt, and black tie, was led from his cell to the gallows erected in a courtyard on the Elm Street side of the Tombs.[32] Despite a sizable police presence, deployed precisely to keep the curious at a distance, onlookers crowded the streets, and the neighbors of the prison filled the open windows overlooking the courtyard to get a better look at the execution.[33] After the drop, at forty minutes past seven in the morning, it took about three minutes for Chacón to die.[34] The body was claimed by his elderly uncle, Manuel López, who the day before had told the priest attending the prisoner that he had no money to pay for the funeral. The priest, Father Byrnes, assured him that the Church would take care of the burial, and he and

López accompanied the hearse carrying the body to Calvary Cemetery, the diocesan cemetery in Queens.[35]

In the stories they filed that day, most reporters wrote empathic postscripts to the Chacón story, with the exception of the *Sun* reporter, who ended his report with the following paragraph:

> Miguel Chacon was an ignorant Negro, born in Cuba 21 years ago. He came to New York six years ago and worked at his trade of cigarmaker. . . . Old Capt. Finley said that this was the thirty-seventh hanging at the Tombs since 1850. . . . A heavier weight was used yesterday than before. It was found to work very successfully. The chances of strangling are less with a heavy weight.[36]

As with Gonzalo Aldama, who committed suicide in 1845, and Félix Sanchez, who was interned the rest of his life at a lunatic asylum, Miguel Chacón's New York story ended tragically, as no doubt also ended the stories of many other Cubans who arrived in the city hoping to live lives they could not live in Cuba. Others would also encounter a similar fate as Cuban New York in the 1880s was transforming itself into a more permanent and diverse community, as many of the elites returned to the island to try to claim their estates.

Félix Govín y Pinto and his brother José were among those Cubans living in New York who in 1871 filed claims against the Spanish government for the confiscation of their properties during the war.[37] The Govíns were descendants of French immigrants who settled in Havana early in the eighteenth century from Villefranche-sur-Mer, east of Nice, and subsequently took advantage of the sugar revolution to establish estates in the Matanzas region.[38] Typical of the island's planter elite, the family had a long history of contact with the city where they sold their sugar, as evidenced by their periodic appearances on passenger lists of ships arriving in Manhattan from Cuba. On March 22, 1853, for example, Félix Govín and his sons, Benigno and Félix, arrived in the city aboard the *Crescent City* from Havana.[39] We also know he visited New York in 1865, and again in 1866 with his brother José.[40] In 1867, before the war had started, José became a U.S. citizen, as did Félix's daughter Luciana.[41] Félix's youngest brother, Rafael, had apparently been sent to New York much earlier to handle the family's business affairs: he became a U.S. citizen in 1858.[42]

The Govíns, therefore, followed the pattern of so many Cuban sugar planters who lived transnational lives, regarding New York as their second home, repeatedly traveling there and even establishing residences in the city. They were also typical of their class in that the outbreak of war in 1868 resulted in a much more definitive migration of entire families from Cuba and a more permanent presence in New York. Félix and his wife appear on the passenger list of the *Eagle*, which arrived in New York on April 15, 1869, at the height of the exodus of elites from Cuba. A large number of Govíns, including José, arrived the following week, on April 21, aboard the *Morro Castle*.[43]

Unlike many of the other planters in New York, however, Félix Govín did not return to Cuba after the war to attempt to reclaim his properties. His legal efforts to seek compensation continued, but from New York, where he amassed a considerable fortune from real estate investments. Perhaps anticipating the debacle in the sugar industry, or realizing the futility of the claims against Spain, he chose to remain where his assets may well have exceeded the value of his family's estates in Cuba. While many other Cuban New Yorkers ate away at their accounts with the counting houses while the war raged on, Félix Govín was buying rent-producing properties in Manhattan, investments that proved far more secure than Aldama's refinery venture in Brooklyn. By the end of the war, Govín was quite possibly the richest Cuban in New York.

Because of a legal dispute over his will, an excellent record has remained of Félix Govín's real estate holdings in the city. When Félix died, in May 1891, the value of his estate was estimated in press reports at between $400,000 and $600,000.[44] That would prove to be a low estimate. He executed a will in 1881 and then amended it in 1887 after his wife, Mercedes, died. The amended will left the entire estate, after the payment of certain obligations, to his (and Mercedes's) heirs. One third of it went to their daughter Luciana, another third to one of their sons, and another third to the children of another one of their sons. The will did provide, however, for a payment of $20,000 and a house in the city to each of three children of a woman named Luz Díaz.[45] The woman came forward after Félix's death and obtained legal representation to challenge the will, claiming she was Luz Díaz Govín, the widow of Félix, and was therefore entitled to one-third of the estate. Govín's children with Mercedes, led by Luciana, the oldest, countered with a petition for probate, rejecting the claim that Luz was ever married to their father.

That Félix Govín had a relationship, and children, with Luz Díaz, is suggested not only by the will but also by the 1870 census, which enumerated Félix in two households, both in the Twenty-First Ward. In one he is listed with his wife, Mercedes, and several of his grandchildren. His age is reported as fifty-four. In the other household his age is given as fifty-five and the other members of the household are Luz Díaz Govín, age twenty-eight, and three children, two girls and a boy, ranging in age from one to seven, all with the last name Govín, and all born in Cuba. The boy's name is listed as Félix.[46]

In the 1880 census, Félix Govín was enumerated in only one household, at the same address as in 1870, 54 West 37th Street, in the Twenty-First Ward, with his wife, Mercedes, his daughter Luciana and her husband, Ramón Miranda (a physician), and Luciana's three daughters. Also in the household were his daughter-in-law, also named Mercedes, and her three children with Govín's son Félix, who is not listed in the household and was apparently deceased by this time.[47] Presumably, those three grandchildren are the ones who directly inherited one-third of their grandfather's estate, since Félix Sr.'s other son, Benigno, was still alive and in fact became a U.S. citizen in New York in 1877, listing his address as 54 West 37th Street on the naturalization form.[48]

Luz Díaz was also still living in the Twenty-First Ward in 1880 with her three children, who now ranged in age from ten to seventeen. No longer do any of them, including Luz, have Govín attached to their names; Luz reported that she was the head of the household, and her marital status appears as "widowed." Their census form, however, has an additional item of information that was available for the first time in 1880: nativity of the respondent's parents. Although Luz is listed in both 1870 and 1880 as "white," she reported that while her mother was born in Cuba, her father's birthplace was Africa, a datum that, placed in its nineteenth-century context, sheds a different light on the nature of her relationship with Félix Govín, a planter, a relationship that evidently started in Cuba, since Luz's children were born there.[49]

On August 10, 1891, nearly three months after Félix Govín's death, the temporary court-appointed administrator of his estate, Frederick

Lewis, convened all parties in the dispute over the will at the vaults of the Mercantile Safe Deposit Company at 120 Broadway to witness the opening of the box Félix kept there. Luz Díaz's attorneys had successfully argued, over Luciana Govín's objections, that they and Luz should be present for the opening of the box, since Luz alleged that she personally saw Félix place their marriage contract in the box soon after they were married following the death of Mercedes. Lewis ceremoniously opened the box and found no piece of paper attesting to a marriage between Félix and Luz, which led Luz to tell the *Times* reporter that she believed that the document had been "abstracted from the box in some way or other."[50] What Lewis did find, and kept in the box for later disposition, were some $600,000 worth of stocks and bonds, a finding that served to revise upwards by quite a bit the estimate of the value of Félix's estate, since it was known that he owned considerable real estate in the city.[51]

Those real estate holdings were detailed in the complaint that Luz Díaz, using the name Luz Díaz Govín, filed in the Supreme Court of New York County on September 3, 1891, against the heirs of the estate: Luciana and Luciana's brother Benigno and her nephews, the children of Félix Jr. The complaint asks the defendants to account for all "rents and profits" that were being accrued from no fewer than twenty-one properties in Félix's estate, and laying claim to one-third of the annual value of the profits of the properties. Fourteen of the properties were clustered in the area of the city where Govín had lived with Mercedes and their children: the west side of Manhattan between 23rd and 38th Streets and Sixth and Tenth Avenues. The others were scattered throughout the city, from Centre Street downtown to as far uptown as 59th and Lexington, including a property on St. Mark's Place.[52]

Luz's failure to produce any proof of a marriage to Félix, as well as the fact that her children, assumed illegitimate under the law, were nevertheless "handsomely remembered in the will" (as the *Times* reported) with $20,000 and a house for each, weakened her case for challenging the will.[53] Two months after filing the complaint, she withdrew it and the will was declared valid and entered into probate in Surrogate Court. She told the *Times* reporter that she would bring action to establish her right to dower, that is, to lifetime support, as widow, from the income from Félix's properties.[54] There is no record that she followed through with such action or that she ever received any money from the estate except what was left to her children in the will.

Although Félix Govín had made attempts to obtain some restitution or compensation from the Spanish for the loss of his properties in Cuba, the war led him to drive some permanent stakes into the Manhattan bedrock. He could have returned to the island after the war but chose to stay where he had developed a substantial fortune. Félix, Mercedes, and Luciana are buried in Green-Wood Cemetery in Brooklyn.[55]

Govín's case was typical of the transition that Cuban New York underwent as a result of the 1868–1878 conflict. Prior to the war, the source of wealth of Cuban elites was in Cuba, as planters or importers of agricultural goods, notably sugar, produced on the island. They traveled frequently between Havana and New York and even kept homes in Manhattan. The war forced a more definitive move to New York and also eventually destroyed their source of wealth in Cuba. Some simply waited for the war to end so they could return to the island, but others developed their lives in their new city by investing their money (as Govín did) or their labor (as the cigar makers did) into a permanent stake in New York. Henceforth, the Cuban presence in New York would be a more permanent one, with subsequent generations of Cubans calling the city their home and planning for burials at Green-Wood Cemetery.

* * *

Buried not far from the Govíns in Green-Wood Cemetery is another family that settled permanently in New York after leaving the island in 1869 in the wake of the conflict. Their burial plot is more imposing than that of the Govíns: a nine-foot-tall sculpted stone structure with a pensive robed figure mounted on a pedestal. The front of the pedestal features prominently the Freemason symbol of a square and a compass with the letter G in the center. On either side of the pedestal are carved depictions of the Cuban royal palm. It is the tomb of Joaquín García Angarica, and it is surrounded by his family and descendants, some of them entombed well into the twentieth century, all sharing space in the burial plot of the Star of Cuba Masonic Lodge.

Joaquín was already in his seventies when he left Cuba during the 1869 exodus, accompanied by his large family aboard the *Morro Castle*, which arrived in New York on March 13.[56] He also brought with him one black and two Chinese "domestic servants," who appear in the 1870 census with the last name Angarica. The entire household, at 308 West 27th Street, had twenty-one persons listed, including two additional domestic servants, both Irish women. The family was enlarged primarily through the marriage of one of Joaquín's daughters, Lutgarda, to a man with the last name of de la Rúa. Many of the members of the household had that last name.[57] Joaquín had several daughters but apparently only two sons, one of whom was José, who had no children of his own. Joaquín's heirs were the many children of his daughters and sons-in law.

Joaquín and José appear as claimants in 1871 before the Joint United States and Spanish Commission on property losses in Cuba.[58] They owned estates in Matanzas, in the Colón area. But as early as 1853, Joaquín became a U.S. citizen, giving as his address another house on 27th Street, evidence of his long-standing connection with the city, and perhaps an indication that he had started buying Manhattan real estate considerably before the war started in 1868.[59] A few years after he was enumerated in 1870, Joaquín was residing at 332 West 38th Street, while José lived at 320 West 23rd Street.[60] Further evidence of their investments in real estate is that for many years after both Joaquín and José died, in 1878, Lutgarda and other heirs were involved in real estate transactions from Joaquín's estate, some of those transactions taking place as late as 1902.[61] But the legacy that Joaquín and José García Angarica left in New York lay primarily in their participation in Masonic lodges. The elder García Angarica had been a lifelong Freemason in Cuba, but because of his advanced age was less active in New York than José, who joined City Lodge No. 408 immediately after his arrival. Three years later, he managed to unite the Cuban Freemasons in the city to form the Star of Cuba Lodge, where he served as Master until his untimely death in 1878 at age forty, only eight months after his father died.[62] At the time of his death, José had reached the thirty-second degree, the Sublime Prince of the Royal Secret, the second-highest level within the Freemasonry hierarchy. His funeral was steeped in the rituals of Freemasonry.[63]

That José García Angarica was able to establish the Star of Cuba Lodge attests to the continued importance of Freemasonry among Cubans in New York. As noted in chapter 3, a Cuban, Andrés Cassard, in 1855 established Fraternal Lodge No. 387 in New York, the first Spanish-language lodge in the United States. No doubt the 1868 conflict served to increase the ranks of Freemasons among Cubans in the city, given the importance of Freemasons among the easterners who initiated the conflict (see chapter 4).

* * *

The remains of ten Moras and several of their in-laws are interred in a large family plot at Green-Wood. The first one was buried before the war started, in 1865, and the last one in 1943, attesting to the long-standing presence of the family in the city.[64] But José María Mora, who faced financial ruin because of his generous support for the outfitting of expeditions during the war (see chapter 6), is not buried at Green-Wood, nor does he appear among those enumerated in New York in the 1880 census.[65] Apparently, his financial situation forced him, and most members of his immediate family, to leave New York. We know from newspaper reports that he died in Rio de Janeiro in 1892, where two of his children, Isabel and Enrique, lived. Two other children, María Josefa and Alberto, lived in Europe at the time of José María's death.[66] But his two oldest boys, José María and José Manuel, did remain in New York. In 1880, when they were both in their mid-thirties, the census found them living as boarders in a house at 38 West 28th Street, far from the old neighborhood on East 12th and 13th Streets, where the Moras had been buying real estate since the 1850s. That their father may have been financially ruined is suggested not only by their condition as boarders, but also by the fact that they were apparently not living from inherited assets, but from the profession they reported in the 1880 census: photographers. The Mora brothers operated a very popular portrait studio at 707 Broadway. Among their subjects were President Chester Arthur and William Cullen Bryant.[67]

Some members of the Mora clan still retained after the war a measure of financial solvency that enabled them to continue residing in the old neighborhood. According to the 1880 census, Antonio Máximo Mora and José Antonio Mora were still living in the same homes in which they lived in 1870: the former at 220 East 12th Street, and José Antonio, his wife, Josefina, and their children at 235 East 13th Street.

* * *

It is not surprising that Cirilo Villaverde and Emilia Casanova did not return to Cuba after the war. The militant married couple, who had been so prominent during the war as the bane of the *aldamistas* and the leading proponents in New York of an intransigent stance against Spanish colonialism (see chapter 6), had lived in New York since the annexationist era, when Cirilo had to leave the island because of his role in the Narciso López expeditions. The 1880 census found Cirilo and Emilia, sixty and forty-five, respectively, living at 46 East 126th Street, across the street from Emilia's father, Inocencio, who lived at number 49. Both Harlem row houses are still standing. Inocencio, who had been a plantation owner in Matanzas, was already seventy-four years old in 1880 and his household was a large one, consisting of his wife and seven children (Emilia's siblings), who ranged in age from fifteen to thirty-eight. Also in the household were two black domestic servants: Antonio Bosaga, forty-eight, a cook born in Africa, and José Díaz, thirty, a waiter born in Cuba.

Cirilo and Emilia lived with their two sons, a teenaged Cuban-born boarder, and two female Irish servants. Their oldest son, who was twenty-one in 1880, was named Narciso (no doubt after the expeditionary López) and his occupation was reported as "railroad clerk." The following year, however, the young Villaverde was engaged in editing a Spanish-language monthly newspaper entitled *El Espejo*. With offices at 4 Cedar Street, the publication listed in its masthead the broad scope of its contents: "Sciences, Arts, Literature, Industry, Instruction, Commerce, Etc." and Narciso was identified as its "Editor and Proprietor."[68]

El Espejo was certainly not in the tradition of the Cuban separatist newspapers that appeared during the war. It was devoid of any politics or controversy. Its twenty-four pages were devoted to both articles and advertising that showcased U.S. manufactured products. The intended readership was clearly importers throughout Latin America and Spain. In every issue there was a list, usually on page 9, of the nearly one hundred "agents" of *El Espejo* located throughout Mexico, Central America, South America, and the Antilles, especially Cuba. Presumably these agents would arrange for the purchases of the featured products. The paper also published a directory with the contact information of all firms whose products were featured in that issue. Among the firms and products advertised were hay mowers from the Victor Mower Company in the Hudson Valley; the George Forbes Company in Massachusetts, manufacturer of wheels for carts and carriages; pneumatic jacks manufactured by Joyce, Cridland and Company of Dayton, Ohio; sewing machines from the National Sewing Machine Company on Pearl Street; and also from New York City, on Liberty Street, the "safe steam-powered hydraulic elevators" of the Otis Brothers. Ads were placed by manufacturers of a wide range of products: baby carriages, organs, hoses, furniture, hardware, corsets, wheelbarrows, even railroad cars. While most of those products were featured in ads, *El Espejo* also ran lengthy articles on new scientific and industrial technologies (e.g., the "processing of iridium"), innovative products, as well as economic and commercial news, such as the 1883 U.S.-Mexico trade agreement. There were also occasional articles of general interest with an international focus: "The Army Ants of the Amazon," or "German Expeditions in Africa."

Judging from the ads, it seems that *El Espejo* was a commercial success, yet it apparently ceased publication in late 1885, perhaps a victim of that success. In some of the last issues, the "Villaverde Brothers" (Narciso and his younger brother, Enrique) announced, in both English and Spanish, to their "friends and patrons" that they opened, also at 4 Cedar Street, a "commission business in connection with *El Espejo* and that we are ready to fill any orders we may be entrusted with, at BOTTOM PRICES. Correspondence solicited. All inquiries cheerfully answered."[69] Narciso and Enrique probably decided that thanks to *El Espejo* they had placed themselves in a position to make more money from commission sales than from publishing a newspaper.

But the most historically significant item to be printed in *El Espejo* was an ad that announced the printing and release, by *El Espejo* itself, of a six-hundred-page novel of "Cuban customs" entitled *Cecilia Valdés ó La Loma del Angel*. The ad was reprinted in every issue of *El Espejo* until the demise of the newspaper in 1885. The novel's author: Narciso's father, Cirilo Villaverde.

The publication of *Cecilia Valdés* in New York is one of the foremost examples of how the city had become in the nineteenth century the premier stage outside Cuba for the unfolding of Cuban political, sociocultural, and intellectual history. Villaverde's novel is not just any novel, but is regarded, as one contemporary scholar of Cuban literature expressed it, as "the most important novel written in nineteenth-century Cuba and perhaps one of the most important works in Latin America during that

Cecilia Valdés

Ó

LA LOMA DEL ANGEL.

NOVELA

DE COSTUMBRES CUBANAS

——POR——

CIRILO VILLAVERDE.

IMPRENTA DE EL ESPEJO, NUEVA YORK, AÑO DE 1883.

Esta novela es del género histórico, no ya solo
por la multitud de hechos y de noticias verdaderas
de que está sembrada, sino tambien por el retrato á
la pluma de varios caractéres públicos de la Isla de
Cuba que en ella figuran mas ó menos prominente-
mente. Forma un volúmen en 8vo de 600 páginas,
impreso con lujo y elegancia, en buen papel y tipos
nuevos de fácil lectura. Va adornada de varios
fotograbados intercalados en el texto á modo de
viñetas. La cubierta lleva un grabado alusivo á la
naturaleza de Cuba. La obra está dedicada á las
cubanas, y tiene un sabor político marcado, carac-
terístico de la época (1812–1831) y del teatro (la
Habana) en que se supone ocurrieron los sucesos.

VENDESE EN

La imprenta de EL ESPEJO á . . . . $1 el ejem.

Figure 7.1. Advertisement for *Cecilia Valdés ó La
Loma del Angel*, by Cirilo Villaverde, in *El Espejo*, April 1883. Source: *El Espejo*, April 1883, 2.

period."[70] Another Cuban scholar judges the work as "our most representative literary myth. It is the equivalent, for Cuban literature, of what the *Quijote* is for Spanish literature, what *Hamlet* is for English literature, and what *Faust* is for German literature."[71]

Cecilia Valdés was a long-postponed literary project. Villaverde first published a two-part short story by that title in Havana in 1839. In the prologue to the "definitive" 1882 edition, Villaverde labels the earlier publication the "first volume" of the work, one that he did not return to until the Ten Years' War was near an end: "It cannot be said in truth that I have spent forty years writing this novel. When I resolved to finish it, two or three years ago, the most I have been able to do has been to finish a chapter, with many interruptions, every fifteen days, sometimes a month, working some hours during the week and all day on Sunday."[72] Villaverde explains to the reader in the prologue that in those forty years he had been otherwise occupied, initially with other literary projects, but once having suffered imprisonment in Cuba and becoming exiled, "I terminated my literary proclivities for higher thoughts: I went from the world of illusions to the world of realities . . . to take part in the enterprises of a free man in a free land."[73] He recounts those enterprises: serving as secretary to Narciso López, editing the annexationist newspaper *La Verdad*, writing countless political tracts, and engaging in the intense activities to which he and his wife, Emilia, dedicated themselves during the war, including "the tumultuous scenes of the Cuban émigrés . . . especially in New York," a reference to the couple's rancorous battle with the *aldamistas* (see chapter 6).[74]

In his 2005 book *Writing to Cuba*, Rodrigo Lazo argues that Villaverde's decision to take up the unfinished *Cecilia* after forty years can only be understood in the aftermath of the defeat of the independence movement: "Villaverde dusted himself off and returned to the novel form to mount a rearguard attack against the enemy. . . . *Cecilia Valdés* is an attempt to seize the nation at a moment when it appears to Villaverde that the military battle for the island has been lost to Spain."[75] The reader learns that the novel was written in New York only because of the reference at the end of the prologue: "New York, May, 1879." Otherwise, there is no indication that it is written by a Cuban émigré who has spent most of his life outside the island. As such, Lazo argues, the novel departs from the tradition of transnational texts in which the attempt is to recapture the lost homeland with an émigré vision, that is, from a location outside Cuba:

> The text of the novel . . . does not acknowledge outright that the vision of *Cecilia Valdés'* Cuba detours through New York. . . . *Cecilia Valdés* can be positioned as a novel solely of Cuba, the ultimate nationalistic fiction.[76]

It is perhaps because of that strictly "Cuban" vision that the novel has endured in the imaginary of the island.

Cecilia Valdés is set in Havana between 1812 and 1831, a time and place that Villaverde can evoke from his memories of the island. It has been regarded by many as an anti-slavery novel, but it is much more than that. To be sure, there are graphic descriptions of the horrors of the slave regime, reflecting Villaverde's conversion to abolitionism after serving the interests of the pro-slavery annexationist movement, but the author is more concerned with recapturing the people, culture, mores, and customs of the homeland while relegating colonialism to the background, in effect claiming the nation from the Spanish. "In this novel, Cuba is not a Spanish colony but rather is its own place," writes Lazo. "Colonialism represents but one of many parts of the picture and does not define the political subject."[77]

The title character is a beautiful *mulata* born of an extramarital liaison between her father, a detestable and morally corrupt plantation owner, and a free *mulata*. Cecilia's light skin permits her to rub elbows with Havana's aristocracy, into which she hopes to marry by parlaying her extraordinary beauty and charm. She is courted and eventually seduced by a young and spoiled aristocrat, Leonardo Gamboa, whose father, Cándido, is (unbeknownst to the couple) none other than Cecilia's father. Of course, Cecilia's half-brother Leonardo does not make good on his promise to marry her and instead marries a white girl from a suitable upper-class family, as he was expected to do. Cecilia is abandoned with a baby girl born of the relationship with Leonardo, and the implication is that the cycle of racial, class, and sexual exploitation starts anew.

But while the novel's "soap-operatic" love story, as Lazo aptly describes it, undergirds the narrative, it is purposely overshadowed by the much broader historical narrative about Cuba that Villaverde set out to write in his attempt to capture the social history of the nation.[78] Tellingly, the advertisement for the novel in *El Espejo* does not sell it as a love story (perhaps a more marketable label), nor even as an anti-slavery novel, but as a

> novel of the historical genre, not only because of the true events in which it is grounded, but also because of the portrait it draws of various public figures of the island of Cuba of more or less prominence.[79]

The most salient feature of Villaverde's portrayal of the novel's characters is the obvious contempt, bordering on disgust, for the behavior of the aristocratic plantation owners, especially Cándido and Leonardo Gamboa. The novel is full of incidents ("confrontations" as Salvador Bueno calls them) in which slaves are treated inhumanely and free persons of an inferior class are treated disdainfully and even humiliated by an arrogant Havana sugarocracy.[80] The Havana elites are depicted by Villaverde with evident scorn, as shallow and despicable characters.

Salvador Bueno, comparing the 1882 edition with its 1839 precursor, argues that the earlier shorter version is much less critical of slavery and slave owners than the novel that was published decades later in New York: "In the definitive [1882] edition the tendency toward realism is stronger, . . . the social vision offered is more critical and the slavery question is inserted into the ample historical mural that unfolds before the reader."[81] William Luis is more direct in comparing the two versions: "Only the 1882 version can be considered an anti-slavery novel."[82]

What experiences during the decades that Villaverde lived in New York after the publication of the original version of *Cecilia* may have led him to arrive at a harsher, more critical view of the entire social system that rested on slavery? The answers given by the literary scholars rest almost invariably on major historical trends that undoubtedly influenced a change in Villaverde: the demise of the pro-slavery annexationist movement and the rise of the anti-slavery independence movement, concerns raised by an "Africanization" of Cuba and the possible rise of slave rebellions, the U.S. Civil War, and the growing number of abolitionists, including Emilia.[83]

The macro-historical analyses of Villaverde's turn toward a more critical anti-slavery stance are certainly valid, but a contributing explanation for his damning portrayal in the 1882 work of the Havana slaveholding elite may also be found in his more immediate environment in New York: the bruising battles he, and especially Emilia, waged in the city with the leading representatives of that very class during the war. Chapter 6 details the conflict with Aldama, Lemus, Mestre, and the other leaders of the Havana sugar elite who emigrated after the outbreak of the war and quickly established themselves, to the chagrin of longtime émigrés in the city, as the representatives of the insurgents. It was a highly acrimonious and personal conflict with evident social class dimensions, as those exiled sugar owners lived grandly on the fortunes they had long deposited in South Street counting houses while the "true" militants for the cause of independence (as Villaverde and Casanova saw themselves) struggled financially. The caustic writings of Emilia Casanova evidenced a strong class-based resentment. Emilia was convinced, as was her husband, that the rich *habaneros'* lack of commitment to the war effort had doomed the cause for independence.

As defeat became inevitable, and Villaverde decided, to borrow Lazo's phrase, "to dust himself off" and, perhaps even more pointedly, lick his wounds, he took up the long-unfinished *Cecilia* manuscript. It would be unreasonable to expect that his protracted clashes with the *aldamistas* in New York would not have influenced the manner in which he portrayed the Gamboas of the 1830s. One could even go as far as speculating that the opportunity to slam the Havana plantation owners may well have factored into his decision to revise and finish the manuscript. The plot of *Cecilia*, which he outlined in 1839, was a perfect vehicle for that. This argument is strengthened by Villaverde's acknowledgment in the prologue that his wife was consulted on "chapter after chapter" as he finished them and the book reflects her advice and suggestions on character development, language and style, and "general tone."[84] There are some critics who believe that Emilia was a coauthor. And in that married couple, as we have seen, the more acerbic pen belonged to Emilia.

Throughout the many years they lived in New York, Cirilo Villaverde and Emilia Casanova always seemed to be teetering on the edge of financial insecurity. They never overcame their lower economic status in comparison with their richer compatriots of the planter class. Maintaining a respectable level of living in the city, which included having a couple of servants, seemed to be a struggle. In every census in which they were enumerated, the composition of their household always included one or more boarders, apparently a source of income on which they depended. The publication of *Cecilia Valdés* did not bring anything close to a windfall of income. Less than two years after the novel came off the presses of *El Espejo*, the couple was living not in Harlem, but at an address where they had resided previously, 39 West 24th Street, apparently trying to make a go of a more ambitious boardinghouse business. They hired "a creole lady" by the name of Elizabeth Story as the manager of the house, but ended up having an altercation with her that required police intervention and a court appearance, and even made it to page 8 of the *Times*.[85] According to the report, Story was paid $1,500 a year by the Villaverdes to run the house and provide "board" for the couple. But, the *Times* reported, "the establishment was not so conducted as to please Señora Villaverde, and last week there was a grand row at the dinner table because the Villaverdes complained of the board."[86] Story reportedly struck Casanova and "pushed her in the doorway of the house and called her names," which resulted in charges of "disorderly conduct and assault and battery" being filed against the hired manager.[87] The matter was resolved in court, with the Villaverdes paying Story $300 "to get her out of the house," after she promised "not to annoy them again."[88]

* * *

Ana de Quesada, the widow of Carlos Manuel de Céspedes, remained true to her bitter vow not to return to Cuba. The 1880 census found her living at the Victoria Hotel on 27th Street between Broadway and Fifth Avenue with her twin children, Carlos and Gloria.[89] She became a U.S. citizen on December 30, 1881.[90] Ignacio Agramonte's widow, Amalia Simoni, was also living in New York in 1880, having returned from Mérida, Yucatán, where in 1873 she had received the news of her husband's death on a Cuban battlefield. Simoni lived at 360 West 45th Street with her two children, Ignacio Ernesto and Herminia.[91] By the time she applied for a U.S. passport in October 1881, she was already a naturalized U.S. citizen.[92] The two widows of the two most revered generals of the war remained in New York.

* * *

On March 27, 1888, the *New York Times*, on page 3, carried a brief dispatch from Havana noting the departure the previous day from the

Figure 7.2. The Aldama mausoleum in Green-Wood Cemetery, Brooklyn. Source: Photograph by the author.

Cuban capital of the steamer *City of Washington*, bound for New York with the remains of Miguel Aldama. The "wealthy Havana merchant and at one time leader of the revolutionists in Cuba," as he was described by the paper, had passed away March 15.[93] His biographer noted that Aldama was unable to rebuild his fortune and died in the most "absolute poverty" as a guest in a friend's house in Havana. Salomé Malagamba, a former slave whom Aldama had freed years earlier, reported the dying words of his once owner: "Do not bury me in this enslaved land, place my bones in a free land."[94] There was a burial spot available to him in that free land: the mausoleum he had built years before near the main entrance to Green-Wood Cemetery in Brooklyn to bury his father, Domingo, and his wife, Hilaria.

The return of the body of Miguel Aldama to New York was a fitting end to the 1880s, a decade that marked a turning point in the history of Cuban New York. In the aftermath of a disastrous war, the landed elites who had spearheaded the exodus to New York found themselves, as did Aldama, in financial ruin, many of them returning to the island, replaced in the city by a growing number of cigar makers, giving Cuban New York a more diverse and proletarian composition. Some elites, such as Félix Govín and the Angaricas, who had invested their money in New York real estate, chose to remain in the city, as did the war widows and committed separatists who could not envision returning to the island. The cigar makers and other workers largely went to New York to stay. They all gave the community a more permanent character that departed from the long-standing pattern of circular migration that had marked the elite presence before the war. With relative peace in Cuba, the level of political activism was much less evident and the volume of political rhetoric was significantly reduced.

* * *

Cuban New York in the 1880s contained the seeds of the major developments that would fundamentally affect the future of the community in the following decade. One of those was the loss, at the beginning of the 1890s, of New York's primacy among Cuban communities in the United States. That would be assumed by an upstart settlement on the outskirts of Tampa, Florida, where, starting in 1886, an entire community of cigar makers arose around the large cigar factories established there by Cuban and Spanish cigar manufacturers. It was Ybor City, the cigar "company town" established by its namesake, the cigar manufacturer Vicente Martínez Ybor.

Although born in Spain, Martínez Ybor joined other Havana cigar manufacturers in relocating their cigar factories to Key West after the outbreak of the war in 1868. During the 1870s and into the 1880s Martínez Ybor manufactured his Príncipe de Gales (Prince of Wales) brand of handmade cigars in Key West, while his principal residence and his distribution office were in New York. He was already sixty years old when the 1880 census found him living at 218 East 14th Street with his second wife, Mercedes (thirty-eight) and seven of his children, ranging in age from thirty-eight to one (the youngest five with Mercedes). The household also included Martínez Ybor's uncle, a Mexican-born female servant, and a black cook born in Cuba.[95]

The backyard of Martínez Ybor's row house on 14th Street abutted the yard of the house facing 13th Street, at number 219. In the Moras' enclave, that house in 1880 was occupied by Eduardo Manrara, thirty-seven, born in Cuba, who listed his occupation as "tobacco merchant." He lived there with his wife, Matilda, thirty-two, also Cuban-born, and their daughter and four young sons. The two oldest children were born in Florida and the rest in New York. Also in the household were two servants: an Irish-born young woman and a Cuban-born black male.

Manrara was not just Martínez Ybor's neighbor; he was his junior partner and right-hand man, and he played a critical role in persuading his older associate to relocate their Key West factory to the outskirts of Tampa. Manrara traveled frequently between New York and the factory in Key West and had opportunity to become acquainted with the town of Tampa and the excellent bay from which he would invariably board the schooner for the last leg of his trip to the Key.[96] Martínez Ybor and Manrara had long been looking to relocate their factory from Key West to a location that would prove less vulnerable to what, from their perspective, was plaguing New York and, eventually, the Key: an organized labor movement that had been galvanized by the strike of 1877 in New York, leading to the creation of the Cigar Makers International Union. In August 1885 another strike paralyzed the factories in Key West, and Martínez Ybor and Manrara became even more convinced that they should relocate to a relatively isolated area and create a "company town," a formula that had proved successful in other industries in limiting union influence.[97]

The owners of the Príncipe de Gales were not the only cigar manufacturers looking to get away from unions. Ignacio Haya and Serafín Sánchez, the owners of one of the largest cigar factories in New York, were also looking to relocate to warmer climates to avoid labor organizers. Their factory, La Flor de Sánchez y Haya, was located at 130 Maiden Lane, literally around the corner from 190 Pearl Street, the offices of Martínez Ybor and Manrara.[98] Both Haya and Sánchez were, as was Martínez Ybor, Spanish-born émigrés from Cuba who had owned factories in Havana. In 1880 Ignacio Haya, thirty-eight, lived with his New York-born wife, Fannie, in an upscale boardinghouse at 57 West 39th Street, while Serafín Sánchez, forty, lived at 165 Bergen Street in Brooklyn with his wife, Regina, and four young children.[99]

It was therefore in New York that the four colleagues and friends—Martínez Ybor, Manrara, Haya, and Sánchez—hatched the plan to create and develop a complete company town on the land they purchased northeast of Tampa. It was named Ybor City, and the first cigar to be produced there rolled off the hands of a cigar maker in the new La Flor de Sánchez y Haya factory on March 26, 1886.[100] The nearby El Príncipe de Gales factory started production a few days later. Other manufacturers followed and cigar factories sprung up, as did houses for the workers. By May 1886, Martínez Ybor's Ybor City Land and Improvement Company had built eighty-nine houses, and a hotel was almost finished. An entire community was thus created by immigrant entrepreneurs, employing immigrant laborers, and processing imported cigar leaves. In the final years of the nineteenth century, Ybor City became the premier Cuban community in the United States. The 1900 U.S. decennial census found 3,533 persons born in Cuba residing in Hillsborough County, the county in which Tampa is located.[101] That was the largest concentration of Cuban-born persons in the United States that year, surpassing New York.[102]

Cuban New York in the 1880s not only sowed the seeds of a bourgeoning cigar-making community in Florida, but also set the stage for the next round of the Cuban separatist struggle. On the third day of that decade, January 3, 1880, José Martí, the protagonist of the definitive push for Cuban independence in the 1890s, arrived in New York. The New York of the 1880s was to be the place and time where he nurtured and honed the considerable intellectual and political talents that he would display when he set his sights on organizing, from New York, the definitive movement for the independence of Cuba.

8

José Martí, New Yorker

You are interested in knowing whether you can find a way
to make a living in New York. In my judgment, that depends
solely on things I assume you master: the language of this
land and your determination. . . . You must summon all your
determination to enter the herd in which the workers of this
city live—but it is a herd of kings.
—José Martí, letter to Gabriel de Zéndegui, October 21, 1882[1]

On a cold January evening in 1895, José Martí walked briskly to Delmonico's Restaurant on 26th Street and Fifth Avenue to celebrate his
birthday. It was a Monday, the twenty-eighth day of the month, exactly
forty-two years after his birth in a modest Havana home. As he walked
into the restaurant, his mind was on the events that he had set into
motion and that at times seemed to overwhelm him. But the sight
of four loyal friends waiting for him at a corner table helped to place
him in a celebratory mood. It was, after all, his birthday and it was his
favorite New York restaurant. He once wrote about Delmonico's that
"everything there is served and prepared with supreme distinction:
. . . moist bottles set on rich napkins, select dishes on elegant plat-
ters, delicate crystal filled with perfumed wines, silver plates with soft
breads."[2] Dinner that January evening provided a much-needed distraction from what Martí had to do on the following day: draft the order
to start a war. Perusing the menu, he recognized many of Delmonico's
signature offerings: red-head roast duck, breast of chicken à la Lorenzo,
terrapin (Baltimore style), filet of beef with stuffed olives, Renaissance
timbales, clear green turtle soup, peaches (or pears) à la Richelieu, and
"fancy cakes."[3]

In some ways he was the same man who fifteen years before, on
another cold January day, had arrived in New York with a mixture of
wonder and trepidation about the great city and with an unshakable

commitment to the future of his homeland. But in other ways he was a very different man, and New York had a lot do with that.

Martí is the towering figure of Cuban history, and he spent most of his adult life in New York. Shortly after his arrival in 1880 he wrote that in New York "one can breathe freely" and "feel proud of one's specie."[4] The city gave him experiences he could not have found anywhere else, experiences that allowed him to develop politically, intellectually, and personally, and made it possible for him to sharpen his vision of the world and his strategy for achieving an independent Cuba. It was in New York that he did his best writing and earned a living from it. It was in New York that he accomplished what no other Cuban émigré had been able to do: build a unified civilian movement that would take a sustainable armed struggle to Cuba. And it was in New York that he was exposed to the best and the worst of what the most important city in the world, the one at the cutting edge of urban modernity, had to offer.

* * *

The manifest of the S.S. *France* lists 192 passengers who boarded at Le Havre and arrived in New York on January 3, 1880. Passenger number 30 is "Mr. Martí," a twenty-six-year-old male "advocate," citizen of Spain, who traveled second-class.[5] José Martí's arrival in New York capped a three-month European journey that he had not willingly undertaken. Arrested in Havana in September 1879 for his activities on behalf of Cuban independence, he was deported by the Spanish authorities and placed on a ship bound for Spain, forcing him to leave behind his wife and infant son.

From the moment he arrived in the Spanish capital, Martí knew that his destiny lay elsewhere. Foremost among his many activities in Madrid was the "tenacious" study of the English language, an indication of where he intended to go.[6] In violation of his deportation orders, he went to Paris, where he stayed just long enough to revisit his favorite people and places: the astronomer and writer Camille Flammarion, the salons frequented by Victor Hugo and Sarah Bernhardt (he met the latter), and the contemplative peace of the Père-Lachaise cemetery.[7] With Christmas approaching, he set off for Le Havre and boarded the New York-bound *France*.

Only five days after arriving in New York, Martí sent a letter to a friend in Havana, Miguel Viondi, asking him to make the necessary ar-

Figure 8.1. José Martí. Source: *Cuba y América*, May 15, 1897, 1.

rangements so that Martí's wife and son could join him in New York as soon as possible. His plan had been to ask Viondi for that favor sometime in April, when he had "thrown down some roots" and was able to support his family. But after only a few days in New York, he became convinced that in the city he would find opportunities, and "it is here . . . that I will live."[8]

For a few days after his arrival, Martí lived with an old friend, Miguel Fernández Ledesma.[9] But he soon took a room at Carmen Mantilla's boardinghouse, 49 East 29th Street.[10] Born Carmen Miyares in Santiago de Cuba, Martí's landlady was a warm and vivacious thirty-one-year-old mother of three young children. Her husband, Manuel Mantilla, was a merchant who had also been born on the island.

The Mantilla household, and especially Carmen, offered Martí a warm haven from the cold and unfamiliar city. There he could find the language, sounds, food, and ambience of his absent homeland and experience a semblance of the family life he had yearned for since his departure from Havana. Carmen's engaging manner, easy smile, and self-assured nature drew Martí to her, especially as February arrived and he favored the warmth of the boardinghouse over the freezing streets.[11]

While he awaited his family's arrival, Martí looked for work in the many large and small publishing houses and printing presses of the city, hoping to capitalize on what he perceived to be his greatest asset: a talent for the written word. But looking for work did not keep him from immediately immersing himself in the world of Cuban separatist politics. And there was no better place for that than New York, yet another reason the city was so attractive to him. An insurgent movement was under way in Cuba, funded largely by the Cuban Revolutionary Committee in New York, the organization Martí had officially represented in Havana until his deportation. Cuban New York was abuzz with the expectation that the veteran military leader Calixto García would soon leave the city to head an expeditionary troop that would energize the armed struggle on the island.

General García was one of the legendary military figures of the long 1868 war. He made his home in New York at 360 West 45th Street, where his family remained during most of the years the general was either in Cuba fighting the Spanish or in one of their prisons.[12] García's participation in the 1868 conflict ended in September 1874 in one of the most bizarre episodes of that war. Surprised and hopelessly surrounded by Spanish troops at his camp in eastern Cuba, he refused to be taken prisoner. Placing his high-caliber revolver under his chin, he fired into his head. The bullet exited through the forehead. He somehow recovered and was sent to a prison in Spain for the remainder of the war.[13] Upon his release in 1878 he returned to New York, where, undeterred by his harrowing experience, he was organizing another military campaign at the time Martí arrived in the city.

As soon as Martí arrived in New York he joined the leadership of the Revolutionary Committee and met with García. On January 24, 1880, at Steck Hall on 14th Street, Martí delivered a two-hour speech to a large gathering of his compatriots, exhorting them to take up the cause of a sovereign Cuba. It was an emotional plea to vindicate the sacrifices of those who gave their lives during the last great war for independence.[14] His eloquence deeply impressed the audience, including the general, and instantly made him a well-known figure among the New York émigrés.

Those first weeks in New York were heady for Martí. Encouraged by the possibilities offered by the city, he worked tirelessly to secure three things: his personal economic self-sufficiency, the success of García's expedition, and having his family join him in New York. Ten months later he could claim limited success accomplishing his first objective, but his hopes for the other two had been utterly dashed, and those two failures would haunt him for his remaining years in the city.

García's expedition left the New Jersey coast in May 1880, but less than three months after it landed in Cuba the entire campaign was finished. Lack of unity among the émigrés, poor planning, few resources, and a limited support within Cuba doomed the effort.[15] García was again imprisoned and deported to Spain. It was a disheartening failure for the émigré community and Martí, who had worked hard in New York to mobilize resources to equip the expedition.

At the same time that Martí had been working to launch García's expedition and struggling to support himself through his writing, he was facing a far greater challenge in his own home. In March 1880 his wife, Carmen Zayas Bazán, arrived in New York with their sixteen-month-old son.[16] The family relocated from the Mantilla boardinghouse to a small Brooklyn apartment that would become the setting for a bitter marital conflict.[17] In contrast to Carmen Mantilla, who one Martí biographer described as a "strong, humble, and giving" woman, Carmen, the wife, was characterized as "high-strung, haughty, and selfish."[18]

Martí welcomed his family to New York with the expectation that it would serve as his anchor in the mission that he believed he was destined to fulfill for his country. Carmen, however, went to New York with the intention of taking her husband back to Cuba so that he would become a respectable lawyer and tend to his domestic obligations. It was an irreconcilable conflict that played itself out every evening for months in the Brooklyn apartment. Fueling the marital crisis was the financial austerity imposed by Martí's limited income as an occasional essayist for the weekly the *Hour* and for the *Sun* newspaper. Worse, from Carmen's point of view, her husband was not even fully engaged in making a living in New York. He busied himself raising money for the García expedition and with the work of the Revolutionary Committee. The eventual failure of the expedition reinforced Carmen's argument that Martí's patriotic activities were futile, based on illusions that were keeping him from his real obligations as a husband and father.

With time, the couple's conflicted expectations opened a bitter chasm between the two. In October 1880, amid a flurry of recriminations, Carmen Zayas-Bazán and her son returned to Cuba. Martí had made a choice between *patria* and family that would prove unwavering in the ensuing years. Ill-fated attempts at reconciliation brought Carmen back to New York twice, in 1882 and 1891. Her last return to Havana proved to be definitive.

On November 28, 1880, Carmen Mantilla gave birth to a daughter, María, the child many believe Martí had fathered not long after he arrived in New York and while he awaited the arrival of his wife and son.[19]

Perhaps there was another place where things would go better for him, a place where he could work for the independence of Cuba, support himself, and where his wife might be more comfortable than in an austere Brooklyn apartment. On January 8, 1881, almost exactly a year after arriving in New York, Martí left for Venezuela. Two days earlier he had served as the godfather in the baptism of María Mantilla in St. Patrick's Church in Brooklyn.

Martí spent seven months in Venezuela. In terms of writing, it was a productive period of his life. He sold stories and essays and even published two issues of a newspaper he founded, *Revista Venezolana*. If, however, he hoped to use Caracas as the base for political activities on behalf of Cuban independence, he soon realized that it was far from the ideal venue. It was far removed from the traditional centers of émigré activism. Furthermore, Venezuela was ruled by an autocrat, Antonio Guzmán Blanco, who discouraged any dissent, something Martí discovered when he wrote a moving eulogy for a Venezuelan writer and friend, Cecilio Acosta, a critic of the regime. Martí was summoned to the presidential palace, rebuked, and pressured to leave. No, in Venezuela one could not "breathe freely," much less organize a political movement within a large community of compatriots. Caracas, in other words, was not New York. On July 28, 1881, Martí boarded the steamer *Claudius* at La Guaira, bound for the city that held so many bad personal memories for him but that he recognized was the best place to realize his aims. By August 11 he was once again walking on the sidewalks of Manhattan.[20]

The failure of the García expedition had taught Martí that a successful revolution could not be improvised on a shoestring. Cuban nationhood would not come about easily, quickly, or cheaply. It would take a lot more than outfitting a military expedition and sending it on its way. The campaign of 1880 and the costly and protracted conflict of 1868–1878 had failed because of the divisions and lack of political organization within the separatist movement.[21] In 1882 Martí wrote that he was rejecting all manifestations of "ridiculous enthusiasm, waiting calmly for the inevitable rise of developments that would lead to a serious, compact, and imposing revolution."[22] "Mobilizing a country, even a small one, is a task for giants," he continued, "and whoever does not feel himself to be a giant in love, or valor, or thought, or patience, should not undertake it."[23]

Martí was readying himself for such a task and by 1881 he realized that it would take patience and many sacrifices, including the ultimate sacrifice. He contemplated not the "useless martyrdom" of the patriots who had fought in the previous wars, but martyrdom in service of a clearly defined and well-planned struggle "worthy of such sacrifice."[24]

One of those sacrifices was the decision to live without his family. Martí would have preferred to have them by his side, where he could draw strength from them in the difficult mission he had set out for himself. There are numerous allusions throughout his writings to the value of having a supportive wife, with envious references to men whose wives commit to helping realize their visions. The most transparent of those allusions is in an article he devoted almost entirely to Emily Roebling, the wife of Washington Roebling, the builder of the Brooklyn Bridge. During the construction, Mr. Roebling had become disabled and was confined to his Brooklyn apartment. For years, Mrs. Roebling worked tirelessly, supervising the work and communicating her husband's precise instructions to the construction crews. In recognition of her contribution, she was selected to be the first person to cross the bridge. Martí heaped praise on her: "Of all her feats, the greatest one was her calm composure as she kept in her feeble body the soul of her illustrious husband . . . to build: that is the work of man—to console, which is to give strength to build, that is the great work of women."[25]

For Martí, Carmen Zayas-Bazán was not a supportive wife. She would not help him build a new Cuba. Her refusal to live in New York and her insistence that he return to Cuba presented Martí with a situation that was impossible to resolve in a way that would salvage the marriage. He had become increasingly committed to the cause of an independent Cuba, and his experience in Venezuela reaffirmed his initial conviction that New York was the best place in which to work toward that end. The city at the time had the largest Cuban émigré community in the world, its burgeoning publishing industry offered many opportunities for making a living, and it was a place where one could freely engage in political activities. For Martí, returning to Cuba meant abandoning his vision for his country and practicing law, a profession he had studied, but despised.[26] Ultimately, therefore, the choice of *patria* over family was not a choice at all, but its consequences were brutal. It weighed heavily on Martí for the rest of his life, though it served to reaffirm his sense of mission.

Martí's choice meant living alone in a city that could be cold, inhospitable, and downright nasty. By 1880 New York was the first American city to reach one million inhabitants. Half of that population, mostly immigrant, was packed into the Lower East Side, where 70 percent of the city's deaths occurred. Middle-class New Yorkers lived in multi-dwelling houses, especially boardinghouses. Even affluent New Yorkers contributed to the crowding, living in brownstones that, although luxurious, typically occupied over 90 percent of their lots.[27] The railroad boom created chaotic public scenes of greed as frenzied trading in the New York Stock Exchange spilled into the adjoining downtown streets.[28] Horses, wagons, and pedestrians clogged Manhattan. In 1881, observed a sanitary engineer, "the city's 40,000 horses produce 400 tons of manure per day [and] 20,000 gallons of urine and nearly 200 carcasses. The odor of horse droppings is everywhere, carried into houses in the form of dried manure that blows into the cuffs of trousers and the folds of skirts."[29] The 1880s would also bring some of the coldest winters in New York history, culminating in the legendary blizzard of 1888.[30] Emerging from that defining period at the beginning of the decade, facing life in New York without his family, Martí looked to the future he had chosen with a mixture of determination and dread: "This is my road. I have faith and take joy in it. Everything ties me to New York. . . . Everything ties me to this cup of poison."[31]

* * *

General Máximo Gómez was already a seasoned veteran of the independence struggle when he arrived in New York in the fall of 1884. Dominican by birth, he had fought long and hard during the grueling war of 1868–1878, but the failure to attain victory had not caused him to relinquish the struggle. In August 1884 he left his home in Honduras and headed for the Cuban communities in the United States to gauge the interest in renewing the armed conflict against Spain.

He was accompanied on that trip by another legendary figure of the great war: General Antonio Maceo. Of African ancestry, Maceo stood for defiance against Spanish rule. He had denounced the pact that had ended the war in 1878, vowing to fight on. Eventually, he was forced to abandon Cuba and withdrew, as Gómez had done, into temporary retirement in Central America.

By 1884 the two venerated generals were eager to get back into the fray. Their trip would take them to New Orleans, Key West, and New York, where they hoped to raise money from wealthy Cuban expatriates for a new military campaign. Their meager resources ran out in New Orleans and they barely had money to feed themselves. Gómez wrote in his diary, "It seems that only the poor are willing to help the revolution in Cuba; not one of the wealthy Cubans who live here has approached me."[32] They were able to continue their trip only because they received a timely contribution from the president of Honduras.

Their spirits were buoyed by the enthusiastic reception they received from the cigar workers in Key West. Gómez wrote at the time that it was "the best" of all the Cuban émigré communities.[33] Eventually, the residents of the small key, both rich and poor, contributed $40,000 toward the generals' revolutionary initiative.[34]

When Gómez and Maceo arrived in New York on October 1, they had every reason to be optimistic. Even before leaving Honduras, they had been promised $200,000 by none other than Félix Govín, the wealthy Cuban discussed in chapter 6. Govín had pledged half of that amount from his own money and promised that he had two other friends willing to come up with the rest.[35]

Upon arrival, the generals went directly to the hotel owned by Madame Marie Griffou, located at 19 West 9th Street.[36] Although actually a small inn or a boardinghouse, it had a venerable tradition of hosting Cuban insurgents and revolutionary conclaves. The Cubans,

Figure 8.2. General Máximo Gómez. Source: *Cuba y América*, December 15, 1897, 1.

always wary of the surveillance efforts of the Spanish government, preferred the hotel's intimacy and its discreet location in a residential neighborhood to the large Manhattan hotels located in high-traffic areas. The French-born Madame Griffou was an especially accommodating hostess to her Cuban guests. She had lived in Cuba before arriving in New York and always employed Cubans at her hotel. Clementine, her New York-born daughter, was married to Marcos Morales, a Cuban who worked in the city's tobacco industry.[37] Unlike many other New York hotels, the Hotel Griffou extended its welcome to guests across the broad spectrum of Cuban racial types. General Maceo had stayed there on a previous visit to New York.[38]

The generals and their small retinue remained in New York, and at Griffou's, during the entire month of October. Not even in the old days, during the war, had the small hotel seen so much insurgent activity. The good Madame must have been overwhelmed as her hotel filled

Figure 8.3. General Antonio Maceo. Source: *Frank Leslie's Popular Monthly*, August 1896, 129.

with thick cigar smoke from the steady stream of visitors calling on the generals.[39] Martí was among the visitors, although he was reluctant to take part in the new initiative. Having learned a lesson in patience, he had reservations about the timing of the effort. But he was probably persuaded to participate by Dr. Eusebio Hernández y Pérez, General Gómez's physician and principal aide during the trip. Hernández y Pérez made the gesture of cabling Martí from Honduras with advance notice of the New York visit because the doctor knew, as he later wrote, that "Martí had become somewhat withdrawn since 1880 when the expedition headed by Calixto failed."[40]

But one New Yorker was slow in dropping by Griffou's to pay his respects to the generals. Félix Govín, the expected benefactor, was, of course, the first person Gómez and Maceo notified of their arrival, asking to meet with him as soon as possible. But days passed and no word arrived from the wealthy businessman. Finally, Govín broke the news to Gómez and Maceo: there would be no contribution, not a cent, from him, nor from his friends. Govín excused himself by saying the timing was not good, since he was involved in a delicate negotiation with the

Spanish government on restitution for property confiscated from him in Cuba during the last war.[41]

The generals, especially Gómez, were furious. Govín's pledge of $200,000 would have been nearly enough to launch the entire revolution and had been one of the reasons they had left their homes in Central America and traveled to the United States. Govín had wasted their time, and, worse, hurt their pride. There they were in New York, two battle-scarred military leaders who had fought for ten years in the Cuban countryside, offering to sacrifice themselves once again and take up arms. And yet they were being rebuffed by the wealthiest community of émigrés, an "exile" community that ostensibly valued the liberation of the homeland.

On October 10, Gómez was warmly welcomed at a large rally of Cubans at Tammany Hall to celebrate the anniversary of the start of the 1868 war.[42] The general, wrote a reporter for the *Herald*, spoke "briefly and pithily of the hopes and fears of their cause," while Martí delivered "a very flowery and eloquent address which was much applauded."[43] Some money was raised from small donations solicited from the audience, but larger contributions would be necessary to get the revolution off the ground.

Gómez decided to send personal notes to more than twenty of the wealthiest Cuban New Yorkers asking for their financial support. Only one responded, with fifty dollars. Gómez wrote in his diary, "I did not anticipate what I have endured here in New York. . . . My disappointment has been very sad; only the poorest Cubans are willing to sacrifice. . . . Once again I must taste bitterness, but I will continue on my road, without fear nor contemplation."[44]

That is precisely what he did. With the money raised so far, especially in Key West, Gómez and Maceo pushed ahead with the organization of the movement. They held meetings at the Griffou with their supporters, drew up a plan, and issued orders to create in the United States, Mexico, and Central America various centers of revolutionary activity that were to outfit expeditions and send them to Cuba in a coordinated fashion.[45] The two generals were, above all, military men and they were organizing the movement with precision and discipline. Within that scheme, Martí was assigned to accompany Maceo to Mexico.

On October 18, Martí went to the Hotel Griffou for a private meeting he had requested with Gómez and Maceo. He anticipated a discussion of the plans for the insurrection. What he encountered was something quite different. In Madame Griffou's little hotel on 9th Street on that Saturday, one of the most pivotal and controversial meetings in Cuban history took place between three icons of that history.[46]

Martí had some misgivings about the plan and his mission in Mexico, so he started the meeting making suggestions on how the generals' strategy could be improved. Gómez, with a bath waiting for him in an adjoining room and a high level of frustration with the whole New York community, found himself facing a poet and writer, a civilian half his age, telling him how to run his campaign. "He allowed himself," Gómez would write later, "to make unsolicited indications to me without good reason, indications that were inappropriate to direct at someone who has been entrusted with responsibility for these matters."[47] When Martí started talking about what he planned to do in Mexico, Gómez could not stand for it anymore. "Look, Martí," he interrupted, "just limit yourself to the instructions. As for anything else, General Maceo will take care of whatever needs to be done." And with that, he picked up his towel and went to take his bath.

Martí was stunned. Maceo immediately tried to give explanations that he thought would soften the brusqueness of his comrade's words: the old man was used to giving orders; it is dangerous to have a military campaign with too many chiefs; commanders are accustomed to being obeyed without question, and so on.[48] Martí said nothing. Maceo's explanations only made matters worse. When Gómez returned from his bath, Martí stood up and respectfully but tersely took his leave, closing the door behind him. Maceo turned to Gómez and said, "General, that man leaves here very upset with us." "Perhaps," said the old soldier, with a shrug.

Maceo was right, although "upset" did not come close to describing how Martí felt. He took two days to settle down before writing a letter to Gómez in which he withdrew from any participation in the planned revolution. The letter became Martí's principal statement on the need for a broad-based civilian revolutionary movement. "A nation cannot be founded, General, as if one were issuing orders in a military camp."[49] He argued for the importance of "conciliating all the work, wills, and elements that make possible the armed struggle."[50] His sharpest words were directed at what he viewed as Gomez's dictatorial tendencies:

What guarantees can there be that public liberty, the only honorable purpose for throwing a country into a war, will be better respected tomorrow? What are we, General? The heroic and modest servants of an idea that warms our heart, the loyal friends of an unfortunate people, or the brave and fortunate *caudillos* that with whip in hand and with spur on the heel are willing to take war to a people, only to assume possession of them later?[51]

He also let Gómez know that Maceo's explanations were even more troubling: "He wanted to make me understand that we should consider the war in Cuba your exclusive property."[52]

Gómez did not reply to the letter, but he wrote in his diary that he had received an "insulting" letter from Martí. Gómez noted to himself that Martí was apparently one of those who "fear dictatorship" and that the charge of authoritarianism was only a pretext so that Martí could resign from a revolution in which he had not been allowed to play a significant role.[53] Eight months after the meeting, and apparently still bristling from Martí's words, Gómez wrote in his diary,

[There is] a lack of manly resolve, for there is even fear of revolutionary Dictatorship. . . . Could there be a more effeminate way of thinking? Can one cite a revolution in the world that has not had its Dictatorship?[54]

A month after arriving, Gómez left Madame Griffou's hotel, and New York, with a profound antipathy for the city's émigré community and, especially, for Martí. Less than three months later he wrote from New Orleans a letter to Juan Arnao, a friend and longtime New York resident, summarizing his experience in the city. He described New York as "always weak," and lamented

the time that the Cubans of New York have made me waste, and even the money, my own, which I foolishly spent under the illusion that I was dealing with men who were willing to do something for their country.

His harshest words were reserved for Martí:

[Martí] is not a man who can get into something without aspiring to dominate it, and when he took my pulse he said to himself "I can't do that with this old soldier . . . who pays little heed to orators or poets and what he seeks is gunpowder and bullets and men to go with him to the battlefields of my country to kill its tyrants." . . . It is important to leave [Martí] alone. We are going on to fight to make a nation for his children. Let us not bother with these petty matters.[55]

The fallout from the meeting at Madame Griffou's had serious implications for the independence struggle.[56] The man destined to craft the civilian movement that would successfully take the revolution to Cuba had become alienated, in a seemingly irreconcilable way, from the most revered military leaders of the separatist cause. During the remainder of the 1880s the struggle for independence was hobbled by the unfortunate encounter of October 1884.[57] The Gómez-Maceo plan failed to materialize, largely for the reasons Martí had anticipated: lack of resources and the absence of a broad base of support.[58] The generals retreated once again to homes in Central America.

Martí also withdrew, as he had done before, from active participation in any movement.[59] The generals' visit and the incident at the Griffou had been yet another formative experience, impressing upon him two lessons. One was that the independence movement had to be a civilian one, inspired by democratic ideals and embodying the very principles upon which a new nation was to be built. Military leaders would be recruited by that movement to lead the fighting, but Martí conceived the struggle as much more than defeating the Spanish. It was about building a nation, not just winning a war. And as he realized from the meeting at the Griffou, the nation he envisioned was not one that could be built "from a military camp."

The other lesson was the now widely held truism that capital is cautious, even cowardly. Many wealthy émigrés were still suffering the consequences of the Spanish embargo of 1869 and had learned to be timid about involving themselves in separatist causes. Martí realized then that the funds for the movement would have to come from the rank and file of the Cuban émigré communities, those who had nothing to lose by lending their support. This awareness influenced the fundraising strategy he would use later, one that closely resonated with his democratic instincts and his affinity for society's less powerful.

Although he continued to write on behalf of independence and to support separatist organizations in New York, more than seven years elapsed after the Griffou incident before Martí fully devoted himself to the cause of independence. In those seven years of relative tranquility, Martí was mostly just a New Yorker, engaged in making a living and enjoying the incomparable cultural, social, and recreational experiences offered by a city plunging headlong into the modern world.

* * *

The simile of the poisonous cup that Martí evoked to characterize his future in New York was no doubt the product of one of his gloomiest moments. The fact is that not long after returning from Venezuela in 1881 he warmed again to the excitement and possibilities of the city that, despite all its hardships, he recognized as the place where he needed to be.

On the domestic front, he did not end up as lonely as he had anticipated when his family left for Cuba. By July 1881, if not earlier, Martí had moved back to Carmen Mantilla's boardinghouse, which she had relocated to 324 Classon Avenue in Brooklyn.[60] Early in 1885 Manuel Mantilla died, leaving Carmen a widow with four children who ranged in age from fifteen to five. There is little doubt, even among the most discreet of Martí's biographers, that during the rest of his days in New York he assumed the roles of husband and father in the Mantilla household, paying special attention to the upbringing of the youngest, María.[61]

Despite finding some measure of family life, Martí remained in many ways a solitary figure in New York.[62] In the political arena, he was estranged from much of the traditional émigré leadership because of his separation from Gómez and Maceo. Intellectually, he was not surrounded by a vibrant literary community of compatriots who were his equals or with whom he had much in common.[63] He never passed up an opportunity to meet with, or attend a lecture by, any prominent intellectual figure of his time who happened to be in New York.

Solitude does not, however, prevent one from living a full life in New York. Martí's withdrawal from participation in organized revolutionary movements lasted until 1891 and gave him the opportunity to live like a consummate New Yorker. To assert that he was very much a New Yorker in no way contradicts the fact that Martí always remained an outsider, a foreigner, in the United States. Then, as now, being a New Yorker is an "extranational" identity, a product of the city's international outreach and character, and marginality and foreignness make up part of that identity. And Martí gave every indication that he was, indeed, a New Yorker, that he felt very much a part of the city, delighting in its cultural, intellectual, and recreational offerings, taking the Mantilla children to Central Park, marveling at the opening of the Brooklyn Bridge, enjoying the culinary offerings of Delmonico's and the attractions of Coney Island, as well as the extraordinary show put on by P. T. Barnum at Madison Square Garden.

But he did more than just enjoy New York: he also wrote about it. Martí's chronicles about life in the United States, especially New York, were an important source of income for him as a regular contributor to newspapers in Latin America. Between 1881 and 1891 he wrote more than 250 chronicles and essays on political, social, and economic events in the United States, many of them about events in the city. They were usually lengthy essays in the form of a letter addressed to the editor and dealing with a variety of topics. Virtually all the chronicles were published in three Latin American newspapers for which Martí served as a correspondent in New York: *La Opinión* in Caracas, *El Partido Liberal* in Mexico City, and *La Nación* in Buenos Aires. They have been compiled as the *Escenas norteamericanas* and account for five volumes of Martí's collected works.[64]

The *Escenas* represent an extraordinary collection of chronicles that rank among the most valuable accounts of life in the United States, and especially New York, during those critical years at the close of the nineteenth century. Roberto González Echevarría regards the North American chronicles as Martí's "greatest literary success."[65] Perhaps because only a portion of the *Escenas* has been translated, their place among the foremost chronicles of the city's history has largely gone unappreciated.[66] As we shall see, however, their impact on Latin American literary trends is widely recognized.

The *Escenas* include reports and reflections on the U.S. political system, electoral contests and candidates, corruption in municipal government, the opulent life of New York's wealthiest families, poor neighborhoods, snowstorms, droughts, and fires in Manhattan, the New York press, Thanksgiving and Easter, U.S. presidents, ice skating, the poet Whitman and the boxer Sullivan, industrial and agricultural fairs, labor strikes, elevated trains, sports, Buffalo Bill, the Wild West and the plight of the Indians, New York schools and theaters, women's suffrage, the South and African Americans, Coney Island, and the Stock Exchange. There are chronicles dealing with historic events: the inaugurations of the Brooklyn Bridge and the Statue of Liberty, the advent of electric light, Oscar Wilde's visit, President Cleveland's wedding, the Charleston earthquake, and Washington Irving's centenary. The assassination of President Garfield and the imprisonment, trial, and execution of his assassin, Charles Guiteau, were the subjects of several essays over a period of months. Immigration and New York's ethnic diversity were recurrent topics, with essays on Chinatown, the Irish, Hungarians, and other groups. There were reflections following the deaths of notables: President Grant, Karl Marx, Emerson, Longfellow, Samuel Tilden, and even Jesse James, among others.

The primary value of the *Escenas norteamericanas* does not rest entirely on their extraordinary variety and range, or even in their style, which may strike modern readers as outdated, ornate, even baroque. What is most notable about the *Escenas* is, as Susana Rotker has noted, Martí's exceptional "gaze" as a Cuban in New York.[67] The *Escenas* are not merely descriptions, nor was Martí a reporter. Although he did write rich descriptive passages, he went beyond that and provided his readers in Latin America with his interpretations and judgments about the emerging colossus to the north. Implicit in the *Escenas*—and sometimes explicit—is an assessment of the appropriateness of the U.S. model for the rest of the hemisphere. That evaluative dimension of the *Escenas* results in a narrative with a constant tension between praise and criticism, admiration and condemnation, which has led to very divergent interpretations among Martí scholars as to his "true" vision of the United States. Some have viewed him as an early denouncer of American imperialism and the threat it posed for Latin America, whereas others have emphasized his admiration for this country's institutions.[68]

Ultimately, however, Martí's interest was not in judging the United States. Writing as an outsider, he did not see a role for himself as a booster or a detractor in a society that was not his own. He never abandoned his "gaze" as a Latin American engaged in the process of building his own nation. The *Escenas*, other than earning Martí income, had the purpose of communicating with Latin Americans the lessons he was learning about the social, political, and economic drama of the United States during the late nineteenth century. New York gave him a front-row seat at that drama, and he used his vantage point to contribute to the development of a modern Latin American identity and sense of national purpose. As Rotker notes, Martí writes as the "small colonial subject" living as an "exile in a city not his own":

> Yet, as admirer *and* critic of the society he writes about, he attempts to reformulate the traditional sense of *Us* and *Them* in order to build for himself an inclusive identity, a "Latin American Us." Furthermore, in *Escenas norteamericanas* the site of the gaze has been displaced: the gaze focuses on New York (a relative model, and at the same time, a threat), not on the pressing issue of Cuba's colonial relation with Spain.[69]

Despite the critical eye Martí casts on New York and the United States, he displays a genuine interest in seeing the American model succeed. But for him, success was not measured by expansionism or by the frenetic growth of personal wealth. Rather, the model would succeed only if progress meant greater social justice and a turn away from materialism.

Martí viewed that progress as constantly in danger of being derailed. One example is his perspective, no doubt disappointing to many of his modern readers, on immigration. He saw it as part of a broader process of European influence that, he argued, threatened to undermine the "noble origins" of the American nation. Those origins were in a colonial struggle that Martí greatly admired, for it had been led by progressive men who had broken with oppressive European traditions and established a free nation governed by modern institutions and values. The Europeans who were crowding into New York in the late nineteenth century were bringing with them "their hatreds, their wounds, their moral ulcers," along with an "anxious desire for money."[70]

Viewed more than a century later, Martí's negative views on U.S. immigration, which he started voicing early in his New York years, do not match the progressive tone of much of his social and political thought. More than anything else, however, those views reflected his perception that the American model was a fragile experiment, one that could easily be corrupted by retrograde European influences.

That point is most evident in a fairly unknown but revealing *Escena* published in 1885 in *La Nación*.[71] In it, Martí commented to his Argentinian readers on the popularity in New York of Monsignor Thomas J. Capel, an English Roman Catholic prelate with a reputation as an inspiring speaker. A traditionalist who had spent some time in Rome and reportedly was close to Pope Pius IX, the monsignor arrived in New York in July 1883 for an extended stay in the United States, intending to make a splash on the American religious scene.[72] The New York press covered his every move, fawning over his fiery oratory, charisma, and good looks.[73]

To Martí, however, the monsignor was a "magnificent fox."[74] The *Escena* critical of Capel was probably motivated by press reports of a sermon the prelate delivered on November 23, 1884, to a packed St. Vincent Ferrer Church on the Upper East Side. Capel offered a revisionist view of the Inquisition, claiming that it "did its duty like the father who would spare its children from iniquity." Further, Capel said, the Inquisition is still alive in the Vatican as a "model institution," and concluded that "the nineteenth century is pretty well the same as twenty centuries ago."[75]

Martí was appalled by the uncritical reception New York gave to the message of the monsignor, as is clear from the opening paragraph of the passage Martí dedicates to assailing Capel:

> In these past few days New York has resembled an echo from Europe and those with some foresight are asking themselves the question: this country so well-equipped by nature and fortune to be original and good, will it ultimately be a genuine and formidable voice . . . forging the world ahead, taking it through new routes, or, without strength to purify and transform that invasion that disrupts it, will it in time become a mere echo?[76]

Clearly, Martí believed in the promise of modernity and was disturbed by the influence of European anachronisms. But he was also disappointed that the American promise was not being fulfilled, corrupted as it was by material excesses, social injustices, and the alienation of the human spirit.[77] That ambivalence between disappointment in the present and faith in the future is the wellspring of the *modernismo* movement in Latin America.[78] Breaking with Spanish literary and artistic traditions, and alienated from the rising bourgeois classes in their own societies, the *modernistas* welcomed the modern age to Latin America, but called for greater subjectivity and spirituality in the face of rationalization and materialism.[79]

Martí's writings from New York, and especially the *Escenas*, are regarded as essential precursory texts in the *modernismo* movement.[80] Written by a Latin American who lived in the heart of the country that had replaced Europe as the source of everything modern, from culture to machinery, Martí's *Escenas* enjoyed enormous popularity throughout Mexico, Central, and South America.[81] Among the avid and "spellbound" readers of the *Escenas* was a young Nicaraguan poet, Rubén Darío, whose small book, *Azul*, first published in 1888, is considered a founding milestone of *modernismo*.[82] The *Escenas* struck a special chord among intellectuals and writers who identified with Martí's rejection of European traditions and anachronisms, his belief in the promise of modernity, and his critical and ambivalent view of the United States as both model and threat. Martí's gaze as a Cuban New Yorker was therefore a crucial element in the impact of his writings on the *modernismo* movement.

The place of the *Escenas* in the annals of Latin American *modernismo* should not keep us from enjoying, at another level, those *Escenas* that take a whimsical look at life in New York and provide a window into Martí as a New Yorker. This is most evident in those *Escenas* in which he displays a fascination with the city's unbounded capacity to amuse and entertain.

Martí had a predilection for Barnum's show, which he mentions several times in his writings. He labeled Barnum a "man of genius": "This world gives rise to so much pain, but it also gives us those who alleviate it. He who discovers ways to attract and entertain others is a benefactor of mankind. Happiness is the wine of the spirit."[83] To Martí, "Barnum's hippodrome" at Madison Square was the site of fantastic sights, which he described in 1887 with childlike enthusiasm:

> Shiny chariots with their hairless coachmen, gladiators smeared in white
> to resemble classical statues, their horses dancing on a wire, . . . women
> hanging by their hair from the highest reaches of the circus, elephants
> prancing and making like clowns until one of them tires of the tamer's
> harassment, . . . breaks down the door and is followed by an infuriated

herd that knocks over musicians and dancers and heads into the stables beneath the seats in a volcanic rumble.[84]

Starting in 1891, Martí devoted himself exclusively to the task of creating a revolution and virtually ceased to write about New York. But even in his earnest last years in New York he rarely passed up an opportunity to let the city amuse him.

In April 1894 he hosted the return visit to New York of General Máximo Gómez, the aging but still respected military leader with whom Martí had had such an unpleasant falling-out in Madame Griffou's hotel. Gómez was returning to New York at Martí's invitation. The young upstart poet and orator who so annoyed the general ten years before was now the head of a unified civilian movement poised to take the revolution to Cuba. Willing to overlook that previous disagreement, Martí hoped to persuade the general to lead the military campaign, and Gómez was ready to be persuaded. Given their past conflicts, Martí realized that it was important to establish a good personal relationship with the general, and to that end he enlisted the help of his favorite New York attraction. One day during Gómez's stay in New York, Martí scribbled a note to his assistant, the young attorney Gonzalo de Quesada, excusing himself for not being able to attend an event that evening because, he wrote, "tonight I am taking the General to Barnum's."[85]

The lens of history renders it an extraordinary sight: the most important builder of the Cuban nation and its most revered military figure, icons both, sitting together taking in the "Greatest Show on Earth." That spring of 1894 Barnum & Bailey's featured attraction was a pair of large chimpanzees, "Chiko and his bride Johanna," whose trained act was a parody of the bliss and agony of human matrimonial life.[86] Judging from the advertisement in the *New York Times*, the three-ring circus at Madison Square that season was an extravaganza:

> Wild and domestic brutes performing at one time, . . . eighty marvelous circus acts, fifty aerialists, twenty acrobats, thirty-three golden chariots, . . . two herds of elephants, two droves of camels, . . . twenty animal clowns and twenty pantomimic clowns, . . . a real Cossack encampment, . . . savage people, black and brown skinned natives from everywhere, . . . truthful, moral, instructive, and historical.[87]

Truly historical was the bond that the writer and the general cemented in those few days in New York. The evening at Barnum's was part of Martí's strategy to gain the trust of the cantankerous but indispensable warrior, who could be a critical player in the revolutionary movement Martí had been assembling since 1891.

* * *

For years Martí had been patient in meeting his destiny. History and experience had taught him that Cuba's independence would not be won overnight and without sacrifice. He was waiting for the right time to devote himself to working for the unity and resources necessary to take the revolution to Cuba.

It is not clear why in 1891 Martí thought the time had arrived to start the long road to revolution. There was no particular political event or combination of economic and social forces that made it the propitious moment to launch an independence movement. In fact, many in New York felt that the timing was all wrong.[88] Perhaps Martí simply ran out of patience. Or perhaps personal circumstances pushed him to the point of no return, the point at which there would be no turning back to his life as a New Yorker.

It was in that same year, in August, that Carmen Zayas-Bazán left New York, and Martí, for the last time. It was a bitter departure, far more rancorous than previous ones. There were no goodbyes. Taking advantage of a short trip that Martí took outside the city, Carmen abruptly left for Havana without his knowledge, taking their son with her. López, in his biography of Martí, argues that the tipping point for Carmen may have been the publication during those days of the *Versos sencillos*, a collection of poems that included some verses that bared his despair at the "wounds" she had inflicted on him.[89] Márquez Sterling, on the other hand, elliptically notes that while Carmen could never reconcile herself to her husband's political choices, during this visit "an inconformity of a more intimate nature intervened," implying that she may have confirmed what she already suspected and most Cubans in New York already knew: that Martí and Carmen Mantilla lived as a couple.[90]

She was abetted in her sudden departure by Enrique Trujillo, a man who had been a close collaborator of Martí, but with whom he started to have political differences. Carmen asked Trujillo to accompany her to the Spanish consulate in Manhattan, where she requested and received permission to return to Cuba without her husband's consent, in accordance with Spanish law.⁹¹ When Martí returned to the city and found her gone and learned of Trujillo's role in her departure, he never forgave him. The rift with Trujillo was not inconsequential. Trujillo ran a newspaper in New York and remained a thorn in Martí's side throughout the rest of Martí's life in the city.⁹²

The anger Martí felt toward what he viewed as Carmen's betrayal by abandoning him was manifested in his relationship with Trujillo. Although Martí always tried to reconcile his differences with his compatriots for the sake of political unity, after Carmen's departure he could not even stand to be in the same room with Trujillo without losing his composure. The deep emotional loss he felt that summer, especially the separation from his son, no doubt made him eager to immediately take up the agenda that ostensibly justified that separation and his continued residence in New York: fulfilling his goal of freeing Cuba.

* * *

Barely two months after Carmen and his son left, on the evening of October 10, 1891, Martí rose to the podium at Hardman Hall on Fifth Avenue and 19th Street as if he were mounting a horse to lead a charge against the Spanish. "We come on horseback this year!" he announced to an audience of more than six hundred of his compatriots who had gathered to observe yet another anniversary of the start of the 1868 conflict: "We have put the bridle on . . . and we will be saddling up soon, and the riders! . . . Misery creates such magnificent riders!" The audience shouted back at the end of his speech when he returned to the riding analogy: "Ride, then, our horse at the invader, dispersing and defeating him."⁹³

It was the most strident speech Martí had yet delivered, a call to arms by an impatient and frustrated man. Although he told his audience on that Saturday night that the charging horses would race silently, "where the enemy cannot hear them," the enemy did hear.⁹⁴ The Spanish consul in New York was able to read all about it the following day, even before receiving the report of the Pinkerton agents hired by his government to shadow Martí. The event, especially Martí's speech, was covered by the *Sun*, the *Daily Tribune*, and the *Times*.⁹⁵ Indeed, the response by the Spanish consul was probably cued by the *Times* article, which identified

Martí as the "Argentine Consul at New York."[96] It was true. For several years Martí had supplemented his income by handling consular matters in New York not only for Argentina, but also for Uruguay. Seizing on such a public identification of Martí's diplomatic status, the Spanish consul, as well as Spanish sympathizers in the city, protested to Vicente G. Quesada, the Argentinian minister in Washington, that an official representative of his republic was engaged in subversive activities against the Spanish government.[97]

Martí moved rapidly to defuse a crisis that, to him, was a mere distraction. He tendered his resignation as consul in an appreciative letter to Quesada, indicating his desire to spare the minister's government any "ungrateful controversy" arising from his own obligation "to secure for my country what the founders of Argentina secured in their time for their country."[98] Martí also promptly resigned as the consul for Uruguay and as president of the Sociedad Literaria, a New York cultural and literary organization. As one of his biographers put it, "Now he felt freer to work for Cuba."[99] Another biographer wrote that "he had burned his ships."[100] On the contrary: he set himself free to outfit the ships that would launch the revolution. He was divesting himself of his New York life so that he could concentrate on what he had always seen as his mission and destiny. He would have patience no longer. After this point his life took on an intense, almost frantic, focus. He was now Martí the revolutionary, not Martí the New Yorker.

Roughly a month later he was among the cigar workers of Ybor City in Florida, the community founded by Vicente Martínez Ybor and other cigar manufacturers only five years earlier (see chapter 7). By 1891 Ybor City already had more Cubans than Key West, a much older center of cigar manufacturing in Florida.[101]

Going to Tampa, and eventually to Key West, reflected a strategy Martí had mapped out for building the movement. An outsider to the established circles of émigré separatism, especially after his falling-out with Gómez and Maceo, Martí bypassed the traditional leadership in New York and went directly to working-class Cubans. He knew he would be welcomed by the politically conscious cigar craftsmen whose dissatisfaction with Spanish rule in Cuba led them to abandon the island.[102] Although Martí's ultimate goal was to unite all sectors of the Cuban émigré community, including the New York elite and the old military leaders, he would build that unity from the ground up, starting with the rank and file.[103] Experience had taught him that the old leadership was fractious and economic elites were cautious with their money.

Arriving in Tampa on November 25 in response to an invitation from a patriotic club, Martí knew he needed to somehow overcome the distrust the Florida cigar workers felt toward New York Cubans. The traditional distance between the two communities was in large measure a class phenomenon: the New Yorkers were viewed in Tampa and Key West as intellectuals, merchants, and elites who always talked a lot about independence but in the end did nothing for Cuba.[104] Martí faced that with his greatest asset: his facility with words. In Tampa, on November 26 and 27, he delivered what are arguably his two most memorable speeches, each around a theme he wanted to impress upon his audience. The first one was on the need for unity and is known by its concluding phrase: "With All, and for the Good of All."[105] On the following day he delivered his "New Pines" speech, a call for a generational renewal in the leadership of the separatist cause. He reminded the cigar workers of their duty to the homeland by telling them that the tall white royal palms of Cuba are "waiting brides," and concluded by describing what he had seen from the window of his train as it traveled toward Tampa:

> Suddenly, the sun broke through over a clearing in the forest, and there, in a flash of light, I saw, growing above the yellow grass and around the blackened trunks of the fallen pines, the joyous sprouts of the new pines. That's us: the new pines![106]

The speeches, especially the first one, "had an electrifying effect."[107] According to one biographer, Martí's "tactical oratory" had accomplished the purpose of stirring his audience with an "order for mobilization":

> The front rows of the audience surged toward the stage, where Martí found himself squeezed by embraces. Standing on chairs, women waved hats, gloves, handkerchiefs. People cried and laughed, and *vivas!* were heard everywhere.[108]

On Christmas Day, 1891, Martí delivered yet another impassioned call for revolution, this time in Key West, where he was invited by the leaders of that community after they learned of his speeches in Tampa.[109] One year later, as 1892 drew to a close, Martí's feverish activity had yielded extraordinary results, creating a revolutionary movement with three components: (1) a duly constituted party, the Partido Revolucionario Cubano (PRC), complete with by-laws, elected officers, and a set of written ideological principles; (2) *Patria*, a weekly newspaper edited in New York that served as the official voice of the PRC; and (3) a network of local clubs, spread throughout the United States, Latin America, and Europe, that responded to the directives of the party, elected the party's officers, and had fundraising as their principal activity.

It was the civilian organization Martí had always envisioned: inclusive, participatory, and democratic, structured to achieve the unity that had always proved so elusive among the émigrés. Centered on a political party, it obviously represented more than just a rebellion against the Spanish. It was also conceived as the basis for constituting a government in an independent Cuba. Having created the organizational basis for the movement, Martí now had to make it work as the vehicle for revolution. It would prove to be, as he had anticipated years earlier, "a task for giants."

The task involved incessant letter writing and travel so as to bring émigrés everywhere into the fold of the organization and raise money to fund the insurgency. Martí's political correspondence after 1891 is so voluminous that it represents a major body of text in his collected works. Starting with his 1891 Florida trips, he was almost constantly traveling until his definitive departure from New York in 1895. He went mostly to the Florida communities, which remained the strongest base for the PRC. But he also took extended trips to Central America and the Caribbean, as well as jaunts to émigré clubs in Philadelphia and New Orleans. This, for a man who, after returning to the city from Venezuela in 1881 had not traveled outside the New York region until he went to Tampa in 1891.[110]

As the organization became stronger in human and financial resources, Martí gained greater legitimacy as the undisputed leader of the separatist movement. This stature enabled him to convince skeptics, such as the military leaders and at least some of the economic elites, to support him and join the movement. But it also made him a target of criticism and attacks by those (especially Enrique Trujillo) who, for ideological or personal reasons, viewed his leadership with suspicion.[111] In the end, those critics did not matter. Martí was able to accomplish what had not been done in the long history of Cuban separatism in New York: organize a unified civilian movement that spearheaded a sustainable insurgency in Cuba. Although he was an influential writer, it is largely for his accomplishments as a political organizer that Martí has occupied the highest position in the pantheon of Cuban national heroes.

But organizing the revolution was an accomplishment so complex and fragile, that until the final moment it could have all failed; and indeed, it nearly did. In the closing days of 1894, Martí had three ships outfitted with men and arms ready to sail for Cuba from Fernandina Beach, near Jacksonville. The expedition had been coordinated with simultaneous landings in Cuba of the military leaders, led by Gómez. But the betrayal of one of the collaborators and the relentless activities of the Pinkertons (who had long been the bane of Martí as agents for the Spanish government) tipped off the U.S. government to the violation of its Neutrality Act, and the vessels were confiscated before they could leave for Cuba.[112]

Through legal maneuvers the movement recovered some of the arms and munitions, but the fruits of Martí's years of fundraising were lost, as was the element of surprise. The Spanish were astounded by the magnitude and organization of the movement and started preparing for an uprising.[113] For the first time, Martí's closest collaborators saw him act in a desperate, even irrational, manner.[114] It would not be easy to raise the money needed to outfit a comparable expeditionary force again. What remained in the treasury of the PRC was not enough. But in a twist of fate, a New Yorker came forward and put up the rest of the money. It was Luciana Govín, the daughter of Félix Govín, the wealthy émigré who in 1884 reneged on his offer to provide support for General Gómez and was by this time deceased. Félix Govín had left his daughter a sizable inheritance, most of it investments in Manhattan real estate (see chapter 7).[115] Luciana Govín handed Martí a blank check and told him he could have up to $100,000, coincidentally the same amount her father had personally pledged to Gómez a decade before.[116]

A new expedition was quickly assembled, awaiting Martí's order to proceed. It was the responsibility of giving that order that weighed heavily on Martí's mind as he walked into Delmonico's on the night of January 28, 1895, to celebrate his last birthday.

During a visit to Key West in 1893, Martí got a haircut at the home of the Figueredo family. The barber told him he had "four or five" gray hairs that could be removed, if he wished. Martí said no: "They are so few that they do not weigh heavily on me and there is little danger they will increase; destiny will not permit others to come and keep them company."[117]

It was that sense of a fatal destiny that made the birthday dinner at Delmonico's a bittersweet occasion for Martí. For him it was much more than a birthday celebration. Enjoying an exquisite culinary evening was a good way to bid farewell to a city that had become a part of him, and that he knew he would never see again.

The day after the dinner, January 29, Martí drafted and signed the order to start the uprising on the island. Gonzalo de Quesada, one of the diners at Delmonico's, carried the order to Key West, where, according to legend, it was rolled into a cigar, taken to the island, and delivered personally to Martí's representative in Havana, Juan Gualberto Gómez.[118]

January 30 was Martí's last day in New York. Since his return from Jacksonville he had been staying at 116 West 64th Street, the home of Luciana Govín and her husband, Dr. Ramón L. Miranda, Martí's physician and a guest at the dinner in Delmonico's. Martí was keeping a low profile so as not to tip off the Pinkerton agents that the uprising was under way.

On that final New York day, Martí found the time to bid a hasty farewell to the Baralt family, who also lived on West 64th Street, in number 135. Blanche Baralt wrote years later that on that day Martí came to her family's house, apologizing for not visiting longer since he did not have a moment to spare. After saying that only God knew when he would see them again, he "dashed off like an arrow into the freezing morning."[119] Days later, Blanche and her sister-in-law discovered an unfamiliar brown winter coat hanging in the cloakroom of their foyer. Upon searching the pockets, they discovered that it was Martí's coat, left there on that last day because he was, Baralt concluded, so preoccupied with his precipitous departure.[120] No doubt. But soon after leaving the Baralt home, the cold January air must have reminded him that he had left his coat behind. He might have momentarily turned back to retrieve it, but then realized that he would never need it again. He was, at last, going back to Cuba.

The most wrenching farewell of that final New York day no doubt took place in the Mantilla household. Two days later, aboard the S.S. *Athos* of the Atlas Line, the steamer taking him away from New York,

Figure 8.4. María Mantilla. Source: Cuban Heritage Collection, University of Miami Library Digital Collections, www.merrick.library.miami.edu.

Martí wrote a letter on the ship's stationery to "my dear girl," the fourteen-year-old María: "Your anguished little face is still before me, and the pain of your last kiss." He asked her to retrieve the *Larousse* from the home of Gonzalo de Quesada and borrow from Blanche Baralt her copy of Bulfinch's *Mythology* so she could look up "Athos" and "Atlas." He signed the letter, "your Martí."[121]

On May 19, Carmen Mantilla and her children received another letter from Martí, one that had been written more than a month earlier in the Cuban countryside. In it, he told them that he carried at all times a picture of María on his chest, next to his heart.[122] The day Carmen received the letter in New York, Martí was killed by a volley of Spanish bullets. The moment is captured in the equestrian statue of him in at Sixth Avenue and Central Park South, in the city that had meant so much to him.

Epilogue

"Martí Should Not Have Died"

The only Cuban prepared to face, politically and culturally, the historical turn of events of '98 was the same one whose death in combat three years before . . . had facilitated that turn.
—Cintio Vitier[1]

> Gentlemen, a voice is missing, the voice of that Cuban
>   mockingbird,
> Of that brother martyr who was named Martí.
> Martí should not have died, ay, have died.
> If he were our teacher today, another rooster would crow,
> The nation would be saved and Cuba would be happy,
> Ay, very happy.
> —popular Cuban song, early twentieth century[2]

Edward H. Boyer, the principal of Grammar School No. 87 on Manhattan's Upper West Side, explained to the *New York Herald* reporter that "what can a principal do when people compliment him by visiting his school? Must he turn them away if he has doubt of their opinions?"[3] The principal was in a predicament that day in early June 1897. His boss, the superintendent of schools, was "exercised" about Boyer's decision, the day before, to allow into the school a group of highly opinionated foreign visitors who tried to "enlist the sympathy of our boys," according to Superintendent John Jasper.[4] "Our children are sent to school to learn history, geography, and the three R's," Jasper charged, "but not international politics or partisanship. . . . It's a matter to be inquired into most carefully when a school principal allows such a thing in his school."[5]

The superintendent was reacting to a report in the *Herald* that "several members of the Cuban Junta" had dropped into the grammar school on June 10 and had been allowed to lecture the youngsters on the abuses and atrocities of the Spanish against the Cuban people and on the need for action by the president of the United States against Spain.[6] It was, as the *Herald* headline described it, an "invasion" of a public school by a delegation of no less than seven members of the Partido Revoluciona-rio Cubano (PRC), including its top leadership: Tomás Estrada Palma, General Julio Sanguily, Benjamín Guerra, and Henry Lincoln Zayas. It was Zayas who delivered the anti-Spain speech to the students and apparently did so very convincingly, for at the end of the Cubans' program, "when the principal asked if there were any whose parents came from Spain," the *Herald* reported, "the boys hissed vigorously."[7]

The grammar school incident is emblematic of the aggressiveness with which the leadership of the PRC in New York placed the cause of Cuban independence before a broad range of private and public audiences in an attempt to garner U.S. support for a war effort that was losing steam on the island. It was José Martí who had founded the PRC as the instrument for civilian control over the independence movement. It was Martí who launched that war effort from New York and then placed himself in the front ranks of his rebel army, leading to his death on a Cuban battlefield on May 19, 1895. But Martí's death resulted in a dramatic and disastrous shift in the strategy that he had laid out for the movement.

The men who inherited the leadership of the PRC were Tomás Estrada Palma and Gonzalo de Quesada. Longtime New Yorkers, they were men whose backgrounds and instincts led them to support the flagging war effort by resorting to the same formula that had been used by generations of Cuban émigrés in New York since the time of the annexationists: aggressively pursuing U.S. involvement in the cause of Cuban independence. It was an approach that Martí, showing extraordinary foresight, had explicitly rejected, breaking with more than half a century of émigré activism. For Martí, calling the attention of the U.S. public, press, and government to the Cuban cause was a dangerous proposition. His abiding preoccupation was that the United States would step into the conflict and end his hopes for Cuban sovereignty. And sovereignty, after all, was ultimately the goal of the entire movement.

"It has had to be in silence," wrote Martí to his friend Manuel Mercado in the last letter he ever wrote, in the camp at Dos Ríos on the night before his death, because there are things that to accomplish them have to proceed hidden, and to proclaim them for what they are would raise problems too serious for attaining the goal. . . . To prevent that Cuba will present the opening of a road . . . of annexation of the people of our America to the convulsed and brutal North that disdains us. . . . I lived in the monster, and I know its entrails well.

Estrada Palma, Quesada, and the other leaders of the PRC in New York, however, departed completely from Martí's strategy of not stirring U.S. interest. Instead, they waged an intense public relations campaign, proclaiming the case for independence to anyone who would listen, including grade-school children in Manhattan. In doing so, they placed the Cuban cause, as the historian Gerald Poyo noted, on "the road to compromised sovereignty."[8] It was a road that would lead to Martí's worst nightmare.

* * *

Tomás Estrada Palma was from Bayamo, a relative and close friend of Francisco Vicente Aguilera. Deeply involved in the war effort that was initiated in 1868 by his fellow easterners, Estrada Palma was arrested in 1877 and deported to a prison in Cádiz. When the war ended in 1878 he was released and made his way to New York, where he eventually served as headmaster of a school for boys in the Hudson Valley, about fifty miles north of New York City. He participated in the activities of the PRC in the city and cemented a close relationship with Martí, who viewed Estrada Palma as a figure who was highly admired by Cubans in New York and who represented a symbolic link with the previous war for independence. Yoel Cordoví Núñez argues, however, that despite Martí's respect for Estrada Palma, he never assigned the headmaster any real leadership role within the PRC, preferring instead to consult on major decisions with Benjamín Guerra and Gonzalo de Quesada, respectively treasurer and secretary of the party.[9]

But perhaps it was Estrada Palma's symbolic stature within the New York community that led Martí, shortly before his departure for Cuba, to anoint Estrada Palma as his successor in New York, asking him to "take care of the party," according to one source.[10] Estrada Palma may well have been the figure most likely, Martí reasoned, to keep the party

Figure E.1 Tomás Estrada Palma. Source: Print Collection, Miriam and Ira D. Wallach Division of Art,
Prints and Photographs, New York Public Library, Astor, Lenox and Tilden Foundations.

united in his absence. When Martí died, Estrada Palma succeeded him
as the leader of the PRC. He was joined in the leadership of the party by
Guerra and Quesada. The new PRC leaders were cut of a similar cloth
as the traditional leaders who had long controlled émigré activism since
annexationism: members of the elite and middle classes who wanted to
avoid a destructive war and who viewed a social revolution with suspicion. They were especially concerned about the scorched-earth strategies of the military leaders in Cuba and the possibility of a *caudillo*-led
government supported by the masses, especially blacks, instead of an
independence process that would deliver a free Cuba, as Gerald Poyo
stated, to the "responsible" classes.[11]

Estrada Palma and the others were therefore predisposed to actively,
indeed aggressively, solicit U.S. intervention in the war, believing that

the conflict could not be won without Washington's help and that the future of Cuba was inevitably tied to the United States. They therefore resisted any effort by the McKinley administration to avoid the war, a war that promised to be short once the United States entered, sparing Cuba any further devastation from what had turned out to be a costly protracted conflict. John Offner argues that "the United States tried to find a peaceful resolution to the stalemated Cuban-Spanish War, but Cuban nationalists were unyielding."[12]

The new leadership of the PRC would not only betray Martí's principle of keeping the United States out of the conflict, but it would fail to replicate what Lillian Guerra has termed Martí's greatest appeal: the discourse of social unity.[13] By the time of the creation of the PRC, there were already fault lines among Cuban émigrés, especially along race and class. As Mirabal has argued, Martí sought "to sustain unity at all costs," minimizing issues of race and labor.[14] His success in promulgating that discourse of unity was evident in the support and loyalty he received from Afro-Cubans, Puerto Ricans, and working-class Cubans whose priorities were on eliminating racism and fighting for labor justice. Martí managed to convince them to lay aside those concerns and work toward the birth of a republic with justice and equality for all.[15]

The death of Martí and the ascension of Estrada Palma to the leadership of the PRC dealt a blow to the unity Martí had so strategically constructed across racial, class, and nationality lines. The new leaders were all New Yorkers who subscribed to Martí's nationalist agenda, but were less committed to the social ideology that had guided Martí's creation of the inclusive and popular revolutionary movement that resonated so much with Afro-Cubans and working-class Cubans, especially those in the Florida cigar-making communities. "The New York PRC leaders embraced a moderate nationalism," Poyo argued, "that envisioned a liberal Cuban republic modeled after the United States."[16] Afro-Cubans and working-class Cubans immediately mistrusted the new leadership. For them, the U.S. model, and the spectre of U.S. control of Cuba, was not the republic Martí had promised. The unity of the revolutionary movement was in crisis.

The figure who best represents the ideological break with the PRC leadership is Rafael Serra, an Afro-Cuban cigar maker, intellectual, and activist. Born in 1858 in Havana to free blacks, Serra became involved

Figure E.2 Rafael Serra. Source: Manuscripts, Archives and Rare Books Division, Schomburg Center for Research in Black Culture, New York Public Library, Astor, Lenox and Tilden Foundations.

early in his life in separatist activities and eventually left the island in 1880, heading first to Key West and later to New York.[17] He continued his activism in the city, writing political and social essays and becoming involved in several organizations that brought him into contact with Martí. On October 10, 1888, Serra became a U.S. citizen, listing his occupation as "cigar maker" and his address as 52 Sixth Avenue.[18]

One of Serra's most important accomplishments was the establishment in 1890 of La Liga, an educational institution housed at 74 West 3rd Street, just south of Washington Square, conveniently located near the predominantly working-class neighborhoods that are now known as the West Village and SoHo, where many cigar workers lived.[19] La Liga was a community center aimed primarily at raising the educational level and political consciousness of working-class Cubans and Puerto Ricans, especially men of color, through classes and lectures.[20] Martí and Serra are listed among the co-founders of the institution, and they taught classes there.[21] It was probably in La Liga where both men developed a close working relationship that made Serra trust Martí as a leader for all Cubans.

Despite his mistrust of the new PRC leadership after Martí's death, Serra did not criticize it directly, maintaining a cordial relationship with Estrada Palma and the others.[22] Instead, he launched an intensive campaign to reaffirm Martí's principles of sovereignty, justice, and a nation for all Cubans. His principal vehicle was a "biographic, political, literary, general interest" periodical he established in mid-1896 and whose title reveals its intent: *La Doctrina de Martí* (Martí's Doctrine). In its pages, Serra and the other contributors to *La Doctrina* cast themselves as the true guardians of the ideology that was supposed to be guiding the PRC: Martí's exemplary life, his teachings, and his efforts to unite and extend justice to all Cubans:

> The illustrious Martí taught us that a people composed of different elements and subjected to the same yoke must be sincerely united and represented equally in all ways that contribute to the creation of the nation. Those of us who as Cubans share the sacrifice, as Cubans we should also share in the benefit.[23]

On the issue of sovereignty, Serra was adamant in his opposition to the efforts of Estrada Palma and the PRC leaders to court U.S. interest in the Cuban conflict. As Deschamps Chapeaux pointed out, "Cubans of dark skin who suffer discrimination in the southern United States know and proclaim that Cuban freedom is, in the words of Serra, a duel to the death that has no other alternatives but triumph or the grave."[24] As Serra wrote in the January 15, 1897, issue of *La Doctrina de Martí*, "Cuba Yankee? Never! Against Spain today, and against all who wish to take away our independence later."[25]

Serra's reminders of Martí's principle of uncompromised sovereignty were ignored by Estrada Palma, who by April 1896 had already dispatched Gonzalo de Quesada to Washington as the PRC's representative to the U.S. government.[26] Quesada was a member of the same national college fraternity at Secretary of State John Hay, and he sought to take advantage of that to gain access to Hay. He would address letters to Hay with the

Figure E.3. Fidel Pierra. Source: *Cuba y América*,
September 1, 1897, 1.

words "Dear Bro."[27] The intense lobbying effort was on, reminiscent of
the Lemus-Aldama agency of nearly thirty years before. The PRC leaders
(the "Cuban Junta," as it was commonly referred to) lobbied Congress
and focused especially on the New York press, constantly seeking opportunities for coverage of their statements or activities.[28] The incident
at the Upper West Side grammar school showed how ubiquitous and
undiscerning that lobbying effort had become.

As early as September 1895, the PRC had already established a "Press
Bureau" (its name appeared exactly like that, in English, in the party's
budget).[29] The bureau was created by Fidel Pierra, a successful Cuban
businessman who became active in the PRC after the death of Martí.
Pierra measured the success of his bureau by how many news and editorial pieces he was able to place in the U.S. press, reporting in March
1896, for example, that his words had appeared in the *Boston Herald*
and in the *Shipping and Commercial List*; the latter, he claimed, inspired

an editorial in the *New York Sun*.[30] In fact he boasted to Estrada Palma in a letter that since the establishment of the bureau he had personally written or ghost-written the equivalent of hundreds of pages that appeared in the U.S. press relating to all aspects of "Cuban civilization" and physical resources, obviously intended to heighten the interest of potential U.S. investors on the island. Pierra also claimed that he was personally funding many of the activities of the Press Bureau, spending $22 of his own money for every dollar assigned to the bureau by the PRC treasury.[31]

Pierra's publicity campaign to push the United States into war, however, would not match the impact of one decisive, and arguably reckless, release that the PRC leadership issued in early 1898: the infamous "de Lôme letter." Written by the Spanish minister in Washington, Enrique Dupuy de Lôme, to a friend in Havana, it contained some insulting personal references to McKinley as well as disparaging observations about the United States. The letter fell into the hands of a Cuban sympathizer, who passed it on to the PRC leaders in New York.[32] Its content was explosive, yet the PRC leadership decided to abandon all discretion, and certainly Martí's dictum of silence, and released it to William Randolph Hearst's *Journal*, possibly the most incendiary paper of the New York sensationalist press. Hearst splashed it across the front page of the *Journal's* February 9, 1898, edition with the headline THE WORST INSULT TO THE UNITED STATES IN ITS HISTORY.[33] It inflamed even further the pro-war press, creating a jingoistic climate that was still reverberating when, six days later, the battleship *Maine* blew up in Havana's harbor. The historian John Offner speculated on how differently subsequent events may have unfolded if the Cuban leadership in New York had decided to suppress the de Lôme letter.[34]

But the PRC leaders did not, and the rest is, literally, history, one that has been written about extensively: U.S. entry into the war, a U.S. military occupation of the island, the Platt Amendment, and a compromised sovereignty that lasted for more than half a century and served to ensconce the seemingly unattainable ideal of a sovereign nation into the historical consciousness of Cubans.[35]

The PRC leaders managed to achieve what the founder of their movement had always feared. The events that unfolded in 1898 caused the veteran General Máximo Gómez to note the critical absence of Martí: "It is a difficult moment, the most difficult one since the Revolution started. Now Martí could have served his country; this was his moment."[36]

* * *

Barely a month after Martí's death, on June 24, 1895, Carmen Zayas-Bazán arrived in New York from Havana aboard the *City of Washington* with her sixteen-year-old son, José Francisco. A reporter for the *New York Herald* sought to interview Martí's widow, but she excused herself, claiming to be tired from the trip.[37] Four days before, the *Herald* reported that Carmen had obtained in Havana certified copies of the burial certificate and affidavits confirming the identification of Martí's body and that "these will be presented to a New York life insurance company, which carried a risk on Martí's life."[38] When the reporter was finally able to interview her, Mrs. Martí was "anxious to deny the report" that she had gone to New York in connection with any insurance money. "Any such report," she said, "was altogether false."[39]

If indeed Carmen Zayas-Bazán did not go to New York to collect on a life insurance policy, then this trip soon after her husband's death is puzzling. She detested New York. She had no family there. Her previous trips to the city had been marked by acrimonious exchanges with her husband over his unwillingness to return to Cuba and assume his domestic obligations. Martí in turn resented her lack of support for what he saw as his mission in life. She had lost her husband in New York and it is hard to imagine she would return to the city so soon after his death unless she had some important business there.

In New York Carmen stayed with Enrique Trujillo and his family on West 39th Street. Trujillo had been Martí's foe in New York and had helped Carmen leave the city in 1891 without Martí's knowledge (see chapter 8). One matter to which Carmen turned her attention in New York was the recovery of her husband's archives. She wrote to Estrada Palma in September requesting the key to her husband's office on Front Street. She conveyed to Estrada Palma that Gonzalo de Quesada told her that because the rent on the office was overdue, no personal property could be removed. A few days later she received the key and was dismayed to find, as she wrote to Estrada Palma on September 19, only books in the office, "no correspondence, no unpublished works or drafts or notes. . . . All the boxes have been opened and carefully emptied; not a single trace is left that reveals the intellectual life of that vast intelligence."[40] She asked for Estrada Palma's help in securing the papers and threatened that she was "willing to go as far as necessary" to rescue what she viewed as her son's legacy.[41] There is no record of Estrada Palma's reply. We know that Gonzalo de Quesada took possession of the papers, possibly with the cooperation of Carmen Mantilla, for the archive eventually came to light as part of an early edition of Martí's works edited by Quesada's son.[42]

Carmen Zayas-Bazán did not return to Havana with her husband's papers, but she likely did return with the insurance money. Martí had always been convinced that he would live a short life. He also had a sense of guilt that his son was growing up without his father. Add to those personal conditions a contextual factor: in the 1890s the life insurance business was booming. Major companies based in the city, such as New York Life and Metropolitan Life, had already established large sales forces and were insuring the lives of an unprecedented number of New Yorkers. In 1890, for example, New York Life alone had sales of $159 million.[43] It would be surprising if Martí had not insured himself before leaving for the Cuban battlefields.

Two years after his father's death, Carmen's son José Francisco enlisted in the Cuban rebel army shortly after he turned eighteen. He reached the rank of captain and later served in various military and government posts during the Cuban Republic.[44] José Francisco and his mother both lived in Havana the rest of their lives. Carmen passed away in 1928 and her son in 1945.

* * *

Carmen Miyares de Mantilla, the woman close to Martí during his New York years, remained in the city until her death. She corresponded with Gonzalo de Quesada, expressing her interest in seeing the publication of Martí's collected works move forward, and she also wrote to Tomás Estrada Palma to ask for financial support from the PRC for Martí's ailing mother in Havana, with whom she was in touch.[45] She continued to pursue the same occupation that had brought Martí to her door when he arrived in New York in 1880: running a boardinghouse. For a time, early in the twentieth century, Carmen operated a large place of lodging catering to summer visitors in Liberty, New York, in the Hudson

Valley.[46] In 1916 she purchased a home at 185 West 74th Street in Manhattan, where she died of pneumonia on April 17, 1925, just shy of her seventy-seventh birthday. She is buried in Woodlawn Cemetery in the Bronx.[47] An appraisal of her estate after her death yielded gross assets of $15,610, almost all of it in real estate.[48]

María Mantilla, Carmen's youngest child and the presumed daughter of Martí, married a military officer in the Cuban rebel army, César Romero, and had four children, one of them the Hollywood actor César Romero. María died in Los Angeles in 1962 at the age of eighty-two. Some of the obituaries published in the Southern California papers include "Martí" as one of her last names.[49]

* * *

Cirilo Villaverde died in New York in 1894 at age eighty-two, eleven years after the publication of his novel, *Cecilia Valdés*. His death did not in any way minimize the impassioned activism that his widow had demonstrated during the nearly half a century of the couple's residence in New York. Emilia Casanova was well-known among New York's Cubans, even feared by some, for her uncompromising militancy for the cause of a free Cuba. Nearly thirty years had now passed since she was the bane of the *aldamistas*, whom she eviscerated with her pen for what she viewed as their lack of commitment to Cuban independence while she and Cirilo used her father's house in Hunts Point in the Bronx to store and smuggle arms to Cuba (see chapter 6).

Upon Cirilo's death, Emilia traveled briefly to Havana to bury her husband in the capital's Colón necropolis, but returned to New York, where she remained, as before, ready to support not just with words, but also with firepower, the new war against Spanish control of the island. In August 1895 she sent a letter to the new head of the PRC, Tomás Estrada Palma, offering to deliver to him in New York a Cuban flag "to be unfurled on the battlefields of Cuba," in addition to six Winchester carbines and two thousand 44-millimeter caps, adding,

> I promise you that whenever it is possible for me to do so, I will place at your disposal an increasingly greater number of carbines to support the "Guerilla of Villaverde," with the expectation that those fighters will triumphantly parade my flag from one end to the other end of a redeemed Cuba.[50]

Estrada Palma expressed his gratitude in his reply, assuring her that he would petition General Máximo Gómez to name a troop of the army after her husband.[51]

Only two years after sending that message to Estrada Palma and while Cuba was still a Spanish colony, Emilia Casanova, the tireless if controversial fighter for independence, died in New York. She was twenty years younger than Cirilo, but survived him by only three years. She was interred in St. Raymond's Cemetery in the Bronx. It was not until 1944 that her son Narciso fulfilled her wish to be buried next to her husband in Havana.[52]

* * *

Ana de Quesada made good on the promise she made in 1874 after the death of her husband, Carlos Manuel de Céspedes, to never return to Cuba. She died in Paris. Her son, also named Carlos Manuel, who was born shortly after his mother's arrival in New York in 1871, was named by Estrada Palma the titular leader of an expedition that bore his father's name and that disembarked in Cuba on October 28, 1895. The young Céspedes was eager to live up to his father's patriotic legacy, but Estrada Palma was concerned about the young man's "inexperience with our type of war" and entrusted a veteran, Captain José López, with the actual command of the expedition and the safety of the patriot's son until the troop could be delivered in Cuba to General Antonio Maceo.[53] After the war, the young Céspedes entered political life in Cuba, serving in the House of Representatives and later as Cuban ambassador to Washington. While serving in that diplomatic post he married in New York an Italian-born woman in a ceremony held in City Hall and officiated by Mayor John Purroy Mitchel.[54] In 1933 he served for less than one month as provisional president of Cuba.

* * *

After receiving the tragic news in 1873 of the deaths of their husbands, Ignacio and Eduardo Agramonte, on the Cuban battlefields, the sisters Amalia and Matilde Simoni returned to New York from Mérida with their children. Amalia became a U.S. citizen on June 13, 1881, listing her occupation as "lady" and her address as 360 West 45th Street.[55] Her son Ignacio Ernesto became a citizen much later in 1893 at age twenty-four and listed his occupation as "civil engineer."[56]

Blanche Baralt, in her 1945 memoir of her youthful days in the New York of the 1880s and 1890s, remembers with affection the Simoni sisters and their children, noting especially the family's joy on the graduation of Arístides, Matilde's son, from the Columbia University College of Physicians and Surgeons. Matilde remarried and had three more children, all girls.[57]

Amalia Simoni, Ignacio's widow, never remarried. During the time she lived in New York as a widow she partially supported herself and her two children by using her talents as a trained soprano. In 1875 the *New York Commercial Advertiser* announced her first public concert with a notice that read,

> Mrs. Amalia Simoni, widow of General Ignacio Agramonte, . . . has seen all her property confiscated by the Spanish government; and in order to support herself, the noble lady is compelled to take advantage of her excellent musical education. She heartily enters the artistical [*sic*] career, and the New York *dilettanti*. . . . A remarkable singer, whom the necessities of exile bring before the American public . . . will give a concert at DeGarmo Hall, Fifth Avenue and Fourteenth Street.[58]

Amalia returned to live in Cuba in 1892, an event recorded in *Patria* by José Martí. After living in Camagüey for many years, she moved to Havana to live in the Havana neighborhood of El Vedado with her daughter Herminia and her grandchildren. She died there in 1918, forty-five years after Ignacio's death, and was buried in the Colón necropolis on January 24, declared by President Mario García Menocal as a national day of mourning.

At the burial, her nephew Arístides, by that time a well-established physician and an important player in the joint U.S.-Cuba effort to eradicate yellow fever in Cuba, thanked the multitude assembled at the gravesite for "accompanying to this sacred place the mortal remains of the exemplary *compañera* of the bravest, most courageous and daring soldier of our liberties, the undiminished hero of Jimaguayú, Mayor General Ignacio Agramonte."[59]

* * *

Calixto García was technically a fugitive from U.S. justice when he arrived in New York on November 21, 1898, from Havana aboard the steamer *Seguranca*. Two years earlier, the general had left the United States on an expedition to join the fighting in Cuba, jumping a $3,000 bail that had been imposed by the federal authorities for violating U.S. neutrality laws. "I am ready to stand trial," he jokingly told the press upon disembarking from the *Seguranca* on that overcast New York afternoon. But he breezed through customs with no arresting official in sight.[60] The U.S. government, as well as the press, was receiving him as the head of a commission appointed by the Cuban Assembly, a body composed of delegates from the thirty-one corps of the Cuban Liberation Army. The war was over, and the Spanish had surrendered to the United States, which in less than two months was to officially assume control of Cuba. The Assembly had instructed García's commission to meet with President McKinley and ascertain the intentions of the U.S. government with respect to Cuba.[61] As four centuries of Spanish colonialism were coming to an end, García and so many others in the Assembly who had dedicated their entire lives to ending Spanish rule in Cuba had no idea what the future held for their country. The general was most deeply concerned that the ideal for which he had fought for so many years, total independence for Cuba, was now compromised by the U.S. entry in the war, a concern shared among the top Cuban generals.[62] He expressed in his halting English one succinct message for reporters at the East River pier: "No annexation!" Through an interpreter he expanded on that message: "The people of Cuba rely upon the good faith of the United States. It is necessary for the American troops to occupy the island until order is established but not forever."[63]

The members of the commission were spending a few days in New York preparing for their important meeting in Washington with President McKinley. They dispersed to hotels in the city, except for General García, who went directly to Harlem to stay with his wife and younger children. The general's family had lived in the city during the many years, dating back to the 1868 war, when he was on the island's battlefields. In 1880 they lived on West 45th Street, but by 1898 the García family had moved to Lenox Avenue.[64]

In Harlem, García was preoccupied with the frail health of his seventeen-year-old daughter Mercedes. But there was work to be done and distractions to deal with. The commission met daily at the Hoffman House, on Broadway and 25th Street, far from Harlem.[65] The distractions came in the form of a growing chorus of prominent Americans calling for a permanent U.S. occupation of Cuba. For the general, the most disturbing of those calls was voiced only a city block from the Hoffman House on November 25 at a banquet in Delmonico's Restaurant. It came from none other than General William Rufus Shafter, who as commander of the Fifth U.S. Army Corps led the U.S. expeditionary forces that had landed in eastern Cuba. In his address to the Sons of the Revolution, General Shafter said, to the audience's overwhelming approval, "The flag is there, and I hope it will stay there forever."[66]

General García first met Shafter five months earlier, on June 20, when the American general, together with Admiral William T. Sampson, who was in command of the U.S. fleet off eastern Cuba, arrived at García's camp at El Aserradero, near Santiago. Shafter's forces, about 16,000, were still offshore in the thirty-two ships that had set off from Tampa a few days earlier. The purpose of the meeting was to coordinate the landing of the Fifth Corps. The disembarkation would be protected from the sea by Sampson's fleet and from land by the Cuban troops commanded by García.

Shafter did not impress García. Obese and sweating profusely in a wool uniform ill-suited to the Cuban summer, the American general would override his judgment on many details of the operation without acknowledging that he had never set foot on the very terrain on which García had been fighting for decades.[67] The Cuban general felt uneasy about placing himself under Shafter's command, but those were his orders. As commander of all Cuban forces in the east, where the Americans had chosen to land, he had been ordered by his superiors in the rebel army to cooperate with U.S. forces and facilitate their operations.[68]

Thanks to García's troops, the American forces landed without having to face a single Spaniard. Throughout the subsequent campaign, the Cubans were critical to the success of the U.S. war effort.[69] It was, however, a contentious partnership. During the siege of Santiago, Shafter ordered that Cuban troops should be used to dig trenches and carry supplies in order to spare the Americans such tasks. García protested.[70]

When the Spanish finally surrendered Santiago, the largest city in the eastern region, General García readied himself for the negotiations of the terms of surrender and the triumphal entry into the city. It was the day the general had long dreamed about after so many years of fighting: occupying the center of Spanish authority in his home region. But no word arrived from Shafter. As it turned out, the American general had already negotiated the surrender and ordered that Cuban troops not be allowed to enter Santiago.

In disbelief, García rode at a gallop to Shafter's camp for an explanation. Shafter informed him that the Spanish had surrendered to the U.S. army and that there was no role for the Cubans in the surrender, occupation, and administration of the city. The American general did not dispel the rumor that he feared García's troops would engage in violent reprisals against the Spanish.

Outraged, García returned to his camp and wrote a long letter to Shafter, denouncing the exclusion of his troops from the surrender and occupation of Santiago and reminding the American of the Cubans' unconditional support during the campaign. Referring to the allegations of possible vengeful violence on the part of his troops, García wrote,

> Allow me, General, to protest against the slightest hint of such a thought. We are not a savage people. We form a poor and tattered army, as poor and tattered as the army of your ancestors in its noble war for the independence of the United States of America. Similarly to the heroes of Saratoga and Yorktown, we respect our cause too much to stain it with barbarism and cowardice.

The general concluded with a statement of his intentions:

> I deeply regret no longer being able to follow the orders of my government, having sent today to the Commander-in-Chief of the Cuban Army, General Máximo Gómez, my formal resignation as commander of this department of our army. I am withdrawing my troops to Jiguaní.
> I remain, respectfully yours,
> Calixto García[71]

On the same day of Shafter's declaration in New York against Cuban independence, García went to the Fifth Avenue Hotel, at 23rd Street, to meet with a member of the commission who was lodged there. As he was entering the hotel, he came face to face with William Shafter. There were reporters present, and the American press had been critical of the disrespectful manner in which Shafter had treated him in June. It was a perfect opportunity to extract a measure of revenge by walking past Shafter and refusing to salute or say a word to him. Or perhaps he would admonish the general for his statement prejudicial to Cuban sovereignty. But General Calixto García was a gentleman, he was representing his army and his people, and he was on a critical mission in this country. The *New York Times* reporter on the scene described what happened:

> There was an interesting meeting of two noted characters in the corridor of the Fifth Avenue Hotel in the early hours of last evening. General Shafter was just about to leave the hotel and was almost at the door when General García alighted from a cab and entered the building. General Shafter and General García recognized each other almost simultaneously and saluted. They then shook hands most cordially and for several minutes engaged in a friendly talk. It was the first time the two Generals met since their rather unpleasant relations during the siege of Santiago.[72]

That same night of the encounter with Shafter, Calixto García's trip to New York took an even more dismal turn. Nearly eight inches of snow fell on the city, with winds exceeding forty miles an hour. Traffic was paralyzed.[73] The following day, November 27, the storm intensified, with snow accumulations nearing ten inches, winds reaching sixty-four miles an hour, and the temperature dropping to twenty-five degrees Fahrenheit. The city came to a standstill as streets were buried under deep snow drifts. The *New York Times* declared it "the severest November snowstorm of which there is any record."[74]

The storm took its toll on General García. By the time the commission boarded the train to Washington on the evening of November 30, he was suffering from a heavy cold.[75] He confined himself to his room at the Raleigh Hotel, located on the corner of 12th Street and Pennsylvania Avenue, NW. On December 2, a Friday, García boarded a carriage for the short ride to the White House. Gonzalo de Quesada's connection with Secretary of State Hay had apparently paid off: commission members were granted an appointment with President McKinley.

Figure E.4. Members of the Cuban commission headed by General Calixto García pose for the photographer George Prince in Washington while they await their appointment with President William McKinley, December 1898. *From left*: Major General José Miguel Gómez, Lieutenant Colonel José Ramón Villalón, General García, José Antonio González Lanuza, and Colonel Manuel Sanguily. Source: *Libro Azul de Cuba* (La Habana: Solana, 1917), 21.

The Cubans were greeted warmly by the U.S. president, but McKinley limited the meeting to the only topic that he wanted to resolve with the Cuban delegation: severance pay for the rebel army so that it could be disbanded. Once that matter was settled, McKinley promptly adjourned the meeting. There was no discussion of Cuban independence. The political future of the island had not even come up. García's troops had not fought so hard for so long for severance pay. They had fought for Cuban independence, and on that December evening in Washington that ideal must have seemed no closer to the general than when he started fighting for it in 1868.

Another cold front moved into the capital. The general stayed in bed at the Raleigh. Two doctors were called in. They diagnosed pneumonia. The Washington newspapers reported daily on his worsening condition.

In its edition of December 12, the *Washington Evening Star* featured on its front page the arrival in Havana of the 202nd New York Regiment, the first U.S. troops to occupy the capital.[76] On page 3, the headline read,

. CUBAN PATRIOT DEAD
General Calixto Garcia, Soldier and Statesman, Passes Away[77]

It happened on the morning of December 11, a Sunday, in the front second-story suite at the Raleigh Hotel. The general's last hours had been spent in a delirium. He called out for his daughter Mercedes. It was reported that among his last mutterings to his son Justo were orders to prepare the men for a surprise attack on a contingent of approaching Spanish troops.[78]

The general's body was taken to a temporary receiving vault at Arlington National Cemetery to await its eventual transfer to Havana. The caisson was draped with the Cuban and U.S. flags and drawn by six horses for the procession to Arlington. The honorary pallbearers included Secretary of State Hay, four U.S. senators, and several commanders of U.S. forces in Cuba: Generals Nelson Miles, Joseph Wheeler, Henry Lawton, and William Ludlow. Another American general designated as a pallbearer, William R. Shafter, sent his regrets at not being able to attend, citing previous commitments.[79]

* * *

On January 1, 1899, in the Palace of the Captain Generals, the same building in Havana where since 1776 Spanish military governors had ruled Cuba, representatives of the Madrid government turned over the island of Cuba to the United States in accordance with the Treaty of Paris. The U.S. flag went up and the Spanish flag came down, and a new military governor installed himself in the palace, except this time he was an American, Major General John R. Brooke, who on that occasion announced the inauguration of the U.S. military government of Cuba.[80] The Cuban army's top general, Máximo Gómez, was not present.[81]

The ceremony marked the end of four hundred years of Spanish rule in Cuba. The island's colonial status had shaped the development Cuban New York. Throughout the nineteenth century the city served as a principal stage for the separatist struggle. Once the United States took over and eventually allowed the establishment of a Cuban government that nevertheless remained politically dependent on Washington, the relationship between New York and Cuba drew even closer. Although Washington pulled the political strings, Manhattan-based corporations launched the huge investments in the island that defined the Cuban Republic, helping to maintain throughout the first half of the twentieth century those long-established economic, social, and cultural connections that made New York that important "other" place in the Cuban consciousness.

ACKNOWLEDGMENTS

This book has been a long time in the making. Most of the research was conducted during the 2004–2005 academic year, when I had the privilege of holding a Mel and Lois Tukman Fellowship at the Dorothy and Lewis B. Cullman Center for Scholars and Writers at the New York Public Library. The Cullman Center at the NYPL is an extraordinary place for researchers and writers, and this book would not have been possible without my residency there. I am deeply indebted to its director at the time, Jean Strouse, and her staff, Pamela Leo and Adriana Nova. That year the center had a superlative cohort of fellows, a community of gifted writers who pushed me to think critically about my topic and, especially, to improve my writing. I was extremely fortunate to be able to be in daily interaction with such creative people. Of that group, I want to make special mention of Hermione Lee, Nathan Englander, and T. J. Stiles. I learned a great deal about nineteenth-century U.S. history from T.J.: his topic overlapped with mine (at the time he was working on what would become a highly acclaimed biography of Cornelius Vanderbilt) and his suggestions and observations were invaluable to me.

During that year in the New York Public Library I received the helpful and constant assistance of NYPL staff, especially Denise Hibay, at that time Latin American bibliographer; Ruth Carr and Maira Liniaro of the Milstein Division of U.S. History, Local History, and Genealogy; and William Stingone and the staff of the Manuscript and Archives Division.

In addition to the fellowship at the Cullman Center, this project was supported by a National Endowment for the Humanities Faculty Research Award, a fellowship from the Gilder Lehrman Institute of American History, and a sabbatical leave from Florida International University (FIU), for which I am especially grateful to the then provost and now president of FIU, Mark Rosenberg.

I wish to acknowledge the support of the staff at the following libraries and collections, in addition to the NYPL: the Special Collections and

Interlibrary Loan Divisions of the Green Library of Florida International University, the New York Historical Society Library, the Manuscript Division of the Library of Congress, and the Cuban Heritage Collection of the University of Miami Library.

The offer extended to me in 2010 by President Jeremy Travis and Provost Jane Bowers of John Jay College of the City University of New York to join the faculty and chair the Latin American and Latina/o Studies Department fulfilled my lifelong dream to live in New York and gave me the opportunity to further expand my knowledge of the city and to have my life enriched by working in the company of an amazing set of colleagues and students.

I am grateful to the many colleagues in the United States and Cuba who provided guidance, suggestions, insights, and, in many cases, much-needed encouragement: Uva de Aragón, Guillermo Grenier, Ana Cairo, Antonio Aja, Oscar Zanetti, Enrique López Mesa, Juan Martínez, Samuel Farber, Eusebio Leal, Mike Wallace, Gerald Markowitz, Rafael Hernández, Ramón Cernuda, Milagros Martínez, Miguel Barnet, Esther Allen, Rafael Rojas, María Cristina García, and Ivan Schulman.

I want to extend a very special thanks to three historians and friends who read an earlier draft of the manuscript and provided immensely useful feedback (in addition to an anonymous reviewer). One is John Gutiérrez, my colleague at John Jay College, who not only made incisive comments, but suggested ways of couching my book within a larger New York narrative. Another reader was Gerald Poyo, who challenged some of my assumptions and conclusions, causing me to rethink several passages of the book. Jerry generously shared with me his vast knowledge of Cuban American history. Emilio Cueto also read a draft of the manuscript. A world-class collector of all things Cuban, with an encyclopedic knowledge of the history and culture of the island where we were both born, Emilio saved me from more than a few gaffes and provided important details. I did not always follow the advice of those three friends, so, needless to say, I am solely responsible for any shortcomings of the book.

My editors at New York University Press, Amy Klopfenstein and Clara Platter, have been wonderful and, perhaps most importantly, very patient with me, more than I could have expected. Amy was especially helpful in solving the many formatting issues that baffled me and in successfully shepherding the manuscript, and me, through every step of the journey from first draft to print. The manuscript owes a great deal to her dedication. I am also grateful to Dorothea Halliday, managing editor, who handled the production process. Deborah Gershenowitz, my first editor at the press, embraced and encouraged the project and provided feedback on some of the initial chapters. Deeply felt thanks also to my student assistant, Angela Reyes, who organized many of my sources and whose help with the illustrations enabled me to navigate the world of pixels and DPIs.

Mi gente never lost faith that I would finish this book, and I really appreciate that. My sons Lisandro José and Julián, and my granddaughter Gabriela are cornerstones in my life and I am very proud of them. My appreciation to my *nuera* Cynthia, whose resilient character I admire, and to my *suegra* Elsa, who kept asking me the dreaded question, "Y el libro?" Her daughter, Liza Carbajo, has been my guiding light ever since she entered my life twenty-five years ago. She has shared the high and low moments of crafting this book and of everything else. I owe her more than I can possibly express here, and I dedicate this book to her.

NOTES

INTRODUCTION

1. The *Morro Castle* and its sister ship the *Oriente* were launched in 1930 and were the mainstays of the Ward Line's profitable New York-Havana route. The *Morro Castle* would make the 1,168-mile run to Cuba in under fifty-nine hours. On September 8, 1934, a little more than a year after it brought my father and his family to the United States, the *Morro Castle* burned off the New Jersey coast as it was returning to New York from Havana. One hundred and thirty four people died in one of the most notable marine disasters in U.S. history. "Burned Ship Built with Federal Aid," *New York Times*, September 9, 1934, 35; and Gallagher, *Fire at Sea*, 280.

2. John Drebinger, "Giants Win Twice, 1st in 18 innings," *New York Times*, July 3, 1933, 7.

3. Louis A. Pérez Jr., *On Becoming Cuban*; and Louis A. Pérez Jr., *Cuba and the United States*.

4. U.S. Bureau of the Census, *Fourteenth Census of the United States: 1920*, Population, New York City, enumeration district no. 551.

5. Louis A. Pérez Jr., *On Becoming Cuban*, 78; and González Echevarría, *The Pride of Havana*, 80–81.

6. Louis A. Pérez Jr., *On Becoming Cuban*, 43.

7. Bender, *New York Intellect*, 6.

8. Louis A. Pérez Jr., *Cuba and the United States*, 207.

9. Alejandro Portes, "Immigration Theory for a New Century: Some Problems and Opportunities," in Hirschman, Kasinitz, and DeWind, *The Handbook of International Migration*, 29.

10. Peggy Levitt, "Migrants Participate across Borders: Toward an Understanding of Forms and Consequences," in Foner, Rumbaut, and Gold, *Immigration Research for a New Century*, 460–61.

11. Nancy Foner, *From Ellis Island to JFK*, 169–76.

12. Nina Glick Schiller, "Transmigrants and Nation-States: Something Old and Something New in the U.S. Immigrant Experience," in Hirschman, Kasinitz, and DeWind, *The Handbook of International Migration*, 99–106.

13. Chan, *Chinese American Transnationalism*.

14. See, for example, Mormino and Pozzetta, *The Immigrant World of Ybor City*; Westfall, "Don Vicente Martínez Ybor"; Castellanos G., *Motivos de Cayo Hueso*; Rivero Muñiz, "Los cubanos en Tampa"; and Greenbaum, *More Than Black*. On the revolutionary activities of Cuban émigrés, first and foremost are the works by Poyo: *"With All, and for the Good of All"*; and "Evolution of Cuban Separatist Thought." See also Casasús, *La emigración cubana*; Mirabal, "De Aquí, de Allá"; Mirabal, "'No Country but the One We Must Fight For'"; Azcuy, *El Partido Revolucionario*; True,

"Revolutionaries in Exile"; Preece, "Insurgent Guests"; Ojeda Reyes, *Peregrinos de la libertad*; Álvarez Estévez, *La emigración cubana*; Ferrer, *Insurgent Cuba*; and Cordoví Núñez, *La emigración cubana*. The bibliography on José Martí is very extensive. Among the works of greatest relevance to his life and activities in New York are the following: Márquez Sterling, *Martí, maestro y apóstol*; Toledo Sande, *Cesto de llamas*; López, *José Martí*; Rotker, *The American Chronicles of José Martí*; Martí, *Todo lo olvida Nueva York*; Quesada y Miranda, *Martí, hombre*; Santos, *Martí a la luz del sol*; Lillian Guerra, *The Myth of José Martí*; Lomas, *Translating Empire*; Zéndegui, *Ambito de Martí*; Oviedo, *La niña de New York*; Mañach, *Martí el apóstol*; Rafael Rojas, *José Martí*; José M. Hernández, "Martí y el liderato del movimiento separatista cubano," in Aragón, *Repensando a Martí*; Pedro Pablo Rodríguez, *De las dos Américas*; Fountain, *José Martí and U.S. Writers*; Castañeda, *Martí*; García Galló, "Martí y los tabaqueros"; and Barbara Ruth Johnson, "Origin of the Partido Revolucionario Cubano in Tampa."

15. Two notable exceptions are: the monograph by Enrique López Mesa on the intellectual and cultural activities of the New York émigrés, *La comunidad cubana de New York*; and the recent book by Mirabal, *Suspect Freedoms*.

16. See, for example, Trager, *The New York Chronology*; and Burrows and Wallace, *Gotham*.

17. See, for example, Binder and Reimers, *All the Nations under Heaven*. This source, a history of New York's racial and ethnic groups, mentions Cubans only once, a passing reference to the post-1959 migration (p. 228). In a recent 734-page work on the history of immigrant New York, Cubans do not appear even once in the index. Anbrinder, *City of Dreams*.

CHAPTER 1. THE PORT

1. Albion, *The Rise of New York Port*, 182.

2. The description of Varela and Madan walking on the streets of lower Manhattan is taken from José Ignacio Rodríguez's biography of Varela, written in the United States and first published in New York in 1878, *Vida del presbítero Don Félix Varela*, 143–44. Madan himself was probably the source of the description, since he was still living in New York at the time the biography was written and Rodríguez knew him well.

3. *New York, 1820–1850 Passenger and Immigration Lists*. José Ignacio Rodríguez was the first one to find the record of Varela's arrival more than 125 years ago in the New York Customs House, citing the date of arrival, the name of the ship's captain, and the names and ages of two Cuban passengers who accompanied Varela (thirty years of age) on the voyage: Tomás Gener, thirty-eight, and Leonardo Santos Suárez, twenty-eight, both of whom had served with Varela as representatives of Cuba before the Spanish parliament. Rodríguez, *Vida del presbítero*, 133.

4. Philip S. Foner, *A History of Cuba*, vol. 1, 102–3.

5. Bradley W. Steuart, ed., *Passenger Ships Arriving in New York Harbor*, vol. 1, *1820–1850* (Bountiful, UT: Precision Indexing, 1991), 11–14.

6. Ibid., 304.

7. *New York, 1820–1850 Passenger and Immigration Lists*.

8. Syrett, *The Siege and Capture of Havana*, xiii.

9. Hugh Thomas, *Cuba*, 1.

10. Louis A. Pérez Jr., *Cuba: Between Reform and Revolution*, 36–37.
11. Syrett, *The Siege and Capture of Havana*, xx.
12. Hugh Thomas, *Cuba*, 6–10.
13. Ibid., 49.
14. Santovenia, "Política colonial," 51.
15. Bernstein, *Origins of Inter-American Interest*, 36–37.
16. Ibid., 36.
17. *Journals of the Continental Congress*, 20 (1781), 370, cited in Bernstein, *Origins of Inter-American Interest*, 35.
18. Ely, *Cuando reinaba su majestad el azúcar*, 56.
19. Fernández de Pinedo Echevarría, *Las balanzas del comercio exterior de La Habana*, 36.
20. Fernández de Pinedo Echevarría, *Comercio exterior y fiscalidad*, 34.
21. Ibid.
22. Bernstein, *Origins of Inter-American Interest*, 37.
23. Moreno Fraginals, *The Sugarmill*, 42.
24. Bernstein, *Origins of Inter-American Interest*, 37.
25. Hugh Thomas, *Cuba*, 12.
26. Moreno Fraginals, *The Sugarmill*, 15.
27. Le Riverend Brusone, "Desarrollo económico y social," 174.
28. Ely, *Cuando reinaba su majestad el azúcar*, 52.
29. Moreno Fraginals, *El ingenio*, 15. The English translation, a single-volume work published in 1964 and cited in previous notes, is a translation of the first Spanish edition. This second Spanish edition is in three volumes and is a significantly expanded revision of the first, which is why both works are cited in this chapter.
30. Le Riverend Brusone, "Desarrollo económico y social," 177.
31. Moreno Fraginals, *The Sugarmill*, 15.
32. Ibid., 15–16.
33. Le Riverend Brusone, "Desarrollo económico y social," 175.
34. Moreno Fraginals, *The Sugarmill*, 15.
35. Le Riverend Brusone, "Desarrollo económico y social," 211.
36. Tornero, "El suministro de mano de obra esclava en Cuba," 318.
37. Moreno Fraginals, *The Sugarmill*, 20–25.
38. Moreno Fraginals, *El ingenio*, vol. 1, 213–14.
39. Moreno Fraginals, *The Sugarmill*, 27–28.
40. Ibid., 19.
41. Ibid., 25, 41, 83–85. Mechanization, of course, refers only to the processing functions. The harvesting side of the mills' operations was still done manually by slave labor.
42. Knight, *Slave Society in Cuba*, 22. Sherry Johnson provides the most detailed description of the population explosion, but argues that, at least until 1809, sugar was not the primary reason for the demographic growth: Sherry Johnson, *The Social Transformation of Eighteenth-Century Cuba*, 52–59.
43. Louis A. Pérez Jr., *On Becoming Cuban*, 20.
44. Portell Vilá, *Historia de Cuba*, vol. 1, 281.
45. Ely, "The Old Cuba Trade," 458.
46. Albion, *The Rise of New York Port*, 187.
47. Ibid., 179, 183.
48. Ibid., 179.

49. Ibid., 180; and Kammen, *Colonial New York*, 169.
50. *Statistics of the New York Sugar Market for Sixteen Years, 1845 to 1861* (New York: Wylie and Wade, 1861), n.p.
51. Moreno Fraginals, *El ingenio*, 25.
52. Albion, *The Rise of New York Port*, 184.
53. Ibid., 180. See also Moreno Fraginals, *The Sugarmill*, 27.
54. Albion, *The Rise of New York Port*, 189.
55. Ibid.
56. Moreno Fraginals, *The Sugarmill*, 29–30.
57. Albion, *The Rise of New York Port*, 182.
58. Louis A. Pérez Jr., *On Becoming Cuban*, 16–24.
59. Portell Vilá, *Historia de Cuba*, vol. 1, 281.
60. Ibid.
61. Ibid.
62. Hodas, *The Business Career of Moses Taylor*, 2–3.
63. Ely, *Cuando reinaba su majestad el azúcar*, 119–20.
64. Barrett, *Old Merchants of New York City*, vol. 1, 314–15.
65. Ely, "The Old Cuba Trade," 460.
66. Ibid., 462.
67. Ely, *Cuando reinaba su majestad el azúcar*, 159–60.
68. Ely, "The Old Cuba Trade," 465.
69. Ely, *Cuando reinaba su majestad el azúcar*, 158.
70. Records of financial dealings with these and other merchants and planters are in boxes 77 and 78, Moses Taylor Papers, New York Public Library.
71. Ely, "The Old Cuba Trade," 476–77.
72. Moreno Fraginals, *El ingenio*, 143.
73. Ely, "The Old Cuba Trade," 476.
74. Ibid., 477.
75. Knight, *Slave Society in Cuba*, 39.
76. Moreno Fraginals, *The Sugarmill*, 30.
77. Letter of Sebn. de Peñalver to Moses Taylor and Company, February 10, 1849, Box 79, Moses Taylor Papers. Although Peñalver does not sign with his full name, this is Sebastián Peñalver identified as the Third Marquis by Santa Cruz y Mallén in *Historia de familias cubanas*, vol. 4, 271–72.
78. Letter of Sebn. de Peñalver to Moses Taylor and Company, February 24, 1849, Box 79, Moses Taylor Papers.
79. Ely, *Comerciantes cubanos*, 142.
80. Roig de Leuchsenring, *La Habana*, 64–65.
81. Letters from José Alcázar to Moses Taylor and Company, 1868, Box 77, Moses Taylor Papers.
82. Ely, *Comerciantes cubanos*, 142.
83. Letter from Aug. F. Nitchy to Moses Taylor and Company, October 5, 1858, Box 77, Moses Taylor Papers.
84. Letter from Torres, Reigadas, and Company to Moses Taylor and Company, May 31, 1858, Box 77, Moses Taylor Papers.
85. Letter from George Tregent to Moses Taylor and Company, March 19, 1860, Box 77, Moses Taylor Papers.

86. Letter from Torres, Reigadas, and Company to Moses Taylor and Company, April 12, 1860, Box 77, Moses Taylor Papers.
87. Letter from Charles Bartlett to Henry A. Coit, January 25, 1849, Box 80, Moses Taylor Papers.
88. Letter from L. Govín to Moses Taylor and Company, August 27, 1858, Box 80, Moses Taylor Papers.
89. R. J. Tellier, "Weekly Report, Martín Ruiz, at St. John's College, 1859," undated, Box 80, Moses Taylor Papers.
90. Letter from Ramón de Céspedes to Percy R. Pyne, March 13, 1855, Box 77, Moses Taylor Papers.
91. "History of West Point Foundry," www.scenichudson.org.
92. Letter from the West Point Foundry to Moses Taylor and Company, December 12, 1871, Box 80, Moses Taylor Papers. This 1871 letter from the foundry was in response to an order from Terry, through Taylor, for two replacement spur wheel segments for the grinder, which, the letter notes, was purchased thirteen years earlier.
93. Letter from Ramón de Céspedes to Percy R. Pyne, April 25, 1855, Box 77, Moses Taylor Papers.
94. Letters from Ramón de Céspedes to Percy R. Pyne, August 7, October 4, and October 9, 1855, Box 77, Moses Taylor Papers.
95. Letter from Ramón de Céspedes to Percy R. Pyne, March 6, 1856, Box 77, Moses Taylor Papers.
96. Thrasher, "Preliminary Essay," 425.

CHAPTER 2. EXILES, SOJOURNERS, AND ANNEXATIONISTS

1. Santa Cruz y Montalvo, *La Havane*, vol. 1, 85.
2. *New York, 1820–1850 Passenger and Immigration Lists*.
3. Santa Cruz y Mallén, *Historia de familias cubanas*, vol. 5, 164–66.
4. Albion, *The Rise of New York Port*, 247.
5. José Ignacio Rodríguez, *Vida del presbítero*, 144.
6. The details of Varela's arrival at Goodhue and Company are told, without reference, by Hernández Travieso, *El Padre Varela*, 292.
7. Santa Cruz y Mallén, *Historia de familias cubanas*, vol. 3, 226–32.
8. Roldán Oliarte, *Cuba en la mano*, 913; and Casasús, *La emigración cubana*, 17.
9. Casasús, *La emigración cubana*, 18.
10. Ibid.
11. Marrero, *Azúcar, ilustración y conciencia*, 38–42.
12. José Ignacio Rodríguez, *Vida del presbítero*, 145.
13. McCadden and McCadden, *Félix Varela*, 63.
14. Hernández Travieso, *El Padre Varela*, 329.
15. Although both José Ignacio Rodríguez (*Vida del presbítero*, 147) and the McCaddens (*Félix Varela*, 59) make reference to the assassination attempt, Hernández Travieso (*El Padre Varela*, 329) is the only Varela biographer who provides details about it. Unfortunately, he is not explicit about his sources.
16. Quoted, without reference, by José Ignacio Rodríguez, *Vida del presbítero*, 144.
17. José Ignacio Rodríguez, *Vida del presbítero*, 144.
18. Ibid., 143.
19. Bayley, *A Brief Sketch*, 109, 114.

20. Varela, *Cartas a Elpidio*, vol. 2, *Superstición*, 154–58.
21. Ibid., 159–61.
22. Ibid., 157.
23. Varela, "Carta del editor de este papel a un amigo," 159.
24. McCadden and McCadden, *Félix Varela*, 78.
25. Ibid., 77.
26. Cheung, *Transfiguration Church*, 4.
27. McCadden and McCadden, *Félix Varela*, 79.
28. Ibid., 78.
29. José Ignacio Rodríguez, *Vida del presbítero*, 143.
30. Bayley, *A Brief Sketch*, 111–12.
31. Navia, *An Apostle for the Immigrants*, 85–89.
32. McCadden and McCadden, *Félix Varela*, 77.
33. Cheung, *Transfiguration Church*, 6.
34. Betty Kaplan Gubert, "Delmonico's," in Jackson, *The Encyclopedia of New York City*, 325.
35. Lately Thomas, *Delmonico's*, 27. The site of the church was across Chambers from where the Tweed Courthouse now stands.
36. "Church Property: Archbishop Hughes to the Public," *New York Times*, May 15, 1855.
37. The house was probably demolished in 1899, when construction started on the ornate Hall of Records, now known as the Surrogate's Court, a municipal building that occupies the entire block bounded by Chambers, Park Row, Reade, and Elk Streets. Brooke J. Barr, "Surrogate's Court," in Jackson, *The Encyclopedia of New York City*, 1144.
38. Cheung, *Transfiguration Church*, 6.
39. McCadden and McCadden, *Félix Varela*, 78.
40. Ibid., 80.
41. The full text of this letter and of all other communications written in relation to the rumored appointment of Varela as bishop are reproduced in José Ignacio Rodríguez, *Vida del presbítero*, 293–97. Rodríguez found them in the Archives of the Indies and in the papers of the Spanish Embassy in Rome.
42. José Ignacio Rodríguez, *Vida del presbítero*, 294.
43. Ibid., 297.
44. The translation of Jefferson's manual was printed by Henry Newton, Chatham no. 157, and the translation of Davy by John Gray and Company. José Ignacio Rodríguez, *Vida del presbítero*, 151, 153.
45. José Ignacio Rodríguez, *Vida del presbítero*, 193.
46. McCadden and McCadden, *Félix Varela*, 79.
47. Ibid., 119.
48. Thomas Gorley v. Felix Varela, judgment filed in the New York Court of Common Pleas, February 25, 1846, Old Records Division, New York County Courts, reference number 1846#976.
49. U.S. Bureau of the Census, *1840 United States Federal Census, New York City*, Sixth Ward.
50. McCadden and McCadden, *Félix Varela*, 101.
51. Guiteras, *Un invierno en Nueva York*, 143–44.
52. Hernández Travieso, *El Padre Varela*, 444.
53. Ibid.

54. Letter of Gaspar Betancourt Cisneros to José Antonio Saco, quoted in McCadden and McCadden, *Félix Varela*, 121.

55. Hernández Travieso, *El Padre Varela*, 364.

56. "Church Property: Archbishop Hughes to the Public," *New York Times*, May 15, 1855, 1.

57. José Ignacio Rodríguez, *Vida del presbítero*, 226–28.

58. McCadden and McCadden, *Félix Varela*, 135.

59. Cheung, *Transfiguration Church*, 9. Bronze plaques honoring Varela adorn the church's facade. On October 2, 1997, a ceremony, led by John Cardinal O'Connor, was held at Transfiguration Church to mark the issuance by the United States Postal Service of a first-class stamp commemorating Varela.

60. *New York, 1820–1850 Passenger and Immigration Lists.*

61. Marrero, *Azúcar, ilustración y conciencia*, 42.

62. López Mesa, *Algunos aspectos culturales*, 16.

63. Bueno, *Figuras cubanas*, 9–23; and Vitier, *Ese sol del mundo moral*, 20–41.

64. Torres-Cuevas, "José Antonio Saco," 27; and Portuondo Zúñiga, *José Antonio Saco*, 70.

65. Trelles y Govín, *Matanzas en la independencia de Cuba*, 13.

66. Garcerán de Vall, *Heredia y la libertad*, 126.

67. Díaz, *Heredia*, 51.

68. Ernest R. Moore, "José María Heredia in New York," 257–58.

69. Letter to Ignacio Heredia Campuzano, New York, October 8, 1824, in Augier, *Epistolario de José María Heredia*, 185.

70. Letter to Ignacio Heredia Campuzano, New Haven, July 17, 1824, in Augier, *Epistolario de José María Heredia*, 165.

71. Letter to María Mercedes Heredia Campuzano, New York, December 24, 1823, in Augier, *Epistolario de José María Heredia*, 90.

72. Letter to Ignacio Heredia Campuzano, New York, March 6, 1824, in Augier, *Epistolario de José María Heredia*, 105.

73. Letter to Ignacio Heredia Campuzano, New York, June 2, 1824, in Augier, *Epistolario de José María Heredia*, 129.

74. Letter to Cristóbal Madan, New Haven, July 10, 1824, in Augier, *Epistolario de José María Heredia*, 163–64.

75. Letter to Ignacio Heredia Campuzano, New York, February 21, 1824, in Augier, *Epistolario de José María Heredia*, 96.

76. Ibid., 96–97.

77. Ernest R. Moore, "José María Heredia in New York," 272.

78. Letter to Ignacio Heredia Campuzano, New Haven, July 17, 1824, in Augier, *Epistolario de José María Heredia*, 167.

79. Letter to María Mercedes Heredia Campuzano, New Haven, July 18, 1824, in Augier, *Epistolario de José María Heredia*, 169.

80. Irwin, *The New Niagara*, xxi.

81. Ernest R. Moore, "José María Heredia in New York," 268.

82. Ibid., 269.

83. Esténger, *Heredia*, 193.

84. "Cronología," in Cairo Ballester, *Heredia entre cubanos y españoles*, 246; and Ernest R. Moore, "José María Heredia in New York," 279.

85. José Ignacio Rodríguez, *Vida del presbítero*, 145; and Ernest R. Moore, "José María Heredia in New York," 279.

86. For an analysis of the content and importance of "Niágara," see Silva Gruesz, *Ambassadors of Culture*, 39–48.

87. Padura Fuentes, *José María Heredia*, 73.

88. Ibid., 75. In Mexico, Heredia continued to garner praise for his poetry, served in various official positions in the government, married a Mexican woman, and had six children. In 1836, after thirteen years living outside Cuba and ill with tuberculosis, Heredia obtained permission to visit the island, and his mother, for a period of thirteen months. The permission was granted by the Spanish captain-general Miguel Tacón in exchange for Heredia's disavowal of his previous pro-independence sentiments and activities, a humiliating act for which he was severely criticized by many of his peers. He returned to Mexico after the visit, but the tuberculosis progressed, and in 1839, at the age of thirty-five, he died in Mexico City.

89. For an analysis of this period in New York's cultural and intellectual history, see chapter 4 of Bender, *New York Intellect*.

90. Timothy Anglin Burgard, "Hudson River School," in Jackson, *The Encyclopedia of New York*, 572; and Irwin, *The New Niagara*, xx.

91. Bender, *New York Intellect*, 124; and Trager, *The New York Chronology*, 64.

92. Ernest R. Moore, "José María Heredia in New York," 280.

93. Ibid., 280, 291; and Cairo Ballester, *Heredia entre cubanos y españoles*, 70. Both Moore and Cairo Ballester reproduce the entire review in their works.

94. See Bender, *New York Intellect*, 119–20, for a discussion of the importance of the arrival of Bryant in New York and his impact on the intellectual life of the city.

95. Garcerán de Vall, *Heredia y la libertad*, 143–44.

96. Ernest R. Moore, "José María Heredia in New York," 281–83. Moore addresses the long-standing polemic regarding the actual role of Bryant in the translation of "Niágara."

97. Letter to Ignacio Heredia Campuzano, Albany, June 7, 1824, in Augier, *Epistolario de José María Heredia*, 133–37.

98. Letter to Ignacio Heredia Campuzano, New York, June 2, 1824, in Augier, *Epistolario de José María Heredia*, 131.

99. Letter to María Mercedes Heredia Campuzano, New York, July 5, 1824, in Augier, *Epistolario de José María Heredia*, 161.

100. For the background on this incident, see Burrows and Wallace, *Gotham*, 513.

101. Letter to Ignacio Heredia Campuzano, New York, April 23, 1824, in Augier, *Epistolario de José María Heredia*, 119–22.

102. Campuzano, "Dos viajeras cubanas," 146.

103. Santa Cruz y Mallén, *Historia de familias cubanas*, vol. 1, 345–46.

104. Méndez Rodenas, *Gender and Nationalism in Colonial Cuba*, 22.

105. Santa Cruz y Mallén, *Historia de familias cubanas*, vol. 1, 348.

106. Santa Cruz y Montalvo, *La Havane*. Three volumes were published in 1844 by the same publisher. A "sanitized" translation, excluding many letters, was published in Madrid the same year as *Viaje a La Habana*. A complete Spanish translation did not appear until 1981: Mercedes de Santa Cruz, Condesa de Merlin, *La Habana*, trans. Amalia E. Bacardí (Madrid: Cronocolor, 1981).

107. Santa Cruz y Montalvo, *La Havane*, 65–66.

108. Ibid., 75.

109. Ibid., 111.

110. Ibid., 112.

111. Ibid., 80–81.

112. Ibid., 72–73.

113. Ibid., 112.

114. Ibid., 127.

115. "Cronología," in Cairo Ballester, *Heredia entre cubanos y españoles*, 252.

116. Cairo Ballester, "Estados Unidos y la construcción del pensamiento cubano"; and Santa Cruz y Mallén, *Historia de familias cubanas*, vol. 2, 275.

117. Gómez de Avellaneda, "A vista del Niágara," 352. I have done a liberal translation of those lines in the poem, converting them to prose.

118. Ibid.; and Campuzano, "Dos viajeras cubanas," 149–50. Judging from her description, the bridge that inspired Gómez de Avellaneda was the Railway Suspension Bridge, which was designed by John Augustus Roebling. When the bridge opened in 1855 it was hailed as an engineering marvel because it doubled the length of all previous railway suspension bridges. Gómez de Avellaneda perceived exactly what the builders had intended, a bridge, as William Irwin noted, that "would crown the landscape with a magnificent human response to nature, . . . an extension of progress and civilization over the broad landscape." Irwin, *The New Niagara*, 32. Years later, Roebling would design the Brooklyn Bridge, a structure that would also be praised by another Cuban writer in New York, José Martí.

119. Albin, *Género, poesía y esfera pública*, 128.

120. Sagra, *Cinco meses en los Estados-Unidos*, 2.

121. Ibid., 255–67.

122. Guerra y Sánchez, *Manual de historia de Cuba*, 312–13.

123. Saco, *Obras*, vol. 1, 308.

124. Quoted in ibid., 309.

125. Ibid.

126. Ramón de la Sagra, "Carta a los editores del *Mensajero* que se publica en New York," in Saco, *Obras*, 310–12.

127. The principal texts of the controversy are reprinted in Saco, *Obras*, 307–413.

128. Guerra y Sánchez, *Manual de historia de Cuba*, 313.

129. Portuondo Zúñiga, *José Antonio Saco*, 70–71.

130. Benítez Rojo, "Azúcar/poder/texto," 104.

131. Guerra y Sánchez, *Manual de historia de Cuba*, 313.

132. "The Flag of Free Cuba," *New York Sun*, May 11, 1850, 2.

133. It has been asserted that the flag flew for the first time in New Orleans, but apparently it was not until May 26 that the flag was displayed there from a window of the offices of the *Daily Delta*. Urban, "A Local Study in 'Manifest Destiny,'" 44. Enrique López Mesa cites a work by Cirilo Villaverde, which I have not been able to consult, as the source for contradictory locations of the Manhattan boardinghouse where the flag was presumably designed and sewn, identifying one location on Warren Street and another on Murray Street. López Mesa, *Algunos aspectos culturales*, 65. Juan Casasús indicates that the flag was designed by López and his collaborators the year before at a meeting in the boardinghouse of Mrs. Clara Levis, 39 Howard Street. Casasús, *La emigración cubana*, 41.

134. *Soundex Index to Petitions for Naturalization*, U.S. District Court, New York, vol. 1, record no. 217.

135. Joyce Mendelsohn, "Madison Square," in Jackson, *The Encyclopedia of New York*, 711; and Burrows and Wallace, *Gotham*, 715.

136. U.S. Bureau of the Census, *1850 United States Federal Census, New York City*, Eighteenth Ward, Second District.

137. Santa Cruz y Mallén, *Historia de familias cubanas*, vol. 5, 166.

138. U.S. Bureau of the Census, *1850 United States Federal Census, New York City*, Eighteenth Ward, Second District.

139. Philip S. Foner, *A History of Cuba*, vol. 2, 21. Foner characterizes O'Sullivan as "a New Yorker who proudly called himself a pro-slavery man."

140. Pratt, "The Origin of 'Manifest Destiny,'" 797–98.

141. Hugh Thomas, *Cuba*, 211.

142. Guerra y Sánchez, *Manual de historia de Cuba*, 439.

143. Marrero, *Azúcar, ilustración y conciencia*, 118; and Hugh Thomas, *Cuba*, 209.

144. Marrero, *Azúcar, ilustración y conciencia*, 154.

145. Poyo, "*With All, and for the Good of All*," 4.

146. Ibid.

147. Philip S. Foner, *A History of Cuba*, vol. 2, 13–14.

148. Cepero Bonilla, *Azúcar y abolición*, 63–64.

149. Philip S. Foner, *A History of Cuba*, vol. 2, 15.

150. Morales y Morales, *Iniciadores y primeros mártires*, 327.

151. Knight, *Slave Society in Cuba*, 22.

152. Poyo, "*With All, and for the Good of All*," 7.

153. Sampson, *John L. O'Sullivan*, 227.

154. Hugh Thomas, *Cuba*, 211–12.

155. Marrero, *Azúcar, ilustración y conciencia*, 166–67.

156. Cited in ibid., 152.

157. Roldán Oliarte, *Cuba en la mano*, 821.

158. Guerra y Sánchez, *Manual de historia de Cuba*, 443.

159. Portell Vilá, *Historia de Cuba*, vol. 1, 368.

160. These points were not presented in the newspaper itself but in an internal document found and examined in the Cuban National Museum by the historian Herminio Portell Vilá and reproduced in volume 2 of his three-volume work, *Narciso López y su época*, 445–46.

161. "Contestación de los cubanos a la carta autógrafa que la Reina de España les ha dirigido con fecha del 8 de octubre de 1851," *La Verdad*, December 15, 1851, 1.

162. Those were the issues of January 20, February 10 and 20, and March 30, 1852.

163. Hugh Thomas, *Cuba*, 214.

164. Guerra y Sánchez, *Manual de historia de Cuba*, 450.

165. Marrero, *Azúcar, ilustración y conciencia*, 159.

166. Guerra y Sánchez, *Manual de historia de Cuba*, 450.

167. Cova, *Cuban Confederate Colonel*, 25–26.

168. Hugh Thomas, *Cuba*, 214.

169. Marrero, *Azúcar, ilustración y conciencia*, 160.

170. Guerra y Sánchez, *Manual de historia de Cuba*, 452.

171. Ibid.

172. Gonzalo de Quesada, *Páginas escogidas*, 219; and Casasús, *La emigración cubana*, 409.

173. Cova, *Cuban Confederate Colonel*, 3.

174. Guerra y Sánchez, *Manual de historia de Cuba*, 452.

175. Kimball, *Cuba and the Cubans*.

176. Ibid., 194.
177. Cova, *Cuban Confederate Colonel*, 30.
178. William Fletcher Johnson, *The History of Cuba*, vol. 3, 66.
179. After printing reports during several days recounting the overwhelming success of the expedition, the *Sun* had to admit on May 30 that it did not have correct accounts of the landing of López, but vowed that "the Cuban movement has not yet come to a close." *New York Sun*, May 30, 1850, 2.
180. Chaffin, *Fatal Glory*, 184.
181. Ibid., 193.
182. José Ignacio Rodríguez, *Estudio histórico*, 155–57.
183. Sampson, *John L. O'Sullivan*, 218.
184. Morales y Morales, *Iniciadores y primeros mártires*, 130; and William Fletcher Johnson, *The History of Cuba*, vol. 3, 93–95.
185. Chaffin, *Fatal Glory*, 199.
186. José Ignacio Rodríguez, *Estudio histórico*, 452–53.
187. "Affairs of Cuba," *New York Herald*, August 26, 1851, 1.
188. "Movements and Meetings in the United States," *New York Herald*, August 27, 1851, 1.
189. Guerra y Sánchez, *Manual de historia de Cuba*, 458.
190. Chaffin, *Fatal Glory*, 217–18. Congress did not actually appropriate the money for the indemnification until March 1853. José Ignacio Rodríguez, *Estudio histórico*, 163–64.
191. Cova, *Cuban Confederate General*, 3; and Gonzalo de Quesada, *Páginas escogidas*, 222.
192. Cova, *Cuban Confederate General*, 361; and Gonzalo de Quesada, *Páginas escogidas*, 223.
193. Poyo, *"With All, and for the Good of All,"* 15.
194. Trelles y Govín, *Matanzas en la independencia de Cuba*, 101–2.
195. Ibid., 102.
196. Ibid.
197. Morales y Morales, *Iniciadores y primeros mártires*, vol. 2, 152; and Portell Vilá, *Historia de Cuba*, vol. 1, 455. Although Madan is an important figure in the development of Cuban New York, I am not aware of any biography or even a chronology of his life. We know of him only when his life intersects with important events or historical figures. It is not clear exactly how long he remained in exile in Spain, but eventually he returned to New York.

CHAPTER 3. AN EMERGING COMMUNITY AND A RISING ACTIVISM

1. Simón Camacho, *Cosas de los Estados Unidos*, 205.
2. "Death by Jumping or Falling from a Roof," *New York Daily Tribune*, February 18, 1845, 2; and "Melancholy Suicide," *New York Evening Post*, February 17, 1845, 2.
3. "City Intelligence," *New York Herald*, February 18, 1845, 2.
4. "Suicide," *Brooklyn Daily Eagle*, February 18, 1845, 2.
5. "City Intelligence," *New York Herald*, 2.
6. "Sane and Suicide: Romance in Real Life," *New York Herald*, February 19, 1845, 2.
7. Ibid.
8. Santa Cruz y Mallén, *Historia de familias cubanas*, vol. 1, 29.
9. Llaverías, *Miguel Aldama*, 6.
10. Álvarez Pedroso, *Miguel de Aldama*, 24.
11. Llaverías, *Miguel Aldama*, 8.

12. Álvarez Pedroso, *Miguel de Aldama*, 25.

13. Lobo Montalvo, *Havana*, 133.

14. I found no evidence in the Moses Taylor Papers that the Aldamas conducted business with the Taylor firm early in their business careers. By 1868, however, Miguel Aldama had an account with Moses Taylor, which he used in the summer of that year to travel to Saratoga Springs and Niagara Falls. Letter from Miguel Aldama to Moses Taylor and Company, August 26, 1868, Box 305, Moses Taylor Papers.

15. *New York, 1820–1850 Passenger and Immigration Lists*. The cousin who traveled with them, Gonzalo Alfonso, also met an untimely death, two years before Gonzalo Aldama, in Paris. Santa Cruz y Mallén, *Historia de familias cubanas*, vol. 3, 13. That cousin was the grandson of Domingo Aldama's father-in-law, Gonzalo Alfonso, and the son of the man (also named Gonzalo) who raised the money that arrived too late to help Father Varela in St. Augustine.

16. U.S. Bureau of the Census, *1850 United States Federal Census*. All references in this chapter to the 1850 U.S. census are to this source.

17. Ibid.

18. All references here to *Mercurio de Nueva York* are derived from the issues I consulted from the microfilm collections in the New York Public Library, which contain scattered issues of the paper from 1828 to 1833.

19. *El Mercurio de Nueva York*, August 15, 1829, 4.

20. *El Mercurio de Nueva York*, May 16, 1829, 3; August 8, 1829, 1; October 31, 1829, 1.

21. *El Mercurio de Nueva York*, August 8, 1829, 4; August 15, 1829, 4.

22. Jan Seidler Ramírez, "Greenwich Village," in Jackson, *The Encyclopedia of New York*, 508.

23. Mendelsohn, "Madison Square," 711; and Burrows and Wallace, *Gotham*, 715.

24. Graham Hodges, "Lower East Side," in Jackson, *The Encyclopedia of New York*, 696; and Homberger, *The Historical Atlas of New York City*, 81.

25. U.S. Bureau of the Census, *1850 United States Federal Census*, New York City, Fifteenth Ward.

26. Santa Cruz y Mallén, *Historia de familias cubanas*, vol. 4, 93.

27. U.S. Bureau of the Census, *1850 United States Federal Census*, New York City, Sixth Ward.

28. U.S. Bureau of the Census, *1850 United States Federal Census*, New York City, Third Ward.

29. Ibid.

30. U.S. Bureau of the Census, *1850 United States Federal Census*, New York City, Ninth Ward.

31. U.S. Bureau of the Census, *1850 United States Federal Census*, New York City, Seventeenth Ward.

32. U.S. Bureau of the Census, *1850 United States Federal Census*, New York City, Twelfth Ward.

33. Ibid.

34. Ibid.; and Alana J. Erickson, "Magdalen Societies," in Jackson, *The Encyclopedia of New York*, 715.

35. *Guía de Nueva York y los Estados Unidos para uso de españoles y sudamericanos donde se esplica cuanto puede interesar a un viajero* (New York: W. & C. T. Barton, 1856).

36. Ibid., 48.

37. Álvarez and Grediaga, *Guía de Nueva York*.
38. Ibid., 153–54.
39. Ibid., 143–45.
40. Ibid., 144.
41. Handwritten flyer dated May 8, 1852, Box 79, Moses Taylor Papers.
42. U.S. Bureau of the Census, *1860 United States Federal Census*. All references in this chapter to the 1860 U.S. census are to this source.
43. Ibid.
44. Casasús, *La emigración cubana*, 58.
45. Calcagno, *Diccionario biográfico cubano*, 398; and *New York, 1820–1850 Passenger and Immigration Lists*.
46. Morales y Morales, *Iniciadores y primeros mártires*, 152.
47. *New York Petitions for Naturalization*.
48. Trelles y Govín, *Matanzas en la independencia de Cuba*, 99–101. Trelles presents official correspondence of the colonial government that documents the amnesty granted to Macías as well as portions of the detailed reports issued and received by the political section and the police regarding his movements on the island. The documents also indicate he was issued a passport to return to the United States in April.
49. H. Wilson, comp., *Trow's New York City Directory, 1861*, 593.
50. Circular and printed notices of corporate changes and addresses sent to Moses Taylor and Company, Box 78, Moses Taylor Papers.
51. *New York Petitions for Naturalization*.
52. The Trustees of the Scotch Presbyterian Church, in the city of New York, against Antonio M. Mora and others, filed in the Supreme Court, City and County of New York, August 15, 1856, Old Records Division, New York County Courts, reference numbers 1856#S-11, 1856#S-12, 1856#S-13, 1856#S-14, and 1856#S-60.
53. *New York Petitions for Naturalization*.
54. U.S. Bureau of the Census, *1860 United States Federal Census, New York City*, Seventeenth Ward, Ninth District; and Wilson, *Trow's New York City Directory, 1861*, 611.
55. Jose M. Mora, Antonio M. Mora, Jose A. Mora and Jose F. Navarro, plaintiffs, against Orlando Moore, judgment filed in the New York Court of Common Pleas, February 15, 1861, Old Records Division, New York County Courts, reference number 1861#1085.
56. Santa Cruz y Mallén, *Historia de familias cubanas*, vol. 1, 283.
57. U.S. Bureau of the Census, *1860 United States Federal Census, New York City*, Seventeenth Ward, Ninth District; and Wilson, *Trow's New York City Directory, 1861*, 26.
58. U.S. Bureau of the Census, *1860 United States Federal Census, New York City*, Twelfth Ward, Third District; and Wilson, *Trow's New York City Directory, 1861*, 730.
59. U.S. Bureau of the Census, *1860 United States Federal Census, New York City*, Ninth Ward, First District; and Wilson, *Trow's New York City Directory, 1861*, 943.
60. U.S. Bureau of the Census, *1860 United States Federal Census, New York City*, Fifteenth Ward, Second District; and Wilson, *Trow's New York City Directory, 1861*, 37.
61. Santa Cruz y Mallén, *Historia de familias cubanas*, vol. 3, 30–32.
62. U.S. Bureau of the Census, *1860 United States Federal Census, New York City*, Fifteenth Ward, Third District.
63. Ibid.
64. U.S. Bureau of the Census, *1860 United States Federal Census, New York City*, Twenty-First Ward, Second District.

65. U.S. Bureau of the Census, *1860 United States Federal Census, New York City*, Eighteenth Ward, Third District.

66. Burrows and Wallace, *Gotham*, 720, 879.

67. "Saratoga," *New York Tribune*, August 11, 1866, 8. I am indebted to T. J. Stiles for pointing out this reference.

68. Simón Camacho, *Cosas de los Estados Unidos*, 82.

69. The invitation is reproduced in Simón Camacho, *Cosas de los Estados Unidos*, 112.

70. "The Marriage of the Season," *New York Times*, October 14, 1859, 4.

71. Van Rensselaer, *The Social Ladder*, 169. Mrs. Rensselaer notes that prior to the 1860s and 1870s, social affairs were "simple."

72. "The Oviedo Nuptials," *New York Daily Tribune*, October 14, 1859, 5.

73. "The Marriage of the Season," *New York Times*.

74. Ibid.

75. "The Oviedo Nuptials," *New York Daily Tribune*.

76. Ibid.

77. "A Very Golden Wedding," *Harper's Weekly*, October 22, 1859, 675.

78. Ibid.

79. "The Oviedo Nuptials," *New York Daily Tribune*.

80. "The Marriage of the Season," *New York Times*.

81. Cantero and Laplante, *Los ingenios de Cuba*, viii.

82. Marta Rojas, *El harén de Oviedo*.

83. The description of the preparations and the ceremony presented here was derived from the overlapping accounts cited above from the *New York Times, New York Daily Tribune, Harper's Weekly*, and Simón Camacho, *Cosas de los Estados Unidos*.

84. "The Oviedo Nuptials," *New York Daily Tribune*.

85. "The Marriage of the Season," *New York Times*.

86. "The Oviedo Nuptials," *New York Daily Tribune*.

87. "The Late Wedding," *New York Times*, October 17, 1859, 4.

88. "The Oviedo Wedding and the Press—Letter from Liet. Bartlett," *New York Times*, October 18, 1859, 8.

89. "The Bartlett-Oviedo Nuptials: A Correction," *New York Daily Tribune*, October 17, 1859, 7.

90. Simón Camacho, *Cosas de los Estados Unidos*, 116.

91. U.S. Bureau of the Census, *1860 United States Federal Census, New York City*, Fifteenth Ward, First District.

92. U.S. Bureau of the Census, *1860 United States Federal Census, New York City*, Fifteenth Ward, Third District.

93. U.S. Bureau of the Census, *1860 United States Federal Census, New York City*, Seventeenth Ward, Ninth District.

94 U.S. Bureau of the Census, *1860 United States Federal Census, New York City*, Eighth Ward, Second District.

95. U.S. Bureau of the Census, *1860 United States Federal Census, New York City*, Twelfth Ward, Third District.

96. U.S. Bureau of the Census, *1860 United States Federal Census, New York City*, Twelfth Ward, Second District.

97. U.S. Bureau of the Census, *1860 United States Federal Census, New York City*, Twenty-First Ward, Fifth District.

98. Baer, *The Economic Development of the Cigar Industry*, 44.

99. Westfall, "Don Vicente Martínez Ybor," vii-viii.

100. Cooper, *Once a Cigar Maker*, 16.

101. *Tobacco Circular*, January 6, 1852, n.p., and January 5, 1856, n.p., Arents Collection, New York Public Library.

102. Schneider, *Trade Unions and Community*, 54.

103. *Directory of Tobacco Men in the United States*, n.p.; and U.S. Bureau of the Census, *1860 United States Federal Census, New York City*, Fifth Ward, Second District.

104. *Directory of Tobacco Men in the United States*, n.p.; and U.S. Bureau of the Census, *1860 United States Federal Census, New York City*, Twentieth Ward, Third District.

105. The account of the crime is derived from overlapping newspaper reports: "Horrible Tragedy in Sullivan Street," *New York Herald*, January 7, 1859, 1; "Another Horrible Murder," *New York Times*, January 7, 1859, 1; and "Terrible Tragedy in Sullivan Street," *New York Daily Tribune*, January 7, 1859, 7.

106. "Another Horrible Murder," *New York Times*.

107. "Terrible Tragedy in Sullivan Street," *New York Herald*.

108. "Another Horrible Murder," *New York Times*.

109. "The Escaped Murderer, Sanchez," *New York Times*, January 13, 1859, 1.

110. Ibid.

111. "City Intelligence: Felix Sanchez, the Murderer Brought to the City," *New York Times*, May 30, 1859, 8.

112. Ibid.; and "Return of Felix Sanchez, the Fugitive Murderer," *New York Daily Tribune*, May 30, 1859, 7.

113. "Return of Felix Sanchez, the Fugitive Murderer," *New York Daily Tribune*.

114. "The Sullivan Street Tragedy," *New York Herald*, June 11, 1859, 1.

115. Ibid.; "Trial of Felix Sanchez for the Murder of His Father-in-Law," *New York Times*, June 11, 1859, 8; and "Trial of Felix Sanchez for Murder," *New York Daily Tribune*, June 11, 1859, 7–8.

116. "The Sullivan Street Tragedy," *New York Herald*, June 12, 1859, 1.

117. "The Murderers in the Tombs," *New York Times*, June 29, 1859, 8.

118. "Persons Charged with Murder in the Tombs," *Brooklyn Daily Eagle*, October 5, 1860, 2.

119. "A Desperate Plot Frustrated," *New York Times*, January 31, 1860, 5; "New York City News," *Brooklyn Daily Eagle*, January 31, 1860, 3; "The Attempted Escape of the Murderers," *New York Times*, February 1, 1860, 8; "Felonious Assault by Felix Sanchez," *New York Times*, November 19, 1861, 5; and "Court of General Sessions," *New York Times*, January 28, 1862, 6.

120. U.S. Bureau of the Census, *1870 Federal Population Census, New York City*, Nineteenth Ward, Thirteenth District.

121. Poyo, "*With All, and for the Good of All*," 19.

122. Willis Fletcher Johnson, *The History of Cuba*, vol. 3, 136–37.

123. "Additional City News," *New York Times*, August 6, 1853, 8.

124. José M. Pérez Cabrera, "From 1851 to 1867," chap. 4 in *Break with the Mother Country*, vol. 4 of *A History of the Cuban Nation*, ed. Ramiro Guerra y Sánchez et al. (La Habana: Editorial de la Nación Cubana, 1958), 124.

125. Marrero, *Azúcar, ilustración y conciencia*, 204.

126. Lazo, *Writing to Cuba*.

127. Ibid., 5–6.

128. "Additional City News," *New York Times*, August 6, 1853, 8.

129. Lazo, *Writing to Cuba*, 21.

130. "Meeting of the Cuban Patriots," *New York Times*, October 20, 1852, 8.

131. Marrero, *Azúcar, ilustración y conciencia*, 196.

132. Santa Cruz y Mallén, *Historia de familias cubanas*, vol. 7, 175–76. In most sources, Goicouría's birth date appears as June 23, 1805, but Santa Cruz y Mallén, a respected Cuban genealogist who evidently examined the birth certificate, indicates in his genealogy of the Goicouría family that Domingo was born five years later, on June 23, 1810.

133. Felipe Goicouria and Gonzalo Goicouria v. Emilio Sanchez y Dolz, filed in Superior Court of New York, New York City, April 21, 1858, Old Records Division, New York County Courts, reference number 1858-#740.

134. Tamayo, *Centenario del sacrificio*, 6.

135. *Conmemoración de Domingo de Goicouría en el trigésimo nono aniversario de su muerte* (Palma de Mallorca: Tipo-Litografía de Amengual y Muntaner, 1909), 20–22.

136. Moreno Fraginals, *El ingenio*, 307.

137. *Conmemoración de Domingo de Goicouría*, 22, 26.

138. Guerra y Sánchez, *Manual de historia de Cuba*, 496.

139. Ibid.

140. Carbonell, *Un héroe pintado por sí mismo*, 14.

141. Casasús, *La emigración cubana*, 58.

142. "Settling Up," *New York Times*, July 4, 1855, 4.

143. Marrero, *Azúcar, ilustración y conciencia*, 210.

144. Domingo de Goicouría, *Al pueblo de Cuba*, printed pamphlet (New York, September 20, 1855), 2.

145. Ibid., 14.

146. May, *The Southern Dream*, 102.

147. Hugh Thomas, *Cuba*, 227.

148. *Conmemoración de Domingo de Goicouría*, 31.

149. Chamorro, *El licenciado Jerónimo Pérez*, 93.

150. Morales y Morales, *Iniciadores y primeros mártires*, 84.

151. Quoted anonymously by Morales y Morales, *Iniciadores y primeros mártires*, vol. 3, 84.

152. Chamorro, *El licenciado Jerónimo Pérez*, 96.

153. Scroggs, "William Walker's Designs on Cuba," 198.

154. "Heading Off a Steamboat Commodore," *New York Times*, November 24, 1856, 4.

155. May, *The Southern Dream*, 104; and "A Patriot Extinguished," *New York Times*, November 22, 1856, 4.

156. Stiles, *The First Tycoon*, 290. See Stiles for a complete account of Goicouría's involvement with Vanderbilt and Walker.

157. "Interesting Correspondence—Goicouria and Walker, et al.," *New York Times*, November 24, 1856, 1.

158. *Conmemoración de Domingo de Goicouría*, 33.

159. Tamayo, *Centenario del sacrificio*, 9–12.

160. *New York Petitions for Naturalization*.

161. *Conmemoración de Domingo de Goicouría*, 35.

162. Ibid., 17; and Carbonell, *Un héroe pintado por sí mismo*, 9.

163. López Mesa, *La comunidad cubana de New York*, 104–5.

164. Lazo, *Writing to Cuba*, 17.

165. Ibid., 141. Lazo devotes an entire chapter to *El Mulato*.

166. Ibid., 148.

167. Poyo, *"With All, and for the Good of All,"* 17. For a detailed discussion of *El Mulato* and the relationship between the Cuban cause, annexationism, and the abolitionist movement, see Mirabal, *Suspect Freedoms*, 25–59.

168. López Mesa, *La comunidad cubana de New York*, 105–106; and Lazo, *Writing to Cuba*, 121–22, 169–91.

169. López Mesa, *La comunidad cubana de New York*, 17–18; and Lazo, *Writing to Cuba*, 127.

170. Lisandro Pérez, "Cuban Catholics in the United States," 147–57. I present five complementary explanations for the relative lack of religiosity and Church influence in Cuban society.

171. López Mesa, *La comunidad cubana de New York*, 18, 67.

172. Ibid., 67.

173. Ibid., 21; and Casasús, *La emigración cubana*, 63.

174. López Mesa, *La comunidad cubana de New York*, 104–5.

175. Armas, "La idea de unión antillana," 141–42.

176. Marrero, *Azúcar, ilustración y conciencia*, 231.

177. Philip S. Foner, *A History of Cuba*, vol. 2, 160.

178. Ibid., 120; and José Ignacio Rodríguez, *Estudio histórico*, 196–210.

179. Poyo, *"With All, and for the Good of All,"* 10.

180. Ibid., 19.

CHAPTER 4. WAR AND EXODUS

1. Soulere, *Historia de la insurrección*, vol. 1, 83.

2. Sedano, *Cuba*, 380.

3. That morning of October 24, Mestre wrote a letter to Miguel Aldama, who was in New York, expressing his expectations about the meeting, although admitting he did not know the purpose of it. José Ignacio Rodríguez, *Vida del Doctor José Manuel Mestre*, 101. Unless otherwise noted, this biography by Rodríguez is the source for most of what is presented here on Mestre and on the meeting of October 24.

4. Letter from Mestre to Nicolás Azcárate, October 15, 1868, reproduced in José Ignacio Rodríguez, *Vida del Doctor José Manuel Mestre*, 99.

5. Carlos Rafael Rodríguez, "José Manuel Mestre," 378.

6. José Ignacio Rodríguez, *Vida del Doctor José Manuel Mestre*, 9.

7. Santa Cruz y Mallén, *Historia de familias cubanas*, vol. 3, 9, 13.

8. José Ignacio Rodríguez, *Vida del Doctor José Manuel Mestre*, 67–69.

9. Marrero, *Azúcar, ilustración y conciencia*, 271.

10. Zaragoza, *Las insurrecciones de Cuba*, 244–46. Zaragoza, a Spanish official, was probably present at the meeting. His account of it concurs in every detail with the one given by José Ignacio Rodríguez in his biography of Mestre, *Vida del Doctor José Manuel Mestre*, 111–14.

11. Carlos Rafael Rodríguez, "José Manuel Mestre," 386.

12. Hugh Thomas, *Cuba*, 241.

13. Marrero, *Azúcar, ilustración y conciencia*, 266.

14. Ferrer, *Insurgent Cuba*, 19.

15. Santa Cruz y Mallén, *Historia de familias cubanas*, vol. 1, 21–22.

16. Moreno Fraginals, *Cuba/España, España/Cuba*, 233.

17. Ferrer, *Insurgent Cuba*, 23.
18. Pánfilo D. Camacho, *Aguilera*, 26; and Marrero, *Azúcar, ilustración y conciencia*, 264–65.
19. Torres-Cuevas, "Vicente Antonio de Castro," 168–72.
20. Torres Hernández, "Céspedes y el 10 de octubre," 94–95.
21. Philip S. Foner, *A History of Cuba*, vol. 2, 171.
22. *Diario de la Marina*, October 15, 1868, 2.
23. Philip S. Foner, *A History of Cuba*, vol. 2, 174.
24. Collazo, *Desde Yara hasta el Zanjón*, 5.
25. Philip S. Foner, *A History of Cuba*, vol. 2, 174.
26. Ibid., 176.
27. Marrero, *Azúcar, ilustración y conciencia*, 286.
28. Quiroz, "Loyalist Overkill," 266.
29. Marrero, *Azúcar, ilustración y conciencia*, 296.
30. Roldán de Montaud, *La restauración en Cuba*, 13–14.
31. Reprinted in Soulere, *Historia de la insurrección*, vol. 1, 60–63.
32. Soulere, *Historia de la insurrección*, 63.
33. Ponte Domínguez, *Historia de la Guerra de los Diez Años*, 159–63; and Marrero, *Azúcar, ilustración y conciencia*, 296–97.
34. Fernández, *España y Cuba*, 136–37.
35. Marrero, *Azúcar, ilustración y conciencia*, 300–301.
36. Quoted in Trelles y Govín, *Biblioteca histórica cubana*, vol. 1, 333.
37. Quoted in Soulere, *Historia de la insurrección*, 96.
38. Saluvet, *Los deportados a Fernando Póo*, 6.
39. "The Cuban Revolution," *Harper's Weekly*, April 10, 1869, 225, 232.
40. [Rodríguez], *The Book of Blood*, 1871 ed., 38–39. There were also students, cigar makers, a tailor, carpenters, clergymen, shoemakers, and a variety of other occupations.
41. Marrero, *Azúcar, ilustración y conciencia*, 322–38.
42. Llaverías, *El Consejo Administrativo*, 11.
43. For a discussion of the cultural and religious contexts of Spanish intransigence, see the following essay by a Spanish Jesuit: Alejandro, "Sobre la intransigencia," 16, 25. In Spanish there is no word that is the precise equivalent of the English word "compromise," that is, an agreement arrived at through mutual concessions to resolve opposing demands.
44. Velasco, *La guerra de Cuba*, 82.
45. Ibid., 83.
46. Almansa y Tavira, *La revolución de Cuba*, 21.
47. Soulere, *Historia de la insurrección*, 63–64.
48. Zaragoza, *Las insurrecciones de Cuba*, 374.
49. Ibid.
50. Ibid.
51. Ibid., 774.
52. Letter from Antonio de la Fuente to Moses Taylor and Company, February 13, 1869, Box 78, Moses Taylor Papers. It appears that Moses Taylor and Company was able to help out Moré, for the company records indicate that from 1869 to 1881 he was a client who made regular remittances to his account, asking Taylor to invest the funds in the United States.

53. *New York Passenger Lists, 1851–1891.*
54. Ibid.
55. Santa Cruz y Mallén, *Historia de familias cubanas*, vol. 2, 361–63.
56. Sedano, *Cuba: Estudios políticos*, 383.
57. José Ignacio Rodríguez, *Vida del Doctor José Manuel Mestre*, 82.
58. Sedano, *Cuba: Estudios políticos*, 381.
59. Ibid., 383.
60. Marrero, *Azúcar, ilustración y conciencia*, 217.
61. Roldán Oliarte, *Cuba en la mano*, 1026.
62. *New York Passenger Lists, 1851–1891*; and Santa Cruz y Mallén, *Historia de familias cubanas*, vol. 6, 175.
63. Zaragoza, *Las insurrecciones de Cuba*, 374.
64. Calcagno, *Diccionario biográfico cubano*, 93.
65. Peraza Sarausa, *Diccionario biográfico cubano*, vol. 1, 30.
66. Calcagno, *Diccionario biográfico cubano*, 93.
67. Castro y Bachiller, *Don Antonio Bachiller y Morales*, 41–42.
68. *New York Passenger Lists, 1851–1891.*
69. Ibid.; and Santa Cruz y Mallén, *Historia de familias cubanas*, vol. 3, 64–65. Bachiller's oldest son, Alfredo, had died the year before of tuberculosis. Also in the Bachiller group aboard the *Columbia* were two teenagers with the last name Bachiller but with an undetermined relationship to the family. Castro y Bachiller also indicated that a servant boy named Ambrosio who had been taken in by the family was aboard the *Columbia*, but he does not appear on the ship's manifest. Castro y Bachiller, *Don Antonio Bachiller y Morales*, 42. The Bachiller party aboard the *Columbia* may therefore have numbered as many as eighteen persons.
70. Unless otherwise noted, the information presented here on Morales Lemus is from Enrique Piñeyro's biography, *Morales Lemus y la revolución de Cuba.*
71. José Ignacio Rodríguez, *Vida del Doctor José Manuel Mestre*, 113.
72. I have not been able to find an entry for Mestre in the *New York Passenger Lists*, but José Ignacio Rodríguez, who knew Mestre well, asserts that on March 13, 1869, he boarded in Havana a ship headed for New York. Rodríguez, *Vida del Doctor José Manuel Mestre*, 123.
73. Llaverías, *El Consejo Administrativo*, 11.
74. All references here to ships and passengers are taken from *New York Passenger Lists, 1851–1891*, previously cited.
75. Santa Cruz y Mallén, *Historia de familias cubanas*, vol. 6, 330–32.
76. Roldán Oliarte, *Cuba en la mano*, 833–34.
77. Two of several memoirs of the odyssey of the Fernando Póo deportees are Saluvet, *Los deportados de Fernando Póo*; and Balmaseda, *Los confinados á Fernando Póo.*
78. Marrero, *Azúcar, ilustración y conciencia*, 380.
79. Ibid., 201.
80. Álvarez Pedroso, *Miguel de Aldama*, 50.
81. Llaverías, *Miguel Aldama*, 8.
82. Moreno Fraginals, *El ingenio*, vol. 1, 243.
83. Zanetti Lecuona and García Álvarez, *Caminos para el azúcar*, 119; and Llaverías, *Miguel Aldama*, 8.
84. Llaverías, *Miguel Aldama*, 8.

85. The genealogical information presented here on the Aldamas is in volume 1 of Santa Cruz y Mallén, *Historia de familias cubanas*, 29–30. The information on the Alfonsos is in volume 3, 8–17.

86. Zanetti Lecuona and García Álvarez, *Caminos para el azúcar*, 117–19.

87. Roldán Oliarte, *Cuba en la mano*, 861–62.

88. Álvarez Pedroso, *Miguel de Aldama*, 14.

89. Llaverías, *Miguel Aldama*, 15–16; and Álvarez Pedroso, *Miguel de Aldama*, 83.

90. *New York Passenger Lists, 1851–1891*. Although most of his family was on the *Columbia*, Miguel Aldama does not appear on the manifest, so he may have traveled separately, probably on an earlier sailing.

91. Letter from Miguel Aldama to Moses Taylor and Company, August 26, 1868, Box 305, Moses Taylor Papers.

92. José Ignacio Rodríguez, *Vida del Doctor José Manuel Mestre*, 100.

93. Letter from Mestre to Aldama, reproduced in José Ignacio Rodríguez, *Vida del Doctor José Manuel Mestre*, 100–101.

94. Ibid., 101.

95. Letter from Carlos de Borbón to Aldama, reproduced in Llaverías, *Miguel Aldama*, 16–17.

96. Letter from Aldama to Carlos de Borbón, reproduced in Llaverías, *Miguel Aldama*, 17–18. Italics for emphasis are in the Llaverías version.

97. Ibid.

98. Llaverías, *Miguel Aldama*, 18; and Piñeyro, *Morales Lemus*, 73.

99. Letter from Miguel Aldama to Moses Taylor and Company, December 18, 1868, Box 305, Moses Taylor Papers.

100. Letter from Miguel Aldama to Moses Taylor and Company, December 26, 1868, Box 305, Moses Taylor Papers. An 1872 ledger sheet in the Moses Taylor Papers showed an entry of $25,000 under the name of José Antonio Echeverría. Ledger Sheet, May 1, 1872, Box 79.

101. Álvarez Pedroso, *Miguel de Aldama*, 89–90. Cesar García del Pino asserts that it was Leonardo del Monte's house, adjacent to the Aldama Palace, that was plundered, not the Aldama residence. García del Pino, "La Habana en los días de Yara," 172.

102. In a letter sent to José Manuel Mestre on April 21, 1869, José Antonio Echeverría indicates that Aldama "cannot travel anywhere" since Hilaria was bedridden from the stroke. Container 61, José Ignacio Rodríguez Papers, Manuscript Division, Library of Congress.

103. *New York Passenger Lists, 1851–1891*. There are many Aldamas on the manifest and not all the first names are legible. Abad, "Las emigraciones cubanas," 154, asserts that Aldama left in June, but does not provide the source. The best evidence that Aldama had indeed boarded the *Morro Castle* on May 2 is a May 20 letter from José Antonio Echeverría in Havana to José Manuel Mestre in New York, which reads, "I am sure you greeted with satisfaction the arrival of Miguel and his family." Container 61, José Ignacio Rodríguez Papers.

104. Abad, "Las emigraciones cubanas," 176.

105. Ledger Sheet, May 1, 1872, Box 79, Moses Taylor Papers.

106. Marrero, *Azúcar, ilustración y conciencia*, 318; and Llaverías, *El Consejo Administrativo*, 34–35.

CHAPTER 5. CUBAN NEW YORK IN THE 1870S

1. Collazo, *Desde Yara hasta el Zanjón*, 149.

2. U.S. Bureau of the Census, *1870 United States Federal Census, New York City*, Seventeenth Ward, Eleventh District. New York City challenged the results of this census and subsequently a second enumeration was taken early in 1871. Ancestry.com has merged the records, maintaining duplicate records only in those cases in which persons changed residence between the two enumerations, moving across enumeration districts. I made every effort to reconcile duplicate records and not count the families twice.

3. Marrero, *Azúcar, ilustración y conciencia*, 329; and Llaverías, *El Consejo Administrativo*, 35. José María Mora may have been among those deported to Fernando Póo aboard the *San Francisco de Borja*. Saluvet lists a José M. Mora in his list of deportees: *Los deportados a Fernando Póo*, 6. Another source, however, lists the name as José Manuel Mora. [Rodríguez], *The Book of Blood*, 1871 ed., 37.

4. Cancela, *Enrique Piñeyro*, 44.

5. Iraizoz y de Villar, *Enrique Piñeyro*, 10–14.

6. Marrero, *Azúcar, ilustración y conciencia*, 330.

7. Cancela, *Enrique Piñeyro*, 50; and U.S. Bureau of the Census, *1870 United States Federal Census, New York City*, Ninth Ward, Ninth District.

8. U.S. Bureau of the Census, *1870 United States Federal Census, New York City*, Ninth Ward, Ninth District.

9. Marrero, *Azúcar, ilustración y conciencia*, 319.

10. Letter from José Antonio Echeverría to José Manuel Mestre, June 14, 1866, Container 61, José Ignacio Rodríguez Papers. The letter lists the group of reformists, including Fesser, which periodically met at the home of José Ricardo O'Farrill, one of the principal figures of the group.

11. Ibid., 326; and Llaverías, *El Consejo Administrativo*, 35.

12. U.S. Bureau of the Census, *1870 United States Federal Census, New York City*, Sixteenth Ward, Seventh District.

13. U.S. Bureau of the Census, *1870 United States Federal Census, New York City*, Sixteenth Ward, Thirteenth District.

14. Santa Cruz y Mallén, *Historia de familias cubanas*, vol. 1, 115–18.

15. Zaragoza, *Las insurrecciones en Cuba*, vol. 2, 245.

16. Guerra y Sánchez, *Guerra de los Diez Años*, vol. 1, 149; Marrero, *Azúcar, ilustración y conciencia*, 325; and Llaverías, *El Consejo Administrativo*, 35.

17. Ponte Domínguez, *Historia de la Guerra de los Diez Años*, 140.

18. Cisneros, *Relación documentada de cinco expediciones*, 16; Guerra y Sánchez, *Guerra de los Diez Años*, 282; and Collazo, *Desde Yara hasta el Zanjón*, 150–51.

19. All of the information presented here on the history of the Jová family is from Joseph John Jová, "The Jová Family of Sitges, Cuba, and the United States," unpublished paper, 1977.

20. Saluvet, *Los desterrados a Fernando Póo*, 13; and [Rodríguez], *The Book of Blood*, 1871 ed., 36.

21. U.S. Bureau of the Census, *1870 United States Federal Census, New York City*, Twentieth Ward, Twelfth District; and *Trow's New York City Directory, 1870–71*. In both the 1870 and 1880 U.S. censuses, this Félix Fuentes and his entire family are identified as white.

It is therefore not clear whether this is the same Félix Fuentes whom Mirabal identifies as an "Afro-Cuban revolutionary." Mirabal, *Suspect Freedoms*, 73.

22. U.S. Bureau of the Census, *1870 United States Federal Census, City of Brooklyn*, Twenty-First Ward.

23. U.S. Bureau of the Census, *1870 United States Federal Census, City of Brooklyn*, Seventh Ward. I interpreted the information in the census schedule by consulting Castro y Bachiller, *Don Antonio Bachiller y Morales*; and Santa Cruz y Mallén, *Historia de familias cubanas*, vol. 3, 63–64.

24. Castro y Bachiller, *Don Antonio Bachiller y Morales*, 42.

25. Marrero, *Azúcar, ilustración y conciencia*, 323, 330, 334; and Llaverías, *El Consejo Administrativo*, 34.

26. Llaverías, *El Consejo Administrativo*, 40; and Santa Cruz y Mallén, *Historia de familias cubanas*, vol. 3, 64.

27. Castro y Bachiller, *Don Antonio Bachiller y Morales*, 44.

28. U.S. Bureau of the Census, *1870 United States Federal Census, New York City*, Twenty-Second Ward, Eighth District.

29. The Simonis were enumerated for the first time on January 4, 1871, as part of the 1870 census recount. Amalia gave birth to her daughter Herminia in New York on February 20, 1871. Santa Cruz y Mallén, *Historia de familias cubanas*, vol. 1, 13–14. The Simonis were probably not in New York when the first 1870 count was taken in the Twenty-Second Ward in late June and early July 1870. Mrs. Simoni and her son José Ramón Jr. arrived in New York on August 9, 1870, aboard a cargo ship, the *Rapidan*, from Havana. *New York Passenger Lists, 1851–1891*. I was unable to find a record of the arrival of Dr. Simoni and his daughters, all of whom may have left clandestinely aboard the *Rapidan* or another vessel at about the same time as Mrs. Simoni.

30. Santa Cruz y Mallén, *Historia de familias cubanas*, vol. 1, 12–13; Guerra y Sánchez, *Guerra de los Diez Años*, 89–90, 256–57; and Marrero, *Azúcar, ilustración y conciencia*, 304.

31. Llaverías, *El Consejo Administrativo*, 34.

32. U.S. Bureau of the Census, *1870 United States Federal Census, New York City*, Sixteenth Ward, Fourteenth District; and Santa Cruz y Mallén, *Historia de familias cubanas*, vol. 1, 13.

33. Boxes 78 and 79 of the Moses Taylor Papers contain files for each of the firm's clients in Cuba, including ledgers listing accounts under the names of those clients. The only person from Puerto Príncipe to appear in those records is one José Miguel Montejo y Hernández, the owner of La Fernandina sugar mill. The only exception in Oriente was Reigadas, Caragol, and Company, exporters in Manzanillo.

34. U.S. Bureau of the Census, *1870 United States Federal Census, New York City*, Eighteenth Ward, Second District.

35. Marquis of Ruvigny and Raineval, *The Jacobite Peerage: Baronetage, Knightage and Grants of Honour* (Edinburgh: T. C. & E. C. Jack, 1904), 144.

36. Márquez Sterling, *Martí, maestro y apóstol*, 102.

37. *New York Passenger Lists, 1851–1891*.

38. Santa Cruz y Mallén, *Historia de familias cubanas*, vol. 5, 166.

39. *New York Times*, August 12, 1869, 4.

40. Quiroz, "Implicit Costs of Empire," 496; and Guerra y Sánchez, *Guerra de los Diez Años*, 222.

41. "Gen. Z. C. Deas," *New York Times*, March 7, 1882, 2.
42. U.S. Bureau of the Census, *1870 United States Federal Census, New York City*, Eighteenth Ward, Twenty-Second District.
43. John Bassett Moore, *History and Digest of the International Arbitrations*, vol. 3, 2638–2642.
44. The letters are found in Container 61 of the José Ignacio Rodríguez Papers in the Manuscript Division of the Library of Congress. Rodríguez had been a student of Mestre and as the trustee of his estate acquired all of Mestre's archives upon his death in 1886.
45. Letter from Cristóbal Madan to J. Nicholson, November 20, 1871, Container 61, José Ignacio Rodríguez Papers.
46. Gerard R. Wolfe, "Randalls Island," in Jackson, *The Encyclopedia of New York City*, 985.
47. This figure was arrived at from a manual tabulation of the census schedules retrieved by a search using place of birth in U.S. Bureau of the Census, *1870 United States Federal Census, New York City*, Seventeenth Ward, Eleventh District. This figure is higher than the 1,565 that the U.S. Bureau of the Census reported in its 1872 printed report as the Cuban-born population in Manhattan and Brooklyn. U.S. Bureau of the Census, *The Statistics of the Population of the United States*, vol. 1 of *Ninth Census, June 1, 1870* (Washington: Government Printing Office, 1872), 388. While my figure may be slightly inflated by possible duplications produced by the 1870 recount, every attempt was made both by me and by Ancestry.com to eliminate those duplications, which in any case would have involved only persons who changed their residence during the five months between the two counts.
48. Burrows and Wallace, *Gotham*, 742.
49. *The Universal Tobacco Dealers Directory*.
50. *Directory of Tobacco Men in the United States*.
51. Schneider, *Trade Unions and Community*, 55–56.
52. *A Directory of the Tobacco Trade*.
53. Schneider, *Trade Unions and Community*, 54.
54. Ronald Mendel, "Cigar Makers' International Union," in Jackson, *The Encyclopedia of New York City*, 224.
55. *The Universal Tobacco Dealers Directory*, n.p.
56. Burrows and Wallace, *Gotham*, 991.
57. Ibid.
58. *A Directory of the Tobacco Trade of the United States*, 122–43.
59. U.S. Bureau of the Census, *1870 United States Federal Census, New York City*, Eighth Ward, Twenty-First District. The last name of the Cuban family is illegible in the census record. That the European families were Jews is only a conjecture based on their places of origin and last names, since the U.S. census does not record religious affiliation.
60. Edwin, *Half a Century with Tobacco*, 84.
61. Schneider, *Trade Unions and Community*, 59.
62. *A Statement of Manufacturers in Opposition to the Proposed Act Abolishing the Manufacture of Cigars in Tenement Houses in the City of New York* (New York: S. Hamilton's Son, 1880), 1–23; and Burrows and Wallace, *Gotham*, 1102.
63. Baltar Rodríguez, *Los chinos de Cuba*, 13.
64. Ibid., 20.

65. Cuba Commission, *A Hidden History of the Chinese in Cuba*, 81.
66. *New York Passenger Lists, 1851–1891.*
67. U.S. Bureau of the Census, *1870 United States Federal Census, New York City*, Seventeenth Ward, Fourth District.
68. U.S. Bureau of the Census, *1870 United States Federal Census, New York City*, Nineteenth Ward, Eighth District.
69. Letter from Federico Martínez to W. N. Adams, July 25, 1870, Box 307, Moses Taylor Papers.
70. Visit of the author to the Colección de Arte Cubano of the Museo Nacional de Bellas Artes, Havana, December 15, 2002; and *Colección de arte cubano* (La Habana: Museo Nacional de Bellas Artes, 2001), 54–55.
71. Electronic communication to the author from Ramón Cernuda, November 4, 2007. In 1992 one of Boudat's paintings, a view of Havana painted in 1864, was sold in an estate auction at Sotheby's.
72. López Mesa, *La comunidad cubana de Nueva York*, 28.
73. *Colección de arte cubano*, 56–57; and Departamento de Educación del Museo Nacional, *Pintores cubanos* (La Habana: Editorial Gente Nueva, 1974), 54.
74. Roldán Oliarte, *Cuba en la mano*, 790.
75. Santa Cruz y Mallén, *Historia de familias cubanas*, vol. 7, 132.
76. Roldán Oliarte, *Cuba en la mano*, 863.
77. Ibid.; and "Edward Alexander MacDowell," *Music Encyclopedia*, www.tribalsmile.com.
78. Peraza Sarausa, *Diccionario biográfico cubano*, vol. 4, 86; and "Andrés Poey Aguirre. Resultados de la ciencia en Cuba: Científicos relevantes," www.resultados.redciencia. cu.
79. Santa Cruz y Mallén, *Historia de familias cubanas*, vol. 5, 230.
80. All the information presented here on the history of the Sacred Heart in Cuba is taken from Raquel Pérez, *Religiosas del Sagrado Corazón*, 26–56.
81. Mike Sappol, "Colored Orphan Asylum," in Jackson, *The Encyclopedia of New York City*, 256.
82. Portuondo, *Historia de Cuba*, 465–66.
83. Beckert, *The Monied Metropolis*, 207.
84. *El Ateneo* 5, no. 26 (September 1876), n.p.
85. Ibid.
86. *El Ateneo* 1, no. 2 (August 1874), n.p., inside front cover.
87. Ibid., back cover.
88. *El Ateneo* 5, no. 26 (September 1876), n.p.
89. *El Ateneo* 1, no. 2 (August 1874), n.p., inside front cover.
90. Santa Cruz y Mallén, *Historia de familias cubanas*, vol. 2, 39.
91. *El Ateneo* 4, no. 21 (March 1876), n.p.
92. *El Ateneo* 5, no. 26 (September 1876), 54.
93. Ibid., 54–55.
94. "Miscellaneous Concerts," *New York Times*, October 17, 1875, 6.
95. Carpentier, *La música en Cuba*, 167.
96. López Mesa, *La comunidad cubana de Nueva York*, 28.
97. Wright, "Violinist José White," 213.
98. Ibid., 214.
99. Gerard R. Wolfe, "Hell Gate," in Jackson, *The Encyclopedia of New York City*, 538.

100. *El Ateneo* 5, no. 26 (September 1876), 55.
101. Ibid., 54.
102. Ibid.
103. Piñeyro, *Estudios y conferencias de historia y literatura*, 247–48.
104. Ibid., 250.
105. Ibid., 69.
106. Ibid., 71, 73–74.
107. Ibid., 76–77.
108. *New York Petitions for Naturalization.*
109. When Bachiller's daughter María de Jesús became a U.S. citizen that same year, she gave her address as 314 West 32nd Street. In 1878 Adela also became a citizen and gave her address as 237 West 23rd Street. *New York Petitions for Naturalization.*
110. For further information on Prieto, and especially his trip to the U.S., see Silva Gruesz, *Ambassadors of Culture*, 196–204.
111. Prieto, *Viaje a los Estados Unidos*, vol. 3, 293–306.
112. López Mesa, *La comunidad cubana de Nueva York*, 20.
113. Ibid., 117.
114. Prieto, *Viaje a los Estados Unidos*, 306.
115. José Martí, "Antonio Bachiller y Morales," *El Avisador Hispano-americano*, January 24, 1889, reprinted in Martí, *Obras Completas*, vol. 5, 149.
116. Bachiller y Morales, *Guía de la ciudad de Nueva York.*
117. Ibid., 3.
118. Ibid., 26.
119. Ibid., 37.
120. Ibid., 206–36.
121. "A Wealthy Cuban Kidnapped," *New York Times*, March 9, 1876, 5.
122. "The Kidnapping of Don Holgado," *New York Times*, March 10, 1876, 5.
123. "The Don Holgado Mystery," *New York Times*, March 11, 1876, 2.
124. "The Kidnapping Mystery," *New York Times*, March 14, 1876, 7.
125. "The Missing Cuban Found," *New York Times*, March 15, 1876, 5.
126. "Senor Holgado's Disappearance Unexplained," *New York Times*, March 16, 1876, 5; and "The Case of Senor Jose Holgado," *New York Times*, March 17, 1876, 5.
127. "The Holgado Mystery Explained," *New York Times*, March 23, 1876, 8.
128. "A Mystery Solved," *New York Times*, March 16, 1876, 4.
129. Ibid.
130. Ibid.
131. Ibid.
132. "The Mysterious Cuban," *New York Times*, October 14, 1876, 4.

CHAPTER 6. WAGING A WAR IN CUBA . . . AND IN NEW YORK
1. Letter of Melchor Agüero to José Manuel Mestre, January 15, 1872, Box 63, José Ignacio Rodríguez Papers.
2. "Ice Cream a Specialty," *Brooklyn Daily Eagle*, April 16, 1869, 2.
3. "Cuban Independence," *New York Times*, October 12, 1869, 8.
4. "Viva Cuba," *New York Herald*, October 12, 1869, 3.
5. Ibid.
6. "Cuban Independence," *New York Times.*

7. Ibid.

8. "Viva Cuba," *New York Herald.*

9. Céspedes unfurled a different flag when he proclaimed independence from his sugar mill, but ironically it was the annexationist flag, largely because of its established history as symbol of rebellion against Spain, that was favored by the Camagüeyanos and adopted in 1869 as the official flag by the constitutional assembly of the rebel forces. Marrero, *Azúcar, ilustración y conciencia*, 307, 381.

10. Piñeyro, *Morales Lemus*, 81.

11. Casasús, *La emigración cubana*, 67.

12. Guerra y Sánchez, *Guerra de los Diez Años*, vol. 1, 340.

13. Cisneros, *Relación documentada*, 6.

14. Poey Baró, *La entrada de los aldamistas*, 24.

15. Cisneros, *Relación documentada*, 67.

16. Herrera Cudello, *Thomas Jordan.*

17. Cisneros, *Relación documentada*, 16.

18. Poey Baró, *La entrada de los aldamistas*, 65.

19. Ibid.

20. Ibid., 72–84.

21. Guerra y Sánchez, *Guerra de los Diez Años*, vol. 1, 346–47.

22. Piñeyro, *Morales Lemus*, 90.

23. José Ignacio Rodríguez, *Estudio histórico*, 224; and Guerra y Sánchez, *Guerra de los Diez Años*, vol. 1, 346.

24. Guerra y Sánchez, *Guerra de los Diez Años*, vol. 1, 339.

25. Masó, *Historia de Cuba*, 257.

26. Guerra y Sánchez, *Guerra de los Diez Años*, vol. 1. 348.

27. Piñeyro, *Morales Lemus*, 87–88. Piñeyro, who was the junta's secretary, is the original source on the meeting between Grant and Morales Lemus. Several Cuban historians subsequently repeat Piñeyro's recollection of the meeting. There is no mention of the meeting, however, by U.S. historians. Hamilton Fish's biographer, Allan Nevins, wrote that in one of the first meetings of Grant's cabinet the issue of the representation of Morales Lemus came up and it was agreed that caution was necessary. Nevins, *Hamilton Fish*, vol. 1, 125, 182. Fish recorded in his diary that when he met unofficially with Morales Lemus on March 24, he flatly refused the Cuban's request to arrange a meeting with the president, but indicated that Morales Lemus was free to meet with Grant during his daily public audiences, in which anyone, as an individual, could approach the president and present his or her concerns. He cautioned Morales Lemus, however, not to impose himself on Grant in any official way. Microfilm reel 3, Container 280, Hamilton Fish Papers, Manuscript Division, Library of Congress. If the meeting did take place, it was probably on those terms, and not, as some have assumed, as a meeting in which Grant "received" or granted an audience to Morales Lemus in an official capacity.

28. Philip S. Foner, *A History of Cuba*, vol. 2, 200.

29. Nevins, *Hamilton Fish*, vol. 1, 3.

30. Ibid., 92.

31. Ibid., 129–30.

32. Ibid., 176.

33. Ibid., 47–48.

34. Ibid., 181–82.

35. Cook, *The Alabama Claims*, 15.
36. Ibid., 185.
37. Cushing, *The Treaty of Washington*, 9.
38. Philip S. Foner, *A History of Cuba*, vol. 2, 203.
39. Nevins, *Hamilton Fish*, vol. 1, 182.
40. Microfilm reel 3, Container 280, Hamilton Fish Papers.
41. Willis Fletcher Johnson, *The History of Cuba*, vol. 3, 202–4.
42. Nevins, *Hamilton Fish*, vol. 1, 193.
43. Ibid., 193; and José Ignacio Rodríguez, *Estudio histórico*, 228.
44. Nevins, *Hamilton Fish*, vol. 1, 194.
45. Guerra y Sánchez, *Guerra de los Diez Años*, vol. 1, 368.
46. The tortuous negotiations that took place involved the U.S. minister sent to Madrid, Daniel E. Sickles, a New Yorker and Civil War veteran with a checkered past and questionable reputation. For details on those negotiations, see Guerra y Sánchez, *Guerra de los Diez Años*, vol. 1, 370–84; and Piñeyro, *Morales Lemus*, 101–28.
47. Piñeyro, *Morales Lemus*, 123.
48. José Ignacio Rodríguez, *Estudio histórico*, 229.
49. Poey Baró, *La entrada de los aldamistas*, 93.
50. More than twenty letters from Morales Lemus to Mestre written during 1870 are in Container 61 of the José Ignacio Rodríguez Papers.
51. Carlos Ripoll, "Morales Lemus y la beligerancia cubana hace un siglo," preface to the 1970 edition of Piñeyro, *Morales Lemus*, xx.
52. Poey Baró, *La entrada de los aldamistas*, 94–95; and José Ignacio Rodríguez, *Vida del Doctor José Manuel Mestre*, 154.
53. Álvarez, *Acerca de Cirilo Villaverde*, 417–18; and Cirilo Villaverde, "Autobiografías," in *Letras: Cultura en Cuba*, vol. 4, ed. Ana Cairo Ballester (La Habana: Editorial Pueblo y Educación, 1987), 7.
54. Cirilo Villaverde, *La Revolución de Cuba vista desde Nueva York* (New York: Cirilo Villaverde, 1869).
55. Ibid., 12.
56. Ibid., 23–32.
57. Horrego Estuch, *Emilia Casanova*, 8.
58. Ibid., 9.
59. [Cirilo Villaverde], *Apuntes biográficos de Emilia Casanova de Villaverde* (New York, 1874), 8. No author is given, but it is widely accepted that the author is her husband, Cirilo Villaverde. Trelles, *Bibliografía cubana del siglo XIX*, vol. 7, 214; and Ana Cairo, "Emilia Casanova y la dignidad de la mujer cubana," in *Mujeres latinoamericanas: Historia y cultura, siglos XVI al XIX*, ed. Luisa Campuzano (La Habana: Ediciones Casa de las Américas, 1997), 232. Cairo also asserts that the publication date of this book is not 1874, but 1884.
60. [Villaverde], *Apuntes biográficos*, 9; and Horrego Estuch, *Emilia Casanova*, 12–15.
61. Horrego Estuch, *Emilia Casanova*, 19.
62. Ibid., 26.
63. Ibid., 25.
64. Jenkins, *The Story of the Bronx*, 387–88.
65. Ibid., 387; and Sean Wilentz, "William Leggett," in Jackson, *The Encyclopedia of New York City*, 662.

66. Jenkins, *The Story of the Bronx*, 388; and Horrego Estuch, *Emilia Casanova*, 26.

67. Jenkins, *The Story of the Bronx*, 388.

68. Prados Torreiras, *Mambisas*, 77.

69. [Villaverde], *Apuntes biográficos*, 15.

70. Ibid., 58–60.

71. Ibid, 17. The meetings with Grant probably took place under the same conditions as those of Morales Lemus with the president, that is, during the public audience hours in the White House.

72. Villaverde, *La Revolución de Cuba*, 9–12.

73. Ibid., 21.

74. Guerra y Sánchez, *Guerra de los Diez Años*, vol. 2, 86.

75. López Mesa, *La comunidad cubana de New York*, 105.

76. Santa Cruz y Mallén, *Historia de familias cubanas*, vol. 6, 263, 276.

77. Philip S. Foner, *A History of Cuba*, vol. 2, 193.

78. Collazo, *Desde Yara hasta el Zanjón*, 20.

79. Guerra y Sánchez, *La Guerra de los Diez Años*, vol. 1, 403.

80. Santa Cruz y Mallén, *Historia de familias cubanas*, vol. 6, 276.

81. Céspedes y Quesada, *Manuel de Quesada*, 101–2.

82. Ibid., 103.

83. Guerra y Sánchez, *La Guerra de los Diez Años*, vol. 2, 86–87. Box 307 of the Moses Taylor Papers contains receipts of numerous reimbursements to General Quesada from this account managed by Carlos del Castillo, including one receipt submitted by Quesada for a payment to Johnson Brothers, "depots for all kinds of Dental Materials and Instruments," at 812 Broadway, dated November 1, 1871 for, among other items, "4 sets whites gum teeth at $2.80 each, and 4 sets whites plain teeth at $1.68 each."

84. [Villaverde], *Apuntes biográficos*, 20–21.

85. Horrego Estuch, *Emilia Casanova*, 38.

86. López Mesa, *La comunidad cubana de New York*, 27–28.

87. Ibid., 118.

88. Santa Cruz y Mallén, *Historia de familias cubanas*, vol. 2, 75–76.

89. Sanguily, *Nobles memorias*, 137–38.

90. Guerra y Sánchez, *La Guerra de los Diez Años*, vol. 2, 101, 108.

91. "Cuban Affairs: A Letter from Mr. Azcárate," *New York Times*, August 28, 1870, 1.

92. Guerra y Sánchez, *La Guerra de los Diez Años*, 119.

93. Ibid., 116.

94. Zenea's mission continues to spark speculation and controversy among historians, with some writers condemning the poet and others defending him. See Piñeyro, *Vida y escritos de Juan Clemente Zenea*; Valverde, *Juan Clemente Zenea*; Vitier, *Rescate de Zenea*; Chaple, "Para una comprensión mejor de Zenea," 68–69; and Estrade, "El puñado de oro de la traición de Zenea," 93–100.

95. Guerra y Sánchez, *La Guerra de los Diez Años*, 116, 119, 131; and "The Fate of Zenea," *New York Times*, September 2, 1871, 2.

96. Ramiro Guerra y Sánchez's explanation of Zenea's execution is based on the divisions between those in power in Havana and Madrid, with the *voluntarios* and other hardliners pressuring Governor Valmaseda to execute Zenea and not honor what they considered a treasonous initiative on the part of liberal elements within the Madrid government. Guerra y Sánchez, *La Guerra de los Diez Años*, vol. 2, 116–31.

97. Casasús, *La emigración cubana*, 110; and Miguel de Aldama, J. A. Echeverría, and J. M. Mestre, "Los comisionados y el agente general de la República de Cuba en los Estados Unidos, a los cubanos" (New York, 1871), 3.

98. Casasús, *La emigración cubana*, 110; [Villaverde], *Apuntes biográficos*, 123–24; and "The Daughters of Cuba," *New York Times*, February 5, 1871, 5. At the time Casanova wrote those words, Zenea had not yet been executed.

99. Aldama, Echeverría, and Mestre, "Los comisionados."

100. Ibid., 10–11.

101. Ibid., 2–3.

102. Álvarez Pedroso, *Miguel de Aldama*, 99–100.

103. Horrego Estuch, *Emilia Casanova*, 37.

104. Emilia C. de Villaverde, "La Liga de las Hijas de Cuba a los cubanos" (New York, September 28, 1874), 4–5.

105. Moses Taylor and Company was the trustee of del Castillo's estate. Most of his papers are indiscriminately integrated into the company's Cuba business papers, primarily in Containers 305, 306, and 307, New York Public Library. See also the letters from Cirilo Villaverde to José G. del Castillo in Ana Cairo, "Epistolario de Villaverde," in Cairo Ballester, *Letras: Cultura en Cuba*, vol. 4, 106–49.

106. "Reservado," anonymous letter, n.d., Container 306, Moses Taylor Papers.

107. Anonymous letter, n.d., Container 306, Moses Taylor Papers.

108. Letter of José Gabriel del Castillo to Carlos del Castillo, n.d., Container 305, Moses Taylor Papers.

109. [Villaverde], *Apuntes biográficos*, 109.

110. In the papers of Carlos del Castillo there is a printed sheet with a poem anonymously written to mock the *aldamistas* that starts, "Gentlemen, let's not eat any more *pasteles*." "Invitación de los firmantes," Container 308, Moses Taylor Papers.

111. Poey Baró, *La entrada de los aldamistas*, 97–99.

112. Letter of José Gabriel del Castillo to Carlos del Castillo, n.d., Container 305, Moses Taylor Papers.

113. Poey Baró, *La entrada de los aldamistas*, 97–99.

114. "New Buildings: The Santa Rosa Refinery," *Brooklyn Daily Eagle*, October 13, 1873, 4. The refinery was located on Hamilton Avenue, just past where Union Street ended, and it backed up on the India Wharf. There are no longer any streets in the area. The site is part of a large lot for storing ship containers, directly above the Brooklyn-Battery Tunnel.

115. Ibid.

116. "Along Shore: A Glance at the Water Front," *Brooklyn Daily Eagle*, August 6, 1875, 3.

117. Villaverde, "La Liga de las Hijas de Cuba," 5.

118. Argüelles, "Prensa cubana de la emigración," 27–36.

119. [Villaverde], *Apuntes biográficos*, 42.

120. "Amusements," *New York Times*, March 23, 1869, 5.

121. "Gran Bazar," *La Revolución*, April 28, 1869, 4.

122. "Meeting in Favor of Cuban Independence," *New York Times*, March 23, 1869, 5.

123. "Cuba and Liberty!," *La Revolución*, April 28, 1869, 4.

124. "City Government," *New York Times*, April 14, 1869, 12.

125. Juan Manuel Macías, *Cuba in Revolution: A Statement of Facts* (London: Hole and Company, 1871), 38.

126. Invoice for membership dues from the American Foreign Anti-Slavery Society to José Manuel Mestre, October 12, 1877, Container 64, José Ignacio Rodríguez Papers.

127. "Sympathy for the Cuban Patriots," *New York Sun*, December 10, 1872, 2. See also "Slavery in Cuba," *New York Evening Mail*, December 13, 1872, 2.

128. "Spain and Cuba—The Freedmen of the United States Rising to the Main Question," *New York Herald*, December 15, 1872, 8.

129. Ibid.

130. Cuban Anti-Slavery Committee, "Slavery in Cuba: A Report of the Proceedings of the Meeting Held at Cooper Institute" (New York, 1872).

131. New York Cuban Junta, "Facts about Cuba" (New York, 1870).

132. José de Armas y Céspedes, "The Cuban Revolution: Notes from the Diary of a Cuban" (New York, 1869), 11–12.

133. José de Armas y Céspedes, "Position of the United States on the Cuban Question: To the Congress and the Press of the United States" (New York, 1872).

134. [Rodríguez], *The Book of Blood*, 1871 ed.

135. [Rodríguez], *The Book of Blood*, 1873 ed.

136. "The Communist Parade," *New York Times*, December 18, 1871, 8.

137. Nicolás Arnao, "La expedición del vapor Lillian, por un expedicionario," typed manuscript, New York, September 1869, 2, Juan Arnao Collection, Manuscript Division, Library of Congress.

138. *Harper's Weekly*, April 24, 1869, 269.

139. Casasús, *La emigración cubana*, 80–81; and "Cuban Junta Arrested," *New York Times*, June 18, 1869, 1.

140. Nestor Ponce de León, "Noticias confidenciales, New York, 1870 y 1871," in Sarabia, *Noticias confidenciales sobre Cuba*, 17–71.

141. Cisneros, *Relación documentada*, 3–31.

142. Ibid., 54–57.

143. Casasús, *La emigración cubana*, 67.

144. Invoice, Charles H. Pond, December 20, 1871, Box 306, Moses Taylor Papers.

145. Cisneros, *Relación documentada*, 26.

146. Invoice, Charles H. Pond, December 20, 1871, Box 306, Moses Taylor Papers.

147. Junta Central Republicana de Cuba y Puerto Rico, handwritten statement, Container 63, José Ignacio Rodríguez Papers.

148. "Recruiting for Cubans in Brooklyn," *New York Times*, June 18, 1869, 1.

149. Tamayo, *Centenario del sacrificio*, 12.

150. Cisneros, *Relación documentada*, 69.

151. Arnao, "La expedición del vapor Lillian," 4.

152. Ibid.

153. Collazo, *Desde Yara hasta el Zanjón*, 153.

154. *New York Passenger Lists, 1851–1891.*

155. Tamayo, *Centenario del sacrificio*, 13.

156. *Conmemoración de Domingo de Goicouría*, 46.

157. "South and Central America," *Harper's New Monthly Magazine*, July 1870, 314; and "Execution of General Goicouría," *New York Times*, May 8, 1870, 1.

158. Nevins, *Hamilton Fish*, vol. 1, 187.

159. Ibid., 344–45.

160. Container 280, microfilm reel 3, Hamilton Fish Papers.

161. Nevins, *Hamilton Fish*, vol. 1, 359.
162. "Message of the President to Congress," *New York Times*, June 14, 1870, 1.
163. Ibid.
164. Philip S. Foner, *A History of Cuba*, vol. 2, 218.
165. There is a large cache of the bonds in Container 64 of the José Ignacio Rodríguez Papers. The terms of the bonds presented here are taken from their reverse side. The bonds were probably printed at the American Bank Note Company, 142 Broadway. In Box 307 of the Moses Taylor Papers there is a memorandum from the company to Carlos del Castillo providing a cost estimate and specifications for the printing of two sets of bonds.
166. Nevins, *Hamilton Fish*, vol. 1, 352.
167. "Message of the President to Congress," *New York Times*.
168. Ibid.
169. José Ignacio Rodríguez, *Estudio histórico*, 231–32.
170. "Message of the President to Congress," *New York Times*.
171. Ripoll, "Morales Lemus y la beligerancia cubana," xix.
172. For his singular role in turning the Grant administration against the recognition of Cuban belligerency and toward a rigorous enforcement of the neutrality laws, Fish has been regarded by many Cuban historians as a veritable villain. For the best example, see Portell Vilá, *Historia de Cuba*, vol. 2, 296–326.
173. Carbonell, *Un héroe pintado por sí mismo*, 45. "Tenement-house" is in quotes and in English in the original.
174. "Decreto firmado por Carlos Manuel de Céspedes, 17 de julio de 1871," in Cruz, *Francisco Vicente Aguilera*, 33–35. It is not apparent that Ramón Céspedes was an immediate relative of President Céspedes, nor is there evidence of any relationship between this Ramón Céspedes and the Ramón de Céspedes who was one of Moses Taylor's charges in Cold Spring some fifteen years before (see chapter 1).
175. Ibid., 35.
176. Aguilera Rojas, *Francisco V. Aguilera*, 66.
177. Untitled and undated written document, Container 64, José Ignacio Rodríguez Papers.
178. Pánfilo D. Camacho, *Aguilera*, 91.
179. Quoted in Céspedes Argote, *Diario de Francisco Vicente Aguilera*, 27.
180. Letter from José Gabriel del Castillo to Aguilera and Ramón Céspedes, October 15, 1871, in Cruz, *Francisco Vicente Aguilera*, 70–78.
181. Aguilera Rojas, *Francisco V. Aguilera*, 207.
182. Céspedes Argote, *Diario y correspondencia de Francisco Vicente Aguilera*, vol. 2, 15.
183. The extent of his activities is evident both in his diary (ibid.) and in his correspondence during this period. Cruz, *Francisco Vicente Aguilera*, 36–94.
184. Francisco Vicente Aguilera, "Cuba al pueblo americano: Declaración de independencia," in Cruz, *Francisco Vicente Aguilera*, 60–67.
185. Francisco Vicente Aguilera and Ramón Céspedes, "Notes about Cuba" (New York, 1872).
186. Pánfilo D. Camacho, *Aguilera*, 91.
187. Letter from Vicente Aguilera to Manuel Rojas, August 29, 1871, in Cruz, *Francisco Vicente Aguilera*, 43.
188. Pánfilo D. Camacho, *Aguilera*, 103, 116–17.
189. Márquez Sterling, *Ignacio Agramonte*, 255; and Casasús, *Vida militar de Ignacio Agramonte*, 83.

190. Letter from Ignacio Agramonte to Amalia Simoni, in Dirección de Cultura, *Ignacio Agramonte y Loynaz*, 171–72.
191. Letter from José R. Simoni to Carlos del Castillo, Box 35, Moses Taylor Papers.
192. "The Cuban Contest," *New York Herald*, March 27, 1873, 3.
193. Letter from Miguel Bravo y Senties to Ramón Céspedes and Francisco V. Aguilera, in Cruz, *Francisco Vicente Aguilera*, 95–99.
194. Aguilera Rojas, *Francisco V. Aguilera*, vol. 1, 387.
195. Guerra y Sánchez, *La Guerra de los Diez Años*, 212–13.
196. Ibid., 213.
197. Ibid.
198. Letter from Salvador Cisneros Betancourt to José Manuel Mestre, November 22, 1873, Container 64, José Ignacio Rodríguez Papers.
199. Villaverde, "La Liga de las Hijas de Cuba a los cubanos," 2.
200. Bradford, *The Virginius Affair*, 25–26. Most of the information presented here on the *Virginius* incident is from this source, unless otherwise noted.
201. Portell Vilá, *Historia de Cuba*, vol. 2, 428.
202. William Fletcher Johnson, *The History of Cuba*, vol. 3, 278–83.
203. "Cuba Libre," *New York Tribune*, November 10, 1873, 7.
204. Portell-Vilá, *Historia de Cuba*, vol. 2, 444; William Fletcher Johnson, *The History of Cuba*, vol. 3, 283; and Philip S. Foner, *A History of Cuba*, vol. 2, 246. In March 1875 the Spanish paid an indemnity of $80,000 to cover all claims arising from their actions in the *Virginius* matter.
205. Nevins, *Hamilton Fish*, vol. 1, 691–94.
206. "The Arrival of the Vessel," *New York Times*, December 29, 1873, 1; and "The Virginius Prisoners," *New York Times*, December 30, 1873, 5.
207. Philip S. Foner, *A History of Cuba*, vol. 2, 247.
208. "Passengers Arrived," *New York Times*, January 17, 1871, 8.
209. Santa Cruz y Mallén, *Historia de familias cubanas*, vol. 3, 120.
210. Pánfilo D. Camacho, *Aguilera*, 91, 96.
211. In Box 307 of the Moses Taylor Papers, there are batches of receipts signed by Ana de Quesada for funds withdrawn from the account of Carlos del Castillo, most of them in the amount of fifty dollars and dated on the first of the month, from February 1874 to April 1878.
212. Letter from Ana de Quesada to Carlos del Castillo, January 11, 1878, Box 305, Moses Taylor Papers.
213. Guerra y Sánchez, *Guerra de los Diez Años*, vol. 2, 223–24.
214. Leal Spengler, *Carlos Manuel de Céspedes*, 1.
215. Castro y Bachiller, *Don Antonio Bachiller y Morales*, 40, 44.
216. "Billiard Entertainment in Aid of the Cubans," *New York Times*, March 3, 1875, 10.
217. "The Cuban Contest," *New York Herald*, March 27, 1873, 3.
218. Katia Valdés, "Francisco Vicente Aguilera: A Man Devoted to Revolution," *Granma Weekly Review*, March 6, 1977, 2.
219. Santa Cruz y Mallén, *Historia de familias cubanas*, vol. 1, 23. It is not clear whether Aguilera's wife, Ana Manuela Kindelán y Sánchez-Griñán, was with him in New York. She is not mentioned in the obituaries. Nine of the children are Doña Ana's. Francisco Eladio, the oldest of his sons and mentioned earlier as his secretary and biographer, was the son of a woman Aguilera did not marry.

220. "Obituary: Francisco Vicente Aguilera," *New York Times*, February 24, 1877, 5; "Obituary: Francisco Vicente Aguilera, Vice President of the Cuban Republic," *New York Herald*, February 24, 1877, 10; "Francesco [*sic*] V. Aguilera," *New York World*, February 25, 1877, 8; "Francisco Vicente Aguilera," *New York Sun*, February 25, 1877, 2; "Obituary: Francisco Vicente Aguilera," *New York Daily Tribune*, February 26, 1877, 5; and "The Late General Aguilera," *New York Evening Post*, February 26, 1877, 4.
221. "Lying in State," *New York World*, February 26, 1877, 8.
222. "Aguilera's Burial," *New York Herald*, February 27, 1877, 5.
223. "The Aguilera Obsequies," *New York Herald*, February 26, 1877, 3; and "The Dead Cuban General," *New York Times*, February 26, 1877, 8.
224. "The Aguilera Obsequies," *New York Herald*.
225. "Aguilera's Burial," *New York Herald*.
226. Ibid.
227. "The Late General Aguilera," *New York Evening Post*.
228. "Aguilera's Burial," *New York Herald*.
229. Louis A. Pérez Jr., *Cuba between Empires*, 4.
230. Ibid.
231. Pichardo, *Documentos para la historia de Cuba*, vol. 1, 403–4.
232. Letter from Ana de Quesada to Carlos del Castillo, March 12, 1878, Box 305, Moses Taylor Papers. Emphasis from the original.
233. In one letter, she referred to Salvador Cisneros Betancourt, who replaced Céspedes as president, as "the great assassin of Carlos Manuel," and in another she calls General Máximo Gómez a traitor. Letters from Ana de Quesada to Carlos del Castillo, March 8, 1878, and March 1, 1878, Box 305, Moses Taylor Papers.
234. Letter from Ana de Quesada to Carlos del Castillo, June 27, 1878, Box 305, Moses Taylor Papers.

CHAPTER 7. THE AFTERMATH OF WAR AND A CHANGED COMMUNITY

1. Roig de Leuchsenring, *13 conclusiones fundamentales*, 15.
2. "Married by the Cardinal," *New York Times*, April 17, 1879, 5.
3. The church is now called Our Lady of the Scapular and St. Stephen and the office address is on 29th Street.
4. "Married by the Cardinal," *New York Times*.
5. "Acquired by a New Company," *New York Times*, August 22, 1889, 8.
6. Álvarez Pedroso, *Miguel de Aldama*, 123–27. Most of the references in this work to Aldama's finances are derived from the unpublished diary of Isaac Carrillo, one of Aldama's sons-in-law, which Álvarez Pedroso consulted.
7. Álvarez Pedroso, *Miguel de Aldama*, 130.
8. Louis A. Pérez Jr., *Cuba between Empires*, 20.
9. For general information on the Newsboys houses, see Mariam Touba, "Newsboys," in Jackson, *The Encyclopedia of New York City*, 807–8. For a novella of the period on the life of New York homeless boys and the shelters that housed them, see Alger, *Ragged Dick*.
10. The two were among Aguilera's unofficial pallbearers identified by his son. Aguilera Rojas, *Francisco V. Aguilera*, 385.
11. "Shot through the Heart," *New York Herald*, June 21, 1884, 3.

12. "The Cuban Murderer," *New York Times*, June 22, 1884, 14; and "Deadly Peril on a Roof," *New York Herald*, June 22, 1884, 12.

13. "Deadly Peril on a Roof," *New York Herald*.

14. "Shot by Her Paramour," *New York Times*, November 22, 1884, 5; "Trying a Negro Murderer," *New York Herald*, November 25, 1884, 5; and "Miguel Chacon's Crime," *New York Times*, July 4, 1886, 3.

15. "Miguel Chacun's [sic] Great Crime," *New York Herald*, November 26, 1884, 4; and "Chacon Pays the Last Penalty," *New York Herald*, July 10, 1886, 6.

16. In addition to the press reports, details of the case can be found in the transcript of Chacón's trial: Court of Appeals, *The People of the State of New York against Miguel Chacon* (New York: C. H. Burgoyne, 1885).

17. Ibid., 104.

18. "Chacon Guilty of Murder," *New York Times*, November 26, 1884, 5.

19. "Miguel Chacun's [sic] Great Crime," *New York Herald*.

20. "To Be Hanged on January 16," *New York Herald*, November 29, 1884, 6.

21. "Asking Chacon's Life," *New York Herald*, June 30, 1886, 3.

22. "A Life for a Life," *New York Herald*, May 18, 1886, 9.

23. "Knife Better Than the Rope," *New York Herald*, July 1, 1886, 9; and "Chacon's Knife Cut," *New York Herald*, July 2, 1886, 9.

24. "Miguel Chacon's Crime, How He Has Come to Be under Sentence of Death," *New York Times*, July 4, 1886, 3.

25. Ibid.

26. "Chacon Resigned to His Fate," *New York Times*, July 5, 1886, 8.

27. Ibid.

28. "Chacon's Last Hope Gone," *New York Daily Tribune*, July 7, 1886, 8.

29. "Two Days More for Chacon," *New York Times*, July 7, 1886, 8; "Chacon's Last Hope Gone," *New York Daily Tribune*, July 7, 1886, 8; "Chacon Still Unmoved," *New York Daily Tribune*, July 8, 1886, 8; and "Has Become Very Devout," *New York Times*, July 8, 1886, 8.

30. "Chacon Must Die," *New York Times*, July 6, 1886, 1.

31. "Chacon's Last Night," *New York Times*, July 9, 1886, 2; "Not Far from the Gallows," *New York World*, July 9, 1886, 8; "Chacon Ready to Die," *New York Herald*, July 9, 1886, 3; "Chacon Must Die To-Day," *New York Sun*, July 9, 1886, 1; and "Chacon Ready for Death," *New York Daily Tribune*, July 9, 1886, 8.

32. "Chacon Pays the Penalty," *New York Times*, July 10, 1886, 8; "Chacon Hanged Decently," *New York Sun*, July 10, 1886, 1; and "Chacon Must Die To-Day," *New York Sun*.

33. "Chacon Pays the Penalty," *New York World*, July 10, 1886, 8.

34. "Miguel Chacon Hanged," *New York Daily Tribune*, July 10, 1886, 8.

35. "Chacon Ready for Death," *New York Daily Tribune*; "Chacon Pays the Last Penalty," *New York Herald*, July 10, 1886, 6; and "Miguel Chacon Hanged," *New York Daily Tribune*, July 10, 1886, 8.

36. "Chacón Hanged Decently," *New York Sun*.

37. "The American and Spanish Claims," *New York Times*, June 5, 1871, 1.

38. Santa Cruz y Mallén, *Historia de familias cubanas*, vol. 2, 185–92.

39. "Arrival of the Crescent City," *New York Times*, March 22, 1853, 6.

40. "Passengers Arrived," *New York Times*, November 6, 1865, 8; and "Passengers Sailed," *New York Times*, August 30, 1866, 5.

41. *New York Petitions for Naturalization*.

Manuel Mestre, Maceo summons Mestre to meet him at "19 y 21 W. calle 9" and at "19 Oeste calle 9," an indication of where he was lodged and also further evidence of the hotel's location on the west side of Fifth Avenue. Antonio Maceo, "Notes to José Manuel Mestre, May 30 and June 16, 1878," Container 63, José Ignacio Rodríguez Papers.

39. Castellanos, *24 de febrero de 1895*, 129.
40. Hernández y Pérez, *El período revolucionario*, 28.
41. Ibid., 30. Félix Govín and his brother José were among those Cubans, purportedly U.S. citizens, who had filed claims against the Spanish government for properties allegedly confiscated or embargoed during the last war. See "The American and Spanish Claims," *New York Times*, June 5, 1871, 1. See chapter 7 for more information on the Govín family. Mañach attributes a duplicitous motive to Govín's original pledge of support, arguing that it was a calculated move to pressure the Spanish to satisfactorily settle his claims. "Govín had played with two cards," wrote Mañach. Mañach, *Martí el apóstol*, 161.
42. Márquez Sterling, *Martí*, 433.
43. "Yara's Sons," *New York Herald*, October 11, 1884, 5.
44. Gómez, *Diario de campaña*, 183.
45. Franco, *Antonio Maceo*, 270–71.
46. The details of this meeting are retold in all biographies of Martí and in other works. Its original sources are Eusebio Hernández y Pérez (*El período revolucionario*, 31), who apparently was a witness to the meeting, and Gómez himself, who wrote his recollection of the meeting on the back of the letter that Martí sent him two days later. Gómez's notes are reproduced by José L. Franco in his biography, *Antonio Maceo*, 272–73.
47. Franco, *Antonio Maceo*, 273.
48. Castellanos, *24 de febrero de 1895*, 132.
49. José Martí, "Al General Máximo Gómez, 20 de octubre de 1884," *OC*, vol. 1, 177.
50. Ibid., 178.
51. Ibid.
52. Ibid.
53. Gómez, *Diario de campaña*, 183.
54. Ibid., 196. The capitalization of "dictatorship" is Gomez's.
55. Máximo Gómez, "Letter to Juan Arnao, January 20, 1885," Manuscript Collection of Juan and Nicolás Arnao, Library of Congress Manuscript Division.
56. Martínez Estrada, *Martí revolucionario*, 190.
57. For example, subsequent initiatives by Maceo, who had not entirely given up on the New York community, encountered the Martí "problem." In an elliptically worded letter written in June 1885 to Juan Arnao in New York, Maceo is seeking Arnao's mediation so as to solicit the cooperation of an organization Martí presides over in New York: "It is not necessary to bring up matters that should be relegated to indifference and best forgotten. . . . I simply solicit your cooperation so that in the event any obstacle should present itself . . . you will intercede with your influence . . . extending to Mr. Martí the consideration he so richly deserves with the purpose of eliminating any personal element that may obstruct the regular course of this delicate matter." Antonio Maceo, "Letter to Juan Arnao, June 5, 1885," Manuscript Collection of Juan and Nicolás Arnao.
58. Castellanos, *24 de febrero de 1895*, 149.
59. Martínez Estrada, *Martí revolucionario*, 190.

60. Martí placed the address on several letters he wrote to inform his correspondents of his mailing address. The first letter bearing the address was to Vidal Morales on July 8, 1881. *OC*, vol. 20, 296–97. The building no longer stands. The site is a playground for an adjacent school.

61. Carlos Ripoll, the most prominent exponent of the view that Martí did not have intimate relations with Carmen Mantilla in 1880 and therefore could not have been the father of María, nevertheless recognizes that the relationship was intimate after the death of Carmen's husband and that Martí helped to raise Carmen's children. However, as would be expected at the time, the couple was always discreet, with Martí maintaining a separate bedroom in the boardinghouse, according to the testimony cited by Ripoll of a childhood friend of María who lived near the Mantilla household in 1893, when it was located at 121 West 61st Street. Ripoll, *La vida íntima y secreta*, 165.

62. Martínez Estrada, *Martí revolucionario*, 253.

63. Rafael Esténger, "Esbozo de Martí," in *Memoria del Congreso de Escritores Martianos, febrero 20 a 27 de 1953*, ed. Congreso de Escritores Martianos (La Habana: Comisión Nacional Organizadora de los Actos y Ediciones del Centenario y del Monumento de Martí, 1953), 99.

64. The *Escenas norteamericanas* are volumes 9 through 12 of the *Obras completas*, while volume 13 contains writings on U.S. literary and artistic trends and events.

65. González Echevarría, "José Martí: An Introduction," xviii.

66. Not only have Martí's writings on New York not received the attention they deserve, but his place among New York's prominent residents has also largely been overlooked. In a book listing the one hundred most prominent New Yorkers of all time, there are only two Latin Americans, Tito Puente and Diego Rivera, and the latter was really only a sojourner in the city. Holmes, *100 New Yorkers*.

67. Rotker, *The American Chronicles*, 84–85.

68. Montero, *José Martí*, 9; and Rafael Rojas, *José Martí*, 49–50.

69. Rotker, "José Martí and the United States," 17–18.

70. Kirk, *José Martí*, 49. Martí's quoted words are in Kirk's text. Even in one of his earliest known published writings in New York, Martí takes a negative view of the city's immigrants, referring to them as a "thirsty foreign population that must not be confounded with the true American people," and "a vulgar storm . . . that brings in strength and possibilities of wealth, what they lack of intellectual height, and moral deepness." Martí, "Impressions in America," 165. It is noteworthy that although Martí is, so to speak, "fresh off the boat," he refers to immigrants in the third person, an optic of Cuban exiles that tends to persist to this day.

71. José Martí, "Cartas," *La Nación*, March 20, 1885, in *OC*, vol. 10, 155–64.

72. "Arrival of Mgr. Capel," *New York Times*, July 31, 1883, 8.

73. Ibid.

74. José Martí, "Cartas," *La Nación*, January 27, 1884, in *OC*, vol. 9, 493. Martí's words were "magnífica zorra."

75. "Aim of the Inquisition," *New York Times*, November 24, 1884, 1.

76. Martí, "Cartas," *La Nación*, March 20, 1885, 155.

77. Kirk, *José Martí*, 48.

78. Rotker, *The American Chronicles*, 7.

79. Ibid.; and González Echevarría, "José Martí: An Introduction," xvi.

80. Schulman, "Modernismo/Modernidad," 20.

81. González Echevarría, "José Martí: An Introduction," xviii-xix; and Rafael Rojas, *José Martí*, 33.

82. Schulman, "Modernismo/Modernidad," 20.

83. José Martí, "El mastodonte," *La América*, September 1883, in *OC*, vol. 8, 409.

84. José Martí, "Gran exposición de ganado," *La Nación*, July 2, 1887, in *OC*, vol. 13, 490–91.

85. José Martí, "Note to Gonzalo de Quesada," *OC*, vol. 3, 130.

86. "Mr. Chiko and Mrs. Johanna," *New York Times*, April 15, 1894, 9. Márquez Sterling asserts that Martí wrote a piece on the two chimps, but I have been unable to find it in the *Obras completas*. Márquez Sterling, *Martí*, 621.

87. Advertisement, *New York Times*, April 2, 1894, 7.

88. Louis A. Pérez Jr., "Meditations on Martí," Occasional Paper no. 1, Latin American and Caribbean Studies, University of South Florida, Spring 2001, 9. José Ignacio Rodríguez, a Cuban New Yorker and committed annexationist, wrote in 1900 that early in 1892, when there was prosperity in Cuba and no one thought of anything but broadening political and economic freedoms through constitutional and peaceful means, Martí's revolutionary movement "appeared suddenly, as if by magic." José Luis Rodríguez, *Estudio histórico*, 278. Gerald E. Poyo disagrees, citing social and economic crises that were leading to an increasing dissatisfaction on the island, making it ripe for revolution. In fact, Poyo argues that the Florida communities were already mobilizing for revolution and that Martí was influenced to start his movement after his visits there. Poyo, *"With All, and for the Good of All,"* 96.

89. López, *José Martí*, 250.

90. Márquez Sterling, *Martí*, 533.

91. Ibid.

92. Enrique Trujillo was the editor of *El Porvenir*, in many ways a rival newspaper to *Patria*. Already estranged from Martí, Trujillo was among the few who objected to what he viewed as the "irregularities" in the way the PRC was established and how Martí assumed leadership of it. López, *José Martí*, 261. A year after Martí's death, Trujillo published in New York his notes and recollections of émigré revolutionary activities between 1880 and 1895. In it he refers to Martí in very positive terms and makes no mention of his personal conflict with him. Trujillo, *Apuntes históricos*.

93. José Martí, "Discurso en conmemoración del 10 de octubre de 1868, en Hardman Hall, Nueva York, 10 de octubre de 1891," *OC*, vol. 4, 259, 266.

94. Ibid., 259.

95. "Cubans Celebrate Their Struggle for Independence," *New York Sun*, October 11, 1891, 4; "Today's News," *New York Daily Tribune*, October 11, 1891, 6; and "Cuba's Independence Day Celebrated by a Gathering of Her Sons and Daughters," *New York Times*, October 11, 1891, 4.

96. "Cuba's Independence Day," *New York Times*.

97. "Consul General Marti Is Out," *New York Herald*, October 20, 1891, 7; and "Signor Marti Has Resigned," *New York Sun*, October 20, 1891, 7.

98. José Martí, "Al Ministro de la Argentina, New York, octubre 17 de 1891," *OC*, vol. 1, 266. Vicente Quesada accepted the resignation with "much regret." Márquez Sterling, *Martí*, 534. A friend of Martí, the Argentinian minister in Washington was an intellectual, writer, and bibliophile. In his periodic jaunts to New York, he recalled years later, "I frequently invited the ill-fated Cuban Martí to dinner in the numerous and

very good restaurants of that large and wealthy city." Quesada also shared with Martí a fondness for Barnum's show at Madison Square. Vicente G. Quesada, *Recuerdos*, 47–49, 53.

99. Márquez Sterling, *Martí*, 534.
100. Mañach, *Martí el apóstol*, 188.
101. Lisandro Pérez, "De Nueva York a Miami," 18.
102. Louis A. Pérez Jr., introduction to *José Martí in the United States: The Florida Experience*, ed. Louis A. Pérez Jr. (Tempe: Arizona State University Center for Latin American Studies, 1995), 3.
103. Castañeda, *Martí*, 22.
104. Poyo, "With All, and for the Good of All," 96–97.
105. José Martí, "Discurso en el Liceo Cubano, Tampa, 26 de noviembre de 1891," *OC*, vol. 4, 267–79.
106. José Martí, "Dircurso en conmemoración del 27 de noviembre de 1871, en Tampa, 27 de noviembre de 1891," *OC*, vol. 4, 286.
107. Louis A. Pérez Jr., introduction to *José Martí in the United States*, 3.
108. Mañach, *Martí el apóstol*, 192.
109. José Martí, "Discurso en Cayo Hueso, 25 de diciembre de 1891," *OC*, vol. 4, 287–90.
110. Instituto Cubano, *Atlas histórico biográfico José Martí*, 97; and Martínez Estrada, *Martí revolucionario*, 224–29.
111. Almodóvar Muñoz, "Martí," 115–34.
112. Márquez Sterling, *Martí*, 646.
113. Ibid.
114. Mañach, *Martí el apóstol*, 232.
115. See chapter 8 for more details on the contested Govín estate.
116. Rodríguez Expósito, *Dr. Ramón L. Miranda*, 36.
117. Figueredo, "Cuatro anécdotas," 201.
118. Deulofeu, *Martí, Cayo Hueso y Tampa*, 292.
119. Baralt, *El Martí que yo conocí*, 62–63.
120. Ibid., 63.
121. José Martí, "Carta a María Mantilla, 2 de febrero de 1895," *OC*, vol. 20, 212–13.
122. José Martí, "Carta a Carmen Mantilla y sus hijos, 16 de abril de 1895," *OC*, vol. 20, 225.

EPILOGUE

1. Vitier, "Martí en el 98," 104.
2. Lyrics by Emilio Billillo, adapted to a popular Cuban tune. Source: Cristóbal Díaz Ayala, "Aquí falta, señores, una voz," *El Nuevo Herald*, February 12, 2009, www.elnuevoherald.com. I am grateful to Emilio Cueto for pointing out that it has now been established that Billillo plagiarized the song, originally composed by José Tereso Valdés for a love interest and with different lyrics, substituting Tereso Valdés's lyrics with these that refer to Martí and taking credit for the entire composition.
3. "Cuban Callers Criticised," *New York Herald*, June 12, 1897, 7.
4. Ibid.
5. Ibid.
6. "Cubans Invade a Public School," *New York Herald*, June 11, 1897, 7.
7. Ibid.
8. Poyo, "With All, and for the Good of All," 112.

9. Cordoví Núñez, *La emigración cubana*, 10.
10. Márquez Sterling, *Don Tomás*, 215.
11. Ibid., 117.
12. Offner, *An Unwanted War*, ix.
13. Lillian Guerra, *The Myth of José Martí*, 6.
14. Mirabal, *Suspect Freedoms*, 131.
15. Lillian Guerra, *The Myth of José Martí*, 6; and Mirabal, *Suspect Freedoms*, 110.
16. Poyo, *"With All, and for the Good of All,"* 116–17.
17. Deschamps Chapeaux, *Rafael Serra y Montalvo*, 41.
18. *New York Petitions for Naturalization.*
19. Deschamps Chapeaux, *Rafael Serra y Montalvo*, 52.
20. González Veranes, *La personalidad de Rafael Serra*, 16–24. For a comprehensive description of the purpose and activities of La Liga, see Mirabal, *Suspect Freedoms*, 113–18.
21. Despradel, *Rafael Serra.*
22. Mirabal, *Suspect Freedoms*, 134.
23. Rafael Serra y Montalvo, writing in the July 25, 1896, issue of *La Doctrina de Martí*, quoted in Deschamps Chapeaux, *Rafael Serra y Montalvo*, 116.
24. Deschamps Chapeaux, *Rafael Serra y Montalvo*, 138.
25. Quoted in ibid., 139.
26. Partido Revolucionario Cubano, *La Revolución del 95*, vol. 4, 35; and True, "Revolutionaries in Exile," 301.
27. Quesada y Miranda, *Documentos históricos*, 285–86. The fraternity was Theta Delta Chi. The two men, of course, did not know each other during their college days. Hay graduated from Brown in 1858 and Quesada from City College of New York thirty years later.
28. Auxier, "The Propaganda Activities of the Cuban Junta," 292–93.
29. Partido Revolucionario Cubano, *La Revolución del 95*, vol. 5, 8.
30. Partido Revolucionario Cubano, *La Revolución del 95*, vol. 3, 237.
31 Ibid., 235–37.
32. Wisan, *The Cuban Crisis*, 380–81.
33. Morgan, "The Delome Letter," 38.
34. Offner, *An Unwanted War*, 227.
35. For a masterful treatment of the role of history and the quest for sovereignty, see Louis A. Pérez Jr., *The Structure of Cuban History.*
36. Máximo Gómez, quoted in Vitier, "Martí en el 98 de ayer y de hoy," 104.
37. "Marti's Widow Here," *New York Herald*, June 25, 1895, 3.
38. "Rebel Guerillas Routed," *New York Herald*, June 20, 1895, 10.
39. "Senora Marti Here for Rest," *New York Herald*, June 25, 1895, 5.
40. Partido Revolucionario Cubano, *La Revolución del 95*, vol. 1, 291–92.
41. Ibid.
42. Octavio R. Costa, "Prólogo: Sobre Gonzalo de Quesada y Miranda y su biografía de Martí," in Quesada y Miranda, *Martí, hombre*, viii.
43. James Bradley, "New York Life Insurance Company," in Jackson, *The Encyclopedia of New York City*, 836.
44. Santa Cruz y Mallén, *Historia de familias cubanas*, vol. 4, 412.
45. Sarabia, *La patriota del silencio*, 75–80.

46. Ibid., 79.
47. "Real Estate Transfers," *New York Times*, June 11, 1916, xx9; and "Obituary 1," *New York Times*, April 19, 1925, E7.
48. "Estates Appraised," *New York Times*, June 30, 1925, 20.
49. Sarabia, *La patriota del silencio*, 88.
50. Partido Revolucionario Cubano, *La Revolución del 95*, vol. 1, 224.
51. Ibid., 225.
52. Horrego Estuch, *Emilia Casanova*, 58.
53. Partido Revolucionario Cubano, *La Revolución del 95*, vol. 2, 52–54.
54. "Cuban Minister Weds," *New York Times*, February 26, 1915, 9.
55. *New York Petitions for Naturalization*.
56. Ibid.
57. Baralt, *El Martí que yo conocí*, 202–3.
58. *New York Commercial Advertiser*, January 15, 1875, facsimile reproduction in Méndez Martínez and Pérez Pino, *Amalia Simoni*, 154.
59. Méndez Martínez and Pérez Pino, *Amalia Simoni*, 222.
60. "Cuban Commission Here," *New York Times*, November 22, 1898, 4.
61. Llaverías and Santovenia, *Actas de las Asambleas*, vol. 5, 45–49.
62. Gonzalo de Quesada's archives, partially published in 1965, contain letters written by Generals Máximo Gómez, Bartolomé Masó, and Carlos Roloff in the period from September to December 1898 in which they express their deep concerns about the future of Cuban independence given the U.S. entry in the war. Quesada y Miranda, *Documentos históricos*, 487–97.
63. "Cuban Commission Here," *New York Times*.
64. Ibid.
65. "Cubans in Conference," *New York Times*, November 24, 1898, 3.
66. "Shafter Tells His Story," *New York Times*, November 26, 1898, 2.
67. Philip S. Foner, *The Spanish-Cuban-American War*, vol. 2, *1898–1902*, 350–51.
68. Ramiro Guerra, *La expansión territorial de los Estados Unidos*, 388.
69. For a detailed eyewitness account of the Cuban army's critical contributions to the success of the Santiago campaign, see Collazo, *Los americanos en Cuba*, 135–217.
70. Philip S. Foner, *The Spanish-Cuban-American War*, vol. 2, 355.
71. The text of the entire letter can be found in Collazo, *Los americanos en Cuba*, 220–22.
72. "Shafter and García Meet," *New York Times*, November 26, 1898, 2.
73. "Effects of the Storm," *New York Times*, November 27, 1898, 1.
74. "The Storm's Ravages," *New York Times*, November 28, 1898, 1.
75. "Cuba's Commission," *Washington Evening Star*, December 1, 1898, 1.
76. "Troops Land in Havana," *Washington Evening Star*, December 12, 1898, 1.
77. "Cuban Patriot Dead," *Washington Evening Star*, December 12, 1898, 3.
78. "Gen. Calixto Garcia Dead," *New York Times*, December 12, 1898, 1.
79. "Consigned to Rest," *Washington Evening Star*, December 13, 1898, 3.
80. Philip S. Foner, *The Spanish-Cuban-American War*, vol. 2, 424; and "Spain Hauls Down Her Flag in Cuba," *New York Times*, January 2, 1899, 1.
81. Philip S. Foner, *The Spanish-Cuban-American War*, vol. 2, 424.

REFERENCES

MANUSCRIPT COLLECTIONS
Juan and Nicolás Arnao Collection. Manuscript Division, Library of Congress.
Hamilton Fish Papers. Manuscript Division, Library of Congress.
Menu Collection. Manuscripts, Archives and Rare Books Division, New York Public
    Library.
Old Records Division. New York County Courts.
José Ignacio Rodríguez Papers. Manuscript Division, Library of Congress.
Moses Taylor Papers. Manuscripts, Archives and Rare Books Division, New York Public
    Library.

DIGITAL COLLECTIONS
Martí, José. *Obras completas*. CD-ROM edition. La Habana: Centro de Estudios Martianos,
    2001.
Patria. CD-ROM edition. La Habana: Centro de Estudios Martianos, 2010.

DATA SETS FROM ANCESTRY.COM
The following data sets were accessed from December 2004 to May 2017 from Ancestry.
com, which combines collections from various sources. Most of the original sources
obtained from Ancestry are from the National Archives and Records Administration
(which keeps the historical decennial census records), along with several others such as
the Church of Jesus Christ of Latter-Day Saints and the U.S. District Court in New York:

New York, 1820–1850 Passenger and Immigration Lists. Original data: *Registry of Vessels
    Arriving at the Port of New York from Foreign Ports, 1789–1919*. Micropublication
    M237, rolls 1–95, National Archives, Washington, D.C.
New York Passenger Lists, 1851–1891. Original data: *Passenger Lists of Vessels Arriving at New
    York, 1820–1897*. Micropublication M237, rolls 95–580, National Archives, Washington,
    D.C.
New York Petitions for Naturalization, 1794–1906.
*Soundex Index to Petitions for Naturalization Filed in Federal, State, and Local Courts
    Located in New York City, 1792–1906*. National Archives and Records Administration,
    Northeast Region, New York.
U.S. Bureau of the Census. *1840 United States Federal Census, New York City*.
———. *1850 United States Federal Census, New York City*.
———. *1860 United States Federal Census, New York City*.
———. *1870 United States Federal Census, New York City*.
———. *1880 United States Federal Census, New York City*.

———. *Fourteenth Census of the United States: 1920.*

U.S. Passport Applications, 1795–1925.

DIRECTORIES

Directory of Tobacco Men in the United States. New York: C. Pfirshing, 1867.

A Directory of the Tobacco Trade of the United States, Great Britain, and Germany. New York: Tobacco Leaf, 1872.

Trow's New York City Directory. New York: J. H. Trow, 1861, 1871.

The Universal Tobacco Dealers Directory for the Year 1867. New York and Philadelphia: Barrett, 1867.

NEWSPAPERS AND OTHER SERIALS

El Ateneo

Brooklyn Daily Eagle

Diario de la Marina

El Espejo

Granma Weekly Review

Harper's New Monthly Magazine

Harper's Weekly

El Mercurio de Nueva York

New York Daily Tribune

New York Evening Mail

New York Evening Post

New York Herald

New York Sun

New York Times

New York World

El Nuevo Herald

La Revolución

Tobacco Circular

La Verdad

Washington Evening Star

BOOKS AND JOURNAL ARTICLES

Abad, Diana. "Las emigraciones cubanas en la Guerra de los Diez Años." *Santiago* 53 (1984).

Aguilera Rojas, Eladio. *Francisco V. Aguilera y la revolución de Cuba de 1868.* 2 vols. La Habana: La Moderna Poesía, 1909.

Albin, María C. *Género, poesía y esfera pública: Gertrudis Gómez de Avellaneda y la tradición Romántica.* Madrid: Editorial Trotta, 2002.

Albion, Robert Greenhalgh. *The Rise of New York Port.* 2nd ed. New York: Scribner's, 1939.

Alejandro, José M. de. "Sobre la intransigencia." *Revista de Occidente* 3, no. 31 (October 1965).

Alger, Horatio, Jr. *Ragged Dick, or, Street Life in New York with the Boot-Blacks.* Reprint of 1868 ed. New York: Modern Library, 2005.

Allen, Esther, ed. and trans. *José Martí: Selected Writings.* New York: Penguin, 2002.

Almansa y Tavira, Juan de. *La revolución de Cuba y el elemento español.* La Habana: Imprenta y Encuadernación de la Sociedad de Operarios, 1870.

Almodóvar Muñoz, Carmen. "Martí en la mirilla de: Trujillo, José I. Rodríguez y Collazo." In *Cuba: La revolución de 1895 y el fin del imperio colonial español*, edited by Oscar Loyola Vega. Morelia, Mexico: Instituto de Investigaciones Históricas, Universidad Michoacana de San Nicolás de Hidalgo, 1995.

Álvarez, Imeldo. *Acerca de Cirilo Villaverde*. La Habana: Editorial Letras Cubanas, 1982.

Álvarez, R., and I. G. Grediaga. *Guía de Nueva York para uso de los españoles e hispanoamericanos*. New York: John A. Gray, 1863.

Álvarez Estévez, Rolando. *La emigración cubana en Estados Unidos*. La Habana: Editorial de Ciencias Sociales, 1986.

Álvarez Pedroso, Antonio. *Miguel de Aldama*. La Habana: Academia de la Historia de Cuba, 1948.

Anbrinder, Tyler. *City of Dreams: The 400-Year Epic History of Immigrant New York*. Boston: Houghton Mifflin Harcourt, 2016.

Aragón, Uva de, ed. *Repensando a Martí*. Salamanca: Universidad Pontificia de Salamanca, 1998.

Argüelles, Luis Angel. "Prensa cubana de la emigración en la Guerra de los Diez Años." *Revista de la Biblioteca Nacional José Martí* 90, nos. 2–3 (April–September 1999).

Armas, Ramón de. "La idea de unión antillana en algunos revolucionarios del siglo XIX." *Anales del Caribe* 4–5 (1984–1985).

Augier, Angel, ed. *Epistolario de José María Heredia*. La Habana: Editorial Letras Cubanas, 2005.

Auxier, George W. "The Propaganda Activities of the Cuban Junta in Precipitating the Spanish-American War, 1895–1898." *Hispanic American Historical Review* 19, no. 3 (August 1939).

Azcuy, Fanny. *El Partido Revolucionario y la independencia de Cuba*. La Habana: Molina, 1930.

Bachiller y Morales, Antonio. *Guía de la ciudad de Nueva York y sus alrededores*. New York: Impresa y Librería de N. Ponce de León, 1876.

Baer, Willis N. *The Economic Development of the Cigar Industry in the United States*. Lancaster, PA: Art Printing Company, 1933.

Balmaseda, Francisco Javier. *Los confinados á Fernando Póo é impresiones de un viaje a Guinea*. La Habana: A. M. Lamy, 1899.

Baltar Rodríguez, José. *Los chinos de Cuba: Apuntes etnográficos*. La Habana: Fundación Fernando Ortiz, 1997.

Baralt, Blanca Z. de. *El Martí que yo conocí*. La Habana: Editorial Trópico, 1945.

Barrett, Walter [J. A. Scoville]. *Old Merchants of New York City*. Vol. 1. New York: Thomas R. Knox, 1885.

Bayley, J. R. *A Brief Sketch of the Early History of the Catholic Church on the Island of New York*. Reprint of 1870 2nd ed. New York: United States Catholic Historical Society, 1973.

Beckert, Sven. *The Monied Metropolis: New York City and the Consolidation of the American Bourgeoisie, 1850–1896*. New York: Cambridge University Press, 2001.

Bender, Thomas. *New York Intellect: A History of Intellectual Life in New York City, from 1750 to the Beginnings of Our Time*. New York: Knopf, 1987.

Benítez Rojo, Antonio. "Azúcar/poder/texto." *Revista Encuentro de la Cultura Cubana* 37–38 (Summer–Fall 2005).

Bernstein, Harry. *Origins of Inter-American Interest, 1700–1812*. New York: Russell and Russell, 1965.

Binder, Frederick M., and David M. Reimers. *All the Nations under Heaven: An Ethnic and Racial History of New York City*. New York: Columbia University Press, 1995.

Bradford, Richard H. *The Virginius Affair*. Boulder: Colorado Associated University Press, 1980.

Bueno, Salvador. "Esclavitud y relaciones interraciales en *Cecilia Valdés*." In *Letras: Cultura en Cuba*, vol. 6, edited by Ana Cairo Ballester. La Habana: Editorial Pueblo y Educación, 1989.

———. *Figuras cubanas del siglo XIX: Selección*. La Habana: Editorial Pueblo y Educación, 2000.

Burrows, Edwin G., and Mike Wallace. *Gotham: A History of New York City to 1898*. New York: Oxford University Press, 1999.

Cairo Ballester, Ana. "Emilia Casanova y la dignidad de la mujer cubana." In *Mujeres latinoamericanas: Historia y cultura, siglos XVI al XIX*, edited by Luisa Campuzano. La Habana: Ediciones Casa de las Américas, 1997.

———. "Estados Unidos y la construcción del pensamiento cubano en el siglo XIX." In *Mirar el Niágara: Huellas culturales entre Cuba y los Estados Unidos*, edited by Rafael Hernández. La Habana: Centro de Investigación y Desarrollo de la Cultura Cubana Juan Marinello, 2000.

———, ed. *Heredia entre cubanos y españoles*. Santiago de Cuba: Editorial Oriente, 2003.

Calcagno, Francisco. *Diccionario biográfico cubano*. New York: Imprenta y Librería de N. Ponce de León, 1878.

Camacho, Pánfilo D. *Aguilera: El precursor sin gloria*. La Habana: Dirección de Cultura, 1951.

Camacho, Simón. *Cosas de los Estados Unidos*. New York: Imprenta de "El Porvenir," 1864.

Campuzano, Luisa. "Dos viajeras cubanas en los Estados Unidos: La Condesa de Merlin y Gertrudis Gómez de Avellaneda." In *Mujeres latinoamericanas: Historia y cultura, siglos XVI al XIX*, vol. 2, edited by Luisa Campuzano. La Habana: Ediciones Casa de las Américas, 1997.

Cancela, Gilberto. *Enrique Piñeyro: Su vida y su obra*. Miami: Ediciones Universal, 1977.

Cantero, J. G., and E. Laplante. *Los ingenios de Cuba*. Edited by Leví Marrero. Madrid: La Moderna Poesía, 1984.

Carbonell, Miguel Angel. *Un héroe pintado por sí mismo*. La Habana: Editorial Guáimaro, 1939.

Carpentier, Alejo. *La música en Cuba*. Reprint of 1946 ed. La Habana: Editorial Letras Cubanas, 1979.

Casasús, Juan J. E. *Calixto García*. 4th ed. Miami: La Moderna Poesía, 1981.

———. *La emigración cubana y la independencia de la patria*. La Habana: Editorial Lex, 1953.

———. *Vida militar de Ignacio Agramonte*. 3rd ed. Miami: La Moderna Poesía, 1981.

Castañeda, Orlando. *Martí, los tabaqueros y la revolución de 1895*. La Habana: Comisión Nacional de Propaganda y Defensa del Tabaco Habano, 1940.

Castellanos, Jorge. *24 de febrero de 1895: Un programa vigente*. Miami: Ediciones Universal, 1995.

Castellanos G., Gerardo. *Motivos de Cayo Hueso*. La Habana: Ucar, García, 1935.

Castro y Bachiller, Raimundo de. *Don Antonio Bachiller y Morales*. La Habana: Editorial Guerrero, 1939.

Cepero Bonilla, Raúl. *Azúcar y abolición*. La Habana: Editorial de Ciencias Sociales, 1971.

Céspedes Argote, Onoria, ed. *Diario de Francisco Vicente Aguilera en la emigración (Estados Unidos), 1871–1872*, vol. 1. La Habana: Editorial de Ciencias Sociales, 2008.

———, ed. *Diario y correspondencia de Francisco Vicente Aguilera en la emigración (Estados Unidos), 1872*, vol. 2. La Habana: Editorial de Ciencias Sociales, 2008.

Céspedes y Quesada, Carlos Manuel de. *Manuel de Quesada y Loynaz*. La Habana: Imprenta El Siglo XX, 1925.

Chaffin, Tom. *Fatal Glory: Narciso López and the First Clandestine U.S. War against Cuba*. Charlottesville: University Press of Virginia, 1996.

Chamorro, Pedro Joaquín. *El licenciado Jerónimo Pérez*. Managua: Editorial La Prensa, 1939.

Chan, Sucheng, ed. *Chinese American Transnationalism: The Flow of People, Resources, and Ideas between China and America during the Exclusion Era*. Philadelphia: Temple University Press, 2006.

Chaple, Sergio. "Para una comprensión mejor de Zenea." *Anuario L/L* 7–8 (1976–1977).

Cheung, Mark. *Transfiguration Church: A Church of Immigrants, 1827–1977*. New York: Park, 1977.

Cisneros, Francisco Javier. *Relación documentada de cinco espediciones*. New York: Imprenta de Hallet and Breen, 1870.

Collazo, Enrique. *Los Americanos en Cuba*. Reprint of 1905 ed. La Habana: Editorial de Ciencias Sociales, 1972.

———. *Desde Yara hasta el Zanjón*. Reprint of 1893 ed. La Habana: Instituto del Libro, 1967.

Cook, Adrian. *The Alabama Claims: American Politics and Anglo-American Relations, 1865–1872*. Ithaca: Cornell University Press, 1975.

Cooper, Patricia A. *Once a Cigar Maker: Men, Women, and Work Culture in American Cigar Factories, 1900–1919*. Urbana: University of Illinois Press, 1987.

Cordoví Núñez, Yoel. *La emigración cubana en los Estados Unidos: Estructuras directivas y corrientes de pensamiento, 1895–1898*. Santiago de Cuba: Editorial Oriente, 2012.

Court of Appeals. *The People of the State of New York against Miguel Chacon*. New York: C. H. Burgoyne, 1885.

Cova, Antonio Rafael de la. *Cuban Confederate Colonel: The Life of Ambrosio José González*. Columbia: University of South Carolina Press, 2003.

Cruz, Marta, ed. *Francisco Vicente Aguilera: Epistolario*. La Habana: Editorial de Ciencias Sociales, 1974.

Cuba Commission. *A Hidden History of the Chinese in Cuba: The Original English-Language Text of 1876*. Baltimore: Johns Hopkins University Press, 1993.

Cushing, Caleb. *The Treaty of Washington: Its Negotiation, Execution, and the Discussions Relating Thereto*. Reprint of 1873 ed. Freeport, NY: Books for Libraries, 1970.

Deschamps Chapeaux, Pedro. *Rafael Serra y Montalvo, obrero incansable de nuestra independencia*. La Habana: Unión de Escritores y Artistas de Cuba, 1975.

Despradel, Lorenzo. *Rafael Serra: Album político*. La Habana: Imprenta El Score, 1906.

Deulofeu, Manuel. *Martí, Cayo Hueso y Tampa: La emigración, notas históricas*. Cienfuegos: Imprenta de Antio Cuevas y Hermano, 1905.

Díaz, Lomberto. *Heredia: Primer romántico hispanoamericano*. Montevideo: Ediciones Geminis, 1973.

Dirección de Cultura, ed. *Ignacio Agramonte y Loynaz: Patria y mujer*. La Habana: Ministerio de Educación, 1942.

Edwin, Morton R. *Half a Century with Tobacco*. New York: James B. Hall, 1928.

Ely, Roland T. *Comerciantes cubanos del siglo XIX*. 2nd ed. La Habana: Editorial Librería Martí, 1961.

———. *Cuando reinaba su majestad el azúcar*. Buenos Aires: Editorial Sudamericana, 1963.

————. "The Old Cuba Trade: Highlights and Case Studies of Cuban-American Interdependence during the Nineteenth Century." *Business History Review* 38, no. 4 (1964).

Esténger, Rafael. *Heredia, la incomprensión de sí mismo*. La Habana: Editorial Trópico, 1938.

Estrade, Paul. "El puñado de oro de la traición de Zenea." *Revista de la Biblioteca Nacional José Martí*, January–April 1978.

Fernández, Aurea Matilde. *España y Cuba, 1868–1898: Revolución burguesa y relaciones coloniales*. La Habana: Editorial de Ciencias Sociales, 1988.

Fernández de Pinedo Echevarría, Nadia. *Las balanzas del comercio exterior de La Habana, 1803–1807*. Bilbao: Universidad del País Vasco, 1984.

————. *Comercio exterior y fiscalidad: Cuba, 1794–1860*. Bilbao: Universidad del País Vasco, 1984.

Ferrer, Ada. *Insurgent Cuba: Race, Nation, and Revolution, 1868–1898*. Chapel Hill: University of North Carolina Press, 1999.

Figueredo, Bernardo. "Cuatro anécdotas de la vida de Martí." In *Memoria del Congreso de Escritores Martianos, febrero 20 a 27 de 1953*, edited by Congreso de Escritores Martianos. La Habana: Comisión Nacional Organizadora de los Actos y Ediciones del Centenario y del Monumento de Martí, 1953.

Foner, Nancy. *From Ellis Island to JFK: New York's Two Great Waves of Immigration*. New Haven and New York: Yale University Press and Russell Sage Foundation, 2000.

Foner, Nancy, Rubén G. Rumbaut, and Steven J. Gold, eds. *Immigration Research for a New Century: Multidisciplinary Perspectives*. New York: Russell Sage Foundation, 2000.

Foner, Philip S. *A History of Cuba and Its Relations with the United States*. Vol. 1, *1492–1845, From the Conquest of Cuba to La Escalera*. New York: International Publishers, 1962.

————. *A History of Cuba and Its Relations with the United States*. Vol. 2, *1845–1895, From the Annexationist Era to the Second War for Independence*. New York: International Publishers, 1963.

————. *The Spanish-Cuban-American War and the Birth of American Imperialism*. Vol. 2, *1898–1902*. New York: Monthly Review Press, 1972.

Fountain, Anne. *José Martí and U.S. Writers*. Gainesville: University Press of Florida, 2003.

Franco, José L. *Antonio Maceo: Apuntes para una historia de su vida*. Vol. 1. 3rd ed. La Habana: Editorial de Ciencias Sociales, 1975.

Gallagher, Thomas. *Fire at Sea: The Story of the Morro Castle*. New York: Rinehart, 1959.

Garcerán de Vall, Julio. *Heredia y la libertad*. Miami: Ediciones Universal, 1978.

García del Pino, César. "La Habana en los días de Yara." *Revista de la Biblioteca Nacional José Martí* 69, no. 2 (May–August 1978).

García Galló, Gaspar Jorge. "Martí y los tabaqueros." *Islas* 3, no. 3 (May–August 1961): 63–69.

Gómez, Máximo. *Diario de campaña del Mayor General Máximo Gómez, 1868–1899*. La Habana: Comisión del Archivo de Máximo Gómez, 1940.

Gómez de Avellaneda, Gertrudis. "A vista del Niágara." In *Biblioteca de autores españoles*, vol. 272, *Obras de Doña Gertrudis Gómez de Avellaneda*, edited by José María Castro y Calvo. Madrid: Ediciones Atlas, 1974.

González Echevarría, Roberto. "José Martí: An Introduction." In *José Martí: Selected Writings*, edited and translated by Esther Allen. New York: Penguin, 2002.

————. *The Pride of Havana: A History of Cuban Baseball*. New York: Oxford University Press, 1999.

González Veranes, Pedro N. *La personalidad de Rafael Serra y sus relaciones con Martí*. La Habana: Editorial La Verónica, 1943.

Greenbaum, Susan D. *More Than Black: Afro-Cubans in Tampa.* Gainesville: University Press of Florida, 2002.

Guerra, Lillian. *The Myth of José Martí: Conflicting Nationalisms in Early Twentieth-Century Cuba.* Chapel Hill: University of North Carolina Press, 2005.

Guerra, Ramiro. *La expansión territorial de los Estados Unidos.* 3rd ed. La Habana: Editorial de Ciencias Sociales, 1975.

Guerra y Sánchez, Ramiro. *Guerra de los Diez Años.* Vol. 1. Reprint. La Habana: Editorial de Ciencias Sociales, 1972.

———. *Manual de historia de Cuba.* La Habana: Cultural, 1938.

Guiteras, Eusebio. *Un invierno en Nueva York.* Barcelona: Gorgas, n.d., ca. 1885.

Hernández y Pérez, Eusebio. *El período revolucionario de 1879 a 1895.* La Habana: Imprenta El Siglo XX, 1914.

Hernández Travieso, Antonio. *El Padre Varela: Biografía del forjador de la conciencia cubana.* Reprint of 1949 2nd ed. Miami: Ediciones Universal, 1984.

Herrera Cudello, Elvis. *Thomas Jordan al servicio de la independencia de Cuba, 1869–1871.* Cienfuegos: Ediciones Mecenas, 2005.

Hirschman, Charles, Philip Kasinitz, and Josh DeWind, eds. *The Handbook of International Migration: The American Experience.* New York: Russell Sage Foundation, 1999.

Hodas, Daniel. *The Business Career of Moses Taylor: Merchant, Finance Capitalist, and Industrialist.* New York: New York University Press, 1976.

Holmes, Julia. *100 New Yorkers: A Guide to Illustrious Lives and Locations.* New York: Little Bookroom, 2004.

Homberger, Eric. *The Historical Atlas of New York City.* New York: Henry Holt, 1994.

Horrego Estuch, Leopoldo. *Emilia Casanova: La vehemencia del separatismo.* La Habana: Academia de la Historia de Cuba, 1951.

Instituto Cubano de Geodesia y Cartografía and Centro de Estudios Martianos, eds. *Atlas histórico biográfico José Martí.* La Habana: Empresa de Cartografía, 1982.

Iraizoz y de Villar, Antonio. *Enrique Piñeyro: Su vida y sus obras.* La Habana: Imprenta El Siglo XX, 1922.

Irwin, William. *The New Niagara: Tourism, Technology, and the Landscape of Niagara Falls, 1776–1917.* University Park: Pennsylvania State University Press, 1996.

Jackson, Kenneth T., ed. *The Encyclopedia of New York City.* New Haven: Yale University Press, 1995.

Jenkins, Stephen. *The Story of the Bronx: From the Purchase Made by the Dutch from the Indians in 1639 to the Present Day.* New York: Putnam's, 1912.

Johnson, Barbara Ruth. "Origin of the Partido Revolucionario Cubano in Tampa: Martí and the Tobacco Workers." Master's thesis, University of Florida, 1968.

Johnson, Sherry. *The Social Transformation of Eighteenth-Century Cuba.* Gainesville: University Press of Florida, 2001.

Johnson, William Fletcher. *The History of Cuba.* Vol. 3. New York: B. F. Buck, 1920.

Kammen, Michael. *Colonial New York: A History.* New York: Scribner's, 1975.

Kimball, Richard Burleigh. *Cuba and the Cubans: Comprising a History of the Island of Cuba, the Present Social, Political, and Economic Condition; Also the Relation to England and the United States.* New York: Putnam, 1850.

Kirk, John M. *José Martí, Mentor of the Cuban Nation.* Gainesville: University Presses of Florida, 1983.

Knight, Franklin W. *Slave Society in Cuba during the Nineteenth Century.* Madison: University of Wisconsin Press, 1970.

Lazo, Rodrigo. *Writing to Cuba: Filibustering and Cuban Exiles in the United States.* Chapel Hill: University of North Carolina Press, 2005.

Leal Spengler, Eusebio. *Carlos Manuel de Céspedes: El diario perdido.* La Habana: Editorial de Ciencias Sociales, 1994.

Le Riverend Brusone, Julio J. "Desarrollo económico y social." In *Historia de la nación cubana,* vol. 2, *Guerras coloniales, conflictos y progresos, desde 1697 hasta 1790,* edited by Ramiro Guerra y Sánchez, José M. Pérez Cabrera, Juan J. Remos, and Emeterio S. Santovenia. La Habana: Editorial Historia de la Nación Cubana, 1952.

Llaverías, Joaquín. *El Consejo Administrativo de Bienes Embargados.* La Habana: Imprenta El Siglo XX, 1941.

———. *Miguel Aldama, o La dignidad patriótica.* La Habana: Imprenta Molina, 1937.

Llaverías, Joaquín, and Emeterio S. Santovenia, eds. *Actas de las Asambleas de Representantes y del Consejo de Gobierno durante la Guerra de Independencia.* Vol. 5. La Habana: Academia de la Historia de Cuba, 1932.

Lobo Montalvo, María Luisa. *Havana: History and Architecture of a Romantic City.* New York: Monacelli, 2000.

Lomas, Laura. *Translating Empire: José Martí, Migrant Latino Subjects, and American Modernities.* Durham: Duke University Press, 2008.

López, Alfred J. *José Martí: A Revolutionary Life.* Austin: University of Texas Press, 2014.

López Mesa, Enrique. *Algunos aspectos culturales de la comunidad cubana de New York durante el siglo XIX.* La Habana: Centro de Estudios Martianos, 2002.

———. *La comunidad cubana de New York: Siglo XIX.* La Habana: Centro de Estudios Martianos, 2002.

Luis, William. "*Cecilia Valdés*: The Emergence of an Antislavery Novel." *Afro-Hispanic Review* 3, no. 2 (May 1984).

Mañach, Jorge. *Martí el apóstol.* 6th ed. Madrid: Espasa Calpe, 1975.

Márquez Sterling, Carlos. *Don Tomás (Biografía de una época).* La Habana: Editorial Lex, 1953.

———. *Ignacio Agramonte, el bayardo de la revolución cubana.* Reprint of 1936 ed. Miami: Editorial Cubana, 1995.

———. *Martí, maestro y apóstol.* La Habana: Seoane, Fernández, 1942.

Marrero, Leví. *Cuba: Economía y sociedad.* Vol. 15, *Azúcar, ilustración y conciencia (1763–1868).* Madrid: Editorial Playor, 1992.

Martí, José. *Todo lo olvida Nueva York en un instante.* Compiled by Jorge de Jesús Aguirre and María Antonieta Juliá. La Habana: Editorial de Ciencias Sociales, 1997.

Martínez Estrada, Ezequiel. *Martí revolucionario.* 2nd ed. La Habana: Casa de las Américas, 1974.

Masó, Calixto C. *Historia de Cuba.* 2nd ed. Edited by Leonel-Antonio de la Cuesta. Miami: Ediciones Universal, 1976.

May, Robert E. *The Southern Dream of a Caribbean Empire, 1854–1861.* Baton Rouge: Louisiana State University Press, 1973.

McCadden, Joseph, and Helen M. McCadden. *Félix Varela: Torch Bearer from Cuba.* 2nd ed. San Juan, Puerto Rico: Félix Varela Foundation, 1984.

Méndez Martínez, Roberto, and Ana María Pérez Pino. *Amalia Simoni: Una vida oculta.* La Habana: Editorial de Ciencias Sociales, 2009.

Méndez Rodenas, Adriana. *Gender and Nationalism in Colonial Cuba: The Travels of Santa Cruz y Montalvo, Condesa de Merlin.* Nashville: Vanderbilt University Press, 1998.

Mirabal, Nancy Raquel. "De Aquí, de Allá: Race, Empire, and Nation in the Making of Cuban Migrant Communities in New York and Tampa, 1823–1924." Ph.D. dissertation, University of Michigan, 2001.

———. "'No Country but the One We Must Fight For': The Emergence of an Antillean Nation and Community in New York City, 1860–1901." In *Mambo Montage: The Latinization of New York,* edited by Agustín Lao-Montes and Arlene Dávila. New York: Columbia University Press, 2001.

———. *Suspect Freedoms: The Racial and Sexual Politics of Cubanidad in New York, 1823–1957.* New York: New York University Press, 2017.

Montero, Oscar. *José Martí: An Introduction.* New York: Palgrave Macmillan, 2004.

Moore, Ernest R. "José María Heredia in New York, 1824–1825." *Symposium* 5, no. 2 (November 1951).

Moore, John Bassett. *History and Digest of the International Arbitrations to Which the United States Has Been a Party.* Vol. 3. Washington, D.C.: Government Printing Office, 1898.

Morales y Morales, Vidal. *Iniciadores y primeros mártires de la revolución cubana,* 2 vols. La Habana: Consejo Nacional de Cultura, 1963.

Moreno Fraginals, Manuel. *Cuba/España, España/Cuba: Historia común.* Barcelona: Grijalbo Mondadori, 1995.

———. *El ingenio: Complejo económico social cubano del azúcar.* Vol. 1. 2nd ed. La Habana: Editorial de Ciencias Sociales, 1978.

———. *The Sugarmill: The Socioeconomic Complex of Sugar in Cuba.* Translated by Cedric Belfrage. New York: Monthly Review Press, 1976.

Morgan, H. Wayne. "The Delome Letter: A New Appraisal." *Historian* 26, no. 1 (November 1963).

Mormino, Gary R., and George E. Pozzetta. *The Immigrant World of Ybor City: Italians and Their Latin Neighbors in Tampa, 1885–1985.* Urbana: University of Illinois Press, 1990.

Navia, Juan M. *An Apostle for the Immigrants: The Exile Years of Father Félix Varela y Morales, 1823–1853.* Salisbury, MD: Factor Press, 2002.

Nevins, Allan. *Hamilton Fish: The Inner History of the Grant Administration.* Vol. 1. Rev. ed. New York: Frederick Ungar, 1957.

Offner, John L. *An Unwanted War: The Diplomacy of the United States and Spain over Cuba, 1895–1898.* Chapel Hill: University of North Carolina Press, 1992.

Ojeda Reyes, Félix. *Peregrinos de la libertad.* Río Piedras, Puerto Rico: Editorial de la Universidad de Puerto Rico, 1992.

Oviedo, José Miguel. *La niña de New York: Una revisión histórica de la vida erótica de José Martí.* Mexico, D.F.: Fondo de Cultura Económica, 1989.

Padura Fuentes, Leonardo. *José María Heredia: La patria y la vida.* La Habana: Ediciones Unión, 2003.

Partido Revolucionario Cubano. *La Revolución del 95 según la correspondencia de la Delegación Cubana en Nueva York.* 5 vols. La Habana: Editorial Habanera, 1932–1937.

Peraza Sarausa, Fermín. *Diccionario biográfico cubano,* vols. 1 and 4. La Habana: Ediciones Anuario Bibliográfico Cubano, 1951.

Pérez, Lisandro. "Cuban Catholics in the United States." In *Puerto Rican and Cuban Catholics in the United States,* edited by Jay P. Dolan and Jaime R. Vidal. Notre Dame: University of Notre Dame Press, 1994.

———. "De Nueva York a Miami: El desarrollo demográfico de las comunidades cubanas en Estados Unidos." *Revista Encuentro de la Cultura Cubana* 15 (Winter 1999–2000).

Pérez, Louis A., Jr. *Cuba and the United States: Ties of Singular Intimacy.* Athens: University of Georgia Press, 1990.

———. *Cuba between Empires, 1878–1902.* Pittsburgh: University of Pittsburgh Press, 1983.

———. *Cuba: Between Reform and Revolution.* New York: Oxford University Press, 1988.

———. *On Becoming Cuban: Identity, Nationality, and Culture.* Chapel Hill: University of North Carolina Press, 1999.

———. *The Structure of Cuban History: Meanings and Purpose of the Past.* Chapel Hill: University of North Carolina Press, 2013.

Pérez, Raquel. *Religiosas del Sagrado Corazón en Cuba.* San Juan, Puerto Rico: Gráfica Metropolitana, 1997.

Pichardo, Hortensia, ed. *Documentos para la historia de Cuba.* Vol. 1. La Habana: Editorial de Ciencias Sociales, 1977.

Piñeyro, Enrique. *Estudios y conferencias de historia y literatura.* New York: Imprenta de Thompson y Moreau, 1880.

———. *Morales Lemus y la revolución de Cuba: Estudio histórico.* Originally printed in 1871 in New York by M. M. Zarzamendi, Impresor. Reprinted with preface and bibliography by Carlos Ripoll. New York: Unión de Cubanos en el Exilio, 1970.

———. *Vida y escritos de Juan Clemente Zenea.* Paris: Garnier Hermanos, 1901.

Poey Baró, Dionisio. *La entrada de los aldamistas en la Guerra de los Diez Años.* La Habana: Editorial de Ciencias Sociales, 1989.

Ponte Domínguez, Francisco J. *Historia de la Guerra de los Diez Años.* La Habana: Imprenta El Siglo XX, 1944.

Portell Vilá, Herminio. *Historia de Cuba en sus relaciones con los Estados Unidos y España.* Vol. 1. La Habana: Jesús Montero, 1938.

———. *Historia de Cuba en sus relaciones con los Estados Unidos y España.* Vol. 2. Reprint of 1939 ed. Miami: Mnemosyne, 1969.

———. *Narciso López y su época, 1848–1850.* Vol. 2. La Habana: Compañía de Libros y Folletos, 1952.

Portuondo, Fernando. *Historia de Cuba, 1492–1898.* 6th ed. La Habana: Instituto Cubano del Libro, 1975.

Portuondo Zúñiga, Olga. *José Antonio Saco: Eternamente polémico.* Santiago de Cuba: Editorial Oriente, 2005.

Poyo, Gerald E. "Evolution of Cuban Separatist Thought in the Émigré Communities of the United States, 1848–1895." *Hispanic American Historical Review* 66, no. 3 (August 1986): 485–507.

———. *"With All, and for the Good of All": The Emergence of Popular Nationalism in the Cuban Communities of the United States, 1848–1898.* Durham: Duke University Press, 1989.

Prados Torreiras, Teresa. *Mambisas: Rebel Women in Nineteenth-Century Cuba.* Gainesville: University Press of Florida, 2005.

Pratt, Julius W. "The Origin of 'Manifest Destiny.'" *American Historical Review* 32, no. 4 (July 1927).

Preece, Carol Ann Aiken. "Insurgent Guests: The Cuban Revolutionary Party and Its Activities in the United States, 1892–1898." Ph.D. dissertation, Georgetown University, 1976.

Prieto, Guillermo. *Viaje a los Estados Unidos*. Vol. 3. Mexico City: Imprenta del Comercio de Dublan y Chavez, 1878.

Quesada, Gonzalo de. *Páginas escogidas*. La Habana: Instituto del Libro, 1968.

Quesada, Vicente G. *Recuerdos de mi vida diplomática: Misión en Estados Unidos, 1885–1892*. Buenos Aires: Librería de J. Menéndez, 1904.

Quesada y Miranda, Gonzalo de, ed. *Documentos históricos: Archivo de Gonzalo de Quesada*. La Habana: Editorial de la Universidad de La Habana, 1965.

———. *Martí, hombre*. Reprint of 1940 ed. La Habana: Seoane, Fernández, 1998.

Quiroz, Alfonso W. "Implicit Costs of Empire: Bureaucratic Corruption in Nineteenth-Century Cuba." *Journal of Latin American Studies* 35 (2003).

———. "Loyalist Overkill: The Socioeconomic Costs of 'Repressing' the Separatist Insurrection in Cuba, 1868–1878." *Hispanic American Historical Review* 78, no. 2 (1998).

Ripoll, Carlos. *La vida íntima y secreta de José Martí*. New York: Editorial Dos Ríos, 1995.

Rivero Muñiz, José. "Los cubanos en Tampa." *Revista Bimestre Cubana* 74 (January–June 1958): 5–140.

Rodríguez, Carlos Rafael. "José Manuel Mestre: La filosofía en La Habana." In *Letras: Cultura en Cuba*, edited by Ana Cairo Ballester. La Habana: Editorial Pueblo y Educación, 1989.

Rodríguez, José Ignacio. *Estudio histórico sobre el origen, desenvolvimiento y manifestaciones prácticas de la idea de la anexión de la isla de Cuba á los Estados Unidos de América*. La Habana: Imprenta La Propaganda Literaria, 1900.

———. *Vida del Doctor José Manuel Mestre*. La Habana: Imprenta Avisador Comercial, 1909.

———. *Vida del presbítero Don Félix Varela*. Reprint of 1878 2nd ed. La Habana: Arellano, 1944.

[Rodríguez, José Ignacio]. *The Book of Blood: An Authentic Record of the Policy Adopted by Modern Spain to Put an End to the War of Independence of Cuba*. New York: M. M. Zarzamendi, Translator and Printer, 1871. Rev. ed., New York: N. Ponce de León, 1873.

Rodríguez, Pedro Pablo. *De las dos Américas: Aproximaciones al pensamiento Martíano*. La Habana: Centro de Estudios Martianos, 2002.

Rodríguez Expósito, César. *Dr. Ramón L. Miranda, médico de Martí*. La Habana: Academia de la Historia de Cuba, 1962.

Roig de Leuchsenring, Emilio. *La Habana: Apuntes históricos*. La Habana: Oficina del Historiador de la Ciudad, 1939.

———. *13 conclusiones fundamentales sobre la guerra libertadora cubana de 1895*. Mexico: El Colegio de Mexico, 1945.

Rojas, Marta. *El harén de Oviedo*. La Habana: Instituto Cubano del Libro, 2003.

Rojas, Rafael. *José Martí: La invención de Cuba*. Madrid: Editorial Colibrí, 2000.

Roldán de Montaud, Inés. *La restauración en Cuba: El fracaso de un proceso reformista*. Madrid: Consejo Superior de Investigaciones Científicas, 2000.

Roldán Oliarte, Esteban, ed. *Cuba en la mano: Enciclopedia popular ilustrada*. La Habana: Ucar, García, 1950.

Rotker, Susana. *The American Chronicles of José Martí: Journalism and Modernity in Spanish America*. Hanover, NH: University Press of New England, 2000.

———. "José Martí and the United States: On the Margins of the Gaze." In *Re-Reading José Martí (1853–1895): One Hundred Years Later*, edited by Julio Rodríguez Luis. Albany: State University of New York Press, 1999.

Saco, José Antonio. *Obras: José Antonio Saco*, vol. 1, edited by Eduardo Torres-Cuevas. Colección Biblioteca de Clásicos Cubanos, no. 12. La Habana: Ediciones Imagen Contemporánea, 2001.

Sagra, Ramón de la. *Cinco meses en los Estados-Unidos de la América del Norte*. Paris: Imprenta de Pablo Renourad, 1836.

Saluvet, Juan B. *Los deportados a Fernando Póo en 1869*. Matanzas: Imprenta Aurora del Yumurí, 1892.

Sampson, Robert D. *John L. O'Sullivan and His Times*. Kent: Kent State University Press, 2003.

Sanguily, Manuel. *Nobles memorias*. Reprint. Miami: International Press of Miami, 1982.

Santa Cruz y Mallén, Francisco Xavier de. *Historia de familias cubanas*. 7 vols. Vols. 1–6, La Habana: Editorial Hercules, 1940–1950; vol. 7, Miami: Ediciones Universal, 1985.

Santa Cruz y Montalvo, María de las Mercedes de (La Comtesse Merlin). *La Havane*. Vol. 1. Paris: Librairie D'Amyot, 1844.

Santos, Mercedes. *Martí a la luz del sol*. Quito: Ediciones La Tierra, 2001.

Santovenia, Emeterio S. "Política colonial." In *Historia de la nación cubana*, vol. 2, *Guerras coloniales, conflictos y progresos, desde 1697 hasta 1790*, edited by Ramiro Guerra y Sánchez, José M. Pérez Cabrera, Juan J. Remos, and Emeterio S. Santovenia. La Habana: Editorial Historia de la Nación Cubana, 1952.

Sarabia, Nydia, ed. *Noticias confidenciales sobre Cuba*. La Habana: Editorial Política, 1985.

———. *La patriota del silencio: Carmen Miyares*. La Habana: Editorial Ciencias Sociales, 1990.

Schneider, Dorothee. *Trade Unions and Community: The German Working Class in New York City, 1870–1900*. Urbana: University of Illinois Press, 1994.

Schulenburg, Chris T. "*Cecilia Valdés*: The Search for a Cuban Discursive Control." *Afro-Hispanic Review* 27, no. 2 (Fall 2008).

Schulman, Ivan A. "Modernismo/Modernidad: Metamórfosis de un concepto." In *Nuevos asedios al modernismo*, edited by Ivan A. Schulman. Madrid: Taurus Ediciones, 1987.

Scroggs, William O. "William Walker's Designs on Cuba." *Mississippi Valley Historical Review* 1, no. 2 (September 1914).

Sedano, Carlos de. *Cuba: Estudios políticos*. Madrid: Imprenta de Manuel G. Hernández, 1873.

Silva Gruesz, Kirsten. *Ambassadors of Culture: The Transamerican Origins of Latino Writing*. Princeton: Princeton University Press, 2002.

Soulere, Emilio A. *Historia de la insurrección de Cuba, 1869–1879*. Vol. 1. Barcelona: Establecimiento Tipográfico-Editorial de Juan Pons, 1879.

Stiles, T. J. *The First Tycoon: The Epic Life of Cornelius Vanderbilt*. New York: Knopf, 2009.

Syrett, David. *The Siege and Capture of Havana, 1762*. London: Navy Records Society, 1970.

Tamayo, Jorge L. *Centenario del sacrificio de Domingo de Goicouría*. La Habana: Academia de Ciencias de Cuba, 1970.

Thomas, Hugh. *Cuba, or The Pursuit of Freedom*. Rev. ed. New York: Da Capo, 1998.

Thomas, Lately. *Delmonico's: A Century of Splendor*. Boston: Houghton Mifflin, 1967.

Thrasher, J. S. "Preliminary Essay." In *Ensayo político sobre la isla de Cuba*, by Alejandro de Humboldt. Revised and translated. La Habana: Publicaciones del Archivo Nacional de Cuba, 1960.

Toledo Sande, Luis. *Cesto de llamas: Biografía de José Martí*. La Habana: Editorial de Ciencias Sociales, 1996.

Tornero, Pablo. "El suministro de mano de obra esclava en Cuba: Estado español y oligarquía criolla, 1765–1820." In *Cuba, la perla de las Antillas: Actas de las I jornadas sobre*

Cuba y su historia, edited by Consuelo Naranjo Orovio and Tomás Mallo Gutiérrez. Madrid: Ediciones Doce Calles, 1994.

Torres-Cuevas, Eduardo. "José Antonio Saco: La aventura intelectual de una época." In *José Antonio Saco: Obras*, vol. 1, edited by Eduardo Torres-Cuevas. La Habana: Ediciones Imagen Contemporánea, 2001.

———. "Vicente Antonio de Castro, el Gran Oriente de Cuba y las Antillas y la ruptura del 68." *Santiago* 32 (December 1978): 168–72.

Torres Hernández, Lázaro. "Céspedes y el 10 de octubre." *Bohemia*, October 6, 1972.

Trager, James. *The New York Chronology*. New York: Harper Collins, 2003.

Trelles y Govín, Carlos M. *Bibliografía cubana del siglo XIX*. Vol. 7. Matanzas: Imprenta de Quirós y Estrada, 1914.

———. *Biblioteca histórica cubana*. Vol. 1. Matanzas: Imprenta de Juan F. Oliver, 1922.

———. *Matanzas en la independencia de Cuba*. La Habana: Imprenta Avisador Comercial, 1928.

True, Marshall M. "Revolutionaries in Exile: The Cuban Revolutionary Party, 1891–1898." Ph.D. dissertation, University of Virginia, 1965.

Trujillo, E[nrique]. *Apuntes históricos*. New York: Tipografía El Porvenir, 1896.

Urban, C. Stanley. "A Local Study in 'Manifest Destiny': New Orleans and the Cuban Question during the López Expedition." Master's thesis, Louisiana State University, 1938.

Valverde, Antonio L. *Juan Clemente Zenea: Su proceso de 1871*. La Habana: Imprenta El Siglo XX, 1927.

Van Rensselaer, (Mrs.) John King (in collaboration with Frederic Van de Water). *The Social Ladder*. New York: Henry Holt, 1924.

Varela, Félix. "Carta del editor de este papel a un amigo." *El Habanero*. Reprint of undated original. Miami: La Revista Ideal, 1974.

———. *Cartas a Elpidio*. Vol. 2, *Superstición*. Reprint of 1838 ed. Miami: Editorial Cubana, 1996.

Velasco, José María. *La guerra de Cuba: Causas de su duración y medios de terminarla y asegurar su pacificación*. Madrid: Imprenta de El Correo Militar, 1872.

Villaverde, Cirilo. *Cecilia Valdés ó La Loma del Angel*. 1882. Rev. ed., with prologue and notes. La Habana: Editorial Lex, 1953.

Vitier, Cintio. *Ese sol del mundo moral*. La Habana: Centro de Estudios Martianos, 2015.

———. "Martí en el 98 de ayer y de hoy." *Debates americanos* 4 (July–December 1997).

———. *Rescate de Zenea*. La Habana: Ediciones Union, 1987.

Westfall, L. Glenn. "Don Vicente Martínez Ybor, the Man and His Empire: Development of the Clear Havana Industry in Cuba and Florida in the Nineteenth Century." Ph.D. dissertation, University of Florida, 1977.

Wisan, Joseph E. *The Cuban Crisis as Reflected in the New York Press, 1895–1898*. New York: Columbia University Press, 1934.

Wright, Josephine. "Violinist José White in Paris, 1855–1875." *Black Music Research Journal* 10, no. 2 (Fall 1990).

Zanetti Lecuona, Oscar, and Alejandro García Alvarez. *Caminos para el azúcar*. La Habana: Editorial de Ciencias Sociales, 1987.

Zaragoza, Justo. *Las insurrecciones de Cuba: Apuntes para la historia política de esta isla en el presente siglo*. Vol. 2. Madrid: Imprenta de Miguel G. Hernandez, 1873.

Zéndegui, Guillermo de. *Ambito de Martí*. Madrid: Escuela Gráfica Salesiana, 1954.

INDEX

abolitionism, 67, 244; American Foreign Anti-Slavery Society, 212; Cuban Anti-Slavery Committee, 212–13; Mestre and, 212; in *El Mulato*, 115. *See also* slavery

African Americans, Cuban independence supported by, 212

Africanization, of Cuba, 67–68

Afro-Cubans, 103; cigar workers, in New York, 246; racial segregation of, 246

Agramonte, Eduardo, 154, 231, 313

Agramonte, Emilio, 169–70

Agramonte, Ignacio, 127, 154–55; death of, 230–31, 313

agricultural products, 24

agriculture: Cuban, 23; in eastern Cuba, 125–26; *estancieros*, 24; sugar cane, 24–25

Aguilera, Francisco Vicente, 125–26, 227, 358n219; *aldamistas* and, 228–29; Casanova and, 228–29; de Céspedes, C., and, 231–32; death of, 237–38; émigré activism and, 226–28; Freemasonry and, 127; funeral of, 238–39; in New York, 226–27; Paris fundraising expedition, 230; *quesadistas* and, 228–29; removal of, 231–32

Alabama (steamship), 193

Albion, Robert Greenhalgh, 27–30

Alcázar, José, 35

Aldama, Gonzalo, 80; death of, 78–79, 251

Aldama, Leonor, 242

Aldama, Miguel, 79–80, 141–42, *196*, 196–97; Assembly of the Cuban Republic and, 232; de Borbón and, 144; burial of, 265–67; Casanova on, 206–7, 209–11; Dulce and, 145; financial hardship of, 243–44; interred at Green-Wood Cemetery, 266, *266*; Mestre and, 143, 343n3; migration to New York, 146, 148, 346n90; on *Morro Castle*, 346n103; Moses Taylor and Company and, 144–45, 338n14; in New York, 153–54; resignation of, 206; Santa Rosa sugar refinery, 243; sugar refineries, 210, 243; war of independence and, 143

Aldama Palace, 66, 79; *voluntario* looting of, 145, 346n101

Aldama y Aréchaga, Domingo, 66, 79

aldamistas: Aguilera and, 228–29; del Castillo, C., and, 355n110; critics of, 197–99, 202, 207–10; de Quesada, M., and, 203; *quesadistas* and, 205, 207–9, *208*, 225; socioeconomic class and, 210

Alfonso, Gonzalo, 51, 122, 141, 338n15

de Allo, Lorenzo, 51, 115

de Almansa y Tavira, Juan, 133

American community, in Havana, 3

American Foreign Anti-Slavery Society, 212

American Revolution, 22–23

annexation movement, 50; Buchanan and, 117; El Club de La Habana and, 66; complexity of, 67; end of, 74–75; failure of, 70; Madan and, 72; O'Sullivan and, 73–74; Pierce and, 106–7, 186; rise of, 66; slavery and, 67–68; supporters of, 68–69; *La Verdad* and, 69

antebellum period, 103, 108, 115–16

anti-Catholicism, 44

anti-slavery sentiment: American Foreign Anti-Slavery Society, 212; campaign, 67; in *Cecilia Valdés ó La Loma del Angel*, 263–64; Cuban Anti-Slavery Committee, 212–13

Apezteguía family, 92–93

Arango, Augusto, 100

arbitration commission, U.S., 157

de Armas y Céspedes, José, 213

de Armas y Céspedes, Juan Ignacio, 174, 176–77

ABOUT THE AUTHOR

A native of Havana, Lisandro Pérez has devoted his academic career to the study of Cuba, especially the Cuban presence in the United States. He is currently Professor of Latin American and Latina/o Studies at John Jay College, City University of New York.